German Jewry and the Allure
of the Sephardic

German Jewry and the Allure of the Sephardic

John M. Efron

PRINCETON UNIVERSITY PRESS

PRINCETON AND OXFORD

Published by Princeton University Press, 41 William Street, Princeton, New Jersey 08540

In the United Kingdom: Princeton University Press, 6 Oxford Street, Woodstock, Oxfordshire OX20 1TW

press.princeton.edu

Jacket art: Leipzig synagogue (exterior). William A. Rosenthall Judaica Collection, Special Collections, College of Charleston

Library of Congress Cataloging-in-Publication Data

Efron, John M., author.
   German Jewry and the allure of the Sephardic / John M. Efron.
      pages cm
   Includes bibliographical references and index.
   ISBN 978-0-691-16774-9 (hardback)
      1. Jews—Germany—Intellectual life—18th century.   2. Jews—Germany—Identity—18th century.   3. Jews—Germany—Intellectual life—19th century.   4. Jews—Germany—Identity—19th century.   5. Sephardim—Social life and customs.   6. Jews—Cultural assimilation—Germany.   7. Haskalah—Germany—History—18th century.   8. Germany—Ethnic relations.   I. Title.
   DS134.24.E37 2015
   305.892´404309033—dc23
2015029524

British Library Cataloging-in-Publication Data is available

This book has been composed in Sabon Next LT Pro

Printed on acid-free paper. ∞

Printed in the United States of America

10 9 8 7 6 5 4 3 2 1

Contents

Acknowledgments

If a book's notes and bibliography reveal one's sources, the acknowledgments reveal one's personal debts. I have incurred many along the way, and they vary in nature and magnitude. Whether discussing the book, critiquing the manuscript, or providing me with lodging and companionship when I was very far from home, colleagues and friends have been remarkably generous. They have helped me when they could and challenged me to think more deeply when they needed to. Were it not for all the assistance I received along the way, this book simply would not exist in anything like its present form.

They say charity begins at home. My friends at the University of California at Berkeley Robert Alter, Martin Jay, Jonathan Sheehan, and Yuri Slezkine really helped shape this study in more ways than perhaps even they realize. They were unfailingly gracious and willing to give of their time, and their critical acumen and wise suggestions have made this a better book than it would have been were they not involved. There is also not one among them with whom I do not share laughter in almost every one of our conversations. They represent the best that life at a university has to offer.

In 2008–2009 I was a fellow at UC Berkeley's Townsend Center for the Humanities. I am grateful to have been chosen to be a part of that stimulating group and for the valuable feedback I received from the other scholars. Berkeley's esteemed Judaica librarian, Paul Hamburg, was with me every step of the way. He responded to my myriad requests with equanimity, immediacy, and kindness, and personifies just what it is to be a *mensch*. I also wish to thank Francesco Spagnolo, director of the Magnes Collection of Jewish Art and Life in Berkeley, and the collection's public services coordinator, Gary Handman, for their assistance and generosity.

Other colleagues and friends in Israel, England, Germany, Canada, and the United States have also left their mark on this book. My thanks to Steven Aschheim, Michael Berkowitz, Richard Cohen, Shmuel Feiner, Shaun Halper, Michael Meyer, Aron Rodrigue, Andrea Schatz, Edwin Seroussi, David Sorkin, Elli Stern, Steve Weitzman, and Steve Zipperstein. I have learned from all of them. Thanks are also due to Derek Penslar and Ivan Kalmar, for hosting an unforgettable conference entitled "Orientalism and the Jews" at the University of Toronto in 2001. It was crucial to helping me develop my thinking about this subject. Midway through the book's gestation period, David Myers asked me a straightforward but tough historiographical question about the nature of this book's contribution. I am very glad he did, for in formulating an answer, I arrived at a place of greater conceptual clarity.

My intellectual and personal horizons were greatly expanded in the course of working on this book. In particular, I owe a huge debt of gratitude to Michael Brenner, for his friendship and much else besides. In accepting his 2006 invitation to take up residency at the University of Munich as the Allianz Visiting Professor of Jewish Studies, I gained the opportunity to teach in Germany for the very first time, which was a remarkably rewarding experience; moreover, Michael inducted me into the life of Munich's Jewish community. I have forged deep friendships as well as very pleasant acquaintances, have become an annual visitor, and feel welcome and very much at home in Munich, something I could not in my wildest dreams have imagined. As a historian of German Jewry, I knew far more about its past than its present. I consider myself privileged to have been able to begin to rectify that imbalance. I have Michael to thank for that.

Much of the book was researched and written in Munich, within the convivial and stimulating environment of the University of Munich's Jewish Studies Program. Special thanks are due Mirjam Triendl-Zadoff, who so generously gave me full use of her office over winter breaks. First in Munich and now in Berkeley as my colleague, Andrea Sinn has been part of this project from its early days. I feel so fortunate that this is the case. Four people in particular have made Munich such a special place for me. For many years now, Michael Brenner and Michelle Engert as well as Eli Teicher and Ute Fackler have opened their hearts and homes to me, just as have John Gerszt and Sue Mandelbaum in both London and Tel Aviv. May this book serve as a token of my gratitude to them and a constant reminder of all the good times spent together.

I am grateful to Brigitta van Rheinberg, editor in chief at Princeton University Press. From the very beginning, her enthusiasm for the book was very validating, and both she and Quinn Fusting have been a pleasure to work with. I also wish to thank Lauren Lepow for her excellent editorial hand and Dimitri Karetnikov, the press's illustration specialist, as well as the authors of the reader's reports for their most helpful suggestions.

My greatest regret is that my father, David Efron, and my Doktorvater, Yosef Hayim Yerushalmi, both of blessed memory, didn't live to see the publication of this book. They both would have cared about the subject and would, I hope, have been pleased with the end product.

There have been many changes at home since work began on this book. Back then, my children, Hannah and Noah, were indeed children. They are now young adults making their own way in the world. It will be a better place for their contribution. It is only fitting that I dedicate this book about beauty to Deborah, whose wisdom, support, and love make it all possible. It is to her that I owe everything, including our newest addition and source of joy, Velvl.

Introduction

This is a book about beauty, about style, about appearance. It is about the German-Jewish quest to be seen as dignified, as refined, as physically appealing. Our story starts in the late eighteenth century, when the Jewish battle for social acceptance and legal emancipation began, and continues through to the late nineteenth century with the explosion of nationalism, mass politics, and racial antisemitism in Germany. In the late eighteenth century, German Jewry began to develop a new and distinctive sense of self, one predicated on its adoption of German language and culture. This was followed in the nineteenth century by the advent of new forms of Judaism, the turn to Jewish scholarship, the acquisition of university education, and the emergence of Jews into the middle classes. All of these innovations intended to or served to change the image and appearance of Jews and Judaism.[1]

One aspect of the great cultural transformation of German Jewry was the special place of honor it accorded medieval Spanish Jewry. Over that span of one hundred years, what began as respect for Sephardic culture developed into adulation, and it is my contention that this sentiment became a constitutive element of German-Jewish self-perception, for this celebration of Sephardic Jewry led simultaneously to a self-critique, often a very harsh one, of Ashkenazic culture. In the eighteenth century German Jewry became increasingly and self-consciously distinct from Polish Jewry. As it went on to form a new type of Ashkenazic culture, the superiority that certain communal leaders claimed was a hallmark of Sephardic civilization offered an ideal that proved inspirational to the shapers of modern German-Jewish identity. I further argue that the intricately interdependent ideas about the Ashkenazic self and the Sephardic Other produced a set of assumptions, beliefs, and prejudices that were marshaled in the process of German-Jewish self-actualization and self-fashioning. The program of remaking German-Jewish aesthetics rested upon establishing a hard cultural line of demarcation between the Jewries of Germany and Poland and invoking the usable and easy-to-celebrate aspects of medieval Sephardic culture, which German Jews considered exemplary. This is the story this book seeks to tell.

From the outset, let me state that I am not suggesting that German Jews gave constant thought to Sephardic Jewry, and I am certainly not suggesting they wanted to imitate them. In fact, given that Christian commentators in the eighteenth and nineteenth centuries frequently dismissed Jews as "Asiatic" or "Oriental," the majority of German Jews were dedicated to a process of occidentalization, not orientalization, and probably paid only scant attention, if any at all, to the Jews of Muslim Spain. What I am saying, however, is that those elites who molded Jewish popular opinion in Germany, those who shaped self-perceptions and created a narrative to go along with those sentiments, did think about medieval Iberian Jewry a lot, and those thoughts were almost always positive. The rays of Spanish Jewry's Golden Age continued to shine long after that community's tragic end, and it may be argued that those rays enjoyed their greatest luminosity in modern Germany.

To a great extent, our own perception of medieval Sephardic Jewry is a cultural legacy bequeathed to us by nineteenth-century German Jews, for their scholarship and popular culture worked in tandem to produce a set of representative images that have enjoyed remarkable staying power, right down to our own day. It was a non-Jewish scholar, the Lutheran theologian and Christian Hebraist Franz Delitzsch, who coined the term "Golden Age" to describe what he said was the period in Spain when "Jewish scholarship and art reached its highest glory." Yet it was the abundant use of the expression in the popular and scholarly discourse of German Jews that made for both its normative use and the nearly universal acceptance of its facticity.[2]

If one could play a retroactive word-association game with nineteenth-century German Jews, the following would have been some of the words and names uttered in response to "Sephardic Jewry": Golden Age, Hebrew poetry, rationalist philosophy, reason, tolerance, openness, Ibn Ezra, Judah Halevi, and Maimonides. If they were then asked to respond to the term "Ashkenazic Jewry," they would surely have mentioned the Crusades, blood libel, ritual murder, martyrdom, intolerance, insularity, superstition, Hasidism, and Yiddish. Beyond Rashi, it would be hard to imagine a modern, secular German Jew naming another medieval rabbi from either Germany or Poland. Every association our German-Jewish participant in this game made about Sephardic Jewry was positive, while nearly every association for Ashkenazic Jewry was negative. This is not to say there is no element of truth in any of these signifiers. Though the intellectual and vernacular cultures of German Jewry greatly exaggerated the extent of tolerance that Iberian Islam extended to medieval Jews, it seems to have been a less oppressive, restrictive, and violent environment than that which Jews experienced in Christian Europe. For example, Jews enjoyed greater economic freedom under Islam, ritual murder charges were invented and flourished in Christian Europe and not in the Islamic orbit, while rationalist philosophy was the preserve of Sephardic, not Ashkenazic, intellectuals. Hebrew grammarians of the first rank were to be found in Spain and to a lesser, or a less well-known, extent in Central and Western Europe.[3] However, the totalizing superficiality of popular perceptions, first crafted, as I will argue, by German Ashkenazic communal elites and intellectuals, fails to recognize uncomfortable realities, principal among them that "the aristocratic bearing of a select class of courtiers and poets . . . should not blind us to the reality that this tightly knit circle of leaders and aspirants to power was neither the whole of Spanish Jewish history nor of Spanish Jewish society. Their gilded moments of the tenth and eleventh century are but a brief chapter in a longer saga."[4]

Also only rarely highlighted was the fact that like the Jews of Spain those of medieval Ashkenaz also had their Hebrew poets, grammarians, exegetes, distinguished political representatives, and physicians, who served Crown and Christian commoner alike.[5] In contrast to the views of those Jews who shaped German-Jewish culture in the eighteenth and nineteenth centuries, the Jewish affinity for Muslim culture was not universally shared by all medieval Spanish Jews. Even among Sephardic elites, there was vehement rejection of rationalist metaphysics, which, they held, was the result of Islam's nefarious influence. There was also considerable Jewish disdain for Islam itself, with many Spanish Jews dismissing it as nothing but idolatry.[6] Harmony, let alone a Muslim-Jewish symbiosis, was far from the norm, and even though some nineteenth-century German-Jewish scholars recognized this, the more historically accurate picture, which included considerable social coercion and theological friction, hardly blurred the romantic portrait they likewise painted.[7]

Perception proved more powerful than reality, and, beginning in the eighteenth century, German Jews saw in the Sephardim of the Golden Age Jews who possessed what the French sociologist Pierre Bourdieu called "cultural capital." As he defined the term, it referred to "all the goods material and symbolic, without distinction, that present themselves as rare and worthy of being sought after in a particular social formation."[8] The emerging middle- and upper-class Jews of eighteenth-century Berlin saw in the Jews of medieval Spain a community that was culturally wealthy, established, and admired by Gentile elites. As evaluated by German Jews, Sephardic "cultural capital" also turned the Jews of Spain into a living expression of Jewish "symbolic capital" and hence generated the idea that they were an ideal community. Endowed with honor and prestige, as befitting their status vis-à-vis other Jewish communities, the Sephardim were a "cultural nobility," to again borrow from Bourdieu, and the measure against which German Jews assessed their own, Ashkenazic self-worth.[9] In what follows we will see how their own forebears, medieval Ashkenazic Jewry, were assayed and found, by comparison, to be of little cultural value. Moreover, it was claimed, they had bequeathed their particular form of cultural penury to their descendents in Germany and Poland. Modern German Jewry sought to shake off that legacy and rid itself of that inheritance by amassing its own cultural capital. The great investment in that project made by maskilim, community leaders, and then the great majority of German Jews would, it was hoped, be transformed into a kind of symbolic capital whereby they would now assume the mantle of prestige and recognition that had once been the possession of Sephardic Jewry.

A central component of the belief system that saw German Jewry value so highly the cultural and symbolic capital of the Sephardim and undervalue that of the Ashkenazim turned on aesthetics and gave rise to the belief that the Sephardim were the most beautiful Jews, and that their culture was aesthetically superior to that of the Ashkenazim. This notion will be our particular focus in this study. We begin in the eighteenth century because that was the moment when appearances first began to matter to German Jews. Long considered to be in religious and thus moral error, Jews faced a new charge at this time, namely, that they were in aesthetic error. In response, the upper stratum of that community began to adopt what the literary theorist Terry Eagleton has called the "ideology of the aesthetic." Speaking principally about eighteenth-century German thought, Eagleton notes that, "in this particular epoch of class-society, with the emergence of the early bourgeoisie, aesthetic concepts (some of them of distinguished historical pedigree) begin to play, however tacitly, an unusually central, intensive part in the constitution of a dominant ideology." In making this claim, Eagleton is principally referring to systems of philosophical thought concerned with art writ large. That is less the case with contemporaneous Jewish thought, for in formulating an ideology of aesthetics, the Jewish Brahmins of Berlin were concerned with the practical application of new ideas about aesthetics as opposed to speculative consideration about them. Eagleton is surely right to note that "aesthetics is born as a discourse of the body. In its original formulation by the German philosopher Alexander Baumgarten, the term refers not in the first place to art, but, as the Greek *aisthesis* would suggest, to the whole region of human perception and sensation, in contrast to the more rarefied domain of conceptual thought."[10] Increasing numbers of German Jews not only preached the ideology of aesthetics but practiced it as well.

Critical theorists have long pointed to the link between aesthetics and politics, some seeing in it an explanatory device for the appeal of fascism, with others seeing it, according to historian Martin Jay, in opposing terms; in this alternative view, "bourgeois culture at its height rather than at its moment of seeming decay is . . . taken as a point of departure for aestheticized politics."[11] In introducing his subject, Eagleton offers the disclaimer that he does "not really intend to suggest that the eighteenth-century bourgeoisie assembled around a table over their claret to dream up the concept of the aesthetic as a solution to their political dilemmas."[12] In contrast to the bourgeois circles of which Eagleton speaks, I will argue that the upper German-Jewish bourgeoisie did assemble, at times physically, at other times through the circulation of texts and letters, to discuss Jewish appearances both for their own sake and "as a solution to their political dilemmas." In doing so, they sought to sculpt a specifically new Ashkenazic aesthetic, taking conscious steps to implement it with a view to becoming refined, cultured, and even beautiful. The larger goal of their "aestheticized politics" was to be deemed worthy of political emancipation and social acceptance. What follows is an exploration of the ways German Jews alternately internalized, rejected, parsed, and negotiated ideas and charges about their own aesthetics. It is about the strategies they adopted to cultivate their aesthetic selves. As such, this is not a study about Sephardic Jewry. Rather, it is about the construction of a particular form of modern Ashkenazic identity, that of the German variety, and the way the trope of the beautiful Sephardic Jew was deployed in the service of German-Jewish identity formation.

Until the modern period there is no evidence that Jews were ever really concerned with, let alone embarrassed by, their particular aesthetic. Their corporeal, sartorial, and linguistic selves were not as they were as a matter of chance but rather were the result of a highly regulated set of proscriptions all considered to be in accordance with either Jewish law, deeply ingrained custom, or social necessity. Biblical laws that regulated everything from permissible fabrics to facial hair were further supplemented over the centuries by a raft of sumptuary laws that regulated Jewish behaviors and appearance. Largely unenforceable and frequently honored in the breach, these laws nevertheless represented a Jewish behavioral and aesthetic ideal.[13]

Even Jewish ideas of beauty and ugliness were shaped by an idealized commitment to the Law. The Jewish masculine ideal, so very different from that of the Christian, revered the pale-skinned, gentle Torah scholar while reviling the ruddy-cheeked, unbooked, Gentile boy, his complexion a telltale sign of his frivolous, outdoor ways. As for their speech, Jews prayed in the very same language that God spoke, and Ashkenazim conducted their daily affairs, including Torah study, in Yiddish, a language that made quotidian the admonitions of the prophets and the wisdom of the sages. There was nothing to be ashamed of, for the Jews appeared exactly as the Lord had commanded them to look. God was the ultimate arbiter of Jewish style.

In the eighteenth century, this long-standing Jewish accommodation to God's fashion sense began to break down. In Germany, the embourgeoisement of Jews was coterminous with the drawn-out process of Jewish emancipation. Many members of the Jewish upper classes began to adopt secular lifestyles and cultivate bourgeois tastes and sensibilities in the hope that in so doing they would come to be considered Germans. Increasing inattentiveness to Jewish ritual as well as certain aspects of popular Jewish culture were likewise losing their hold on this social stratum. Knowledge of Hebrew was in sharp decline, and what would become a long-running assault on the Yiddish language began with German maskilim. Sartorially, Jewish men were increasingly clean-shaven, and traditional Jewish dress was abandoned in favor of contemporary fashions. Writing about eighteenth-century England, the historian Dror Wahrman has observed that "fashion signified the constant manufacturing and remanufacturing of identity through clothes."[14] This applies to German Jews as well. Thanks to changes in dress and language, they came to increasingly look and sound more and more like their Christian neighbors.

These cultural transformations were hastened and intensified by increasing fraternization between upper-class Jews and non-Jews.[15] Exposure to the latter's culture was intoxicating, leaving Jews full of both admiration and desire. Among Jewish social elites in Central Europe, that exposure to bourgeois culture occasioned among them a crisis of aesthetic confidence. Self-doubt turned into self-scrutiny, and nearly every aesthetic particularity, corporeal and otherwise, was examined. Ashkenazic accents, languages, cognitive capacities, posture, deportment, and even history itself were examined and evaluated according to a non-Jewish scale of aesthetic worth. In almost all categories, Jews found themselves to be deficient. These beliefs made German Jews hyper-self-conscious, acutely aware of how they sounded, how they looked, and how they carried themselves. The German Enlightenment philosopher Immanuel Kant (1724–1804) characterized the dominant intellectual imperative of the age in which he lived when he declared, "Our age is, in especial degree, the age of criticism, and to criticism everything must submit," while the romantic poet and literary critic Friedrich Schlegel (1772–1829) pithily echoed Kant, announcing, "One cannot be critical enough."[16] For German Jews at this time, Schlegel's dictum might well be paraphrased: "One cannot be self-critical enough."

What made Jewish self-criticism so acute in Germany has to do with the quest for civic equality and social acceptance. In contrast to developments in France, Jewish emancipation in Germany was not the result of legislative action in the context of political and social revolution. Rather, emancipation in Germany was piecemeal, an uneven process that entailed a carrot-and-stick approach whereby increasing liberty was to be the reward for Jewish self-improvement. Of course "self-improvement" was never a quantifiable category of analysis. When was enough enough? Neither Germans nor Jews really knew the answer. In this environment, appearances, physical as well as moral, counted for much. Outward signs became critical markers of change, and thus German Jews, prior to emancipation, and in fact thereafter, felt themselves to be under surveillance, with Germans looking for signs of positive change and Jews seeking to trumpet the actualization of such.

Of course, Jews have not been the only minority group subject to the watchful, judgmental eye of the majority. Here we can turn with profit to the African American historian, public intellectual, and civil rights activist W.E.B. Du Bois, for he provides us with a theoretical underpinning that helps explain the responses of German Jews to the cold stare of the majority at the dawn of emancipation. In 1903 Du Bois published his seminal work *The Souls of Black Folk*, wherein he developed his theory of "double consciousness," which he defined as "this sense of always looking at one's self through the eyes of others, of measuring one's soul by the tape of a world that looks on in amused contempt and pity." The consequence of this is that "one ever feels his two-ness,—an American, a Negro; two souls, two thoughts, two unreconciled strivings; two warring ideals in one dark body, whose dogged strength alone keeps it from being torn asunder."[17] In speaking so poignantly about his own people and their particular suffering, Du Bois gave voice to the dilemma of all minorities seeking acceptance on the one hand while seeking to avoid self-effacement on the other. If we exchange the words "American" and "Negro" for "German" and "Jew," Du Bois provides us with the critical tools with which to come to a better understanding of the dilemma that manifested itself in what was at times a painful expression of German-Jewish "double consciousness."

Du Bois was very clear that the "American Negro" did not wish to disappear but rather sought "to merge his double self into a better and truer self." His was not so much an act of being as one of becoming. It was about fashioning a new identity, one that was composed out of the bifurcated self. The story told in this book maps onto the Du Boisean ideal, for it seeks to explicate the process by which German Jewry sought to remake itself, in response to the self-perception that its aesthetic debasement disqualified it from self-fulfillment and acceptance by the dominant society. What held true for the African American was equally applicable to the German Jew: "He simply wishes to make it possible for a man to be both a Negro and an American, without being cursed and spit upon by his fellows, without having the doors of Opportunity closed roughly in his face. This, then, is the end of his striving: to be a co-worker in the kingdom of culture, to escape both death and isolation, to husband and use his best powers and his latent genius."[18] For both African Americans and German Jews, the juggling act was made all the more difficult because of the surveillance that comes with "double consciousness." Excessive scrutiny, or at least the sense that one was being constantly observed, bred an acute self-consciousness.

Over the century or so covered by this book, German Jews underwent a radical aesthetic transformation, largely in accordance with new tastes, sensibilities, styles, and fashions. Those changes were determined by many things including then-current theories of language and rhetoric, new musical tastes, emerging architectural styles, the Protestant worship service, the internalization of antisemitic tropes about Jewish physicality, and new ways of writing Jewish history that served to identify those moments in the past when Jews led aesthetically exemplary lives and when they did not.

Across the German-Jewish social and cultural spectrum, the aesthetic transformation was informed by a celebration of all things Sephardic. Our focus is on Ashkenazic perceptions of Sephardic appearance, and we will see how, in both high and vernacular Jewish culture, a portrait was drawn of both Sephardic and Ashkenazic Jews that promoted an image of the former as authentic, desirable, attractive, and worthy of emulation, while the culture of Ashkenaz was most frequently considered regrettable and in need of radical correction. To repeat, this phenomenon did not manifest itself in some form of German-Jewish Kabuki where they pretended to be that which they were not. Their goal was to become the best German Jews they could be. However, what it does mean is that with the dissolution in the eighteenth century of what might be considered a pan-Ashkenazic culture, German Jewry struggled with the felt need to distinguish itself from the rest of Ashkenazic Jewry, namely, their brethren to the East, and they enlisted the Sephardim to help them achieve their liberation.

The relationship of German to Polish Jewry is at the core of our story. Freud coined the term "narcissism of small differences" to describe the process whereby one nation or ethnic group distinguishes itself from their nearly identical neighbors by highlighting distinctions between the groups. For German and Eastern European Jews, what had been a shared religious culture, a shared vernacular language (Yiddish), as well as commercial and familial links, began to unravel in the late 1700s, and the uneven, sometimes slower, sometimes faster, but unmistakable trend toward differentiation and separation set in. To be sure, there had always been regional differences in religious customs, foods, and pronunciation of Hebrew and Yiddish between German Jewry and Eastern European Jewry, as well as within those respective communities. However, it is also true that in the realm of Jewish folk culture, those differences never impeded mutual intelligibility. Indeed, depending on geographic location, German Jews retained many Eastern European Jewish traits, while Eastern European Jewish culture exhibited many Western forms. This syncretism continued into the twentieth century. As historian Steven Lowenstein has observed, "Whatever the differences, German and Polish Jewish folk cultures were more similar to each other than either were to the folk cultures of Jews in southern Europe or in the Muslim world."[19]

However, as German and Eastern European Jewry began to drift apart in the eighteenth century, the two most visible markers of that separation, the advent of Hasidism—which never appeared as a mass movement in Germany and, by contrast, swept Poland by storm—and the continued use of Yiddish in Eastern Europe along with its slow but steady abandonment in Germany and the adoption of German in its stead, meant the emergence of two distinct forms of Ashkenazic culture.[20] Two further developments brought the real differences between German and Polish Jewry into sharp relief. They were the adoption of Gentile high culture among German Jews and their greater economic success, which saw them rise into the middle class, while the majority of Eastern European Jews did not aspire to Polish culture and remained mired in poverty, just as Poland itself did not enjoy the level of affluence found in the West. What had once been the narcissism of small differences now became that of big ones, as German Jews became vigilant practitioners of a cultural politics of Jewish difference. In fact they brought into microcosmic relief an intra-Jewish version of the larger syndrome Du Bois described. However, where the analogy meets its limits is in the fact that in myriad ways, both subtle and obvious, by constantly reaffirming the distinction between German and Polish Jewry, I would argue, they inadvertently instantiated the connectedness between the two communities.

The most important distinction was that of language, a theme that will recur throughout this study. The proximity of German to Yiddish explains what made the Jewish enlighteners of eighteenth-century Berlin disparage it so, leaving behind them a sad legacy of prejudice. It is also what made them such staunch advocates of German. For other large Ashkenazic communities that traced their roots to Eastern Europe, be it Anglo or American Jewry, English was so far removed from Yiddish that the relationship between the respective speakers of these languages was not especially fraught. By contrast, the shame and embarrassment that German Jews felt toward Eastern European Jews, feelings that were exacerbated by the physical proximity of Germany to Poland and the presence of Eastern European Jews in Germany, were especially keen. The fear that one's roots would be uncovered by the presence of Eastern European Jews in Germany, or just the very reminder that there had once been a pan-Ashkenazic culture, led to discomfort and protestations of difference that were heard more frequently and more loudly in Germany than elsewhere.[21]

The insecurity born of shared culture and in many cases origins, and made most manifest by language, was extended to other expressive forms, principally body language. The Herderian idea that the *Volksgeist*, or spirit of the nation, resides in language meant that the way one spoke was indicative of much more than a mere mode of communication. Some of the cultural critics we will encounter in this study operated from the premise that language reflected inner character and morality. It also reflected the extent to which Jews interacted with the world beyond the Jewish community. Indeed language was constitutive as well as determinative of aesthetics. Since these ideas appeared around the same time that the quest for Jewish emancipation in Germany began, aesthetics came to play a central role in the cultural transformation of German Jewry.

It was in the context of the split between German and Polish Jewry that German Jewry turned to the medieval Jews of the Iberian Peninsula, for their overall aesthetic bespoke a Jewish community whose sounds, appearance, comportment, and levels of cognition revealed a *Volksgeist* that had been forged from a sparkling yet strong alloy of Jewish and Spanish culture.

It was an experiment that had taken place in the laboratory that was Muslim Spain, where, it was believed, Jews, Muslims, and Christians thrived together in harmony.

The adulation of the Sephardim emerges during the era of romanticism and may be considered a central element of that movement's early Jewish incarnation. Romanticism spanned the period from the late eighteenth century until the 1830s and challenged some of the fundamental tenets of the Enlightenment, especially the latter's devotion to neoclassicism and its negative view of religious enthusiasm, as well as history—in particular the Middle Ages, which it dismissed as a time of barbarism and ignorance. It rejected the Enlightenment's drive to understand natural law, politics, and social relations in terms of systems, order, hierarchies, and classification, as static entities untouched by history. Instead, romanticism stressed a dynamic world of possibility, progress, intuition, and the importance of history.[22] It also cultivated what scholars of romanticism refer to as "sensibility," a term used to denote "sensitivity or emotional responsiveness, bordering on sentimentalism."[23] However, despite these real differences, romanticism actually shared important features with the Enlightenment: it was not an enemy of reason; it likewise sought to weed out superstition; it opposed religious obscurantism as well as political injustice and disorder. Among German Jews, the cultural, economic, social, and religious transformations that began in the late eighteenth century and took hold by the mid-nineteenth were rooted in reason, a devotion to history, and a profound desire to do away with the discrimination Jews faced in nearly every sphere of life.

A notoriously difficult term to define with any precision, "romanticism" has accrued as many definitions as there have been commentators on the subject.[24] The philosopher Isaiah Berlin has given us numerous working definitions of romanticism, including this particularly apt one: "It is nostalgia, it is reverie, it is intoxicating dreams, it is sweet melancholy and bitter melancholy, solitude, the sufferings of exile, the sense of alienation, roaming in remote places, especially the East, and in remote times, especially the Middle Ages."[25] For those German Jews who sought a palatable, domesticated, and glorious medieval past, Iberian Jewry answered their need for "intoxicating dreams" that emanated from the East, and certainly no Jewish community better conjured up positive feelings of "nostalgia" or more completely exemplified "the sufferings of exile" than did the Sephardim.

German Jews do not appear to have been swept up by romanticism, nor did they produce any romantic poets or artists—Heinrich Heine may perhaps be considered an exception to the rule. What can be claimed is that to sing the praises of Sephardic beauty to the extent that German Jewry did and simultaneously decry the aesthetics of Ashkenazic culture was to ride the wave of intense emotion characteristic of romanticism's excesses. These feelings first took hold among Jewish elites during the Berlin Haskalah, or

Jewish Enlightenment, which, while not a romantic movement *tout court*, nonetheless emerged at the time of German romanticism's first incarnation, which lasted from approximately 1760 to 1830.[26] The Berlin Haskalah was characterized by a blending of Enlightenment and certain romanticist sensibilities and tendencies, and it was with what has been called "Sephardism" that both inclinations are brought into starkest relief.[27]

In the realms of religious and social life the program of the Haskalah sought, like the Enlightenment, to cultivate taste, beauty, and the senses with a view to the promotion of virtue, goodness, refinement, respectability, and reason. As we will see, the maskilim and those like-minded thinkers who followed in their wake repeatedly ascribed these qualities to the Sephardim, almost as if they were congenital. For example, a striking characteristic of the Berlin Haskalah was its cult of reason. Order, tempered emotions, and logic were repeatedly invoked to praise Spanish Jewry, indict Polish-Jewish culture, and serve as aspirational goals for German Jewry. In this respect, the Sephardim served as a Jewish analogue to the way figures of the German Enlightenment viewed the Greeks, whom they glorified as the epitome of reason, controlled passions, and beauty.[28] Beyond this, the way maskilim depicted the Sephardim allowed Iberian Jewry to be presented as ideal intermediaries, Jews who were capable of breaking down the age-old Hellenic-Hebraic divide. The other romantic feature of the Haskalah that played a leading role in the formation of modern German-Jewish culture was its profound and unprecedented attraction to Jewish history. The cult of the Sephardic Jews was made possible only thanks to the Haskalah's appreciation of the Jewish past and the development of a sentimental, pathos-filled attachment to Jewish suffering, a trope that repeatedly manifested itself into the early twentieth with German-Jewish culture's highly confected representations of Spanish Jewry.

There was one further component that set in motion the new Jewish sensibilities to be explicated in this study, and it is directly linked to the changing intellectual and political culture of the late 1790s. The generation of romantics in Germany, which included the poets Novalis and Hölderlin, the theologian Schleiermacher, the philosopher Schelling, and the Schlegel brothers, both poets and philosophers, had become disillusioned with the French Revolution, of which they had been staunch supporters. However, the unending violence and instability provoked a change of attitude, and the romantics began to assert the "need for some form of elite rule, for a more educated class to direct and control the interests and energies of the people."[29] According to the romantics, the problems in France were brought about by the fact that there had been no prerevolutionary preparation of hearts and minds that would make it possible for the people to cope with the radically new social and political conditions of postregicide France. Germany could not be allowed to go the way of its chaotic neighbor, and the romantics believed that the way to introduce social change—to which they were still committed—while maintaining stability in Germany was through education, the goal of which was to inculcate virtue, self-control, refinement, and a sense that actions undertaken for the greater good should trump individual desire. The educational program to promote these qualities was called *Bildung*, a term denoting the all-encompassing cultivation of the self through the acquisition of education, critical reason, good taste, and an appreciation of beauty.[30] For the poet and playwright Friedrich Schiller (1759–1805), who, Gershom Scholem remarked, had an "incalculable" impact on "the formation of Jewish attitudes towards Germany," "Beauty alone confers happiness on all, and under its influence every being forgets that he is limited."[31] With Schiller as their guide, the march of German Jews into modernity would be, among other things, a quest for beauty.

The changing attitudes of the romantics and their prescription to avoid political and social calamity in Germany were coterminous with the Haskalah and came to inform it. As the distinguished historian George Mosse observed, "*Bildung* and Enlightenment joined hands during the period of Jewish emancipation; they were meant to complement each other."[32] *Bildung*, like any ennobling imperative, is by definition a transcendent force, capable of creating potential unity and productive tranquillity among diverse peoples. If Herder believed that the acquisition of *Bildung* could contribute to the elimination of differences between the aristocracy and the bourgeoisie, German Jews believed deeply that it could surely erase any nonreligious barriers that separated them from Germans. Proceeding from the assumption that Jews were deficient in terms of virtue and refinement, the maskilim were that self-appointed vanguard that would bring *Bildung* to the people. In their writings they repeatedly referred to *shlemut*, the Hebrew word for "perfection" or *Vollkommenheit*, its German equivalent. The attainment of an impossible-to-achieve perfection, or at least the adoption of it as a noble and ongoing exercise, was the intended goal. If, as they diagnosed, the Jews were suffering from an acute case of imperfection, the maskilim saw in romanticism's ideals combined with Haskalah and *Bildung* a curative elixir.

Just as the dating of Jewish history does not easily map onto the dating schema for general European history, so too Jewish romanticism is not exactly coterminous with the European variant nor does it share all of its features, even its most important ones. The aesthetic preference we will examine in this study lingered on long after the romantic era had ended. The preference persisted, first, because the era of Jewish romanticism exceeds the chronology of the European romantic movement by some decades, and, second, because the protracted struggle for Jewish emancipation in Germany, which officially ended in 1871, abuts the emergence of the antisemitic movement, which in turn gave rise to a more robust expression of

Jewish self-assertion.[33] (In Eastern Europe that self-assertion manifested itself in Jewish nationalism.) At this political and cultural moment we will see that the adoration of the Sephardic Jews, initially a trope of German-Jewish self-realization, becomes one of self-defense, and, finally, an important article of faith for Zionism's founding Ashkenazic fathers, mostly, though not all, from Eastern Europe.

No one better exemplifies the romantic tendency to venerate the Sephardim in the service of all three goals than Theodor Herzl. With his vivid imagination and highly developed theatrical sense, this Budapest-born resident of Vienna constructed for himself an imaginary lineage, wherein he claimed to be the descendant of Sephardic Jews. He told several versions of the story. In one, he confided to the English Zionist Jacob de Haas that his paternal great-grandfather, a rabbi named Loebl, had been forcibly converted to Catholicism. After fleeing the Iberian Peninsula, Loebl emerged in Constantinople, whereupon he returned openly to Judaism. Just prior to his death in 1904, Herzl told the Hebrew author Reuven Brainin that he was descended from one of two Jewish brothers, both of whom had risen high in the ranks of the Catholic clergy. When sent on an important mission outside the country, they decided to make their departure a permanent one and embraced the faith of their ancestors. For his own sense of self and his own self-image Herzl concocted this fantasy wherein Loebl was no longer the Slovenian Jew of reality but the Spanish Jew of Herzl's desires. Not only was this move a singular act of artifice; it must also be seen in relation to Herzl's extremely negative and frequently disgraceful descriptions of Eastern European Jews. That is to say, Jews not unlike the ones from whom he was descended.[34] Having absorbed the dominant stereotypes about Jews circulating in the Vienna of his day, Herzl saw in his make-believe past a way to escape the taunts and jibes that he could pretend were reserved for the *Ostjuden*.

With his regal bearing, his piercing black eyes, olive skin, and thick beard, Herzl had the look of a leader, a Jewish leader. Years later, David Ben-Gurion, first prime minister of the State of Israel, recalled his reaction to Herzl's appearance: "One glimpse of him and I was ready to follow him there and then to the land of my ancestors."[35] It was an image Herzl did much to cultivate. Herzl was portrayed, whether by friend, foe, or himself, as a Jew with exotic origins and flamboyant designs: as a biblical figure; or as a latter-day Shlomo Molcho—the sixteenth-century Portuguese mystic of Marrano parentage who declared himself the Messiah—or Shabbtai Zvi, the seventeenth-century false messiah from Izmir, both of whom were Sephardic Jews. Herzl longed to be anything but an ordinary Ashkenazic Jew from Central Europe.[36]

In terms of its specific features, the German-Jewish romanticism of which we speak here differed from the larger European movement of the same name, especially in terms of the latter's impact on European nationalism. Where, for example, European nationalists of the later nineteenth century looked to the distant past and linked themselves to their ancient forebears, the myth of Sephardic supremacy was an Ashkenazic invention and it was one that highlighted distance and difference from the object of their paeans and not linkage to this mythical culture. In fact, what we might call the Sephardicist turn was built upon what was at times brutal Ashkenazic self-rejection. Its fundamental claim was that because they had lived in backward, medieval, Christian Europe, with its endless cycle of torment, debasement, and persecution, Ashkenazic Jews had been physically and psychologically scarred. Indeed, it was claimed that they even bore the aesthetics and physicality of a people cowed by history. The Sephardic Jews, who were said to have lived freely, thriving in Muslim Spain, gave birth to a superior culture and, in contrast to the Ashkenazim, evinced the proud carriage of a people that flowered in this propitious medieval environment.

Among Jews, romanticism, which emphasized instinct and emotion, was never permitted to supersede the Enlightenment values German Jewry so deeply cherished. Instead, Jews combined certain aspects of romanticism with an unshakable commitment to the culture of the Enlightenment, praising the Sephardim as an exemplary Jewish community. With its rationalist philosophers, secular Hebrew poets, prominent courtiers, and distinguished rabbis, medieval Iberian Jewry provided an ideal social and cultural template for a German Jewry that was becoming increasingly cognizant of its own ascent out of the ghetto. However, beset with doubts and anxieties occasioned by the antisemitic backlash that came about in the wake of Jewish embourgeoisement and success, many German Jews internalized claims about Jewish difference, cultural inferiority, and even bodily deformity.

In the political realm the Sephardism of German-Jewry was employed in the service of a liberal, cultural, and social politics. Unlike Christian romanticism, Jewish romantic sensibilities in Germany were used to bolster not Jewish nationalism but, in fact, its very opposite. Sephardism was intended to promote an ideology of Jewish acculturation, accommodation, and compatibility with the majority.

A study such as this naturally leads us into an engagement with the subject of orientalism, another theme that runs through this book. The term was popularized by Edward Said in his influential study *Orientalism* (1978). Taking his cue from Foucault, Said claimed that orientalism is "a Western style for dominating, restructuring, and having authority over the Orient."[37] But he is able to formulate such a sweeping indictment only by employing a limited definition of orientalism and by ignoring entire episodes within the intellectual history of the modern East-West encounter that do not conveniently conform to Said's orientalist-as-imperialist thesis.

One episode is that of German orientalism. For Said, the determining motive behind the orientalist enterprise was imperialism, hence his focus on Britain and France, the two principal colonial powers in the Middle East. Because it lacked significant colonial holdings, Said excluded Germany from his purview.[38] In fact, Germany came to lead the field of orientalist scholarship, proof that orientalism and imperialism as understood by Said simply did not need each other. Rather, as Suzanne Marchand, the leading historian of German orientalism, has conclusively demonstrated, that country created a field of Oriental studies that was largely motivated by the search for Christian religious origins and not the desire for imperial domination.[39] Germany also developed a rich orientalist literary canon that can be read as a challenge to any singular, monolithic definition of orientalism. Indeed, scholars of orientalism, especially if their focus is Germany, prefer to speak of "orientalisms."[40] One aim of this study is to expand our conception of orientalism, to indicate that just as it may have been, in some instances, an intellectual adjunct to imperialism, it was not always that and, for most genuine orientalists, especially German ones, never that. Many orientalists pursued their work long before the era of imperialism properly began, or if they worked during its heyday, they were often among the most dogged opponents of imperialist adventurism.

This brings us to the second episode in the history of orientalism that was left out of Said's intervention and that of subsequent scholarship on the history of orientalism, namely, its Jewish dimension. It is the argument of the present study that the German-Jewish Sephardicists, whether communal leaders, anthropologists, novelists, scholars of Islam or of the history of Jews in Muslim lands, serve as significant counterexamples to the typical orientalist imagined by Said. For Central European Jewish scholars, in particular, orientalism did not function as an intellectual justification for a political system of domination. Rather, it was often celebratory and inspirational, for Jewish orientalism more often than not entailed a valorization of the Muslim Other. This was because, for German-Jewish orientalists, like their Christian counterparts, orientalism was often tantamount to a search for religious roots, for authenticity, and for Oriental role models.

Among Jewish orientalists, this undertaking, rather than a straightforward means of asserting colonial, corporeal, and cultural authority, could be, as this book will demonstrate, a profound expression of one's own cultural anxiety and insecurity, one that could provoke deep-seated fears of inferiority and, ironically, Jewish chauvinism at the same time. Not only did the German-Jewish orientalists come from a country without a significant empire, but as Jews, they were entirely marginal to the official political and academic structure. They were not, in other words, agents of the state, and their scholarship did not serve its ends. In fact, their professional marginality as well as the overall social marginality of German Jewry served as an impetus for their approach to Islam and to the Jews who hailed from that environment. The example of the German-Jewish orientalists we will encounter, especially in chapter 5, and the Sephardic triumphalists who appear throughout this study demonstrates that knowledge does not always equal power, especially state power.

I will argue that the Ashkenazic orientalists who promoted the cult of the Sephardic Jews did not look at the Muslim world and its subjects as ripe for imperial domination, but, rather, as a place from which contemporary Europe could learn lessons about tolerance and acceptance. According to the Ashkenazic Sephardicists, it was on the Iberian Peninsula under Muslim rule that the Jews of Spain flourished as they had nowhere else in the history of European Jewish settlement. It is for this reason that nineteenth-century German-Jewish historians were among the most energetic promoters of an image of Muslim Spain's *convivencia*, that harmonious and productive interaction among Muslims, Christians, and Jews.[41] The image that these scholars painted was of an open political and cultural environment that made for Jews who were proud, dignified, respectable, and, indeed, physically beautiful.

There is no denying that the Sephardim proved alluring to German Jews, that they were possessed of a certain "mystique," and there is a well-established albeit brief historiographical paper trail that attests to this phenomenon. One of the first to identify this was the historian of medieval German Jewry Ivan Marcus. In a 1985 essay entitled "Beyond the Sephardic Mystique," Marcus noted the role played by nineteenth-century German-Jewish historians in touting the supposed superiority of Spanish Jewry. Moreover, he also incisively pointed to the unfortunate persistence in scholarship of mythologizing medieval Sephardic history. After Marcus, the distinguished historian of German Jewry Ismar Schorsch penned "The Myth of Sephardic Superiority" (1989). In this concise yet rich article, Schorsch noted that "with the advent of emancipation in Central Europe . . . German Jews came to cultivate a lively bias for the religious legacy of Sephardic Jewry forged centuries before on the Iberian Peninsula." Both before and after Schorsch, other scholars have examined one or another of the categories that he touched upon in that important essay. In 1981, the German architectural historian Harold Hammer-Schenk's monumental two volumes on the history of synagogues in Germany contained a relatively brief but valuable section on the neo-Moorish synagogues that began to appear in the nineteenth century. His work was followed in 1984 by the more detailed study of Islamic style elements in German synagogue architecture by Hannelore Künzl. More recently, literature scholars Florian Krobb, Jonathan Hess, and Jonathan Skolnik have focused their attention on nineteenth-century Sephardic-themed German-Jewish fiction. However, with the exception of Carsten Schapkow's German-language volume on the place of the Sephardim in modern German-Jewish culture, most studies of this general subject have been brief and schematic or the work of one scholarly specialist or another. Despite the undeniable value of such works, this is a story best told comprehensively and against the larger backdrop of modern German history as well as modern Jewish history, as it unfolded in both Central and Eastern Europe. However, there is more involved than just this. In what follows I seek to demonstrate that German Jewry did not so much "cultivate a lively bias for the religious legacy of Sephardic Jewry," as Schorsch claimed, as it cultivated a lively bias for the aesthetic and thus secular legacy of Sephardic Jewry. What most attracted the attention of German Jewry was its own invention of Sephardic beauty, which it imaginatively constructed as a reflection of Jewish history, "as it actually happened," to paraphrase the great German historian Leopold von Ranke.[42]

To provide the broadest perspective on the Sephardicist dimension of German-Jewish culture, this study will consider a variety of orientalist cultural productions, among them the work of Enlightenment-era Jewish intellectuals and nineteenth-century anthropologists, ethnographers, synagogue architects, novelists, and historians. Chapter 1 addresses one of the most obvious and, for German Jews in particular, vexing makers of Jewish identity, namely, language. Beginning in the eighteenth century among a small elite and then expanding into the nineteenth century among all classes of German Jews, an obsessive concern with and indeed fear of Yiddish became a central element of what it meant to be a German Jew. This is not the principal subject matter of this chapter but it was a constant presence when it came to the Jewish Enlightenment's attitude toward Hebrew. The Haskalah venerated that language, and we see in Berlin in the 1780s the first important steps toward turning Hebrew into a secular language. That process begat a discussion about the correct way to pronounce Hebrew. This chapter examines this discourse, one wherein advocacy for the Sephardic over the Ashkenazic mode of pronunciation—the latter was perceived as too reminiscent of the sound of Yiddish—was one of the earliest expressions of the Sephardicist turn among German Jews.

Language, it was believed, reflected inner moral health and outward physical appearance. Chapter 2 takes up this theme as we examine moral, behavioral, and physical descriptions of Sephardim and Ashkenazim as depicted by maskilim, as well as anthropologists and ethnographers. Taken together, these various discourses lent themselves to the widespread representation of Sephardim as the most physically beautiful Jews; moreover, such depictions were frequently juxtaposed with negative descriptions of Ashkenazim, especially those from Eastern Europe. While they sometimes borrow heavily from the then-current tropes of racial antisemitism, they depart from the biological determinism inherent in that discourse and suggest instead that even the least attractive of Ashkenazic Jews can, with the right education and speaking the right language, shed their loathsome characteristics and become beautiful like the Sephardic Jews of the Middle Ages and the German Jews of late. Beauty and language are linked in another way. The Sephardic pronunciation of Hebrew was considered authentic by many commentators because they claimed, or at least assumed, that the way Iberian Jews pronounced it was closer to its original form than the Ashkenazic accent. A similar argument was made about physical appearance. In this chapter we will see how archaeological evidence depicting ancient Israelites was used to make the claim that there was a physical line of descent from ancient Judea to the medieval *Juderia*.

Chapter 3 continues with the theme of Jewish beauty but moves the discussion from bodies to buildings. From the 1830s to the 1860s, the growth of German cities, the expanding Jewish population, and a loosening of restrictions on the appearance and location of Jewish buildings led to the construction of many new synagogues. Among Germans, urban expansion occasioned a long, complex, and at times bitter debate about the ideal style of German architecture. Jews were implicated in this debate because of their own building boom, and with it we see the appearance of various Oriental architectural styles employed in these new synagogues. This chapter traces the evolution of these various designs, which at first appeared modest and subtle but finally came to full-blown maturity and splendor with the appearance of grand, neo-Moorish synagogues. While such buildings would later come to appear across the world, it is in Germany that they originated, and at a particular moment in architectural history unique to that time and place. These houses of worship were built in an entirely fictitious Sephardic style and were almost always designed by Gentile architects. In the design phase, the plans and rationale for the way these buildings would look were tied to questions of Jewish origins in the Land of Israel, their history in the Diaspora, and the nature of German-Jewish identity.

The final two chapters of the book take up the subject of history writing in two distinct but deeply intertwined genres—the historical novel and historical scholarship. For German Jews these were two new literary forms that emerged almost simultaneously in the nineteenth century, their link personified, for example, by an author like the poet Heinrich Heine (1797–1856), who not only wrote important novellas and poetry centered on Sephardim and Marranos but also was a member of the founding circle of young university students that in 1819 established the Association for Jewish Culture and Scholarship, the first learned society dedicated to researching and writing Jewish history.

In chapter 4 we enter squarely into the realm of German-Jewish popular culture as we see how belles lettres contributed mightily to the dissemination of a set of images of Sephardic Jews that became a fixed part of the German-Jewish imagination. For the most part, the Jewish public's view of the Sephardim was shaped by the scores of novels, poems, and short stories that were frequently published in serialized form in Jewish newspapers. Fast-paced adventure stories with vulnerable Jewish damsels who reject the advances of Christian suitors, Marranos who hold true to their faith despite the threat posed by terrifying inquisitors, and Sephardim who resurrect their successful lives in the lands of their dispersion after 1492 are the protagonists of these extremely popular and influential tales.

However, such stories were not mere exercises in romanticization—though that certainly happened—for the depictions of Sephardim were tailored to suit divergent German-Jewish sensibilities. So, for example, where Reform Jews tended to see Marranos as courageous adherents of the faith, Orthodox authors tended to be less forgiving, seeing them as weak and all too easily seduced into remaining in Spain even if it meant apostasy. These differing interpretations notwithstanding, such stories, whether written by Reform or Orthodox authors, agreed on one thing, namely, it was the Catholic Reconquista that had brought devastation upon what had been an ideal community, composed of beautiful, refined, successful Jews, products of their preexpulsion Muslim environment.

Chapter 5 focuses on the representations of Islam and the Spanish-Jewish past as constructed by Jewish historians. Beginning in the 1830s historians started to "package" the notion of a Jewish "Golden Age," a concept that has enjoyed remarkable staying power, a result of the idea's being promoted simultaneously in popular and academic culture, the one symbiotically reinforcing the other. Here too we will see history written under the influence of the personal religious sensibilities and cultural biases of the historians themselves. Their frequent juxtapositions of Sephardic and Eastern European Jewry, always involving the denigration of the latter, exemplify yet again the powerful hold of Sephardic Jewry over German Jews and the utilitarian uses to which the Iberian-Jewish past could be put. Likewise, the historians' repeated emphasis on the tolerance extended to Jews in the Islamic world was a foil for their hostile feelings about Christianity and the contemporary antisemitic movement. In other words, the orientalism of these pro-Islamic and pro-Sephardic Ashkenazic Jews formed the basis of a profound critique of the European state.

In the end, I hope to demonstrate how all the German-Jewish Sephardicists we will encounter in this study were engaged in a complex process of orientalist and neo-romantic self-fashioning, wherein they sought to change the aesthetics of German Jewry by lionizing those of the Sephardim while simultaneously distancing themselves from the majority of their fellow Ashkenazim—the Jews of Poland. The goal of this aesthetic makeover was the promotion not of assimilation but, rather, of acculturation, and the creation of a new form of German-Jewish identity, ironically enough, inspired by a Sephardic model.

CHAPTER ONE

The Sound of Jewish Modernity

SEPHARDIC HEBREW AND THE BERLIN HASKALAH

For at least a century, historians have depicted the Berlin Haskalah as a textual, hortatory, and pedagogic revolution in Jewish intellectual life. In books, journals, manifestos, and plays, the goals of the Haskalah were written down or performed, serving as how-to guides to Jewish self-improvement. In the felicitous expression of the historian Shmuel Feiner, the figures of the Jewish Enlightenment formed a "republic of letters."[1] As such, the Haskalah is chiefly recalled as a literary enterprise. But there is another dimension to the Haskalah, one that has received little or no attention from scholars, and that is the Haskalah as an auditory experience. While it was intimately bound to the purely intellectual manifestations of Jewish Enlightenment thought, the auditory was also distinct in that it represented the sensory aspect of the Haskalah.

Specifically, nearly all those who were either involved in or later influenced by the Berlin Haskalah of the late eighteenth century were preoccupied with language generally but, more particularly, by the very sound Jews made when talking. The Haskalah arose amid the drive of centralizing European states to promote the standardization of the written and the spoken word. Both the command Jews had of various languages and the particular accents they possessed became important markers of social, economic, and even religious status. Because accents laid bare one's geographic origins and cultural orientation, nearly all those who wished to refashion the Jewish people turned their attention to the way Jews spoke, the sounds they uttered, and the impact of those sounds on the listener. Advocates of reform went so far as to express the belief that cognitive and moral improvement of the Jews would accompany language and accent change.[2]

To consciously alter one's accent implies a sense of knowing exactly the way one wants to sound in the future. It requires an aural template, a sonic frame of reference, onto and against which the desired metamorphosis can take place. The Berlin Haskalah set out such a model in the course of its advocacy on behalf of the revitalization of the Hebrew language. A major concern of the maskilim on this score was the felt need to discourage Jews from uttering Hebrew with their normative Ashkenazic forms of pronunciation. Rather, for aesthetic reasons, ones deeply implicated in the way the Hebraically literate elite came to see themselves and their coreligionists, they encouraged Jews to discard their mode of speaking Hebrew and replace it with Sephardic pronunciation. The project of changing the sounds Jews made when speaking, for the purpose of enhancing the delight of listeners, was informed by a particular kind of internal Jewish orientalism, one that was characterized by phonological self-abnegation, on the one hand, and sonic celebration of an alternative mode of Jewish speech, on the other. The promotion of Sephardic Hebrew went beyond making a case for its preeminence and entailed some of the earliest Central European paeans to Sephardic culture and the superiority of Jewish life under Islam.

Expanding knowledge of Sephardic culture and traditions came about with the noticeable increase in the number of medieval Sephardic works appearing on Ashkenazic bookshelves. Across Europe in the eighteenth century, Iberian philosophical, scientific, kabbalistic, halakhic, and liturgical texts increasingly occupied and fascinated Ashkenazic intellectuals. Even among those quintessential Ashkenazic Jews, the Hasidim, Sephardic practices were incorporated into the new forms of religious observance that emerged in the wake of their pietistic revolution. Elsewhere, secret Sabbatean cells encouraged religious subversion, while kabbalists and mystics inspired by their Sephardic predecessors were to be found throughout the Ashkenazic world.[3]

To be sure, not all Ashkenazim were Sephardic triumphalists. But paradoxically, for those who were, the turn to medieval Sepharad was one marker of the Ashkenazic path to modernity in that it expanded the intellectual canon, introducing old ideas that were now read afresh against the backdrop of a rapidly changing European world, while the exposure to Sephardic culture helped give structure and substance to Ashkenazic self-critique.[4] The Haskalah left nothing untouched. There was disaffection expressed with the Ashkenazic educational system, the rabbis, the morality and dignity of Jews, their lack of appreciation of nature and of beauty, their appearance, and even their diet.[5] The litany of withering self-criticism was not the end of the story, for if it represented the thesis whose antithesis was the Ashkenazic championing of Sephardic culture, the synthesis was to be the refashioning of the Ashkenazic Jews by having them emulate Sephardic manners. The ideological impulse and strategy of those advocating the Ashkenazic makeover manifested itself in an enthusiastic, largely ahistorical celebration of the social conditions under which the Sephardim lived, conditions held to be so propitious that they gave rise to the gloriousness of Sephardic culture, which in turn meant that such Jews had been the beneficiaries of a sensory education that had historically been unavailable to Ashkenazic Jews.

That education and the Ashkenazic myth of Sephardic superiority that was its ideological ballast began in Berlin. As it pertained to Hebrew and the way it was supposed to sound, this mode of thought began in the late eighteenth century and reached its apotheosis at the end of the nineteenth with the advent of Zionism. This view did not emerge out of nothingness, and in what follows I examine the intellectual context and scholarly debts and social networks that influenced the maskilic project of making the Jews a euphonious people. There was, to be sure, a textual Haskalah, but there was also an acoustic Haskalah.

• • • • •

In the beginning was Hebrew. The struggle over language use was paramount to the modern Jewish experience. That struggle was often seen as a simple battle between the proponents of Hebrew and those of Yiddish or, and this was less acute, between Hebraists and those who advocated that Jews adopt European vernaculars. But in truth, the earliest concerns had to do with Hebrew itself. The issue turned on the suppleness, indeed the very usability, of Hebrew. Already among Sephardim in the Middle Ages, authors such as Moses ibn Ezra, Judah Halevi, Maimonides, and Samuel ibn Tibbon had noted some of Hebrew's inadequacies when it came to expressing secular ideas, inadequacies that were particularly conspicuous when Hebrew was compared to Arabic.[6] Deeply dedicated to Hebrew, they lamented that Exile had led to its abandonment as a living vernacular, and thus had it remained frozen in time.[7]

By contrast, among Italian Hebraists of the Renaissance and thereafter, there was a feeling of greater confidence about Hebrew. For them, the language of the Bible was pure, its structure, syntax, and grammar all perfect. For distinguished rabbis such Yehuda Messer Leon, Yehuda Aryeh Modena, and, later, Moshe Hayyim Luzzatto, proper biblical Hebrew was so rich, so precious, that it was to be quarantined off from the importation of borrowed words—and the reference here was not to Gentile languages but to mishnaic Hebrew, which some authorities saw as separate from, though obviously connected to, the Hebrew of the Bible.[8] Especially in the domain of poetry, they cautioned, only biblical Hebrew was to be used, hence their rejection of medieval liturgical poetry, known as *piyyut*. They considered the authors of such works to have disregarded the basic grammatical and syntactical rules of Hebrew; most unforgivably, those authors introduced foreign words instead of relying on biblical terms. The charge that maskilim and later Hebraists leveled at Yiddish, namely, that it was a corrupted language (*la'agei safah*), was also directed at medieval Hebrew by those who championed the singular use of biblical Hebrew.[9] Purity, as we will see, was central to eighteenth-century notions of aesthetic beauty, and languages whose purity had been compromised were regarded as an assault on aural sensibilities.[10]

With the Haskalah of the eighteenth century, promoters of Hebrew faced a linguistic crisis. Though most of them held Hebrew to be the original language of humanity (as did many Christians) and still considered it sacred, they also recognized its limitations thanks to its comparatively small and antiquated vocabulary. Considered incapable of expressing recently coined terms drawn from the natural sciences, technology, and philosophy, Hebrew, in its current state, was deemed quite unable to meet the needs of the modern Jew. Moreover, the problem was compounded by the fact that Jews were no longer contributing to Hebrew's vitality. The impression of the London physician Mordechai Gumpel Schnaber (1741–1797) was typical of this line of thought. In his short Hebrew encyclopedia of mathematics and natural science that appeared in 1771, Schnaber lamented that

> we have lost our Holy Tongue; no one studies it and no one longs for it. If we look at all the nations around us, both near and far, [we see that they] neither rest nor remain silent and keep on composing books and expanding their languages . . . why do we squander the bequest of our fathers and abandon our Holy language? We have become idle . . . our language is poor and deficient because there is no one among us who knows how to call a thing by its name in Hebrew, or how to describe it, unless it is found in the Torah or Prophets, and even then there are few among us whose language is pure and whose speech, pleasant (*tsekhi ha-melitsa ve-ne'imei ha-dvarim*).[11]

The polemical nature of Ashkenazic self-criticism demanded that Schnaber ignore the fact that other languages wanted for modern words as well. More pointedly, however, of Schnaber's many claims it is his desire for "pleasant"-sounding speech that goes to the heart of the auditory dimension of the Haskalah, for according to eighteenth-century linguistic theory, language that was pleasant to the ear tended also to be "pure."[12] With the passage of time, this sentiment only strengthened. As race science and linguistic theory converged in the nineteenth century, the pleasantness (read superiority) of a language became increasingly predicated on the imagined (racial) purity of the speakers of that language.[13]

The paradox engendered by Hebrew was that its antiquity, which endowed it with prestige, also consigned it to limited, largely liturgical use.[14] Rectifying the problem posed in the present by Hebrew's deep past was of major concern in maskilic circles. The challenge lay in expanding and modernizing Hebrew while at the same time taking care not to compromise the deeply held belief in the purity and perfection of biblical Hebrew.[15] In contrast to their Italian Jewish predecessors, Central and Eastern European rabbis such as Shlomo Zalman Hanau (1687–1746), Israel ben Moshe Halevi of Zamosc (1710–1772), Shlomo Pappenheim (1740–1814), and Isaac Satanow (1733–1805) regarded mishnaic Hebrew as pure Hebrew and argued that incorporating it in order to expand the possibilities of biblical Hebrew was entirely permissible.[16] Thus the linguistic problem for Pappenheim was not caused by anything intrinsic to the language of the Bible. Rather, "it is not Hebrew that is poor ... but we whose knowledge is inadequate. We are ignorant of the many books that perished, the 'Histories of the Kings,' for instance, the 'Midrashim of the Prophets' and their like, all of which were written in Hebrew. In addition, after Hebrew ceased to be a spoken language, parts of it ... were forgotten and equally lost."[17] We thus begin to see that the self-critique of Ashkenazic intellectuals did not spare Hebrew. However, in what would become a mantra among ideologues of all modern Jewish persuasions, chief responsibility for the sad state of affairs lay with the people. In the realm of language, it was they, not Hebrew, who were deficient.

The people did indeed need help, and it is not surprising that over the course of the eighteenth century one can detect an increasing preoccupation with Hebrew. In Germany, many scholarly and instructional books on Hebrew grammar appeared, written in both Hebrew and Yiddish, aimed at both adults and schoolchildren. The goal of course was to promote familiarity with, if not mastery of, Hebrew's grammatical rules and thus facilitate comprehension of the Bible. There was a widely held view that ignorance of Hebrew grammar had compromised Jews, and it was up to them to recapture this lost wisdom.[18] None of the authors of these texts would have agreed with the assessment of Hebrew grammar expressed in Johann Gottfried Herder's *Spirit of Hebrew Poetry* (1783). Herder, a man fascinated by Jews, their history, and their ancient language, and an advocate of their legal emancipation, constructed in this work a dialogue about the nature of Hebrew between Alciphron and Euthyphron, the former lamenting, "How imperfect [a language] is it! How unfixed and uncertain are the tenses of the verbs! One never knows whether the time referred to by them be today or yesterday, a thousand years ago, or a thousand years to come."[19]

The exchange recorded by Herder echoes, to some extent, the dialogical interchange between Al Khazari and the Rabbi in Judah Halevi's twelfth-century *Kuzari*. Interrogating the Rabbi on all things to do with Judaism, Al Khazari asks, "Is Hebrew superior to other languages? Do we not see distinctly that the latter are more finished and comprehensive?" The Rabbi concedes that "it shared the fate of its bearers, degenerating and dwindling with them." But this was merely a consequence of the ravaging effects of Exile. The Rabbi then offers a ringing defense of Hebrew, one that the doubting Al Khazari comes to accept: "Considered historically and logically, its [Hebrew's] original form is the noblest."[20] Among Jews, Hebrew was referred to as *leshon ha-kodesh* (language of holiness), or *lashon elohit* (language of God) and, as both names suggest, was simply considered perfect. There was no Jewish Alciphron.

That did not mean that the maskilim failed to recognize the reason for contemporary Hebrew's deficiencies. History, they maintained, had been cruel to the Jews. Most saw Exile, with its discriminatory pressures and its assimilatory power, as responsible for the overall poverty of Jewish culture and the particularly depressed state of Hebrew. They looked with envy at other nations and noted that those peoples that engaged in the full panoply of occupations and arts, and pursued philosophical and scientific endeavors, also saw their languages enriched by the sheer diversity of such experiences. The fuller the cultural and economic life of a people, the richer, more layered, and more deeply textured were its means of written and oral communication. This was precisely the view of the prolific Polish maskil Yehuda Leib Ben-Ze'ev (1764–1814).

In his account of the history of the Hebrew language, Ben-Ze'ev identifies its beginnings with Sinai (as opposed to the creation of the world) and observes that it fell into disuse with the Exile and underwent a rebirth (*leda sheniyah*) in medieval Spain but was lost again in early modern Ashkenaz, albeit recognizing the efforts in that era of a coterie of scholars, Jews and non-Jews alike, who strove to keep Hebrew alive. Among them were the German-Jewish Hebrew grammarian Elia Levita; the Christians Johannes Buxtorf the Elder, professor of Hebrew at Basel, and the Göttingen orientalist and biblical scholar Johann David Michaelis; and the poet Herder. While he acknowledged the efforts of the philosopher Moses Mendelssohn (1729–1786) to revitalize Hebrew, Ben-Ze'ev, who from 1787 to 1790 lived in Berlin, nonetheless lamented that the youth of his own generation had lost both interest in and facility with the language.[21]

According to Ben-Ze'ev, the crisis became most acute after about 1500 and had continued into his day. During this time, it was not only the discrimination Jews faced from the outside world that narrowed the frame of their experience. Jews too were responsible for their low cultural level. The rise of religious mysticism, along with the neglect of Torah study and, particularly, of the rules of grammar, all conspired against the Hebrew language. Under normal social conditions, however, a different, more hopeful outcome was to be expected:

> As long as a nation maintains its independence and its people live in peace in their own land, following their own political and ethical norms—wisdom and the arts multiply among them, giving rise to thinkers and artists, scientists and writers, rhetoricians, poets, and authors of books on all kinds of subjects. As a result, the language expands . . . gaining the capacity to express any idea. Indeed, the beauty of the language and its perfection are then taken as an indication of the perfection of the nation.[22]

In his attempt to define enlightenment, Moses Mendelssohn noted similarly that, "generally, the language of a people is the best indication of its education, of its culture as well as its enlightenment, in terms of both its extent and its strength."[23]

This was far from an exclusively Jewish idea. At least since the seventeenth century, European languages had come in for similar scrutiny. In his study of the German language since the Reformation, *Ausführlich Arbeit von der Teutschen Haubt-Sprache* (A Detailed Account of the Standard German Language; 1663), the baroque grammarian Justus Georg Schottel (1612–1676) argued that German, contrary to widespread belief, was not inferior to Greek, Latin, and Hebrew, and, in fact, surpassed them in its suppleness. He urged his readers to "pay attention to our German and note how the German language speaks with powerful short expression and pleasing sound . . . [that] the roots are nearly everywhere univocal, clear, bright, evident, perfect, yes their quality such that nature has performed its master stroke in them." The reason for this was that "our age-old forefathers have not obtained them by begging from foreign nations and enemies." Finally, Schottel observed, any "unwelcome deficiencies with a German oration cannot be attributed to the deficient properties of the language but to the deficiencies of the speaker."[24]

The philosopher Gottfried Wilhelm Leibniz (1646–1716), who was familiar with both Schottel's work and that of his contemporary, the prolific poet and language theorist, Georg Philipp Harsdörffer (1607–1658), employed the urgent title *Ermahnung an die Teutsche, ihren Verstand und Sprache besser zu üben* (An Exhortation to the Germans to Better Cultivate Their Intellect and Language; 1679, first published 1846) to inextricably link the two elements.[25] Leibniz followed this with an influential essay entitled *Die Unvorgreiflichen Gedanken betreffend die Ausübung und Verbesserung der Teutschen Sprache* (Modest Thoughts concerning the Practice and Improvement of the German Language; 1709, first published 1727). Appealing to their sense of patriotism, Leibniz enjoined Germans in both works to use a refined form of German in order to better compete with the English, French, and Italians. He held that "languages are the best mirror of the human mind," and were thus the source of cultural and ethnic identity.[26] Leibniz also believed that proper German usage was central to the project of national reawakening. In an essay he penned in the 1680s entitled "Einige patriotischen Gedanken" (Some Patriotic Thoughts), Leibniz wrote, "I am of the opinion that the nations (*Nationen*) that develop and perfect their languages thereby have a great advantage in sharpening their intellect."[27] Currently, he observed, Germany suffered from cultural backwardness, a direct consequence of the people's poor use of the national language.[28] Whatever particular sentiments of dismay and frustration the Berlin maskilim expressed over the way Jews spoke must be seen in the broader context of contemporary German language politics, which was similarly replete with mixed feelings—a sense of inferiority about the way German was currently spoken by the majority and great confidence that if learned properly, German and thus Germans could take their rightful place in Europe.

The notion that language was a tool of cognition, which, when properly used, had the power to elevate and ennoble, was a key principle of both the Enlightenment and the Haskalah. The connection between language and thought and their mutual influence upon one another were concerns of such urgency that in 1759 the Prussian Academy of Sciences held an essay contest to investigate this very subject. The winner was the Hebrew Bible scholar Johann David Michaelis, a man who, in the 1780s, would come to publicly reject the idea of Jewish emancipation, earning himself an adversary in Moses Mendelssohn. But for now, Mendelssohn's views of Michaelis's essay "Beantwortung der Frage von dem Einfluss der Meinungen in die Sprache, und der Sprache in die Meinungen" (Response to the Question of the Influence of Opinions on Language and of Language on Opinions) were wholly positive.[29] Contestants were expected to provide practical suggestions on how to modernize languages so as to allow them to accommodate modern ideas, a subject already under discussion with regard to Hebrew. Mendelssohn was greatly impressed and influenced by Michaelis's essay, writing a very appreciative review of it.[30] The essay would reflect some of Mendelssohn's most deeply held beliefs about the faculty of speech and its relation to reason, and the capacity of both working in tandem to contribute to human perfectibility.[31] In a practical sense Mendelssohn and other advocates of Hebrew expected Jews to reap the cognitive rewards of knowing Hebrew well, but especially of pronouncing it properly.

The implementation of practical language reforms in the eighteenth century also colored the early Haskalah's attitude to Hebrew. In England, France, and Germany, school reformers, educators, and bureaucrats agitated for the introduction of formal language education into the curriculum.[32] Various historical interpretations locate the eighteenth-century drive to create uniform national languages, designed to replace minor languages and dialects, at the center of fundamental processes such "social disciplining," "rationalization," and "state centralization." The sociologist Norbert Elias also recognized language mastery as a crucial part of both the "civilizing process" and the social transformation away from the dominance of the "culture of the court." With reference to Germany, Gerhard Oestreich deemed the goals of language politics less benign, as he considered the forcible acquisition of a common language to be an important element in the "repression of the individual" and his forcible yielding to the "absolutist state," while ensuring the development of "class differentiation" and "class consciousness." For Joachim Gessinger, the promotion of "language facility" and "language consciousness" was integral to the cultivation of "social commerce" and "collective experience."[33] More recently, Andreas Gardt has identified the eighteenth-century consolidation of High German (*Hochdeutsch*) as a consequence of certain factors that, as was the case with maskilic critiques of Hebrew, identified history and its institutions as having conspired against the development of German. Changes that began in the sixteenth and seventeenth centuries led to the eventual adoption of a uniform national language. Among the major factors influencing this development were Luther's Bible translation; the rise of new territorial and administrative structures; incipient capitalism; the growing sense that one's mother tongue was an expression of political and cultural identity, especially in the wake of the decline of the Holy Roman Empire; the desire of advocates of language reform to rid German of the empire's arcane legal and chancery argot in favor of a language that more closely approximated that which people actually spoke; the emergence of an educated bourgeoisie; and the rise of increasingly standardized scientific method and discourse.[34] And as German-language theorists had claimed for over a century, their mother tongue was just as suitable for scientific and philosophical discourse as Latin, French, and English. It was simply up to the people to master it.

It is in the context of eighteenth-century German pedagogical reforms and highly publicized programs that focused on "proper" language usage, and its material as well as moral benefits, that we must understand the language politics of the Berlin Haskalah. Indeed, the later Zionist program that aimed at the Hebraization of the Jewish people was likewise indebted, though not exclusively, to the ideological and intellectual impulses that came to the fore during the Enlightenment. In the Jewish context the emphases that were at play among the majority society were adapted to specific Jewish needs. Where European monarchs saw the introduction of a single national language as necessary for the successful creation of the centralized state, the promise of civic emancipation informed Jewish attitudes to language; where the economic trend pointed to growing forms of capitalist mercantilism, various non-Jewish advocates, such as Joseph II of Austria, sought to promote occupational change among Jews along with the Germanization of Jewish business discourses, while certain Jews were also concerned to expand the spectrum of Jewish economic activity; and where the existence of dialects and minor languages was regarded as a hindrance to the civilizing process, we can detect a similar impulse among Jewish proponents of High German and Hebrew.[35]

Closely related to the belief in the capacity of language to act as a civilizing agent and the Herderian view of language as a key to "national character" is the vituperative maskilic condemnation of the Jewish lingua franca, Yiddish, which runs like a red thread through all Jewish discourse concerning Hebrew from the eighteenth to the twentieth century.[36] To take the views of a native Yiddish speaker such as Moses Mendelssohn as emblematic, we must recall that he declared that Yiddish was in part responsible for the immorality of the common man (read Jew) and then went on to proclaim the salutary benefits to be expected with the adoption of High German (*Hochdeutsch*) among Jews.[37] The irony that Mendelssohn conversed almost daily in Yiddish with other Jews and corresponded with his wife, Fromet, in Yiddish, seems to have been lost on him. But for Hebraizers of the Berlin Haskalah, the civic and moral improvement of the Jews had to begin not merely with eliminating Yiddish and cultivating Hebrew but with making the sound of the Holy Tongue commensurate with its inherent perfection. Beyond the link between language and ethics lay the connection between language and aesthetics, and it is here that we can begin to more closely attend to the speech of Jews.[38]

The relatively sudden concern of maskilim about the aesthetics of the Jewish people, generally speaking, and the focus on their accents in particular, constitute a set of ideas that had rarely been expressed by Jews before this time. Here again, we must turn to the larger German intellectual and cultural context in order to properly situate and elucidate emerging Jewish concerns. These concerns, or, more properly put, anxieties, were informed by three intellectual trends central to the German Enlightenment: aesthetic experience, art criticism, and music appreciation. And in turn, our interest lies with the way political and cultural elites in Germany sought to channel such experiences toward Jewish *bürgerliche Verbesserung*, or civic improvement.

Although aesthetics had been subject to philosophical speculation since classical times, in 1735 a young art historian named Alexander Gottlieb Baumgarten (1714–1762) published his *Philosophical Meditations on Some Requirements of the Poem* and in it designated aesthetics a new discipline within philosophy. Baumgarten takes up the distinction between the higher and lower mental faculties, or, put differently, between the rational and the sensitive, as applied to art, especially poetry. The aim of poetry was the cultivation of "perfect sensory discourse."[39] Baumgarten begins the *Meditations* with a number of linked definitions of what constitutes "discourse": (1) a "series of words that bring to mind (*intelligimus*) connected representations," (2) "sensible representations" as ones "received through the lower part of the cognitive faculty," (3) "sensible discourse" as a "discourse of sensible representations," and finally (4) a "poem" as an example of "perfect sensible discourse." In turn, sensible discourse has three components: "(1) sensible representations, (2) their interconnections, and (3) the words, or the articulate sounds which are represented by the letters and which symbolize the words." For Baumgarten, the perfection of a poem resides in both its medium, namely, the words used, and the imagery the poem evokes. These two spheres are not separate but are indeed linked.[40]

In a later work, *Aesthetica* (1750 and 1758), Baumgarten begins his treatise with the following definition of his subject: "Aesthetics (as the theory of the liberal arts, as inferior cognition, as the art of beautiful thinking and as the art of thinking analogous to reason) is the science of sensual cognition."[41] Baumgarten regarded aesthetics as a science of sensual cognition, as well as a theory of art,[42] and identifies three different potential sources of beauty in a work of art: "the harmony of the thoughts insofar as we abstract from their order and their signs," or means of expression; "the harmony of the order in which we meditate upon the beautifully thought content"; and "the harmony of the signs," or means of expression, "among themselves and with the content and the order of the content."[43] Here Baumgarten deploys the traditional rhetorical categories of *inventio*, *dispositio*, and *elocutio*, and conceives of the latter two, the harmony of the thoughts and the harmony of the expression of those thoughts, as indivisible parts of a single rhetorical whole.[44]

Beginning in the eighteenth century, the Jewish world also became deeply concerned with aesthetics, particularly in a Baumgartian sense. The outer appearance of Jewish life came under assault by those Jews, the intellectual elite, who felt that their own ideas and language, by which they meant Hebrew, were purer and more beautiful than the language of the majority of their coreligionists, by which they meant Yiddish, and that rectifying the myriad cultural deficiencies in all Jews was a sine qua non for acceptance by the Gentile world and was imperative for self-improvement. Maskilim held to the belief that Hebrew, if spoken properly, would help restore to the Jews their lost dignity. To again become worthy of their noble biblical origins would lead Christians to see them in a more positive light. Therapeutically speaking, the adoption of correctly articulated Hebrew would begin to reverse the ill effects of Exile.[45]

Moses Mendelssohn was profoundly influenced by Baumgarten, and by the latter's student Georg Friedrich Meier, who introduced and explicated Baumgarten's dense Latin writings to the German-reading public. In his writings on aesthetics but also in those on language, Mendelssohn reiterated "the harmony of the thoughts and the harmony of the expression" credo but went further.[46] In his book *Jerusalem* (1783), Mendelssohn characterized Judaism as a religion of the spoken rather than the written word, its "living tradition passed on by oral instruction."[47] Thus the role of orality in Judaism was to temper blind faith by the use of reason, because for Mendelssohn, the laws were unintelligible without reasoned explication. The precision with which Hebrew was articulated is paramount and could never be compromised.

Mendelssohn believed that the Bible represented the spoken word, and, as with the law itself, he believed that the Hebrew accent was given at Sinai. There, at that place and time, Moses had heard the Torah spoken by God, with "full emotion, inflection and intonation." Moses in turn faithfully transmitted the law to Joshua, and from there it was passed on for all time to the Jewish people. God had spoken, the people had heard, and it was good. What ensured that the people would speak with God's pronunciation is that the Bible's system of accents was written into the text. All languages, Hebrew included, begin as oral forms of communication. According to Mendelssohn, Hebrew's uniqueness lay in the fact that no other ancient language had bequeathed to future generations exact instructions on how the language was supposed to sound.[48]

For Mendelssohn, the Bible as sonic primer was effective only so long as the Jews lived in their own land and spoke the language of the Bible as a vernacular tongue. However, history had intervened, and with the Babylonian exile "the Jews mixed with heathens, took foreign wives, and forgot their language." Mendelssohn sought to help salvage Hebrew. In the introduction to his Pentateuch translation, which contains his apologia for translating scripture into German, *Or la-Netiva* (Light for the Path; 1782), Mendelssohn returned to a well-worn theme to outline why Hebrew had fallen into disuse and why, sadly, Bible translation was necessary: "So long as the children of Israel never changed their language and this was the common language of the land, [the one] in which all people, both great and small, were well versed, there was no need for a Bible translation. All who heard the Bible read [aloud] by the [official] reader paid heed to the exact vocalization, the melody, and the accent, as it was intended. On their own they were able to understand the intention of the text according to its simple meaning."[49]

In his project of Hebrew and thus Jewish rehabilitation, Mendelssohn paid heed to translation, grammatical principles, and exegesis, all of which he deemed to be inseparable. In setting out his theoretical propositions on language and his understanding of Hebrew's unique architecture of pronunciation, Mendelssohn drew from two sources: the lively eighteenth-century German philosophical discourse on language criticism and medieval Andalusian scholarship on Hebrew, including the work of Maimonides, Judah Halevi, Ibn Ezra, and Nachmanides.[50] His views on Hebrew and language more generally would have a decisive impact on the young maskil Naphtali Herz Wessely (1725–1805), whose treatise *Divrei Shalom ve-Emet* (Words of Peace and Truth; 1782) "set out the ideology of the Jewish Enlightenment for the first time" and will be the focus of our attention below.[51]

Mendelssohn wrote widely on aesthetics and other related philosophical categories that were in vogue in the eighteenth century, such as taste, pleasure, and sensations.[52] Amid the constellation of aesthetic writings with which Mendelssohn was engaged were also those of the art historian Johann Joachim Winckelmann (1717–1768), whose *History of Ancient Art* (1764) largely shaped contemporary European views of classical art and beauty.[53] Mendelssohn was a great admirer of Winckelmann, whose championing of the superiority of Greek art would have inspired Mendelssohn to see in the poetry of biblical Hebrew an art form equal in worth, if not superior, to that of the Gentile ancients.[54] Though Mendelssohn kept overt reference to Jewish matters out of his aesthetic writings, he nonetheless had aesthetics in mind when considering Jewish matters, perhaps foremost among them Hebrew.

While sight had long been the most privileged of the senses, a heighted interest in sound became a key focus of Enlightenment-era natural and experimental philosophy as well as science. Alain Corbin, who has studied the cultural significance of sound and smell, has taught us the extent to which these senses came to symbolize notions of disgust, desire, and difference.[55] All three of these categories can be applied to the subject of Jews and sound. Poorly spoken or accented Hebrew evoked disgust, in contrast to the desired beautifully sounding Hebrew, while the difference between the maskilim and the masses could be heard in the way they spoke. Outside of Jewish society, the ridicule to which Jews were subjected thanks to their rudimentary command of German, whether real or imagined, or because they spoke Yiddish, became an important part of popular culture; the poorly spoken Jew, with a nasally or high-pitched voice, became a stock character in German theater, especially in the genre of farce.[56] There is no doubt that the very public nature of the lambasting made German Jews hypersensitive to these charges and thus played a major role in the development of Jewish self-perceptions of they way they sounded.

To go beyond the spoken word to sound more generally, a long-standing charge—one that first emerged in second-century Christianity—held that Jews were discordant noisemakers. Their penchant for making what was to Christian ears an unintelligible din was yet a further sign of their rejection by God. In the *perfida synagoga*, the heterophony so characteristic of non-Western musical forms grated on the ears of Christians. So offensive were such sounds that in Germany they became the benchmark for all that was an assault on the ears. There, unpleasant sounds, whether made by Christian or Jew, adult or child, were analogized in a popular expression still in widespread use into the twentieth century, namely, that what was being heard was *Lärm wie in einer Judenschule* (noise as in a synagogue).[57]

In light of this perception, one might also be entitled to wonder about the role music played in the changing auditory sensibilities of eighteenth-century German Jews and the impact this may have had on Mendelssohn, his maskilic disciples, and their notions of Hebrew's euphony. The Jewish Enlightenment took place against the background of a musical revolution, a high point in the creation of modern music, and Berlin's elite Jews were deeply involved in the creation and promotion of new musical forms. The music historian Anselm Gerhard has gone so far as to claim that it was Jews who were largely responsible for changing the nature of Prussia's music by moving it away from its courtly domain and into the realm of bourgeois culture.[58]

Within the network of Jewish musical connoisseurs there were some who were either devotees of the Haskalah or part of its larger friendship and familial circles. The Haskalah journal *Sulamith*, for example, published sheet music for "the joy of the journal's music lovers."[59] At the heart of the Berlin music scene was the wealthy Itzig family, headed by its patriarch, Daniel Itzig (1722–1799). Both at his home and in the musical salons of his daughters Sara Levy and Hanna Fliess in Berlin, as well as in the home of their sister in Vienna, Fanny von Arnstein, who was a patron of Mozart, the new music was performed and promoted, while aspiring musicians were provided with stipends.[60] As members of the many musical societies and clubs already in existence, most of which were then absorbed into the Berlin Singakademie, newly founded in 1791, the Itzigs and many other Jews, including Moses Mendelssohn's son, Abraham, stood at the center of a circle of like-minded Jews whose assimilatory impulses had a direct impact on their changing auditory tastes.[61] It was change that was also being institutionalized among Jewish youth. At Mendelssohn's suggestion, Daniel Itzig, together with his son-in-law David Friedländer, established the Berlin Jewish Free School in 1778, the prototype of the maskilic school, where along with secular subjects, the students were taught to pronounce Hebrew with Sephardic accents. Among the group of Jewish music lovers was Carl Bernhard Wessely, an accomplished pianist and the nephew of the Hebrew scholar Naphtali Herz Wessely. Carl Bernhard, who lived in Hamburg, enjoyed a deeply close relationship with the intellectual Elise Reimarus, who in turn became extremely close with Mendelssohn late in the philosopher's life.[62] Wessely is perhaps best known as the composer of the mourning cantata in honor of Moses Mendelssohn's death.[63]

David Friedländer (1750–1834) was a wealthy and learned Jewish industrialist from Königsberg and, after Mendelssohn, was the leading figure of Prussian Jewry. A fighter for Jewish emancipation and radical maskil, Friedländer also actively promoted the reform of Jews and Judaism along aesthetic lines, stressing the need for Jews to attend to their oral and auditory deficiencies.[64] In 1819 he published a report on the state of those Polish Jews who had come under Prussian rule as a result of the partitions of Poland that had taken place in 1772, 1793, and 1795. He found them culturally wanting in almost every way possible, disparaging them as distinct, offensively exotic, and utterly unassimilated despite decades of Prussian governance. Friedländer made a number of pointed recommendations for the improvement of Polish Jewry, placing the adoption of the German language above all else. Following the stipulations enshrined in Joseph II's Edict of Toleration of 1782, Friedländer insisted that all oral and written communication by Jews, without exception, be conducted in German. Speech, according to Friedländer, was "not only the most powerful organ, it was the only one that could increase and refine cognition and ennoble one's sensibilities." All of this involved dispensing with not only Yiddish but Hebrew too, which in Poland he found to be "a dark, rabbinic-Aramaic dead language" that "aside from a few Talmudists hardly anyone understands." He predicted that instituting these changes would lead not only to social, cultural, and occupational change but also to religious reform. Among the innovations Friedländer recommended be instituted were praying in the vernacular and the introduction of music into synagogue services. Echoing Rousseau, who had declared that "the French have no music," Friedländer inexplicably asserted that neither did Polish Jewry.[65] As such, they had to develop *Tempellieder*, tunes for the synagogue, because "music should accompany the liturgy." The end result of all these auditory changes will be "the cultivation of true religious devotion," which in turn will see the "buds of humanity bloom and bear beautiful fruit."[66] In short, better speech and better music would make for a better Jew. In many ways, Friedländer, who described himself as a "friend and disciple" of Mendelssohn—the latter expressed reciprocal feelings of warmth, loyalty, and friendship—was profoundly influenced by the so-called Sage of Dessau, and one can see in Friedländer's recommendation the impact of Mendelssohn's understanding of music in general, liturgical music in particular, and the aesthetic history and capacity of the Jews.[67]

For Mendelssohn, music was the highest art form insofar as it comports with what he regarded were the three principal sources of pleasure: sensuous beauty, the accord of sensuous and metaphysical perfection, and, finally, the improved state of the body. In his essay "On the Sentiments" (1755), Mendelssohn, who played piano, studied musical harmony, and became a noted theoretician of music, declared, "Divine musical art, thou art the only one that astonishes us with every kind of pleasure."[68] In this work, Mendelssohn addressed various forms of "beautiful arts," among which were rhetoric, elocution, and music. Mendelssohn's own piano teacher was Johann Philipp Kirnberger, a contemporary music theorist and *Kapellmeister*, as well as piano teacher of Bella, another of Daniel Itzig's daughters. Mendelssohn had been introduced to Kirnberger by the maskilic physician Aaron Salomon Gumpertz in 1756. Gumpertz taught Mendelssohn French and English, introduced him to Pierre-Louis Moreau de Maupertuis, the head of the Prussian Academy of Sciences, attended lectures with him at the *gymnasium*, and introduced Mendelssohn to the man who would soon become his best friend, the writer and philosopher Gotthold Ephraim Lessing. A member of the learned and economic Jewish elite, Gumpertz was the author of a Hebrew study of the Jewish calendar, as well as a supercommentary on a commentary on the five *Megillot* by the medieval Spanish rabbi Ibn Ezra, yet he was also perfectly at home in the world of foreign languages, literatures, and music. Gumpertz was, in all ways, a role model and mentor to Mendelssohn, despite being only six years his senior. He introduced Mendelssohn to foreign languages, philosophy, science, and music and showed him how exposure to general culture did not necessitate abandoning or even compromising one's attachment to Jewish culture and the Jewish community.[69]

Gumpertz also inducted Mendelssohn into Berlin's intellectual high society, which provided him with a network of important friends and acquaintances drawn from the sciences and the arts. In the 1750s at places such as the Scholars' Coffeehouse and the Monday Club Mendelssohn discussed the latest philosophical and scientific ideas in a relaxed and convivial atmosphere.[70] It was in these settings that he also entered into intensive debates with theorists and musicians over the aesthetics of music and the subject that was core to those contemporary discussions, namely, the affective "impact of music." Like most of the *philosophes* in France and the *Aufklärer* in Germany, Mendelssohn saw music as a language and, somewhat conservatively, considered its purpose to be determined by its influence on the poetic arts.[71] Mendelssohn's ideas about "musical syntax" were not his alone. Rather, he was deeply influenced by the work of Johann Philipp Kirnberger, who in his monumental *Die Kunst des reinen Satzes in der Musik* (The Art of Strict Composition in Music; 1771–1779) observed: "The chords are to music what words are to speech; just as out of several interconnected words and one idea perfectly expressed, a sentence is formed, so too is a harmonious musical composition or cycle created out of chords arranged in a unified way."[72]

Mendelssohn was more than just Kirnberger's piano student and a like-minded theorist; he actually collaborated with Kirnberger on the latter's study *Odes with Melodies*, published in 1773. For this work, which was intended to be a paradigmatic study on how to set speech to music, Mendelssohn contributed a German translation of Psalm 137 from the original Hebrew.[73] This undertaking was not so much a new musical turn for Mendelssohn as it was a return to an authentic form of expression. Mendelssohn believed that, originally, it was intended that the psalms be chanted to the accompaniment of instrumental music. This was further proof for Mendelssohn that in their original state the Jews possessed an auditory aesthetic so sophisticated that Europeans were only now attempting to approximate that which the ancient Israelites had long ago consecrated, namely, the marriage of instrumental music and poetry. Mendelssohn was less confident about contemporary musicianship than he was about the sweet singers of Israel:

> Do not compare our contemporary art of music to the magnificent art cultivated by those perfect ones [i.e. the leaders, sages, and prophets of Israel], for it seems that there is no comparison between them at all. To this art happened what happened to the art of poetry. Excellence of meaning and thought, in which the improvement of the rational soul lies, has been abandoned in favor

of excellence in sound, which makes only for sensual pleasure and the delight enjoyed by the ear.

Mendelssohn lamented that poetry and music had been divorced from one another and that music was no longer guided by what should be its ultimate aim—the cultivation of reason and morality. Instead, "instruments upon instruments had been invented, melodies upon melodies have been composed that are no longer guided by reason but are a mere jingling of sounds that flatter the ear."[74] In making this claim, Mendelssohn, according to his biographer, Alexander Altmann, betrayed the influence of the greatest of the Sephardic poets, Judah Halevi, who rejected poetry that was no more than mere artifice, designed to please to the ear.

So wedded was he to the idea that the Torah was first and foremost an oral expression written down that Mendelssohn placed great stress on accents both for exegetical reasons and for the purpose of translation. He was deeply concerned with rendering into German as close an approximation as possible of the sound and emotional quality of Hebrew. On some occasions when translating, Mendelssohn added exclamation marks to the German text in order to convey meaning and accent.[75] In working so closely with such a respected public figure as Kirnberger, Mendelssohn surely felt the weight of responsibility in attempting to transmit to a non-Jewish audience that which he took to be the authentic and thus divine sound of Hebrew. If, as was often the case in Germany, all eyes were upon the Jews, now all ears would hearken to their sounds as well.

To trace a direct link between the newly expressed love of music of this generation of German Jews and the coterminous cultivation of Sephardic Hebrew is highly elusive. But the circle of Jewish music lovers and maskilim intersected, bound by mutual aesthetic interests, marriage, and a desire to escape the perception of Jews as cacophonous. What we can say with certainty is that many of the most prominent Berlin, Königsberg, and Hamburg Jews in the eighteenth century were deeply attracted to the beauties offered by the new music and by Hebrew, becoming patrons of both. The Enlightenment and integration into high society led, among other things, to the cultivation of the Jewish ear, as it became increasingly sensitive to beautiful sounds.[76] Mozart and *melitsa* were not mutually exclusive.

In 1758, the same year that the second volume of Baumgarten's *Aesthetica* appeared, Mendelssohn began to turn out a Hebrew monthly entitled *Kohelet musar* (Preacher of Morals), considered to be the first modern journal in Hebrew. Mendelssohn's aim was to present Judaism from an enlightened perspective (all the while adhering to tradition), to foster morality, and to promote the renaissance of Hebrew, which Mendelssohn and others believed was being eroded by the growing influence of Enlightenment thought and European culture.[77] In language typical of the maskilim, Mendelssohn lamented that Hebrew had fallen into decline, and counsels the following remedy: "Let us learn from the other nations, each one with their own national language. They never rested until the limits of their languages had been expanded. Why should we remain in a dreamlike state and not do the same with our language, the most noble and time honored [of all]."[78]

According to Alexander Altmann, Mendelssohn's sparking a revival of classical Hebrew was "bound to create a sense of aesthetic pleasure and, thereby, of national pride as well." Even more revealing of these original intentions is a Hebrew note entered on the last page of the first number of *Kohelet musar* by the Hebraist and tutor to Mendelssohn's children Solomon Dubno (1738–1813). Altmann estimates that it was written sometime between 1778 and 1780 when Dubno and Mendelssohn were in close contact. In it, Dubno, who had written a book on Hebrew accents, makes very clear the link between language and morals, writing that the editors' "intention was . . . to train them [those Jews ignorant of Hebrew] in the ways of morality and in the improvement of their character; also to enthuse their hearts with the beauty of the style of the Holy Tongue." But beyond the cultivation of morality lay aesthetics, for, as Dubno predicted, the categorical imperative behind the acquisition of Hebrew was "so that the tongue of the stammering might soon speak with elegance."[79] In writing this, Dubno anticipated his contemporary Immanuel Kant, who understood beauty to be nothing less than "the symbol of morality."[80]

Because aesthetics stands at the center of Jewish attempts at individual and communal reform, and language has played a crucial role in all modern Jewish ideologies, we see that beyond what would become the general desire of many for the resuscitation of Hebrew as a vernacular language, the issue of how that language should sound when spoken was of paramount importance. Thus one of the most interesting discussions to emerge among modern Jews concerned the differing pronunciations of Hebrew by Sephardim and Ashkenazim. And here the perfect and the imperfect, and not in a grammatical sense, are everywhere to be detected. In fact, it was the sound rather than the structure or potential of Hebrew that animated much discussion. In the Middle Ages, little seems to have been made of the different pronunciations, but by the seventeenth century we can see stirring defenses of Ashkenazic pronunciation in the writings of prominent rabbis. Judah Loew ben Bezalel (ca. 1520–1609), the leading rabbi of Prague, urged his fellow Ashkenazim to "maintain the pronunciation that has been handed down to us by our forefathers as of old, and not to change anything, God forbid, because of what is found in the books of the later Sephardi grammarians who even among themselves do not agree."[81] Further east, the Grodno rabbi Mordechai Jaffe (ca. 1530–1612) likewise objected to any change in the pronunciation of certain Hebrew vowels, invoking the authority of Proverbs 1:8, "Listen, my son, to your father's instruction and do not forsake your mother's teaching.[82]

By the eighteenth century in Germany, however, a somewhat less defensive attitude is apparent. Jacob Emden (1697–1776), the distinguished Talmudist from Altona—notably, in nearby Hamburg there resided a substantial Sephardic community—adopted a more self-critical position. Warning against mispronunciations, Emden emphasized the need to avoid substituting one letter for another (*aleph* and *ayin* and *heh* and *khet*) and not to do "as we Ashkenazim do with the pronunciation of the letter *tav*, which to our great shame sounds like the letter *samekh*. However, with regard to the pronunciation of the vowels happy are we and goodly is our portion, unlike the Sephardim who do not distinguish between a *kametz* and a *pathah*, thus making the holy profane."[83]

On the matter of correct Hebrew pronunciation, Emden can, then, be considered somewhat of a transitional character. While he was a man deeply wedded to tradition, he nonetheless displayed traces of openness to the acquisition of secular knowledge, attempting, albeit with limited success, to learn Latin and Dutch. His willingness to accord authority to some Sephardic pronunciation, especially in light of his virulent battle against followers of the false messiah and Sephardic Jew Shabbtai Zvi is, therefore, significant. So too is the case of Nathan Adler (1741–1800) from Frankfurt. A pietistic devotee of the sixteenth-century kabbalist Isaac Luria, Adler was one of the first Ashkenazim to adopt the Sephardic pronunciation of Hebrew. So dedicated was he to learning it correctly, he is said to have hired a Yemenite Jew—some sources suggest a Jew from either Palestine or India —to come to Frankfurt, live with him, and teach him the Sephardic pronunciation. His contemporary Pinhus Horowitz, the head of the Frankfurt Beit Din, is likewise said to have prayed according to the Sephardic manner.[84] While these remained isolated cases, the appeal of Sephardic Hebrew was beginning to gain traction in Ashkenazic circles.

By the 1780s, the Haskalah's abiding concern with Jewish aesthetics became more pronounced, hence the emergence of a more fully developed discourse of Ashkenazic self-criticism. Correct Hebrew pronunciation was part of the overall critique. For the early generation of Berlin maskilim, language reform lay at the center of their attempts to refashion Ashkenazic Jewry. Because this meant abandoning the use of Yiddish, even Hebrew pronunciation in the Ashkenazic style was rejected, for it lay so deeply embedded in spoken Yiddish.[85]

Naphtali Herz Wessely (1725–1805) was one of the finest Hebrew stylists of his generation and played a seminal role in the revitalization of the Hebrew language.[86] In 1782 he published *Divrei shalom ve-emet* (Words of Peace and Truth), a work intended to promote modernization of the Jewish school curriculum, based on the inclusion of foreign language instruction and secular subjects. Wessely also sought to encourage Galician Jews to accept the terms of the Edict of Toleration, which was issued in that same year by Emperor Joseph II of Austria. Along with its liberating intent, there were elements that can be seen as restrictions on Jewish freedom, one of which had to do with language. The edict stipulated that Jews stop using Hebrew and Yiddish in legal and commercial documents and instead adopt the local language. Wessely did not engage this aspect of imperial policy overmuch. Instead, he spilled a great deal of ink on Hebrew, the need for Jews to learn it, and, in particular, the way it should sound when properly articulated.

The views expressed in *Words of Peace and Truth* are crucial because it was one of the seminal texts of the Berlin Haskalah and Wessely was one of its leading figures, a man whose opinions on the Hebrew language counted for much.[87] He was also a close friend and collaborator of Moses Mendelssohn, the two men enjoying a relationship built on mutual respect and mutual influence. As a measure of the tight-knit circle of maskilim and the circulation of like-minded ideas among them, it was David Friedländer who translated *Words of Peace and Truth* from Hebrew into German.[88] The impact of Mendelssohn's theories on language, aesthetics, and music are fully in evidence in Wessely's work. In addition to the traditional reading of *Words of Peace and Truth* as a text promoting Jewish educational and behavioral reform, it can also be read as a maskilic guide to transforming the cadence of the Jews. And the sonic quality that Wessely sought to inculcate among Ashkenazim comprised those Hebrew sounds that had been perfected by Sephardim during Spanish Jewry's Golden Age under Islam.

In their critique of traditional Jewish life, maskilim were wont to deride Jews for their perceived irrationality and their language, which, in the eighteenth century, was seen as a window onto the state of a speaker's mind and cultural level. Throughout the text, Wessely returns again and again to speak in the most disparaging terms about Yiddish. By turns he accuses it of being an aesthetic assault and a cause of cognitive ills. He claims that the widely used Yiddish Bible translations do not convey the poetry of the original and must seem "cumbersome and repulsive to the students." When Yiddish is used in daily life, Wessely claims that "[the Jew's] speech in worldly affairs will not be in conformity with reason," while as far as Hebrew is concerned, he asserts that "those among us who dwell in Germany and Poland . . . are ignorant even of the grammar of the Holy Tongue, and they do not discern the beauty of its diction, the rules of its syntax and the purity of its style."[89] After reciting what would become a standard complaint of maskilim, namely, that of the poor educational standards of the Jewish people—"we don't have authors and books on metaphysics and ethics and even theology; students do not learn these things in school as part of the curriculum"—Wessely nonetheless absolves his "Ashkenazi brothers" of responsibility for this situation: "We are not blaming them and do not have complaints because in the past there were nations that made life so difficult, [and who] lowered us to a level that was subhuman (*lehiot lamata mimadrigat ha-adam*)."[90]

For Wessely, responsibility for the debasement of Jews lay with the larger and inhospitable social environment. "Here in our difficult exile (*be-galut kashah*) in the lands of Ashkenaz, we arrived a long time ago (*mizman kadmon*) among nations that possessed neither memory nor knowledge (*yad vashem*), wisdom or civilized practices. Their speech was primitive and unwritten." And things only worsened with the passage of time, for "afterwards, when they became Christians, they became haters of Israel." The maltreatment that soon followed—Wessely claimed that it was even worse in Poland than in Germany—included blood libels, many expulsions, and forced conversions. These humiliations "hurt the heart and struck at the soul." Moreover, "[the Christians] also limited our commerce and we were turned into the wretched poor (*ve-na'asinu ani'im merudim*) as well as cowards (*ba'alei morekh lev*); the custom of charitableness did not stay with us and we [displayed] no respectable characteristics (*midot nekhbadim*)." It is at this point that Wessely offers what may be the first historical and anthropological explanation for the different contemporary Hebrew pronunciations of the two main branches of the Jewish people. Beyond the behavioral consequences of restricted economic activity were those of Jewish euphony. Because Germany and Poland "were landlocked and [Ashkenazim] did not conduct business with lands that had access to the sea and only had contact with those around them and no more," the Jews of these two countries inhabited a small cultural universe, and thus their language became impoverished.[91]

In stark contrast to this was the state of the Jews who lived in the lands of Islam, which permitted "monotheists (*ba'alei emunot*) to live under their rule [and] Jews could believe as they wish and follow the customs of their fathers." Muslims also permitted Jews (and Christians) to engage in all kinds of occupations. Commercial activity in these wealthy lands saw Jews trading with "a number of countries overseas, France, Spain, Portugal and all the Greek lands, Sparta, the Mediterranean islands and all of Italy." Wessely observed that commerce at this level and over such great distances demanded excellent communication skills and literacy, and that a consequence of the robust social and commercial traffic among them was that "[Jews] saw one another and learned from one another and learned to be articulate (*tsakhut hadibur*)."[92] The relative freedom enjoyed by the Sephardim not only allowed for self-expression in the most reasoned and orderly manner, but their superior speech was accompanied by correct Hebrew pronunciation. With his privileging of Sephardic Hebrew, Wessely gave voice to the notion that speech was more than just a means of communication, that it was, in fact, a key to moral character. And for Wessely, what contributed more than anything to the development of moral perfectibility was freedom, a right long denied the Jews of Central and Eastern Europe but previously enjoyed by Sephardic Jews.

Though denounced by opponents as a dangerous modernizer, Wessely was, in fact, a deeply pious, conservative yet modern, man.[93] While his brief on behalf of Hebrew and its correct pronunciation was in keeping with typical maskilic views on Jewish self-improvement, he also insisted that command of Hebrew was a religious obligation. In the fourth "letter" of *Words of Peace and Truth*, Wessely observes that "God gave [man] a living soul in order to speak with knowledge and wisdom. It is appropriate that he uses this honor to praise and crown (*le-atarat*) [God] and each word that he speaks should be thoughtfully expressed so that it be pleasant to the ear of the listener and be understandable without [the listener] making an effort (*bli amal*)." This then was Wessely's ideal depiction of social intercourse—lofty words, pleasantly expressed and well chosen. However, the social reality, as it struck his ears, was very different insofar as "when we pay attention to the regions (*glilot*) of Ashkenaz and Poland and how they pronounce words we find many faults (*kilkulim rabim*)."

Ironically, or perhaps instrumentally, if only for its polemical force, Wessely decried the fact that even among the learned, Yiddish was not spoken correctly (*she'eina ke'tikuna*). And so the way Jews spoke, was, for Wessely, an even deeper problem than their merely lacking mastery of Hebrew. By their incorrect manner of talking, Ashkenazic Jews were depriving themselves of the just reward that comes to those who are articulate, for "when you speak clearly (*tsakhot*) and know how to speak about all things in a proper manner you give honor to your Torah [and thus] will you have the respect of your fellow man."[94]

Wessely observes that it was widely known that those Jews in the lands of Islam, as well as those in Italy, Holland, and England, "say the letters and vowels of Hebrew with a different accent (*be-havarah aheret*) than the Jews of Ashkenaz and Poland."[95] But unlike an earlier age when there was no qualitative judgment issued on Jewish accents, the Haskalah, informed by contemporary aesthetic standards, now heard things differently:

> It is impossible to believe how superior and lofty the correct accent is among the Sephardim compared to the deficient accent that is found among us (*havarah hakhsarah she-beyadeynu*). Because of the beauty of the sound of the vowels and the pleasantness to the ear (*ne'imutan le-ozen*) it will be bequeathed unto the soul of the speaker and the listener and will awaken the powers of their soul. [These sounds will be heard] in the reading of the Torah and the holy texts, in the words of prayer and in the joy of holy song. But what can we do? The accent that has been rooted in our mouths is ancient and there is no

longer any hope that we can be saved from it. If we were to agree to change our accents the whole [Ashkenazic] Diaspora would have to agree to choose teachers to instruct the next generation from their youth to pronounce the vowels in the manner that they are pronounced by those from the East and the West [Sephardim] and [the chances of] this are remote and well-nigh impossible (*zeh rakhok ve-kimat i efshar*).[96]

Wessely spends considerable time discussing Hebrew vowels, emphasizing that parents were "duty bound to teach our children from their youth to draw out of their mouths the letters as is according to the true nature of the Holy Tongue." The various trope and stress signs had been explicated by the Sephardi grammarians (*ba'alei ha-lashon*), and it was their rules that were to be followed. Knowing the difference between the penultimate stress (*milel*) and the ultimate stress (*milra*) meant the difference between correct and incorrect pronunciation and determined one's intelligibility and whether one was thus able to bring pleasure to the ear of the listener.[97]

Rules, said Wessely, exist for all languages, and, most surprising of all in this seminal Hebrew text, he provided Yiddish as the example of where its rules needed to be followed, as, for example, in the case of its syllables, which can alternately be shortened or lengthened. "For example, in Yiddish (*leshon ashkenaz*) the words, *gegangen, gestanden, gekomen* and the like, the stress is on the middle syllable (*yarichu be-tnuah ha-emtsait*)—*gan, shtan, kom*—and will thus shorten the others. And the person who changes the order [by stressing the ultimate syllable] his speech is incorrect (*mekulkal*) and will not be easily understood (*eino muvan heitev*). And this is well known." Similarly, Hebrew, like Yiddish, should be spoken according to its rules, especially important in the case of "the Holy Tongue, where one needs to accent the letter where there is a trope or a stress and shorten the other letters. Anyone who disregards this rule, it is as if he does not speak the Holy Tongue."[98] Again, Wessely combines the aesthetic and the religious, for to compromise the former would contravene the latter. Now shifting the blame, he laments that the chief responsibility for the faulty Hebrew speech of Jews lay with their teachers. They, he charged, had been delinquent in their responsibilities and therefore "the people spoke in a garbled way" (*medabrim sefat ilegim*).[99]

Wessely, as critical of Ashkenazic as he was laudatory of Sephardic culture, did not live to hear the sonic changes for which he called. Like many other aspects of the eighteenth-century cultural revolution that were promoted in the name of Jewish "regeneration," Sephardic pronunciation of Hebrew by Ashkenazim (more imagined than real) would not come into widespread use until the twentieth century. Nevertheless, Wessely stands at the forefront of one of the most important aesthetic changes that modern Ashkenazim have undergone. Just before he passed away in 1805, at the age of eighty, Wessely made one final and most unusual request, one that exemplified the cultural distance that he as an elite Ashkenazic Jew had traveled. The communal authorities granted him his wish and he was buried in the Sephardic section of the Jewish cemetery in Hamburg's sister city, Altona.[100]

Within the new aesthetic theory of the eighteenth century, leading figures such as Hume and Kant focused more on the response to the object than on the object itself, and on judging rather than producing art. But within contemporary Jewish aesthetic theory as it applied to Hebrew, such a neat divide was neither possible nor desirable. As a Holy Tongue Hebrew's inherent "art" or nature and its production, namely, the way it was spoken, could not be separated, let alone demoted or ignored in favor of the response to it or how it sounded to listeners. In fact, as Wessely and other maskilim stressed, both elements, Hebrew's production (speaking it properly) and the response to it (how pleasurable its sounds were), were given equal weight—the former out of respect for Jewish tradition, the latter out of concern for the Jewish future, a future whose success, the maskilim claimed, was dependent on Jews being rational, logical, and articulate. Correct pronunciation, syntax, and modes of expression were all properties that, if acquired by Jews, would promote a new sentiment, one that was crucial to Jewish "regeneration," namely, an appreciation of beauty. The process would begin at the most personal level, with the way one pronounced Hebrew, thus simultaneously making oneself sonically attractive to listeners while paying homage to the holy and the perfect. The aesthetics of orality and aurality were of central concern to Mendelssohn, Wessely, and the rising German-Jewish bourgeoisie. As an aniconic people, the Jews would create great art through the sound of their ancient words. About eighteenth-century aesthetic theory, Martin Jay has observed: "Objects were admired not for what they were in themselves, but for what they could do to or for us. The telos of this Copernican reversal was an increasing indifference to the inherent qualities of the object as such, perhaps extending even to its very existence."[101] While Sephardic Hebrew was believed beneficial for speaker and auditor alike, there was a limit to the Jewish appreciation of modern aesthetic theory. It was not possible to become indifferent to Hebrew's "inherent qualities" or "nature," as Wessely called it, because to do so was to become indifferent to God's language and thus to Judaism itself.

In maskilic and, later, Reform circles, the Sephardic pronunciation for the transcription of Hebrew words in secular texts took hold, although the unique German pronunciation of spoken Hebrew, which was very much Ashkenazic, held sway for the overwhelming majority of German Jews. Still, it is a measure of the extent to which modern German Jewry became deeply invested in the program of aesthetic improvement that the Reformers, like some traditionalists, saw in Sephardic pronunciation a more articulate and pleasing way to God's ear. In 1815, early exponents of the Reform movement resolved to change their pronunciation of Hebrew and adopt the Sephardic mode.[102] In the contemporary circles of *Wissenschaft des Judentums*, however, a more scholarly, as opposed to ideological, position is apparent. Their focus on the glories of Sephardic Hebrew culture notwithstanding, Jewish historians passed a more detached judgment on Hebrew pronunciation, claiming that both Sephardic and Ashkenazic versions were of equal antiquity and merely reflected what had been the different pronunciations of the Jewish communities in Palestine and Babylonia, respectively. However, their concentration on works produced by the Jews of Spain clearly indicated their cultural and aesthetic preferences.

It remains to take note of an important tension at the heart of the eighteenth-century attempt at a sonic makeover of the Jews. If the Haskalah represents a movement aimed at the Europeanization of the Jews, then the reconstitution of their Hebrew accents after the Sephardic fashion represents their orientalization. After physical appearance, the most obvious marker of Ashkenazic identity was language, whether Yiddish or Ashkenazic pronunciation of Hebrew. It is no accident that the drive by the maskilim of Berlin to eliminate both took root simultaneously, nor is it by chance that to replace both required a new form of Jewish expression upon which to model one's sound, appearance, and behavior. It was Sephardic Jewry, European by birth but Oriental by virtue of their having lived under Islam, as well as their perceived connectedness to an authentic Hebrew past that served as the archetype for a new Jew.

Thus it was the Haskalah of the 1780s that ushered in the modern beginnings of Ashkenazic intellectuals' infatuation with Sephardic culture. To cultivate the Jews' senses according to European norms was integral to the maskilic "civilizing process." But this did not mean the abandonment of some of Judaism's most fundamental attributes in favor of European ones. This is not what the Haskalah advocated. Comprehensive salvation, said the maskilim, required both Europeanization and reconnecting with authentic Oriental expressions of Jewishness. This led Ashkenazic intellectuals to look to the Orient for inspiration, in particular to the glorious Hebrew culture that flourished under Islam. Where Europeans at this time discovered and celebrated all that was sublime about Indian culture, especially Sanskrit, Central and Eastern European Jews had an exotic and highly esteemed Hebrew culture from which to draw in their quest to reclaim their authentic cultural and sensory selves, attributes that they claimed had been long compromised by the vicissitudes of history.[103] And in Muslim Spain, where the past was considered to have been kinder to the Jews, both their language and their moral worth were considered superior to that of their benighted and sensuously deprived Ashkenazic brethren.

CODA

Since our temporal focus in this chapter has been on the eighteenth century, we were not able, in the main body of the text, to pursue the afterlife of the Haskalah's first attempts to make Ashkenazim appreciative and imitative of Sephardic sounds. In addressing the acoustic Haskalah, we have dealt with the multiple influences that informed this wish, and I have argued that the German musical revolution was one of the most influential sources for Jewish elites wishing to cultivate the Jewish ear, central to whose endeavor was the promotion of the Sephardic pronunciation of Hebrew. It is only appropriate, then, that I append a coda to this story, one that will indicate the direction that the Ashkenazic Sephardicization of Hebrew took after the Berlin Haskalah.

While it does not fit into the main structure of a work, the function of the musical coda, coming as it does at the end, permits one to revisit but not needlessly reprise what has preceded it, while it simultaneously provides balance and closure via prolongation. In the case before us, the coda to our story, one that will round it out, focuses on how the Haskalah's sonic desire for the Jews progressed from an expression of longing to actual innovation and change in the musical and spoken sounds Jews made.

Indeed, in Germany the advent of Reform Judaism in the early decades of the nineteenth century led to radical changes in liturgical music. The call to adopt new melodies was accompanied by a critique whose very language was reminiscent of the discourse that addressed Jewish languages. The seemingly informal, unstructured, and improvised tunes of the traditional liturgy were to be replaced by predictably structured melodies, the overall goal of which was to promote decorum within the synagogue. Musical performance was considered so important that the rules governing it were formally set down in a synagogue's bylaws, known as the *Synagogenordnung*. For example, in the "Proclamation concerning the Improvements of the Worship Service in the Synagogues of the Kingdom of Westphalia," published in Cassel in 1810, we note the following in paragraphs 14 and 15: "Every cantor shall endeavor to enunciate every word of the prayers clearly. The unsuitable *traditional* [my emphasis] singing which interrupts the prayer is to be avoided. Every accompaniment [of the cantor] by singers and bass-singers, employed by some congregations for that purpose, is to cease altogether," and "the members of the congregations are reminded and ordered to follow the cantor's prayers quietly and silently. They must refrain from the illegal and cacophonous *shouting* [my emphasis] which so frequently disturbs peaceful and true devotion."[104] These rules—and there were many more, including explicit prohibitions against "laughing, talking, joking, irrespective of time and occasion, noisily standing around, or even leaving one's seat"—were typical and were intended to Westernize the synagogue service as much as possible.[105] Put otherwise, they were intended to eliminate traditional modes of Ashkenazic conduct and worship.

Musical and behavioral innovations such as these within Reform Judaism went hand in hand with proposed changes in Hebrew pronunciation. There were two new sources of influence on synagogue music in the early nineteenth century. These were Protestant choral works and Sephardic traditions. Together they led to a radical change in the sonic ambience of Jewish worship services. In 1801, in the provincial Westphalian town of Seesen, Israel Jacobson (1768–1828) opened the first new school that followed the principles of incipient Reform Judaism. A founding figure of Reform Judaism, Jacobson created a new children's synagogue service replete with new hymns based on Protestant chorales. In 1810, he erected a temple on the grounds of the school. In imitation of churches, it had both a bell and an organ, the latter used for the accompaniment of Hebrew and German hymns. However, the traditional chanting of Torah was abolished, for Jacobson considered it too Oriental and unmusical. He elected to read the service himself.[106]

Outside of the religious realm, other Christian influences may have had a significant impact on the German-Jewish preference for Sephardic pronunciation of Hebrew. In his monumentally important study *Hebräische Grammatik* (Hebrew Grammar; 1813) the leading nineteenth-century Christian Old Testament and Hebrew scholar Wilhelm Gesenius (1786–1842) observed: "The pronunciation of Hebrew by the modern German Jews, which partly resembles the Syriac and is generally called 'Polish', differs considerably from that of the Spanish and Portuguese Jews, which approaches nearer to the Arabic. The pronunciation of Hebrew by Christians follows the latter (after the example of Reuchlin), in almost all cases."[107] When Gesenius, a distinguished biblical critic and professor of Oriental studies at the University of Halle, speaks of the way Christians in Germany pronounce Hebrew, he is referring to the way it was taught in university faculties of theology. Given Gesenius's authority and the great esteem held for the German professoriate in general, it is reasonable to assume that Germans' having employed Sephardic pronunciation since the sixteenth century, while it was not a motivating factor, would have pleased Jewish advocates by reassuring them that their own choice had the imprimatur of the educated Christian elite.

Jacobson's first efforts at reforming the Jewish worship service were the foundation for what would blossom into a broad movement over the course of the nineteenth century. The first stand-alone Reform temple to employ a comprehensive Reform liturgy opened in 1818 in Hamburg. New German and Hebrew hymns were composed by the temple's two preachers (the word "rabbi" was strictly avoided), but the majority of new songs were written by Christians, and it was Christian musicians who played the organ that had been donated to the temple by Salomon Heine, the uncle of lyric poet Heinrich Heine. The boys who made up the choir, however, were all Jewish. The congregation adopted what was referred to as "Portuguese" pronunciation of Hebrew—the new prayer book bearing transliterations to assist the worshippers. The congregation also employed various Sephardic melodies and appointed as its first cantor a Sephardic Jew named David Meldola.[108] Those melodies were officially transcribed by the congregation's organist and were used until World War I.[109] All in all, "the result was a strange combination of Sephardi modes in the Hebrew together with the contemporary style of church music in the German hymns."[110] In his midcentury series of portraits of Spanish-Jewish dramatic poets, the distinguished historian of Spanish and Portuguese Jewry Meyer Kayserling (1829–1905) declared that "most of the songs of praise that we sing in our synagogues today are of Spanish origin."[111] It is noteworthy that at the Hamburg Temple, Torah chanting according to the ancient form of cantillation was reintroduced only in 1879, while Ashkenazic pronunciation was reintroduced in 1909, a signal that the Sephardic turn among German Jews had just about run its course.

One outcome of this chapter has been to unsettle a commonly held view that it was Eastern European Zionists at the end of the nineteenth century who were the first Jews to privilege Sephardic pronunciation of Hebrew. As we have seen, they were anticipated by at least a century by elite Jewish circles in Germany. Some historians of the Hebrew language have even posited that there was a substantial Hebrew-speaking population in Palestine before the arrival of the Zionists. That story is not ours, however.[112] Nevertheless Germany's maskilim were unable to effect a change in the way the majority of Jews uttered Hebrew words, and German Jewry retained its unique form of Ashkenazic Hebrew pronunciation until the very end. Zionism, by contrast, refused to accept the existence of Ashkenazic Hebrew, and the Sephardicists enjoyed their greatest success in Palestine/Israel.

Among all Hebraists, whether maskilim or Zionists, Sephardic pronunciation was considered authentic and, as important, the one least reminiscent of Yiddish's spoken Hebraic content. And with Zionism's commitment to transforming the *yehudi* (Jew) into the *ivri* (Hebrew), a Sephardic pronunciation that proponents imagined most closely comported with the way ancient Jews spoke was given the stamp of approval. The link between an imagined pronunciation of ancient Hebrew and the preference for Sephardic Hebrew was drawn by romantic inference from the physical appearance of Sephardim in the eyes of Ashkenazic observers. Even those European immigrants who arrived in Palestine speaking Hebrew with an Ashkenazic accent set about dispensing with it in favor of adopting a pronunciation that sounded, to their ears, Sephardi, that is to say, authentic.[113] There were at least three ideological reasons for this. The Ashkenazic pronunciation was too intimate a reminder of the Yiddish that cultural Zionists so despised; the adoption of Sephardic pronunciation promised to eliminate the sharp distinctions that separated one Ashkenazic dialect of Hebrew from another in Palestine; and, finally, cultivating a Sephardic accent would, it was believed, draw the European immigrants closer to their fellow Jewish immigrants from the Middle East.[114] It thus represented a sonic "homecoming," one that would complement the physical return of Jews to their homeland.

But practical considerations, such as the desire for unity of pronunciation, were usually secondary to aesthetic ones. And principal among them was the belief that speaking Hebrew with a Sephardic pronunciation was essential to the larger restorative project that would see a more complete return of the Jews to their original cultural and thus psychological state. For Eliezer Ben-Yehuda (1858–1922), one of the principal architects of the revival of modern Hebrew, hearing Sephardi Hebrew for the first time was a transformative experience. It came from the mouth of a young Lithuanian Jew, Getzl Zelikovitz, who later went on to become a prominent journalist in the American Yiddish press. Having spent some time among the Jews of Tunisia and Morocco, Zelikovitz had picked up their accent, which enchanted Ben-Yehuda as they spoke with one another. While conversing with Zelikovitz, Ben-Yehuda recalled the mighty impression made upon him by Avraham Mapu's biblical epic *Love of Zion* (1853), which was one of the first historical novels to be written in Hebrew. So enraptured was he with the dialogue, Ben-Yehuda claimed that he and a friend from the *bet ha-midrash* would sometimes "go out into a field, so as not to be overheard," where they "tried to really speak Hebrew like Amnon and Tamar [the novel's two protagonists] with all that artificial flowery Biblicism that Mapu put into the mouths of his characters." Now, speaking with Zelikovitz, Ben-Yehuda again did so "in the manner of Amnon and Tamar," but what made him especially happy was that Zelikovitz responded with "simple words spoken naturally" and in his acquired Sephardic accent.[115] That Zelikovitz had managed to sound authentic when speaking Hebrew filled Ben-Yehuda with confidence that the resurrection of Hebrew as a daily language and with Sephardic pronunciation was a genuine possibility.

In 1881 Ben-Yehuda immigrated to Ottoman Palestine. Dismayed that he had landed in a polyglot environment where many languages were spoken, he was always focused on those individuals who already had facility with Hebrew and, just as importantly, the way it sounded. His views on language also governed his overall impressions of the Jews he encountered, in particular their physicality. In Jerusalem, he kept company with Israel Dov Frumkin, the Hasidic editor of the Hebrew journal *Havazelet*. It was the festival of Sukkot, and Ben-Yehuda recalled the many Jews from all sectors of society who visited Frumkin in his home on the holiday. Observing them all he declared:

> Why should I deny it? The Sephardim made the best, the most pleasant impression upon me. Most of them were handsome (*ba'alei tsura*), elegant figures in Oriental dress, with a lovely manner and almost all of them spoke Hebrew. Their speech was fluent and natural, rich in vocabulary and idiom, and spoken with original accents that were so sweetly Oriental! The Ashkenazic visitors, who came from all classes, mostly looked as if they were from the ghetto. Only the older ones from among them, those that had immigrated when the Ashkenazim were still a minority among the Jewish ethnic groups of Jerusalem, had assimilated a little to the Sephardim and resembled them a bit in dress and manners and the impress of the ghetto had been somewhat erased from their faces. They all spoke Yiddish with Frumkin, but in my honor they also spoke some Hebrew; the older ones among them spoke with a measure of naturalness, and with Sephardic pronunciation, but everywhere one could hear that it was not a Sephardi who was speaking.[116]

Ben-Yehuda, however, went further, positing linkages among language, pronunciation, and behavior. Without a hint of irony or self-reflexivity this Lithuanian Jew, influenced by the concept of *Sfaradi tahor* (pure Sephardi), observed: "How much the Sephardi Jews love cleanliness and how strict they are about it even in the secret places, the most private rooms. . . . And all household and cooking utensils were truly sparkling with cleanliness."[117] Their language, their bodies, and even their homes were models of aesthetic perfection.

Finally, this universe of new Jewish ideas was governed by an unsettling cultural equation: beauty + purity = strength. The perceived power of Sephardic speech and the imagined weakness of Ashkenazic pronunciation meant that for men such as Ben-Yehuda, Menakhem Ussishkin (1863–1941), the zealous Hebraist and head of the Jewish National Fund, and David Yellin (1864–1941), cofounder in 1903 of the Hebrew Language Association and first president of the Hebrew Teachers Seminary (founded in 1912), the Sephardi mode was preferable: if adopted by Jews, it would translate to a complete metamorphosis, one that would see the disappearance of what their contemporary, the assimilated German Jew Walter Rathenau, had called the Jews' "sloppy, roundish shape."[118]

Worshipping at the altar of all things Oriental, the Hebrew Language Association (Va'ad ha-lashon ha-ivrit), which was established in 1889 as a branch of Safa Brura (Clear Language), oversaw the revival of spoken Hebrew.[119] In a guide to the organization's mission written by Ben-Yehuda in 1912, it was clearly stated that one of the body's two main objectives was "to preserve the Oriental quality of the language and its special form of pronunciation," and to that end it recommended that teachers of Hebrew be drawn from among those Oriental Jews who spoke both Hebrew and Arabic, and, in particular, those who were fluent in the dialect of Syrian Jews.[120] The reason Ben-Yehuda gave was that "[because we, Ashkenazim, lost the Oriental ring of the letters, *tet, ayin, kuf*] we deprive our language of its force and power by the contempt we have for the emphatic consonants, and because of that, the whole language is soft, weak, without the special strength the emphatic consonant gives to the word."[121] David Yellin also expressed his preference for Sephardic Hebrew, but not because of any allegiance to or belief in the idea that there was an "original" Hebrew accent; he claimed that there were multiple varieties, none more authentic than another. In antiquity, there were accent differences between "those from the north and those from the Negev, and Galilean pronunciation was similar to that of Syria while the accent of the Judeans was similar to Arabic."[122] He likewise claimed, as did Ben-Yehuda, that Ashkenazic Hebrew was as valid in many respects as the Sephardic, and it is impossible to tell which is historically more accurate. Rather, his choice of the Sephardic accent stemmed from its "pleasant ring to the ear" and his desire to impose some kind of unity of pronunciation upon the embryonic Hebrew nation, a pronunciation that differed from Ben-Yehuda's in significant ways. Yellin believed that the accent should comport with the written word, and thus he favored a kind of biblical-sounding Hebrew, while Ben-Yehuda was open to including Hebrew forms drawn from the language's long history, which meant the inclusion of mishnaic and rabbinic Hebrew. Among Hebrew pedagogues there were many other positions taken on the subject of how Hebrew had sounded in antiquity, and how it should now be taught and nurtured among the newcomers to Palestine.[123] The many differences notwithstanding, there was consensus that auditory aesthetics demanded the replacement of traditional Ashkenazic pronunciation.

The Hebrew Language Association also arrogated to itself responsibility for "fashioning new words and adding elasticity to the language in order that a person can express humane thoughts."[124] As we have seen above and will see again in the next chapter, the expression in Yiddish or Ashkenazic Hebrew of logical, humane thoughts was considered impossible by the maskilim of Berlin and their ideological successors, the Hebraists.[125] For the former, the use of High German would come to be seen as the elixir that would rejuvenate the Jews. For the Zionists, whose critique of Jews was often even harsher, Sephardic Hebrew promised to rehumanize them. For others, the adoption of the Sephardic accent would even drive a desirable wedge between young Ashkenazim and their fathers. Yehuda Grizovsky, a teacher from the new settlement of Ekron, informed the Hebrew Language Committee: "The fathers will speak in their [Polish or Lithuanian] accents and the children will understand their mistakes. . . . The child will speak with a correct Sephardic accent, will become accustomed to it and it will do no harm that he will not understand his father's accent."[126] Here was a radical expression of the Zionist revolution and the role that Sephardic Hebrew would play in it. Differences in accent would bring about a welcome rift between fathers and sons, one that would separate old from new, correct from incorrect. For Grizovsky, it promised nothing less than a reconfiguration of the Jewish family. The father, trapped in his Ashkenazic-ness by his language, must surrender his son to the new Hebrew culture, here, in the Land of Israel, where he has been instructed to express himself in a more "correct" and more "authentic" Hebrew manner.[127]

The Ashkenazic orientalizers, all from Yiddish-speaking backgrounds, had their way, as Sephardic pronunciation of Hebrew was taught in schools and became normative. This became as true for the Diaspora as it was for the Land of Israel. It was, as Benjamin Harshav has observed, among only two groups that resistance to this trend could be observed: religious Jews, who saw both the revival of Hebrew as a spoken language and the use of Sephardic pronunciation as a challenge to religious authority and tradition; and the early Zionist poets, individuals who had an ear for Ashkenazic Hebrew's rhythm, lyricism, and musicality.[128]

The Hebrew accent that was created in Israel was not really Sephardic at all; it was, rather, a blend of Sephardic vowels and stress patterns, on the one hand, and Ashkenazic consonants, on the other. What emerged, by a mixture of accident and design, was an accent that, to the ears of the Ashkenazic revivers of Hebrew, was Sephardic.[129] From a linguistic point of view, the true nature of modern Hebrew is not the issue for us here. What matters is the Ashkenazic impulse to self-orientalize, to remake oneself in the image of an imagined (and better) Jewish Other, for to do so was to bring about more than a mere change of pronunciation. Going beyond mere words, the linguistic makeover was to be an act of purification whereby the Ashkenazic Jew would lose himself as he took on the qualities of the *Sfaradi tahor*. The hard word endings and contracted vowels of Sephardic Hebrew pronunciation were to replace the soft word endings and elongated vowels of Ashkenazic Hebrew in the same way that, ideally, the hardened, matter-of-fact *ivri* would replace the imagined, effeminate *yehudi*, whose exaggerated mellifluousness bespoke his diasporic softness and shapelessness.

CHAPTER TWO

"Castilian Pride and Oriental Dignity"

SEPHARDIC BEAUTY IN THE EYE OF THE

ASHKENAZIC BEHOLDER

Valorization of the beautiful sounds that Sephardic Jews were purported to make, ones that delighted the ears of their interlocutors and bespoke their own superior comportment, also extended to a wholehearted appreciation of their character and, later on, their bodies. And in keeping with the eighteenth-century view of things as established by the new science of physiognomy and, shortly thereafter, phrenology, outward appearances were said to reflect inner character.[1] Outer calmness evinced inner peace; outward dishevelment reflected inner disorder; poor posture typified a servile nature; and speaking an impoverished language signified limited cognitive powers. Starting with the Haskalah of the eighteenth century and extending into Zionist ideology of the early twentieth century, the belief in the interconnectedness of outer form and inner character informed Ashkenazic views of the self and the Sephardic Other. In a variety of literary genres and media, a composite and wholly complimentary picture of Sephardim was drawn. Simultaneously, Ashkenazic Jews were also represented *en tout*, invariably cast in a negative manner, the exact opposite of their Sephardic coreligionists. Where Ashkenazim were hunched, ugly, unkempt, unruly, petty traders, middlemen, or Hasidic rebbes, the Sephardim walked upright, were beautiful, immaculately dressed, manicured, and coiffed, and were respected international merchants or worldly intellectual giants. How and why the aesthetics of the Sephardic body became the ideal Jewish type, and why it was Ashkenazim who created it, is the story to which we now turn.

Even as the Enlightenment held out the promise of emancipation for Jews, the majority of Europeans still had an overwhelmingly negative impression of them, and as Jews began to inch ever closer to the threshold of bourgeois society, their cultural and physical differences from Europeans were mostly interpreted as deficiencies. A host of Europeans from social commentators to statesmen began to talk of the need to "improve" or "regenerate" the Jews.[2] Having internalized such critiques, Jewish intellectuals began to talk in similar terms, and the goal of the Haskalah was the eradication of whatever social, cultural, and physical defects Jews were said to possess. This was embarked upon with a view to making them more complete, more perfect, more like Europeans.[3]

Jews in Central and Western Europe responded to the intense scrutiny imposed upon them in a variety of ways that included acquisition of the vernacular, the recasting of Judaism in more universalistic terms, and—the most radical of all responses—conversion to Christianity.[4] Our interest here lies in another response: elite Jews strove desperately to prove to Christian critics, as well as fellow Jews, that the kinds of Jews bourgeois Christians were calling for already existed—and had existed for a long time. Seeking to set the record straight for Christians and promote feelings of intense pride or even "improved" behavior among their fellow Jews, maskilim began to identify Jews who were virtuous, dignified, often prosperous, and who did not conform to the stereotypical depictions of the Jewish masses. Most frequently it was Sephardic Jews who were selected as the exemplary Jewish types. In a host of genres, including private correspondence, memoirs, communal regulations, and official publications, note was taken of the supposedly different morality and physicality of Sephardic Jews that distinguished them from Ashkenazim.

Such comparisons were facilitated by the increased contact between the two Jewish groups, a result of Central European, that is, Ashkenazic, migration to the Sephardic-dominated centers of Western Europe. Since the seventeenth century, relations between the two groups had not been good, the Sephardic Jews being particularly keen to minimize social contact with Ashkenazim. Adopting an attitude of haughty superiority toward them, expressive of a mind-set and a language drawn from the ethnocentric culture of the very Iberian Peninsula where their forebears had experienced persecution and then expulsion, the Sephardim practiced what has been termed *la mimesis de l'antagonisme*.[5] Emphasizing their "purity of blood" and constantly repeating the need to "conserve" the "nation," the leaders of the Sephardic diaspora of Western Europe jealously sought to guard the integrity of their communities by erecting myriad barriers to entry and by discriminating against anyone they considered to be of different stock.[6]

It is ironic that the celebration of the supposed superiority of Sephardic Jews became increasingly full-throated at the very time that their numerical predominance vis-à-vis Ashkenazim was in decline, communal disintegration among them was quite advanced, and levels of poverty among Sephardim were on the rise. In Paris, for example, Isaac de Pinto, a financier and economic theorist, carried on a vibrant correspondence with major figures of the Enlightenment, among them David Hume, Voltaire, and Diderot. With the first of these, de Pinto mostly dealt with economic and social matters, while with the latter two the interaction largely took the form of an apologetic dialogue in which de Pinto challenged the offensive charges the two Frenchmen made against Jews.

In focusing on the declining economic status of Sephardic Jews in Northern Europe, de Pinto noted that their poverty would be greatly alleviated should they begin to emigrate to the West Indies or North America. He also proposed that wealthy Sephardic Jews establish a fund to support the poverty-stricken Sephardim who remained in Europe. As a syndic of the Sephardic community, de Pinto concerned himself with the economic state of his community, which he attributed to specific policies such as unfair taxation, the prejudicial policies of the banks and the stock market, rules regarding the import and export trade that negatively impacted some of the wealthier Portuguese-Jewish families, unfair competition promoted by the guilds, and policies that discriminated against Jewish commercial agents.[7]

The historical explanations offered by de Pinto naturally led him to more general considerations of the character of the Jews because it was that which was mercilessly attacked by Voltaire and Diderot. In 1762 he saw fit to respond to their all-encompassing diatribes, attacks that knew neither subtlety nor nuance. In his retort to Voltaire's vulgar encyclopedia entry on Jews, de Pinto highlighted the differences between Sephardim and Ashkenazim, beseeching the philosophe to be mindful of the distinctions when attacking Jews. These were differences that he as a Sephardic Jew considered indisputable, and as such, de Pinto's essentializing of Jews was no less egregious than that of his interlocutor:

> Are there any imputations which can be laid on a people in general? Can a whole nation be accessory to a crime? . . . How is it possible to give the moral picture of a nation with one dash of the pen? If this be true with regard to nations in general, it is much more so with respect to the Jews in particular. They have been scattered through so many nations, that they have, we may say, adopted in each country, after a certain time, the characters of the inhabitants; a Jew in London bears as little resemblance to a Jew in Constantinople, as the last resembles a Chinese Mandarin! A Portuguese Jew of Bordeaux and a German Jew of Metz appear two beings of a different nature!
>
> If M. Voltaire had acted according to that principle of sound reason which he affects to do, he would have begun by distinguishing from the other Jews the Spanish and Portuguese, who have never mixed or incorporated with the crowd of the other sons of Jacob. . . . M. Voltaire cannot be ignorant of the scrupulous exactness of the Portuguese and Spanish Jews not to intermix in marriage, alliance, or any other way, with the Jews of other nations.[8]

De Pinto's challenge to Voltaire concerns the latter's failure to distinguish between Sephardim and Ashkenazim, his tarring them both with the same brush, and perhaps, above all, his ignorance of even the stark biological split between the two groups, a separation instigated by Sephardic Jewry's heightened and protective sense of self. It is a self-consciousness of which de Pinto is very proud. Having established radical differences among groups of Jews, especially those distinguishing the Sephardim from the others, de Pinto begins to assign qualitative values to those differences, claiming that

> the manners of the Portuguese Jews are also very different from those of the rest: the former have no beards nor anything peculiar in their dress. The rich among them vie with the other nations in Europe in refinement, elegance and show, and differ from them in worship only. Their variance with other brethren is at such a height that if a Portuguese Jew in England or Holland married a German Jewess, he would of course lose all his prerogatives, be no longer reckoned as a member of their Synagogue . . . [and] be absolutely divorced from the body of the nation and not even buried with his Portuguese brethren. They think, in general, that they are descended from the tribe of Judah, and they hold that the chief families of it were sent into Spain at the time of the Babylonian captivity. This is the cause of those distinctions and of that elevation of mind which is observed among them, and which even their brethren of other nations seem to acknowledge. By this wise policy they have preserved purer morals, and have acquired a certain importance, which helps even Christians distinguish them from other Jews.[9]

De Pinto goes on to directly address the German and Polish Jews, speaking of them in terms typical of the Enlightenment. He concedes to Voltaire that they are, as whole, "debased and degraded," and that they lack "virtue and honor," but these character flaws are a result of Christian mistreatment. And in spite of all this de Pinto applauds the Ashkenazim for their fortitude, courage, and resoluteness in remaining true to their faith. And then, at the conclusion of his letter, he addresses Voltaire in the third person: "Let him consult his reason and his heart, and I am confident he will employ all his talents in recanting his errors: he will show in a masterly way that the mean characters of certain Polish and German Jews are not to be laid to the charge of that ancient, divine, and sacred religion. Want, persecution, various accidents, render them such as other people would be if they professed a different faith, but found themselves in the same circumstances."[10]

De Pinto's response to Voltaire resonated beyond France, providing inspiration to those German Jews who were agitating for emancipation. Like de Pinto, David Friedländer also wrote descriptively about Jews; however, he did so not as part of a one-on-one polemic but in response to great political change. On three separate occasions, in 1772, 1793, and 1795, Poland was partitioned among Russia, Austria, and Prussia. In all, Prussia inherited about 160,000 Polish Jews. It is to this changing demographic reality that Friedländer was responding. He was a wealthy Königsberg industrialist—son-in-law of the above-mentioned Daniel Itzig, community leader and disciple of Moses Mendelssohn—and his own prosperity and social station informed his reformist agenda for Jewish worship and the Jews themselves. A man consumed by issues of class, social propriety, and aesthetics,

Friedländer also deeply internalized the negative Christian assessments of Jews. Taken together, these factors helped shape his attitudes toward Polish and German Jews, and they play a seminal role in our story of Ashkenazic self-perception and the role of Sephardic Jews within a nascent modern German-Jewish identity.

In 1793, on the occasion of the second Polish partition, Friedländer published a set of documents with a lengthy introductory essay outlining the political and cultural steps he considered necessary for the reform of the newly acquired Polish Jews. Referring to the tract *On the Civic Improvement of the Jews* (1781) by the Prussian bureaucrat Christian Wilhelm Dohm, which advocated for their emancipation, Friedländer gratefully related how Dohm had thoroughly addressed every charge laid at the Jews' door by their enemies. He applauded the fact that Dohm had even taken advice from those friendly toward Jews, and this, said Friedländer, made the text all the more "valuable and remarkable because it is a mirror that accurately shows us our form (*Gestalt*). Consequently, we can learn how to cast off those defects that really do lie within us."[11]

Like de Pinto, Friedländer fretted over the generalized character of negative representations of Jews. Rhetorically, he asked whether it was possible for the millions of Jews, living among all sorts of peoples, cultures, and political systems, to be all the same. Of course they were not. There were Jews who were to be celebrated, and there were those, such as Polish Jewry, in desperate need of corrective measures. From their use of Yiddish and their ignorance of "pure Hebrew" to their schools and their synagogue services, Friedländer advocated for wholesale change. Absurdly he declared that "they have no educational institutions," and outrageously he believed them to be "incapable of speech," while "not a single one of them knew the aesthetic value of Oriental poetry." In fact they had "not produced a single poet, and the feel for poetry had died out among them." This, he said, was a measure of the great distance that separated them from their coreligionists in Germany. Still, he conceded, they were "religiously scrupulous, and had among them barely any murderers, thieves, gluttons and drunkards. They were intelligent and sharp even if subtlety of thought had deserted them." All in all, however, these Jews were the most "useful, capable and necessary class of people" in all of Poland and sat on an incomparably higher intellectual, moral, and cultural level than their neighbors, the Polish peasantry.[12]

Where Friedländer, the Ashkenazic Jew, parted company with de Pinto, the Sephardi, is that integral to the former's argument is the chasm that he establishes between Jews from Poland and those from Germany. Where de Pinto lumps them together, Friedländer prizes them apart. In fact the role that German and Polish Jews played vis-à-vis Sephardim in de Pinto's representation to Voltaire was reserved for Polish Jews in Friedländer's work, for it was they who were most socially and aesthetically poverty-stricken. One might paraphrase de Pinto and say that to Friedländer a German Jew of Berlin and a Polish Jew of Kalisz appear two beings of a different nature.

To highlight the distinction between the two groups of Ashkenazim, Friedländer identifies the Jews of Berlin with the Sephardic Jews of Bordeaux. And here his class consciousness comes to the fore: "Even if we are all marked with the name Jew, tinged as it is with contempt, and even if the great mass of us are judged negatively ... the enlightened non-Jew still distinguishes [on the one hand] between the [Sephardic Jew] of Bordeaux, who has earned the honor of being a [military] captain, and the [Ashkenazic] Jew of Berlin who has been deemed worthy of a seat in the Royal Academy and [on the other hand] the Jews in Poland and Bohemia." With reference to the latter group, Friedländer noted that even the enlightened "friends of humanity (*Menschenfreunde*)" were unable to overcome their prejudices and could not imagine Eastern European Jews as anything but incorrigible. By contrast, as a Jew dedicated to the liberal principles of the Enlightenment, Friedländer observed that "without any doubt all possible perfectibility can be attained by them and one can be confident our brethren will become [culturally, morally, and spiritually] refined."[13] Friedländer's belief in the capacity of all Jews to improve was steadfast and total. After all, had not Prussian Jewry, or at least Jews in his social and intellectual circles, emerged from the darkness and into Enlightened Europe and been so successful in doing so that they were now able to take their place alongside the Sephardim? In terms of *Bildung*, he pursued a policy of "no Jew left behind": as he saw it, Eastern European Jewry stood poised, because they were inherently capable of improving, to join the ranks of the refined, cultivated, and widely admired Sephardic and German Jews.

Beginning in the eighteenth century, German Jewry started to develop a sense of its uniqueness. It was a difference that was increasingly built upon a foundation that necessitated their separating themselves from their fellow Ashkenazim, those in Eastern Europe. At the center of this process of identity formation sat language and religious practice, the former conditioned by similarity, the latter by difference. German-Jewish hostility to Yiddish was a sentiment made all the more neurotic because of the proximity of the two languages. Linguistic familiarity bred contempt. For Friedländer, Yiddish was the source from which all the other defects flowed, and "it must be eradicated completely. . . . [because] once the child is stuck into the so-called Judeo-German language he cannot have any correct conception of a single thing in this world."[14] This maskilic view struck a chord, and in the eighteenth century German Jews began to discard Yiddish as their vernacular and in its stead adopt German. An uneven and long process, quicker in some places than others, it was a significant factor in the breakdown of what had been a pan-Ashkenazic culture, especially given that Eastern European Jewry continued to use Yiddish as its national language.[15] In the religious sphere Hasidism, the great pietistic movement, swept through Polish Jewry beginning in the eighteenth century, thus entirely changing the religious culture.[16] By contrast, Hasidism never crossed the border into Germany. Instead, the late eighteenth century saw the first steps toward Reform Judaism, an undertaking with which David Friedländer was deeply involved.[17] These developments essentially split the Ashkenazic world into two distinct branches.

The German-Jewish fascination with Sephardic culture that begins in the eighteenth century and gains strength during the nineteenth was an important dimension of this internal Ashkenazic split. For Friedländer, the Jew worthy of taking his seat in the Royal Academy—he was referring to Moses Mendelssohn—was comparable only to the Jewish military captain from Bordeaux, a man he does not name. That the pious and tradition-bound Mendelssohn could be portrayed as having nothing in common with any Eastern European Jew and was, according to Friedländer, closer to a Sephardic soldier from France was not only a means of celebrating the Sephardic Jews; it was an important part of the creation of a German-Jewish mystique.

There was a third feature that also served to deepen the divide between German and Polish Jewry, and that has to do with the deep impact of the Enlightenment and secular culture on elite German Jews, an influence not really in similar evidence to the east at this time.[18] Much of what came to characterize German Jewry—its acquisition of *Bildung* (self-cultivation); its appreciation for the German language, German music, and the aesthetic ideals of classical antiquity, especially its notions about bodily perfection; and general openness to the non-Jewish world—animated eighteenth-century Berlin's salon culture. At the center of this glittering world of studied performance, intellect, and Jewish and Gentile social and sexual relations were Marcus Herz and his wife, Henriette née de Lemos. Marcus Herz was born in Berlin; upon turning fifteen, he moved to Königsberg, and not long thereafter the teenager was welcomed into the home of David Friedländer. The exposure to European culture and manners profoundly changed Herz, who quickly outgrew his insular upbringing.[19] After having studied philosophy with Immanuel Kant at the University of Königsberg, Herz decided instead on a career as a physician. It was David Friedländer who financially supported Herz's medical studies at the University of Halle.[20] Unlike Mendelssohn, Herz responded to his exposure to philosophy, but especially science, by moving away from religious practice, trading the religious orthodoxy of his youth for the orthodoxy of Enlightenment rationalism.[21]

Herz and his brilliant, beautiful, wife, Henriette, led a glittering life in Berlin and at their home hosted one of the most renowned of the Jewish salons of the 1780s. There on those convivial evenings Henriette expounded on the latest works of literature and art, while in another room

Marcus lectured on natural science, medicine, and philosophy.[22] She also assisted him in the scientific experiments he performed for the edification and amusement of their guests. The two complemented each other, and Henriette was highly cognizant of the fact, later writing that "through his intellect and as a famous doctor Herz attracted people, and I attracted them through my beauty and through the understanding I had for all kinds of scholarship."[23]

The couple came from totally different Jewish backgrounds. Henriette was Sephardic and came from a wealthy family of Portuguese origin that had migrated to Berlin from Amsterdam in the seventeenth century. A polyglot, this woman from a culturally open background had command of French, English, Latin, Hebrew, Italian, Portuguese, and Danish, and was familiar with Turkish, Malay, and Sanskrit. Marcus, like his mentor, Moses Mendelssohn, was from a poor, parochial background and was also the son of a Torah scribe. And like Friedländer, despite his rejection of Jewish ritual, Herz was an active community worker who enjoyed a stellar reputation as a doctor and in 1782 became director of the Jewish Hospital in Berlin, a position previously held by his father-in-law, Benjamin de Lemos.[24]

While Herz became a man transformed, leaving his family background behind, his wife, by contrast, never lost her pride in her origins, this despite the fact that she converted to Protestantism in 1817 at the urging of her dear friend, the theologian Friedrich Schleiermacher. This seeming incongruity was possible for the reasons outlined above, namely, that one's Sephardic identity was considered superior to one's Judaism, which people like Henriette felt was culturally inferior. Religious conversion, they believed, could wash away its stain. By contrast, one's Sephardic identity was both indelible and precious. In particular, what Henriette found so enduring and endearing were her father's Sephardic physical features and his manner of speech. In her memoirs Henriette wrote of this "deeply religious man" who frequently read the Bible in Hebrew, with his "soft, most mellifluous expression," and noted that he possessed "the most beautiful foot and hand," that he had a "noble bearing," and that "his language was pure because like all the Portuguese Jews he had absolutely none of the Jewish jargon and its sound."[25] She was aware of her own beauty and frequently referred to it, sitting for many portraits and carefully crafting and managing her public image, and she was clearly conscious of her linguistic powers: in addition to her multilingualism, she herself is said to have taught Alexander von Humboldt Hebrew.[26] The desirable physical and cognitive qualities she venerated in her father appear to have come to her by inheritance.[27]

With Henriette Herz we go beyond the praise of Sephardic morality and essential difference that we heard so fulsomely expressed by Isaac de Pinto, and beyond David Friedländer's celebration of German Jewry's cultural superiority to Polish Jewry (a superiority that was symbolic of its move toward the level of Sephardic Jewry), to an enraptured description of Sephardic beauty and euphony. Admittedly this is the memoir of a loving daughter, but two factors argue against our seeing it only in that light. The first is that this was written after her conversion to Christianity, and so one might have expected less of a paean to her father's piety and the source of the physical nature of her father's Jewishness—his Iberian origins. Significantly, despite her apostasy, the stark juxtaposition of Sephardic and Ashkenazic aesthetics retained its resonance with her. And second, although filial bonds may have initially prompted Henriette's admiring portrait of her father, she was an integral part of the intellectual and social universe of maskilim where such descriptions became standard for all later Ashkenazic (and even Gentile) observers of the Sephardic body. Henriette was thus not unusual in praising Sephardic looks; she was only early in doing so.

Before moving on to the nineteenth-century discourse on Sephardic beauty, we must consider another crucial Enlightenment-era source that contributed to the composite portrait being drawn of Sephardic Jewry. In German Haskalah journals we see regular features on what were called "Great Men of the Nation." Whether in the Hebrew periodical *Ha-Me'assef* (The Gatherer), which appeared intermittently from 1784 to 1811, or the German-language *Sulamith*, published from 1806 to 1848, biographical portraits of distinguished Jews frequently featured Sephardic notables. They were portrayed as exemplary figures, worldly, wise, true to their faith, paragons of virtue. Such articles increased in number with the explosive growth of Jewish newspapers and journals over the course of the nineteenth century. Very often the figures profiled were Marranos who had attained fame in various fields of endeavor, refused to abandon the faith of their fathers, even under the threat posed by the Inquisition, and often fled the Iberian Peninsula to emerge as Jews in Northern Europe. These were especially appealing to the elite, acculturated German-Jewish readership of these publications, who found they could relate to the Sephardic paragons.

They were, in short, ideal types. Among those frequently featured were Hebrew poets, philosophers, rabbis, and statesmen, among them Solomon ibn Gabirol (ca. 1021–ca. 1058), Moses ibn Ezra (ca. 1055–ca. 1138), Judah Halevi (ca. 1075–1141), Maimonides (1135–1204), Don Isaac Abravanel (1437–1508), and Menasseh ben Israel (1604–1657). The *Me'asfim*, the authors of *Ha-Me'assef*, did not exactly present these characters as forerunners of the Haskalah, irrespective of how well they combined their worldliness with faithfulness to Judaism. They had few of the genuine characteristics of the maskil. But these Sephardim were "noble" and "good," and given that the publishers of *Ha-Me'assef* called themselves the Society for the Promotion of the Noble and the Good, bearing these characteristics is what counted. Above all, though, in addition to being revered within their own communities, it was their ability to reach out beyond the confines of Jewish society that was most highly valued. They were able to interact with and be respected by the non-Jewish worlds in which they lived. And that is what the maskilim wanted for themselves—to be held in high regard among non-Jews.

What the Berlin writer and book dealer Friedrich Nicolai said of Moses Mendelssohn in a letter to the dramatist and philosopher Gotthold Ephraim Lessing became a genuine aspiration of all Jews who sought acceptance beyond the Jewish world: "I am indebted to [Mendelssohn] for the most cheerful hours of the past winter and summer. I never left him, regardless of how long we were together, without becoming either better or more learned."[28] But for men as dedicated to the ideals of the Enlightenment as Lessing and Nicolai, and the myriad others who made his acquaintance, Mendelssohn was always seen as exceptional. They never imagined that one could find his character, his behavior, and his intellect in another Jew. The yoke of prejudice that encumbered even men of goodwill was simply too heavy to easily cast off.

It is true that Ha-Me'assef was written in Hebrew and was thus not intended for non-Jewish consumption, but, battered and influenced by popular perceptions of Jews, the authors first sought to reassure and bolster the spirits of their Jewish readership by providing them with a veritable gallery of Jewish notables who fit the ideal typology.

What was the Jewish ideal that the Me'asfim constructed, and what was the basis for their mythical Jew? He was a rationalist, took a democratic approach to Jewish institutions, was a proponent of secular education, had mastery of the Holy Tongue and vernacular languages, and was committed to having Jews pursue productive labor. Some of these, of course, were modern qualities, but others were not. When searching the annals of Jewish history for figures who best personified the ideals of rationalism, Jewish learning, and possession of secular wisdom, the Me'asfim turned to Maimonides more often than to any other figure. In fact he was the only medieval commentator they ever quoted.[29] Maimonides provided the authors of Ha-Me'assef with ample support for their ideological positions. Rhetorically, they asked, had he not "grown in all the sciences and the various disciplines, natural and divine, legal and ethical, as well as astronomical?" And did he not have command of "Aristotle, Plato, Galen and Themisteus?" And was he not "exceedingly wise in the medical sciences?"[30]

The maskilim were also deeply impressed by Maimonides's demand that languages be kept pure, and lauded the fact that he wrote in the vernacular. This was the historical precedent they used as justification for their demand that German Jews learn the purest biblical Hebrew and Hochdeutsch. While it is true that Maimonides's Commentary on the Mishnah and the Guide for the Perplexed were both written in Arabic, as were his medical treatises, most of his philosophical works were written in Judeo-Arabic. The

Me'asfim did not make anything of the distinction between those works written in Judeo-Arabic and those in Arabic, for to do so would have, by implication, given sanction to Yiddish.

It was the journal *Ha-Me'assef* that drew a straight line from Moses Maimonides to Moses Mendelssohn, coining the adage that "from Moses to Moses there was none like Moses."[31] Despite the many philosophical and theological differences between the two paragons, the maskilim attributed Maimonidean qualities to Mendelssohn and vice versa. Where Friedländer aligned his master, Mendelssohn, with the Sephardic military officer from Bordeaux, the *Me'asfim* saw him as the latter-day embodiment, indeed the fulfillment, of the greatest of Sephardic Jews, Moses Maimonides.[32]

While Maimonides was the second individual to have received a biographical treatment in *Ha-Me'assef*, the first person chosen was Don Isaac Abravanel (1437–1508), and in many ways, even more fully than Maimonides, he exemplified the German-Jewish image of the Sephardic hero.[33] Despite the fact that he had been a distinguished Bible commentator and philosopher, the *Me'asfim* paid little heed to Abravanel the scholar. Instead, it was Abravanel the wealthy statesman and distinguished representative of his people that caught the fancies of the maskilim; in particular, it was his welcome presence in the company of Europe's Gentile elites that they wished to convey to the readers of *Ha-Me'assef*. Although Abravanel was a polyglot and worldly man—he was appointed treasurer by Portugal's King Alfonso V and later occupied the same post under Ferdinand and Isabella until the expulsion of 1492, finally ending his life as a councillor of state in Venice—he was opposed to formalized secular education for Jews and was a philosophical antirationalist. He was, in other words, the opposite of Maimonides and very far from the Haskalah's image of the ideal Jew.

As such, he was revered by the maskilim for what he achieved, not for what he thought, for his status rather than his intellect, his acculturation as opposed to his parochialism. In their loving portraits of Abravanel, the *Me'asfim* cast him as a symbol of all that a Jew could become. Although he failed, despite desperate efforts, to have the expulsion order of 1492 rescinded, all of his intercessory efforts and charitableness on behalf of his people were seen as praiseworthy and exemplary:

> All his life he was a God-fearing man, able to get along in society, interceding on behalf of his people. Although we see in his works his opposition to the Christian faith . . . nevertheless, he loved those among them who were good, enjoyed their company, and was concerned with their welfare. This is the way of the truly wise man, as can be seen from the example of Abravanel. All those who seek wisdom and love mankind should do the same.[34]

As popular myth had it, Abravanel was descended from the House of David. Thus for the *Me'asfim*, Abravanel was part of a royal line, and they depicted him as a genuine Sephardic aristocrat. A Jewish nobleman: nothing could have been more appealing for an unemancipated but already acculturated German Jewry. And in a land where titles counted for much, this "Prince of the House of Israel," as he was called, became an iconic figure, a totem not only for the maskilim but also for later generations.

Into the twentieth century he was the subject of plays and biographies in a variety of languages, including a Yiddish biography written for children, and even in their hour of unspeakable torment or perhaps because of it, in 1937, on the five hundredth anniversary of his birth, the Jewish community of Berlin organized an exhibit on Abravanel.[35] A man of dignity, he preferred exile to apostasy and joined the rest of the Spanish Jews in departing the country in 1492.[36] Apostasy was not an option under the Nazis; that distinction notwithstanding, Abravanel's qualities as a political and moral leader resonated with a community already in the midst of its own tragedy. There were many Sephardic myths about Abravanel, but the image of the courageous Sephardic man of action that the Jews of Nazi Germany inherited was an Ashkenazic one, first sketched out for them by the *Me'asfim*. Abravanel was a man for all seasons.[37] At a time of hope and confidence that the future was bright, *Ha-Me'assef* presented its readers with the story of a Jew who stood for all that was possible in a world where goodwill prevailed. In a desperate time when only ill will was to be found, for another Jewish community in another age Abravanel appeared as a Moses to lead the Jews out of bondage.[38]

The *Me'asfim*'s adulation of Sephardic men of distinction did not stop with Maimonides and Abravanel. Many other such characters were featured, but that which appeared in Hebrew would only ever be read by what was an ever-shrinking pool of readers. By contrast, beginning in 1806, the German-language journal *Sulamith* became the main publication dedicated to the promotion of the values of the Haskalah. Published in the city of Dessau, Moses Mendelssohn's birthplace, the periodical trumpets in its subtitle its commitment to the ideals of that city's leading Jewish son—*Journal for the Promotion of Culture and Humanism among the Jewish Nation*.[39] A driving theme of the journal was to emphasize the essential humanity of the Jews. With utter faith in the times and complete confidence in his fellow man, Joseph Wolf, one of the journal's two editors, observed: "Thank God the era of [injustice] is over. No longer will the concepts 'Jew' and 'human being' be considered as heterogeneous."[40]

Wolf repeatedly stressed the capacity for all human beings, if treated well, to improve, for "the laws of equality had conquered the sentiments of all nations."[41] But the improvements that Jews had to make would not be de novo. Rather than become refined and civilized, Jews had merely to return to that state. There had been a period when, remaining true to the religion of their fathers, the "Jewish people could be counted among the most fortunate on earth." But that was when the "most propitious circumstances" obtained, and the "Israelites attained a certain level of perfection," one characteristic of which was the Jewish people's "love of all humanity." Again we return to the theme of Jewish-Christian relations, the breaking down of walls, and a plea for an age of comity. Israel did not have to learn but, rather, relearn how to flower, not just within a non-Jewish world but in full partnership with it.

Wolf seems to have been fully aware of *Sulamith*'s potential to influence its readers. Appearing in German guaranteed *Sulamith* a broader readership than *Ha-Me'assef* because it was now accessible to non-Jews. Thus, not entirely designed for internal Jewish consumption, *Sulamith* was arguably more influential, for among those who subscribed to it were government officials and representatives of various princely houses.[42] That is to say, those who were in policy-making positions could now read about Jewish history's most exemplary characters.

In the journal's programmatic statement those characters named were Sephardic Jews—"Maimonides, Aben Ezra, and Manasseh ben Israel." Despite what it had done to Ashkenazic Jews, Exile had not caused these Spanish Jews to become insular, had not turned them against the acquisition of knowledge and away from interaction with the rest of humanity. One assumes that this was the case because, like the ancient Israelites, these men were the bearers of a culture that had been originally formed under "propitious circumstances," in this case, those afforded by Islam. Wolf promised his readers that future issues of the journal would publish excerpts of their writings, which were full of "instructive wisdom and useful knowledge."[43]

The term "useful knowledge" was used as a counterpoint to what Wolf called "religious zealotry." It is noteworthy that a certain form of Talmudic argumentation, *pilpul*, a method of reconciling apparent conceptual differences of textual readings, was frequently dismissed as "useless." *Pilpul* first appeared in sixteenth-century Poland and indeed garnered many virulent enemies from within Polish rabbinic circles. For Enlightened German Jews such as the *Me'asfim* or the editors and Jewish readers of *Sulamith*, however, it was not just one particular mode of textual study but Talmudic scholarship itself that was the focus of their ire. The Sephardic Jews so lionized in *Sulamith* were depicted as free of the taint of Talmudism. Here were rational, learned, productive, and refined Jews, such as Menasseh ben Israel, whose tolerant homeland, Holland, was extolled by the author Joseph Löwisohn, for it was a haven for the "most brilliant minds of the Israelite nation, [those who] were engaged with literature and scholarship.... One need not wonder why almost all that is beautiful and useful, and, moreover, that which was ushered forth in the Hebrew language, came from Holland beginning in the seventeenth century until the [start] of the Mendelssohnian epoch."[44]

All that was required for Jews to thrive was a tolerant, welcoming land. All of those Sephardim featured in *Sulamith* were like Maimonides, who, before any consideration was given to his scholarship, was described by one author in an extended biographical portrait as one of those men with "a warm heart full of human dignity and love of man . . . [with a] great reputation especially among Christian scholars."[45] Here was the ideal model for the kind of rejuvenated Ashkenazic Jewry that the Haskalah promoted.

What we have been concerned with thus far is the theme of character formation. There was a deep-seated sense among the maskilim that the character of Ashkenazic Jews was deformed. Persecution bred insularity, superstition, ignorance, and petty trade; it stunted their personal aesthetic development and their general appreciation of beauty. They did not seem to know what beauty was, nor did they care to know. By contrast the Sephardim were seen as possessing a distinct sense of self and being open to the world, and, in return, the world was open to them. Whether in Muslim Spain or Calvinist Holland, Iberian Jewry found itself in happy circumstances, free to worship, free to trade, and free to mingle with non-Jews. These circumstances bred cosmopolitanism, rationalism, wisdom, prosperity, and an aesthetic sense that made its presence felt in their speech, their philosophical tradition, their religious culture, and their profound command of the Hebrew language.

In the value system of the German maskilim these attributes were understood as the victory of morality and good character over immorality. They allowed for what the maskilim called for time and time again, whether it was *shlemut* in *Ha-Me'assef* or *Vollkommenheit* in *Sulamith*. Both words mean "perfection," and its attainment was, said Isaac Euchel, a founder of *Ha-Me'assef*, "the purpose of man."[46] In the typologies of the two main branches of the Jewish people established by the Haskalah, Sephardic Jewry had come much closer to their idea of perfection than had Ashkenazic Jews. To sharpen the point further, the new elite of German Jewry had come far nearer the Sephardic ideal than had Polish Jewry—the group the maskilim were so desperate to distance themselves from and simultaneously rehabilitate, because the Berlin Jewish elite so steadfastly believed in the Enlightenment ideology that held out the possibility of human *Verbesserung*, or regeneration.

• • • • •

If the eighteenth century was an age concerned with the refinement of one's character, the focus in the nineteenth century was on bodily form and its perfection. This is not to suggest that character was no longer of importance. It most certainly was, but physical features counted more than ever before, with Jews taking real note of how they looked, attaching great significance to their own appearance as well as to the physical differences among Jewish groups. This is a turning point in Jewish *mentalité*, for it marks a critical and novel dimension to Jewish self-perceptions. To that list of qualities that Jews had long understood as being characteristic of them as a people—Exile, their religious beliefs, their sacred texts, their languages, and their historic suffering—one could now add their physical appearance. But more than this, Jews began to stress the importance of beauty, of looking good, of making a positive physical impression.

Thus the Ashkenazic discourse about Sephardim and Ashkenazim takes on a different hue from that which preceded it. By the late nineteenth and into the early twentieth century, we see a full-blown Ashkenazic glorification of the physical appearance of their Sephardic coreligionists. Eighteenth-century notions of beauty were very much the product of contemporary intellectual currents, particularly philosophy, art history, and language politics, as well as the imperatives of the Enlightenment, the Haskalah, and the aesthetic demands they impressed upon Jews in their quest to be considered Europeans.[47] One hundred years later, however, Jewish notions of Jewish physical beauty came to be defined by a new set of contemporary sensibilities. These were not drawn from the sea of speculative philosophy that had generated aesthetic notions in Moses Mendelssohn's day. Rather, at the fin de siècle, ideas about Jewish beauty were influenced principally by politics, science, modern scholarship, and mass culture. Subsumed under these broad categories we can identify nationalism, in its Jewish and non-Jewish forms, Jewish acculturationism, antisemitism, the practice of history, and the emergence of archaeology and race science, all of which influenced changing notions of Jewish physicality.

In fin de siècle Central Europe, under the influence of the dominant culture's focus on physical prowess and well-being, Jews began to pursue recreational activities, visiting spas and participating in organized sports, particularly gymnastics and fencing. These new avocational pursuits all worked together to reflect and shape new concerns about the physical appearance, strength, health, and beauty of Jews.[48] In addition, with its elaborate honor codes, its emphasis on manliness and stoicism, and its goal of scarring the face of an opponent, the *Mensur*, or duel, practiced by university fraternities in German-speaking Europe, further sharpened both the Jewish and non-Jewish focus upon Jewish physicality. By and large Jews were barred from membership in Christian dueling fraternities and were mostly denied "satisfaction" upon receipt of an insult because they were considered unworthy. Even though Jewish fraternities tended not to duel, their members were deeply impacted by the masculinist culture of the *Mensur*.[49] Furthermore, a rapidly changing visual culture, exemplified by the rise of photography, magazines, newspapers, illustrated journals, and postcards depicting Jews, all helped give substance to new conceptions about the Jewish body.[50]

As a consequence of all these developments, the way Jews were now seen by non-Jews and the way they saw themselves—the latter often contingent upon the former—underwent significant change. In both popular culture and politics, Jewish and non-Jewish alike, the physical appearance and condition of Jews came in for intense scrutiny, which took alternate forms of praise and ridicule.[51] This, however, was far from the end of the matter, for the increased self-consciousness and emerging inferiority complexes Central and Eastern Europe European Jews began to develop about their appearance set in motion a reflexive response that accepted the judgment of Jewish bodily imperfection but simultaneously challenged it by establishing a new model of Jewish beauty. In a vast array of nineteenth-century sources—among them learned journals, popular literature, and visual depictions—the case was repeatedly made that Jewish beauty did indeed exist, and that not all Jews were by turns grotesque or enervated. The belief that the Sephardim embodied Jewish aesthetic perfection gripped the popular Ashkenazic imagination, shaping a set of ideas about Jews that became enshrined in Jewish codes of self-understanding and, in powerful ways, still obtain down to our own day.

Interrogating Ashkenazic as well as non-Jewish discourse on the Sephardim affords us the opportunity to explore more deeply the powerful neoromantic impulse expressed by European Jews at the fin de siècle. As part of a response to the tribal and medievalist element at the heart of various expressions of European nationalism, Jews pursued their own claims to antiquity by celebrating the links between contemporary Jews and ancient Israelites. What was novel in this process was that it was an entirely secular undertaking: not a focus on Judaism as the religious patrimony of the ancient Near East, it entailed instead a series of claims about the physical verisimilitude of modern and ancient Jews. This discussion will also allow us to broach the subject of orientalism and begin to explore some of its Jewish dimensions. In the end, the detour along the ancient pathway in modern Jewish culture will bring us back to the Sephardim, as they were considered by many to be the most direct and authentic descendants of the Israelites.

Let us begin by considering how two new, seemingly unconnected products of late nineteenth-century culture were brought together to help animate the discourse on Jewish physicality: archaeology and photography. The rise of the former as a new academic discipline contributed greatly to nationalism, romanticism, and the era's fascination with bodily form and its links to racial and ethnic roots.[52] As it relates to Jewish history, archaeology was often pressed into service to establish the ancient lineage and biblical pedigree of modern Jews. In particular there was a concerted effort to claim that modern Jews betrayed their racial origins insofar as they looked identical to those Israelites depicted on ancient reliefs. Examining ancient monuments for signs of contemporary Jewish physiognomy in order to establish the Semitic origins and permanency of Jewish appearance was not the preserve of any one constituency. It was, rather, an ecumenical exercise practiced by Zionists, liberal Jews, and well-meaning Christians, as well as notorious racists and antisemites. All of them used this highly malleable evidence in ways that supported their widely differing political agendas.

The impetus for Jews to make claims of biological continuity between past and present derived from the contemporary Jewish neo-romanticist impulse to seek out their roots and embrace their Israelite origins. In an act of nonstatist nationalism this was the Jewish version of a larger European undertaking; but whereas the Christian search for ethnic or racial roots had the desired effect of narrowing the definition of national identity among Europeans, for Jews committed to social and cultural integration, archaeology, when used in this way, served the purpose of enlarging the definitions of what it meant to be European. Orientalist archaeology deployed in this manner provided Jews with a means of challenging reified and constricted categories of Europeanness. With their glorification of ancient, and by extension Sephardic, Jewry, Central European Ashkenazim were able to celebrate an illustrious branch of the Jewish people and simultaneously lead Europeans to consider a more expansive definition of what it meant to be an Occidental. One might add that the higher Bible criticism of the nineteenth century, dedicated as it was to historicism, stood to remind Europeans of Christianity's Oriental, indeed Jewish, roots, even if many Christians, including the Bible critics among them, wished to deny this.[53] In this light, comparison of the modern appearance of Jews with the portraits of Israelites found on recently discovered antiquities can be interpreted variously, without recourse to a simplistic Saidean reading of orientalism. Instead, the appeal to recognize the physical verisimilitude between ancient and modern Jews might be seen as a politically progressive statement that demonstrated the capacity of Jews to acculturate to European manners, despite their so-called Oriental origins, which non-Jews in fact shared, via the Judaic origins of Christianity.

The new practice of photography abetted archaeology and contributed to evolving notions of Jewish physicality and beauty.[54] In its infancy photography's value was that it could capture for posterity the single, unrepeatable instant. But with time, photography was capable of doing more, of producing a series of images that was more akin to writing. Narratives in pictures, what might be referred to today as the "photo essay," were capable of telling stories in new ways. Among the stories that Europeans and Americans sought to tell were those drawn from the Bible; thus photographic images of the Holy Land and ancient Near East were an important new tool with which to establish the Bible's veracity.[55] As such, photography provided a new way to address the nature of Jewish physicality and even shed light on Jewish origins.[56]

In 1885, the Australian-Jewish author Joseph Jacobs delivered an address to the Royal Anthropological Institute entitled "On the Racial Characteristics of Modern Jews," in which he stressed the permanent character of

Jewish appearance and based his claim upon what he considered to be in-controvertible evidence garnered from photography. He analyzed photographs of ancient reliefs, as well as composite contemporary photographs of students taken at London's Jews' Free School and the Jewish Working Men's Club by Francis Galton, the great English polymath and cousin of Charles Darwin. It was Jacobs's conclusion that "[the Jewish expression] may be traced throughout the history of Art, and I may refer to one of the earliest representations of the Jews in Art, the Assyrian *bas relief* of the captive Jews of Lachish (B.C. 701).... The subject is undoubted and well-known, and the persistency of the Jewish type for the last 2,600 years is conclusively proved by it." In fact, asserted Jacobs, "the female slaves behind Sennacharib's throne might have been taken from the synagogue galleries of to-day.... The *relief* then shows not only the permanency of the Jewish type, but its practical identity with the ordinary Semitic type of those days."[57]

What made Jacobs's claims believable was the deeply held belief that the photograph represented objective truth. According to the historian of photography Mary Warner Marien, "no prior medium fully presaged the common photograph's ability to externalize remembrance, or to produce images conceived of as genuinely akin to actual experience."[58] As photography's appeal grew and the idea that one could possess a copy of one's likeness became more widespread, the notion of owning images of distant peoples in far-off lands also made logical sense. In our context, this made the use of photography in the quest to identify Jewish racial origins all the more compelling. It was as if one could travel across time and space to establish that there existed an unbroken chain of Jewish peoplehood from antiquity to the present: here were the photos to prove it.

Galton and Jacobs profoundly disagreed on what the photographs showed. According to Galton, "the feature that struck me most, as I drove through the ... Jewish quarter, was the cold scanning gaze of man, woman, and child.... I felt, rightly or wrongly, that every one of them was cooly appraising me at market value, without the slightest interest of any other kind." Galton published this in the journal *The Photographic News*; Jacobs countered that with the composites, "here we have something ..., more spiritual than a spirit.... The composite face must represent this Jewish forefather. In these Jewish composites we have the nearest representation we can hope to possess of the lad Samuel as he ministered before the Ark, or the youthful David when he tended his father's sheep."[59] In fact, Jacobs concludes with this reference to an ideal Sephardi, whose looks and intelligence conjured up an ideal portrait of a modern Jew: "On my showing this [the photographs] to an eminent painter of my acquaintance, he exclaimed, 'I imagine that is how Spinoza looked when a lad.'"[60] Where Galton saw the Ashkenazic ghetto Jew as a huckster, Jacobs saw biblical heroes living exemplary lives according to the code of Hebrew morality and responsibility. The

2.1. Judean women captives. From the frieze depicting the Assyrian king Sennacharib's siege of Lachish in 701 B.C.E. The caption reads, "South Palestinian Women from the Eighth Century." J. M. Judt, *Die Juden als Rasse*, 124.

2.2. Judean male captives. From the frieze depicting the Assyrian king Sennacharib's siege of Lachish in 701 B.C.E. The caption reads, "Racial Type of a South Palestinian Jew." J. M. Judt, *Die Juden als Rasse*, 118.

artist, and Jacobs seems to approve of the description, then sees a portrait of a Sephardi as a young man, a soon-to-be modern Jewish hero. It was no co-incidence that Jacobs, who was a polymath, wrote on many different themes including Spanish-Jewish history, the poet Judah Halevi, and the man he repeatedly called his hero, Baruch Spinoza.[61]

The view Jacobs expressed here was typical. In his study *Die Juden als Rasse* (The Jews as a Race; 1903), the Polish-Jewish anthropologist Ignacy Maurycy Judt likewise drew upon the extant archaeological evidence to claim that contemporary Jews bore striking resemblance to those portraits of ancient Israelites appearing on the antique friezes and monuments of Egypt and Assyria.[62] For Judt, the pictorial evidence showed the close phys-iological relationship of the Jews to the various peoples of the ancient Near East. In fact, he sought to play down the influence of both "the ghetto" and, more recently, "European civilization" on Jews, noting that what they im-parted to the Jews in either a physical or intellectual sense was of secondary importance, and that it was the ancient world that stamped the Jew as such, something that was clear from the ancient monuments.[63]

Writing in 1907, the German-Jewish Zionist Elias Auerbach noted that "the pictorial representations of the Assyrians and the Babylonians that we have not only show a great conformity with the ancient representation of Jews, but also a striking similarity with today's Jewish type. We are also jus-tified in speaking of a general Semitic type, to which Jews belong."[64] In the mind of this liberal Zionist, Jews and Arabs shared the most fundamental of biological features. The return of Jews to Palestine to again live in close proximity to one another and alongside Arabs was, therefore, a return to the natural order of things.

Another liberal Zionist from Germany, Arthur Ruppin, echoed these views. A founder of Brit Shalom, an organization formed in 1925 that ar-gued for a binational Jewish-Arab state in Palestine, Ruppin recognized the sui generis nature of Zionism, noting that there was no case of an indige-nous people willingly allowing another nation to come and settle alongside it while simultaneously securing equal rights and national autonomy on that same land.[65] Normative theories and practices of nationalism à la Herzl could not accommodate Zionism, and so Ruppin was drawn to the idea of race, for as a concept it rose above mundane notions of nationhood. For a while at least—that is, until he became convinced that a binational state was an unrealistic goal—Ruppin was certain that the shared biological and morphological characteristics of Jews and Arabs could form the basis of a cooperative relationship between them. And in particular, Ruppin believed that Sephardic and Middle Eastern Jews had a special role to play. They were to serve as a conduit between Ashkenazic Jews such as himself and Arabs. Ruppin even planned to visually depict the grounds for this racial fraternity. Having set sail from the United States on his way back to Palestine aboard the S.S. *Aquitania*, Ruppin noted in a diary entry of April 13, 1923:

> It appears to me that Zionism is possible only if it possesses a completely different scientific foundation. Herzl's conception was naive and makes sense only given his ignorance about conditions in Palestine. We must once again take our place among the Oriental peoples and produce a new cultural community in the Near East, in cooperation with our racial brethren, the Arabs (and Armenians). Increasingly, I believe that Zionism is justified only on the basis of the fact that the Jews belong racially to the peoples of the Orient. I am now collecting material for a book on Jews, the basis of which will be the racial question. I wish to include in it drawings that will present the ancient peoples of the Orient and the present-day population and describe the types that ruled and still rule among the people living in Syria and Asia Minor. I wish to show that these types still persist among the Jews of our time.[66]

It was axiomatic among many early Zionists that the Jewish return to the Land of Israel was not merely a homecoming; it was to be a reunion. History had torn the Jews not only from their native soil but from their Arab neighbors, who were, in fact, their racial and cultural brethren. According to a Zionist physician named Baruchov writing on the eve of World War I, Zionism was a cure to the ailment that was Europeanness, and he warned that Jews in Palestine were to "stand on guard and be careful not to plant the seeds of European decay in the land of our rebirth." In unison, Arabs and Jews would work together to keep Palestine Oriental.[67] Ironically, nothing more clearly bespoke an anti-European, anticolonialist strain of Zionist thought than those arguments drawn from the discourse of race, based as they often were on archaeological and photographic "evidence."

Non-Jews likewise weighed in on the appearance of the Jews; long before the advent of Zionism, they too had deployed archaeology to make assertions about the antiquity of the Jewish type and its affinity with Arabs. In his influential work *The Inequality of the Races* (1853–1855), the father of modern polygenist thought, Arthur, comte de Gobineau, asserted that whatever their current provenance, all Jews "look alike" because they stemmed from the one place:

> I have had the opportunity of examining closely [a Polish Jew]. His features and profile clearly betrayed his origin. His eyes especially were unforgettable. This denizen of the north, whose immediate ancestors had lived, for many generations, in the snow, seemed to have been just tanned by the rays of the Syrian sun. The Semitic face looks exactly the same, in its main characteristics, as it appears on the Egyptian paintings of three or four thousand years ago, and more; and we find it also, in an equally striking and recognizable form, under the most varied and disparate conditions of climate.[68]

At the same time that Gobineau spoke of the permanency of the Jewish racial type, an American surgeon from Mobile, Alabama, Josiah Clark Nott, published his revealingly titled *Types of Mankind: or, Ethnological Researches, Based upon the Ancient Monuments, Paintings, Sculptures, and Crania of Races* (1854). Nott related that he was an acquaintance of a respected member of the city's Jewish community, and he assured his readers that not only would Mobilians recognize the man as a local dignitary but anyone familiar with archaeology would also instantly recognize the man's racial provenance: "Still, after 2,500 years, so indelible is the [Hebrew] type, that every resident of Mobile will recognize in this Chaldean effigy [a colossal bust found near Nineveh] the facsimile portrait of one of their city's most prominent citizens."[69]

Nearly all who appealed to the archaeological finds that they had come to know through the medium of photography drew upon such evidence to claim that the morphology of Jews was everywhere identifiable, and that they were a Semitic racial group whose Near Eastern origins stamped them as permanently different. For Richard Wagner's son-in-law, the rabid English antisemite Houston Stewart Chamberlain (1855–1927), and others of his ilk, the Jews' geographic origins—"the Jewish people is and remains alien to our part of the world"—ensured their essential difference, their unassimilability, indeed, the danger they posed for Aryan Europe. In Chamberlain's words, "almost all pre-eminent and free men from Tiberius to Bismarck have looked upon the presence of the Jew in our midst as a social and political danger."[70]

Chamberlain drew upon the work of historians, Bible critics, anthropologists, and archaeologists to make his case against the Jews. Like Gobineau, he was a racist who considered all the superior races to have been of mixed descent. The Jews, for Chamberlain, were not so much a mixed race as they were a "mongrel" race. The distinction for him was that the mixture in the latter was among races at great remove from one another, while healthy race mixing was among different but kindred racial types. Jews were 50 percent *Homo syriacus* (Hittite), 10 percent Indo-European (Amorite), 5 percent Semite (Bedouin), and 35 percent "indefinable mixed forms."[71] The negative consequence of all this was made manifest by the power and control Jews wielded over European civilization. For Chamberlain, archaeology revealed telltale signs of the Jewish character when one considered what traits Jews inherited from the Hittites: "On the Egyptian pictures the Hittites look anything but intelligent. The exaggerated 'Jewish' nose is continued upwards by a retreating brow and downwards by a still more retreating chin. . . . To judge from the few pictures he must also have been shrewd, in fact extremely cunning (which of course has nothing to do with brilliant intellect, on the contrary). His history, too, shows him to be shrewd: he has known how to rule and how to submit to an alien power where the conditions were favourable."[72] Of the noble Aryan qualities to be found among the Israelites, next to nothing was left in either the behavior or the physical appearance of most Jews. Those qualities had been bred out of this "mongrel race."[73] The extent to which the purported physical and social characteristics of the ancient Hittites corresponded precisely to the contemporary antisemitic description of Jews and Jewish behavior is impossible to miss.

Chamberlain was uncompromisingly hostile to Jews, a fanatical Germanophile, a central figure in Wagner's Bayreuth Circle, and a man of such influence in the pantheon of antisemites that Hitler visited him on his deathbed. Despite his unswerving consistency when it came to Jews, there was, nevertheless, one exception—Iberian Jewry: "This is nobility in the fullest sense of the word, genuine nobility of race! Beautiful figures, noble heads, dignity in speech and bearing.... That out of the midst of such people Prophets and Psalmists could arise—that I understood at the first glance, which I honestly confess that I had never succeeded in doing when I gazed, however carefully, on the many hundred young Jews—'Bochers'—of the Friedrichstrasse in Berlin." Here we have comments at no great remove from those of the maskilim of the late eighteenth and early nineteenth centuries and, as we will see, from Chamberlain's Jewish contemporaries.

The question is, however, why Chamberlain privileged the Sephardim when, after all, "our governments, our law, our science, our commerce, our literature, our art.... practically all branches of our life have become more or less willing slaves of the Jews."[74] The answer, as evidenced by many factors, including the archaeological and pictorial record, is that "Jews," according to Chamberlain, were a product of the Diaspora, the religion largely formed in Babylonian exile by the prophet Ezekiel. We now come to the crux of the matter:

> The course of Jewish history has provided for a peculiar artificial selection of the morally higher section: by banishments, by continual withdrawals to the Diaspora—a result of the poverty and oppressed condition of the land—only the most faithful (of the better classes) remained behind, and these abhorred every marriage contract—even with Jews!—in which both parties could not show an absolutely pure descent from one of the tribes of Israel and prove their strict orthodoxy beyond all doubt.... *And when at last the final dispersion of the Jews came, all or almost all of these sole genuine Jews were taken to Spain.* (my emphasis)[75]

Not only did those from the "morally higher" classes hail from Judea, but that territory, according to Chamberlain, was where the "Amorites were more numerous," and among the Israelites there was a "constant infiltration of genuine Semitic blood from Arabia." The Amorites, he had explained, were an Aryan people, and from the Egyptian monuments "we see.... an open countenance so full of character and intelligence." From the Semites

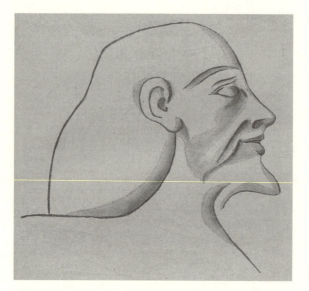

2.3. "Drawing of a South Palestinian Jew of Amorite [Racial] Type" J. M. Judt, *Die Juden als Rasse*, 129.

the Judeans inherited their intensity of religious feeling and "Gothic blood."[76] That by even so warped a figure as Chamberlain Sephardic Jews could be distinguished from the Ashkenazim and depicted as "noble" and "beautiful" speaks volumes for the seductive appeal of Spanish Jewry. Not even one of the most steadfast and influential antisemites of the nineteenth century was immune to their allure.

Only the racists among those observers who believed that they saw contemporary Jewish faces on ancient monuments held to a view that the Jews were all of a piece and unchangeable. By contrast, among Jews, even those who imagined that they could see their own likenesses on temple sculptures from the Nile valley, there was no attempt to suggest that just because their physical features remained unaltered, their behavior likewise followed suit. Despite the Jews' geographical origins their contemporary culture was proof that their Near Eastern beginnings were not a hindrance to their becoming Western.[77] The neo-romanticist impulse among Ashkenazim demanded a sensitivity to the past while being at the same time forward-looking, seeing in Jewish history mores and manners that were exemplary, and that could be harnessed for the purposes of emancipation, social and cultural integration, and, if necessary, self-defense. The Jewish past, in other words, could point the way forward.

It was not just within the confines of Jewish history that the Sephardim were said to have occupied a special place. Archaeology's focus on ancient

Israel and its link to Iberian Jewry extended even to its impact on Spain itself. For Max Grunwald, who in the late nineteenth century was the founding father of the field of Jewish ethnography, the Semitic Hamites were among the original inhabitants of Spain, with evidence of the country's Jewish roots residing in Hebrew place-names and monuments, and in the appearance of the Spaniards who "are descended from King David." Even the dance of the Israelites around the Ark of the Covenant was, he declared, "still performed in Spanish churches."[78] Gone and forgotten by Spaniards, the Sephardim nevertheless lived on courtesy of the legacy they bequeathed to Spain and its culture.

One of the most compelling features of the Jewish discourse on the Ashkenazic-Sephardic split is that it involves a complete inversion of a model of orientalism that presupposes Western triumphalism. The modern Jewish claims of ethnic and aesthetic kinship with the Jews of antiquity was of a piece with the impulse of eighteenth- and nineteenth-century Europeans who, in the spirit of romantic nationalism, began to popularize their own myths of origin. Christian Europe, of course, traced all humanity back to Adam, through Noah and his sons, Japhet, Shem, and Ham, the three of whom were said to have begotten the different races of mankind. This Christian teaching was incorporated into preexisting myths of origin, which by the nineteenth century became vital components of that era's nationalist ideologies. Tracing their own roots all the way back to the Aryans—via groups such as the Visigoths, the Franks, the Celts, the Jutes, the Angles, the Saxons, the Gauls, the Huns, and the Slavs—modern Europeans, from the British Isles in the West to Russia in the East, glorified themselves by celebrating their imagined ancestors. Expressing a universal human condition, each nationality claimed to have a noble and distinct lineage. And central to these genealogies was the claim that they shared the values, creative spark, and, very often, the martial spirit of these earliest Europeans.[79] In fact in his study of antisemitism, *Israel among the Nations* (1895), the French historian Anatole Leroy-Beaulieu noted the difference between the value systems bequeathed to future generations of Jews and of Christians by their ancestors: "The scholar, says the Talmud, 'takes precedence over the king; the learned bastard over the ignorant high-priest.' What a contrast to this is afforded by our Western barbarians, the Franks, the Goths, and the Lombards."[80]

The Ashkenazic celebration of Sephardic Jews is of a different order from the European genealogies. Crucially, Ashkenazic Jews did not claim descent from Sephardim; they did, however, bestow upon them the crown of Jewish authenticity and aristocracy. The way they walked as well as the way they talked revealed what many Ashkenazim considered to be an original Jewry with a noble bearing. That demeanor was born in antiquity, and they had been able to maintain it throughout history; as the distinguished

Russian-Jewish anthropologist Samuel Weissenberg observed, "The Sephardim have maintained the Semitic type more purely than the Eastern European Jews."[81]

On the other hand—so the argument went—Ashkenazim, though likewise the descendants of the ancient Israelites, had seen history strip them of the original nobility and grace that so manifestly characterized the Sephardim. In other words, in stark contrast to claims about the continuity of behavior between modern Europeans and their ancestors, the Ashkenazic infatuation with Sephardic bodies was built upon the notion of historical rupture, and on concomitant distinctions between beautiful and ugly Jews, the physical dimension to the morality question discussed above—namely, the juxtaposition between those who were dignified and those who lacked self-respect, those who were praiseworthy and those who were in desperate need of excoriation and improvement. The Ashkenazic myth of Sephardic supremacy was the product of anxieties about the aesthetics of Jewish peoplehood that gained traction in a world beset by competing nationalisms, racial tensions, and intense antisemitism.

Assessing the Jewish body in order to establish where it was to be situated on the scale of human beauty is the aspect of second-wave Jewish romanticism that owed its greatest debt to the discourse and iconography of contemporary antisemitism. Because antisemitism served as the cornerstone of an entire political and ideological worldview, the wide dissemination of negative images of and tropes about Jews served as the glue that connected and fortified antisemitic movements across the length and breadth of Europe. By the late nineteenth century, antisemites, irrespective of religion, nationality, and class, spoke a mutually intelligible language of hate.[82] While our focus in this chapter will remain on Germany, the Jewish contribution and response to this discourse was global, and we will have occasion to go beyond Germany's borders to take account of modern Jewish aesthetic sensibilities elsewhere. Local variations notwithstanding, the fundamental representations of both Ashkenazic and non-Ashkenazic Jews were transnational and were shaped by a shared historical romanticism and distorted sense of self.

Through the mass media of the late nineteenth century, images were disseminated widely, ensuring that European culture became ever more visually oriented. Amid this flood of images iconographic representations of Jews became more accessible than ever before. The mass reproduction of negative images of Jews was without precedent and thus was a crucial development in the history of antisemitism. Mass-circulation newspapers and other propagandistic media published sensational and scurrilous stories about Jews, and used photography and caricature to embellish those tales. Modern print culture was the vehicle by which Jew hatred was secularized, popularly scientized, and made an ideology that could be graphically depicted. The unique ability to deploy illustrations on a massive scale to promote hatred of Jews is one of the defining characteristics of modern antisemitism because texts, both ancient and modern, describing Jewish failings and flaws could now be enhanced with or simply replaced by lurid and frightening pictures.[83]

This was a moment of radical innovation in the history of Judeophobia. In the long, premodern history of antisemitic discourse and representation, Jews were charged with a litany of crimes, including misanthropy toward Gentiles, the killing of Jesus, the murder of young children for ritual purposes, well poisoning, Host desecration, and charging usurious rates of interest. It is noteworthy then that when such crimes were depicted, Jews were only infrequently characterized with criminal miens. They were rarely pictured, for example, as ugly or deformed. This is not to say such depictions did not exist. The anonymous English caricaturist who in 1277 doodled a depiction of a Jew in the margins of the Forest Roll of Essex, with the caption "Aaron Son of the Devil," gave him a pronounced hooked nose, black eyes, curly hair, and thick lips. In so doing he set a precedent for a negative image of Jews that has persisted down to our own times.[84] There are other exceptions, but throughout the course of the High Middle Ages, Jews more often than not appear quite normal looking.[85] In fact, before the eleventh century, Jews were rarely depicted with distinctive features. They were almost never portrayed as weak, sickly, or misshapen; they are often indistinguishable from Christians, save for their clothing and beards or—as is the case in some French and English illuminated Bibles of the thirteenth century—where the Jews are identifiable because they are the ones being beaten with clubs.[86] According to art historian Sara Lipton, in French *Bibles moralisées* the faces of Jews, who are certainly portrayed as being in theological error, exhibit "distress, regret, and indifference."[87] In twelfth-century art, increasingly prevalent are Jews who appear with "fierce, scowling expressions, heavy brows, squinting or staring eyes, and a variety of distorted beast-like noses." These features reflected the Jews' moral turpitude and their enmity toward Christ. They were not of a different physiological order from Christians and were still mostly identified by their hats and beards. However, by the middle of the thirteenth century, Lipton observes that what has been called the "Gothic face" of the Jews, consisting of a long, thin bony nose and pointed beard, became ubiquitous in Christian art. However, even then, other figures in medieval art that were rendered as religious or social enemies often had such features. They were not yet unique to Jews.[88]

Even the notorious *Judensau* images, those uniquely German depictions of Jews engaged in acts of bestiality with pigs, largely represent Jews with what might be termed normative human features, even when the figures are shown performing the deeply transgressive act of coprophilia and other forms of bestiality. To be sure, Jews in such portrayals are sometimes seen as

"*Aaron fil diaboli*"

Forest Roll of Essex (1277)

2.4. "Aaron Son of the Devil." First known caricature of a Jew. Taken from Forest Roll of Essex, 1277.

possessing talons or cloven feet, but these are so phantasmagoric that they cannot be said to be depictions of real Jews.[89]

Even in early modern texts seeking to "expose" Jewish rituals, Jews were depicted performing their ceremonies, which the authors belittled, but the illustrations accompanying such texts were for the most part straightforward, the Jews appearing quite normal.[90] In the seventeenth century, members of the Sephardic community of Amsterdam, among them its leading figure, Menasseh ben Israel, began to have portraits of themselves painted; Rembrandt's dignified and frequently majestic depictions of Jews are only

2.5. Rembrandt, portrait of the Sephardic doctor Ephraim Bueno, 1647.

the most famous of these paintings.[91] In eighteenth-century Germany, a second wave of rather lavishly illustrated texts began to appear that focused on the ethnography of Jews, explaining and illustrating their customs. Produced by Christians, the representations were for the most part respectful, the Jews depicted with objective sincerity, even if the commentary on the rituals was sometimes critical.[92]

This was not the case in the nineteenth century. To be sure, the Jewish bourgeoisie in Western and Eastern Europe commissioned portraits, and even more Jews had themselves professionally photographed. However, in Gentile representations of Jews, in a world becoming increasingly secular, Jewish rituals held less interest and focus shifted to depicting Jewish economic and political activities. This was part of a larger and more sinister development in European political culture. De-emphasizing the charge of deicide and theological error, modern antisemitism replaced its traditional anti-Jewish sermons with a secular liturgy that trumpeted the Jews as aggressive conspirators, whether sexual predators, rapacious capitalists, or, into the twentieth century, Bolshevik revolutionaries. No longer wearing distinctive clothing such as the badges and conical hats that were found in medieval depictions of Jews, modern antisemitic representations focused on Jewish physical features as a marker of Jewish difference, promiscuity, and criminality.[93]

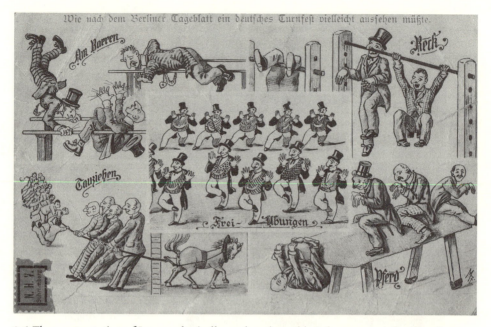

Wie nach dem Berliner Tageblatt ein deutsches Turnfest vielleicht aussehen müßte.

2.6. The representation of Jews as physically weak and unathletic became a staple of modern antisemitism. The caption reads, "What a German gymnastics tournament might look like according to the *Berliner Tageblatt* [newspaper]." Courtesy of The Magnes Collection of Jewish Art and Life, Berkeley, CA.

At the same time, another image of the Jew (most frequently depicted as a male) emerged, one that was in many ways the exact opposite of the Jew as threatening menace. In this version he was effete, delicate, unmanly, lacking in valor, and decidedly unathletic. He was, in other words, the opposite of the way Europeans saw themselves, as healthy, strong, salt-of-the-earth representatives and defenders of their respective nations. These positions were reinforced by the *völkisch* movement of the late nineteenth century, which stressed, among other things, ideas about ethnic essentialism and bodily perfection, both largely understood in racial terms. Accordingly, *völkisch* ideology demanded that Jews be excluded from membership in the *Volksgemeinschaft*, or national community. Divorced from its language, its poetry, its songs, its religion, and its historical destiny, Jews were not considered bearers of the nation's true spiritual identity; irrespective of how long they had been in any one place, they could never become part of the *Volk*.[94]

With the rise of mass culture all these images, whether of menacing or of cowardly Jews, were dispersed globally, in newspapers through cartoons and caricature, in paintings, posters, political pamphlets, and postcards.[95] Beyond the published depictions of Jews there was a bustling market for

2.7. Late nineteenth-century smoking pipe with the bowl carved as an anti-semitic depiction of a Jew. Courtesy of The Magnes Collection of Jewish Art and Life, Berkeley, CA.

antisemitica in the nineteenth century, with vile representations of Jews found in the form of porcelain, ceramic, bronze, and wood figurines; the visual slurs were etched on medallions, carved into smoking pipes, and portrayed on tobacco cases, ashtrays, the heads of walking sticks, letter openers, paperweights, ink pots, bowls, plates, dishes, salt and pepper shakers, drinking glasses, beer steins, beer coasters, match holders, candlesticks, playing cards, stickers, stamps, and much else besides.[96] Such antisemitic images were ubiquitous. Impossible to avoid and appearing in multiple media, they were the stuff out of which a stock impression of the Jews was established and repeatedly reinforced.

The stereotyped physical features of the Jews—they were depicted as unhealthy looking, frizzy haired, swarthy, now corpulent, now frighteningly scarecrow-like, heavy lidded, large nosed, and thick lipped—betrayed their non-European origins. Whether portrayed as effeminate dandies, urban intellectuals, corpulent businessmen, rapacious gynecologists, or unkempt peddlers, they were all hideous. To their enemies, ugliness became a characteristic Jewish trait.[97] By contrast, the idealized image of Northern Europeans was the very opposite. They were tall, powerful, lithe, and beautifully proportioned.[98] Here were blond, muscular Christians who tilled the soil. They were, in other words, the essence of the nation, paragons of Nordic racial perfection.[99]

The cumulative impact of all this was an unending assault on the Jewish body, a body that was almost always prototypically Ashkenazic. The lampooned Jews were from Central and Eastern Europe. It is they who were

2.8. Late nineteenth-century greeting card with antisemitic caricatures of Eastern European Jews. The caption reads "Peaceful Lions." Courtesy of The Magnes Collection of Jewish Art and Life, Berkeley, CA.

caricatured as unattractive, ignoble, and unhealthy. Notably, the Sephardic Jew was largely left unscathed and could even be celebrated by an antisemite such as Houston Stewart Chamberlain. In fact, the iconography of antisemitism in southeastern Europe—lands where the Jews were predominantly Sephardic—was drawn directly from Central and Eastern Europe. There simply was no antisemitic iconography that formulated a negative physical stereotype of Sephardic Jews.[100]

Just as the Ashkenazic Jews served as a countertype to Christian manhood, so too did the Sephardim serve as a beautiful, noble, and healthy countertype to the Ashkenazim. Yet for many observers, the outlandish claims of the British prime minister and Sephardic chauvinist Benjamin Disraeli, or the fanciful attempts to imagine the mannerisms and accents of ancient Jews via inference drawn from Sephardic physical and cultural characteristics, was an impressionistic undertaking that lacked the rigor that the nineteenth century demanded.[101] It was an era that laid stress on scientific verifiability and statistical certitude, and thus it was fortuitous that there arose yet another academic discipline, one that was capable of helping turn subjective judgments about Jewish bodies into believable, objective

2.9. Postcard from the Kölner Hof Hotel proudly declaring itself to be the "only Jew-free hotel in Frankfurt," which, because of the sizable Jewish presence in the city, is referred to as the "New Jerusalem on Franconia's Jordan River." The Jew is depicted as short, swarthy, with a hooked nose and thick lips. To the right of the hotel is a giant fist and boot indicating that the Jew, who is flying through the air, has been kicked out. He is a traveling salesman, his open suitcase revealing his wares now lying on the ground before him. Courtesy of The Magnes Collection of Jewish Art and Life, Berkeley, CA.

facts. That new field was physical anthropology, or race science as it was also called.

Because of its emphasis on aesthetics, physical anthropology contributed much to promoting the Sephardic dimension of Jewish romanticism. In general the methodology of race science encouraged an almost irresistible urge to compare the physical appearance—and, by extension, moral worth—of one group with another. Through close scrutiny and measurement, race scientists were able to identify and then quantify human difference, thus swaddling popular instinct and prejudice in the garment of hard science.[102] The dizzying array of Jewish types meant that within Jewry, observers could identify groups with widely different morphological traits and, true to the inherent assumptions of contemporary race science, draw conclusions from them about beauty, character, and morality.

2.10. "The Family Löwy." Postcard depicting a German-Jewish family,
the caption playing on the name Löwy, which approximates the
German word for "lion." Courtesy of The Magnes Collection of
Jewish Art and Life, Berkeley, CA.

Physical anthropology as a discipline played a central role in the discourse
on the Sephardic-Ashkenazic split. At the end of the nineteenth century the
myth of Sephardic superiority emerged in the larger context of what was then
called the Jewish "racial question." In anthropological terms this involved a
detailed discussion about the origin of the Jews, and identifying their physical
and psychological characteristics in order to ascertain whether these differed
fundamentally from those of non-Jews. The debate over the physical nature
of Jewishness also revolved around determining whether the Jews were composed of one or more racial types, and how those types had arisen.[103]
It is this that occasioned intense focus on the origins and nature of the
Sephardic-Ashkenazic divide; in the midst of this general debate, a fascinating subtext emerged that addressed the urge—inherent in all discussions
about race—to create a racial hierarchy. What came to the fore in the anthropological literature was once again the theme of Sephardic beauty and
idealization.[104] Moreover, we will see that the language of anthropologists,
whether in academic journals, in talks before learned societies, or in popular encyclopedias, differed little from the impressionistic observations that
to them would have seemed unscientific. However, in the hands of the cre-
dentialed such pronouncements sounded authoritative.[105]

The propagation of racial myths, that is, the making of claims that were not really open to empirical investigation, was central to race thinking and nationalism at the fin de siècle.[106] Ashkenazic Jews, whether committed to the Diaspora or adherents of Jewish nationalism, engaged in the process of countering racial myths about themselves by creating new racial myths, at the center of which stood the Sephardic Jew, who served not only as a foil for the Ashkenazic Jew, but also as the model for a future, rejuvenated Jewry.

In this discourse, the Sephardi serves as the Jewish equivalent of the "Aryan," a glorious figure, characterized by his nobility, breeding, poise, and creativity. Here was portrayed the physical counterpoint to the ignoble Jew of Central and Eastern Europe. In fact in the nationalistic and racially charged atmosphere of the late nineteenth century, where great emphasis was placed on the idea of racial authenticity, for many Jewish scientists the Sephardic Jew represented the *Urjude*, the original Jew.

Most non-Jewish scientists also extolled the beauty and virtues of the Sephardim even as they painted a disagreeable portrait of Ashkenazic Jews. Almost all such descriptions are similar to that of the German ethnographer and geographer Richard Andree, who in 1881 wrote of the two major Jewish types: "The one is the more dignified and nobler, with a fine nose, black, shining eyes, and graceful extremities; this type predominates among the Sephardim or Spanish Jews. The other is the less noble, mostly with a big mouth, a thick nose, deep furrows around the nose and mouth, and often has curly hair. . . . This type predominates among the Ashkenazim or German-Polish Jews."[107]

Beyond their positive appreciation of Sephardic beauty, a subtle religious sentiment impinged on the work of Gentile anthropologists. As we have noted, the division and classification of the Jews into two separate "Jewish types" served to draw a distinction between contemporary Jews and ancient Israelites. In this way, the modern Jew of Central and Eastern Europe, a figure long vilified, was juxtaposed with the more praiseworthy ancient Hebrew (read contemporary Sephardic Jew). By doing this, modern anthropological theory incorporated a form of traditional Christian antisemitism, which expressed its hostility primarily toward rabbinic, rather than biblical, Judaism. Just as Christianity had long preached the ugliness and corruption of Judaism, modern anthropology saw Ashkenazic unsightliness as a mirror of the ugliness of their religion and behavior. Though Sephardic Jews no less than Ashkenazic ones practiced rabbinic Judaism, their physical appearance rendered them more easily imaginable as Israelites, noble and heroic looking, as if they had just stepped out of the pages of the Bible.

The myths that Jewish scholars constructed about Sephardim and Ashkenazim were just as subjective as those of their non-Jewish counterparts but in a different way. Jewish appraisals exhibited the same anthropological descriptions of Sephardic beauty and Ashkenazic coarseness, frequently adding the aside and thus the implication that the Sephardim look as they do because they are most likely direct descendants of the tribe of Judah. However, thanks to the Jewish literacy of these observers, they enlarged upon their assessments of Jewish physicality with the addition of extensive cultural critiques. As such this was a uniquely inner-Jewish conversation, one that linked bodily form and behavior.

In his address (read in absentia) to the Royal Anthropological Institute in 1885, the distinguished Oxford scholar and bibliographer at the Bodleian library Adolf Neubauer (1831–1907) focused on the apparent differences between Ashkenazim and Sephardim. In the typical language of contemporary race science, Neubauer wrote that there were "1st, those with a well-developed nose, black and striking eyes, and fine extremities—in one word, the noble race of the Sephardim, or the Spanish-Portuguese Jews; 2nd, those who have a thickish nose, large mouth, and curled hair, features which are represented amongst the Ashkenazim, or the German-Polish Jews." Tellingly, Neubauer noted that the division of the two Jewish types "is only a revival of the old legend which existed for a long time amongst the Jews themselves in the middle ages, viz., that the noble Spanish race are descended from the tribe of Judah and the rougher German-Polish Jews from the tribe of Benjamin. This legend had such effect that intermarriage between the Spanish and German Jews was for a long time avoided."[108] De Pinto's epistolary boast to Voltaire was now publicly affirmed in Britain's Royal Anthropological Institute.

Part of the racial myth involved juxtaposing group behavior with physical descriptions of the people under the anthropologist's gaze. Neubauer's highly subjective evaluations of the behavioral and cultural level of, respectively, the Sephardim and Ashkenazim clearly betray a preference for Sephardic customs. Although Neubauer has made perfectly clear his belief that the myth of Sephardic superiority stems from the Sephardim themselves, it is a myth that Neubauer not only accepts but propagates even further. Although he was a Hungarian Jew, Neubauer vilified the Jewish culture and behavior of the Ashkenazim, in other words, his own culture:

> What is curious to notice is that the manners and habits of the so-called distinct tribes are also different, in accordance with the features, viz., the Spanish and Eastern Jews have a kind of refinement in speech and gesture, while the German-Polish Jews are rougher in both; and the Italian Jews lie again between the two. But this also must be attributed to the manners and speech of the nations amongst whom they lived, and with whom they are in daily contact. We shall go further; there is even a difference in the literature of the mediaeval Jews of the two so-called tribes. The Spanish Jews are much more logical and clear in their casuistic compositions, and dislike scholastic discussions, whilst the contrary is the case with the German-Polish Jews, whose

casuistry reaches the climax of logical mistakes, of scholastic torture, and absurd thinking. The Italians stand again between these two in this matter. Can this be attributed to a difference between the two tribes, or rather not to the character and tone of the nations amongst whom they lived?[109]

With echoes of Naphtali Herz Wessely and David Friedländer, both of whom attributed the supposedly lower cultural level of the Ashkenazim to the nature of the non-Jewish cultural space they inhabited, Neubauer's descriptions are representative of a kind of scientific writing about race in the late nineteenth century that, even if not wedded to a belief in biological determinism—and they are not in his case—nevertheless employed the language of scientific racism to make sweeping assessments of physical appearance, national character, intelligence, and aesthetics. Neubauer combines this with the discourse of the Haskalah and its critique of Polish rabbinic culture. Implicit in this criticism is that the casuistic mode of Torah study is incompatible with the norms of modern Jewish critical scholarship, which was already well established, and of which he was a distinguished practitioner. He also employed the language of a learned, classically trained, but now secular Jew from what was a small Hungarian town, and who sought to make sure that he would not be mistaken for a Polish Jew.[110]

After a long stay in England, the Australian scholar Joseph Jacobs (1854–1916) immigrated to the United States in 1900, in order to take up a position as revising editor of the great *Jewish Encyclopaedia*. Jacobs enjoyed an international reputation for his work on the physical anthropology of the Jews, some of it, as mentioned above, undertaken in tandem with Sir Francis Galton. Jacobs's research interests left their mark on the *Encyclopaedia*. Never before had such a reference work on the Jews paid so much attention to Jewish anthropology, both physical and cultural, nor had one focused so attentively on different Jewish types and the Jewish racial question.

The man chosen to contribute the entry under "Sephardim" in the encyclopedia's eleventh volume was Meyer Kayserling (1829–1905), the German-born, liberal rabbi of Budapest. He was also one of the nineteenth century's leading historians of Iberian Jewry.[111] Kayserling's article borrows heavily from the contemporary scientific (and at times antisemitic), discourse on the Jews. Noting that vis-à-vis the Ashkenazim, the Sephardim "considered themselves a superior class, the nobility of Jewry," Kayserling actually reaffirmed the claim, declaring that "this sense of dignity which the Sephardim possessed manifested itself in their general deportment and in their scrupulous attention to dress. Even those among them whose station in life was low, as, for example, the carriers in Salonica, or the sellers of 'pan de España' in the streets of Smyrna, maintained the old Spanish 'grandezza' in spite of their poverty."[112] As evidence of the ubiquity of such notions, it is highly revealing to know that in his tireless antisemitic screed, Houston

Stewart Chamberlain expressed a sentiment that was identical to Kayser-ling's: "Now whoever wishes to see with his own eyes what [a] noble race is, and what it is not, should send for the poorest of the Sephardim from Salonici or Sarajevo (great wealth is very rare among them, for they are men of stainless honour) and put him side by side with any Ashkenazim [sic] financier; then will he perceive the difference between the nobility which race bestows and that conferred by a monarch."[113] Chamberlain's reference here is to the Rothschilds, who, despite their wealth and their having been ennobled, remain forever marked as children of the Frankfurt ghetto. By contrast, even the poorest Sephardic Jew possesses true nobility; it is not bestowed from without but comes from within. It is organic, derived from nature, indeed from race.

So deeply ingrained were the characteristics of the Sephardim that they appeared to be impervious to changes of environment. The noble bearing Kayserling detected among them seems to have been an inheritable trait. He drew a straight line from Sevilla to Salonika, from the Islamic caliphate to the Ottoman Empire, depicting a Jewry that withstood the debilitating effects of poverty and discrimination. Few, if any, authors prior to World War I ever remarked on the nobility of penury-stricken Ashkenazic Jews in the Pale of Settlement.[114] However, Sephardic Jews, because of their glorious past, retained a mystique and remained exceptional in the eyes of Jewish scholars like Kayserling. And where class difference conditioned so much of the eighteenth-century Haskalah's response to those Jews that it deemed to be in need of improvement, nineteenth-century responses like Kayserling's display a willingness to actually highlight Sephardic poverty not in order to demean or excoriate but, rather, to demonstrate that privation could not extinguish Sephardic nobility and dignity.

Language, the subject with which we began this study, was, as we have seen, a fundamental component of the myth of Sephardic superiority. According to Kayserling, unlike Ashkenazic Jews the Sephardim had remained linguistically beyond reproach because "the rabbis, who, in common with all the Sephardim, laid great stress on a pure and euphonious pronunci-ation of Hebrew, delivered their sermons in Spanish or in Portuguese."[115] Voicing a typically banal maskilic view of Yiddish, Kayserling declared that "from Tangier to Salonica, from Smyrna to Belgrade, and from Vienna to Amsterdam and Hamburg, [the Sephardim] preserved not only the Spanish dignity, but the Spanish idiom also; and they preserved the latter with so much love and with so much tenacity that it has remained surprisingly pure up to the present day. It must be remembered that Judæo-Spanish, or Ladino, is in no wise as corrupt a language as is the Judæo-German."[116]

In collapsing categories such as race and language, Kayserling's argu-ment was in keeping with the then-contemporary misconceptions that associated the two with each other.[117] In turn, the unspoken assumption surrounding his praise of Ladino because of its supposedly greater purity was that that virtue extended to its speakers. In other words, like that of other Jewish and Gentile scholars of his day, Kayserling's praise of the vernacular language and Hebrew pronunciation of the Sephardim implied their greater racial purity. By extension, the suggestion that Yiddish was impure was also a judgment about the imperfection of the Ashkenazic body. Kayserling would have done well to be more attentive to his contemporary Max Müller, the great German philologist, orientalist, and Indologist, who in 1888 stated: "When I say Aryas (Aryans) I mean neither blood nor bones nor hair nor skull; I mean simply those who spoke an Aryan language. To me an ethnologist who speaks of Aryan race, Aryan blood, Aryan eyes and hair, is as great a sinner as a linguist who speaks of a dolichocephalic dictionary or a brachycephalic grammar."[118]

This association of race and language, along with the extrapolation drawn that speakers of certain languages are biologically connected to their linguistic ancestors, was a central component of the racial myth.[119] Because Indo-European languages (of which German was one) and Semitic languages (of which Hebrew was one) were two entirely different linguistic categories, with different origins, many race theorists believed that the speakers of those tongues must differ to the same extent. Just as there was no identifiable linguistic root that could link Indo-European with Semitic languages, so too did a biological or racial gulf separate Germans and Jews.

This theory was deployed over and over again by antisemites in German-speaking Europe. Jews were frequently told that they lacked the intuitive capacity to master the German language, because Jews are racially Semites, and not Aryans (the originators of Indo-European, and therefore the racial ancestors of the Germans), and that even those Jews who spoke it fluently were merely engaged in an act of mimicry.[120] It is in the context of this myth of language that we must interpret Kayserling's denigration of Yiddish and adulation of Ladino. Yiddish was mimicry of German, poorly executed, while Ladino was presented as pure and, most importantly, independent of Spanish. All this naturally extended to Hebrew, with Kayserling noting that

the Sephardim, who speak a purer Hebrew than do the Ashkenazim, do not attribute great value to the "*ḥazzanut*," [cantorial singing] and their form of cantillation is simpler than that of other Jews. The main point in which they differ from the Ashkenazim is, however, their liturgy. The Sephardic liturgy originated in part with the *Geonim* [the presidents of the two great Babylonian Talmudic academies at Sura and Pumbedita]; it is more natural and elevating than the Ashkenazic, and also less burdened with *piyyutim* [liturgical poems]. The Sephardim admit into their liturgy only the *piyyutim* of Spanish poets, which are characterized by Rapoport as "mediators between the soul and its Creator," while the Ashkenazic *piyyutim* are "mediators between the nation and its God."[121]

Again, locating the "soul" as an organic site where culture resides and from which it emanates was a staple of late nineteenth-century racial thought. The distinction that Kayserling here endorses is crucial because it identifies the Sephardim as those Jews for whom the soul is the operative link to God. The Ashkenazim may communicate with God as representatives of the nation, but the Sephardim possess a more profound, more mysterious means of communion, one that makes them the bearers of the authentic Jewish racial soul.

In two other realms Kayserling established the superiority of the Sephardim over the Ashkenazim: in economic life and religious practice. In contrast to the Ashkenazim "the Sephardim never engaged in chaffering occupations nor in usury, and they did not mingle with the lower classes. With their social equals they associated freely, without regard to creed, and in the presence of their superiors they displayed neither shyness nor servility." Here Kayserling continues the link between class and character that we have seen was established by David Friedländer and his fellow maskilim:

> They were received at the courts of sultans, kings, and princes, and often were employed as ambassadors, envoys, or agents. . . . The Sephardim occupy the foremost place in the roll of Jewish physicians; great as is the number of those who have distinguished themselves as statesmen, it is not nearly as great as the number of those who have become celebrated as physicians and have won the favor of rulers and princes, in both the Christian and the Mohammedan world.

Promoter of past Sephardic glories, Kayserling uses the present tense to describe the achievements of Sephardic doctors: "The Sephardim occupy the foremost place in the roll of Jewish physicians." Kayserling was living in a time when, in Germany and Austria, there were more Jews engaged in medical practice than in any other profession, their success was extraordinary, and it had been in large part responsible for a complete transformation of the mentality, culture, and economic well-being of German Jews. This professional efflorescence was also being replicated among Hungarian and Eastern European Jews.[122] Yet in Kayserling's presentation, it was if this had never happened. His pronouncement is a measure of the extent to which the celebration of Sephardic Jewry was totally removed from contemporary or even historical social reality. Not only was the picture of Ashkenazic culture and physicality distorted, but so too was that of the Sephardim.

It is interesting and instructive to note that the *Jewish Encyclopaedia*, an undoubtedly brilliant work, carries no corresponding article on the

"Ashkenazim." This lacuna would further reinforce the proposition that the Sephardim were thought, by nineteenth-century Jewish scholars, to be of greater ethnological worth.[123] That this was so should not be surprising. Since all the Jewish physical anthropologists writing on the Jews were European Ashkenazim, the Sephardim represented, for them, the Jewish Other. Jewish physical anthropology at the fin de siècle was a microcosm of race science in general, in that it too had its superior and inferior types. Moreover, in the main, anthropology was not yet self-reflexive. It was still driven by the need to go out and discover (even if only in a figurative sense) people who are "not like us."

However, this did not translate into an Ashkenazic presentation of the Sephardic Jew as a kind of noble savage. It did not entail the same process of distancing and sense of fascination that modern anthropologists once adopted toward preindustrial peoples. This was not an act of orientalizing the Sephardic Jew in order to have authority over him. In fact it was quite the other way round. The Ashkenazic discourse placed the Sephardic Jew in the position of authority, while the Ashkenazic Jew played the role of subjugated subaltern.

Like archaeology, anthropology in the late nineteenth century was given impetus by rising nationalism. The anthropological study of the Sephardim was greatly impelled by one of the major concerns for any late nineteenth-century nationalist group, including Zionism, namely, the problem of establishing origins and antiquity.[124] Like the maskilim before them, Zionist authors also tended to see in the Sephardim an ideal type of Jew, one who was worldly, yet whose Jewish identity or "racial instinct," to use the language of the day, remained intact. For example, in 1907, the aforementioned German-Jewish physician and early settler in Palestine Elias Auerbach spoke vaguely about there being a particular Jewish survival instinct, one that was especially well developed among the Sephardim.[125]

Influenced heavily by contemporary *völkisch* ideology, he referred to the group-survival instinct of Spanish Jews in his long discussion of large-scale intermarriage in Germany.[126] Auerbach juxtaposed medieval Jewish society on the Iberian Peninsula with that of his contemporary Germany and claimed that the high rate of intermarriage among German Jews demonstrated that they had abandoned their racial instinct, a sign that they had lost the will to survive.[127] According to Auerbach, Spanish Jews provided an example of an acculturated Jewish community, which still preserved intact its separatist identity, both cultural and racial, while German Jews had become assimilationists, destined to disappear and blend insensibly into the German nation.[128] That there was a world of difference between medieval Spain and modern Germany, especially with reference to the permissibility of intermarriage, was a major distinction that Auerbach failed to recognize. Sephardic separatism was simply presented in terms of that old saw—the superior morality of Sephardic Jews. Where a Zionist like Auerbach differed from the maskilim is that the low intermarriage rate among Polish Jews was, for him, a sign of their spiritual superiority over German Jewry, and they were, on this score, the Ashkenazic group that most closely resembled the Sephardic moral economy.[129]

It was not only in Europe that the political and cultural exigencies of Jewish life led scientists and scholars to idealize the Sephardic Jew. The belief in the superior beauty of the Sephardim was a global idea. In the United States, Maurice Fishberg (1872–1934) was an internationally renowned physician, physical anthropologist, and clinical professor of medicine at New York University and Bellevue Hospital Medical College. An active and dedicated member of the Jewish community, Fishberg was medical examiner to the United Hebrew Charities of New York City. He was also an anthropological consultant to the Bureau of Immigration, and it was in this latter capacity that he undertook two trips to Europe in 1905 and 1907, on behalf of a U.S. congressional committee, to study the immigration problem.

Deeply involved in Jewish communal life, Fishberg was also dedicated to the thorough Americanization of immigrant Jews. An examination of his anthropological work relating to Jewish racial types reveals that for Fishberg, just as it had been for German-Jewish maskilim and social commentators, it was the Sephardic Jew who offered the ideal model for Jewish acculturation, this time in an American key. Since the 1890s, Fishberg's important anthropological works had, for the most part, appeared only in scientific journals. By contrast, his study *The Jews: A Study of Race and Environment* (1911), which was based on a massive amount of data about Jews across the entire world, made his work widely accessible and, simultaneously, the authoritative source on the anthropology and pathology of the Jewish people. It was especially influential in Germany, where the work appeared in German translation in 1913.[130]

Fishberg's anthropological descriptions offer us perhaps the starkest example of how deeply the myth of Sephardic aesthetic superiority had penetrated into both serious scientific discourse and Jewish popular opinion and culture:

> The Jews of Germany, Russia, Poland, etc., known as the Ashkenazim, are generally of a type which differs much from [the Sephardim]. Their features are not as elegant, not as graceful as those of the Sephardim. Indeed, . . . most of the beautiful Jewesses, irrespective of the country in which they are encountered, are of the Sephardi type. A blond Jewess, no matter how charming she may be, is not in conformity with what one would expect a Jewess to look like. . . . Her face is round, with prominent cheek bones, and the nose medium-sized, broad, with fleshy wings, often narrow and depressed at the root, appearing generally somewhat pear-shaped. . . . The chin is heavy, the mouth

Fig. 52. Fig. 53.

Fig. 54. Fig. 55.
POLISH JEWESS, MONGOLOID TYPE.
Figs. 52-55.—ASHKENAZI TYPES OF JEWESSES.

2.11. "Ashkenazi Types of Jewesses." Maurice Fishberg, *The Jews*, 113.

large, and the lips thick, all of which give a rather heavy expression to the countenance.[131]

Jewish beauty is Sephardic beauty. It cannot be any other way, for Sephardim hold the lien on Jewish aesthetic perfection. By contrast, Fishberg's Ashkenazic woman, with her large mouth, thick lips, and generally fleshy appearance, conformed to the standard antisemitic rendering of Jews. Such were the images to be found everywhere and on everything, whether drawn, sculpted, carved, or represented by actors in the theater.[132] To grant the "blond Jewess" her due as a beautiful woman was to contradict nature.

We get a sense of the extent to which the images of Sephardic and Ashkenazic Jews were so deeply engrained as part of Jewish self-perception

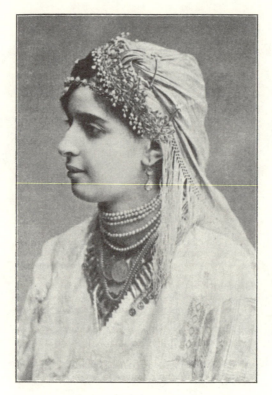

Fig. 1.—JEWESS OF ALGIERS.

2.12. "Jewess of Algiers." Maurice Fishberg, *The Jews*, 5.

that the politics and cultural agenda of the individual observer did not seem to alter the universal Ashkenazic preference for the Sephardic aesthetic. Whereas men such as Fishberg and Kayserling were committed to Jewish acculturation, the aforementioned anthropologist Ignacy Maurycy Judt was a Zionist. When the latter studied the Jewish racial question in 1903, he did so with an exhaustive examination of all the scientific literature that had been produced on the subject. His conclusions were generally based on the mountains of anthropometric data that scientists had been accumulating over the previous three decades. Likewise, his interpretations of Sephardic origins were based on the weight of accumulated statistics. In the end, however, when he drew a composite portrait of the Sephardic Jew, the numbers and scientific method no longer counted for much. Instead, the subjective power of the stereotype informed Judt's conclusions. The Sephardic Jew is the "genuine Semite with a long skull, raven-black hair and eyes, dark skin and a graceful nose. He is a type that stands closest in form to the Arab Bedouins. It is the same form that we find in Rembrandt's paintings of the Jews of Amsterdam." The Ashkenazim, by contrast, possessed a "low brow, often blond hair, blue eyes, a thick nose, large mouth, a slightly protruding lower jaw and prominent cheekbones."[133] It is stunning to recall that this description of the Ashkenazim, with their simian-like features, is the work of a Warsaw Zionist and does not differ all that much from the descriptions of an American liberal like Fishberg or any number of non-Jewish anthropologists, or, in fact, antisemites.

In returning to Fishberg, we note that he was not content to draw a distinction between Ashkenazim and Sephardim purely on the basis of outward appearance, for what began with looks was merely an external symbol of a deep inner difference, one that could be observed in comportment and behavior:

> They are medium-sized, slender, narrow-shouldered, but graceful people, with a somewhat melancholy expression. Only very rarely is to be seen a Spanish Jew displaying a servile or cringing attitude in the presence of superiors, as is often to be seen among German and Polish Jews. The Sephardim are very proud, and their sense of dignity manifests itself even in their dress and deportment, to which they pay scrupulous attention. These traits, which they acquired while living for centuries among the Castilians, have been transmitted to their descendants of today. [In addition], they look down on their German co-religionists and consider them an inferior race.[134]

According to fin de siècle race science, characteristics such as conduct and deportment were inheritable and fell largely under the rubric of "national character," and thus it should not surprise us to learn that for Fishberg, Sephardim have "transmitted [these traits] to their descendants of today." Here were Jews who were physically beautiful and graceful; their manner was especially commendable in that they mixed with and learned from their Christian neighbors, while never relinquishing a dignified pride that bespoke a knowing self-confidence and a mature aesthetic sensibility.

The distinctiveness of the two groups' manners was crucial to a man such as Fishberg, dedicated as he was to the project of Americanizing the multitude of Eastern European Jewish immigrants to the United States. The Sephardim acquired their traits as a result of "living for centuries among the Castilians." It was to be hoped that living among Americans would have the same salutary effect on the newly arrived Jewish immigrants. Fishberg was tapping into what he identified as a recurring and welcome phenomenon in Jewish history. His was nothing more than a recapitulation of David Friedländer's century-old assimilatory dream for those Eastern European Jews who now found themselves in "civilized" Prussia thanks to the partitions of Poland in the eighteenth century. What had begun with the His-

Fig. 64.   Fig. 65.

Figs. 64, 65.—POLISH JEW, MONGOLOID TYPE.

[*Photo lent by Elkind.*]

Fig. 66.   Fig. 67.

Figs. 66, 67.—GALICIAN JEWS, NEGROID TYPES.

2.13. Polish Jews, "Mongoloid" and "Negroid" Types. Maurice Fishberg, *The Jews*, 117.

panization of the Sephardim, followed by the Prussianization of the Polish Jews, would now see Americanization domesticate and civilize the masses of Russian Jews pouring into New York harbor.

The metamorphosis of Jewish physicality was a cherished goal. Pleas for it could be heard across the Jewish political spectrum. The famous Zionist call to transform the enervated, cowardly, Diaspora Jew into a strong, courageous, and proud figure was not *sui generis*. The effectiveness of early Zionist propaganda and subsequent historiography has tended to mask the fact that the Jewish critique of the Jewish body was ecumenical, coming insistently from all quarters. In 1897, the same year as the founding of the Zionist movement in Basel and the Jewish Labor Bund in Vilna—both ideologies seeking to transform Jews and Jewish society—an assimilationist call rang out urging Jews to take stock of their bodies and transform them.

Fig. 100.—TUNISIAN JEW.

2.14. "Tunisian Jew." Maurice Fishberg, *The Jews*, 138.

In the journal *Zukunft* (Future), the Jewish industrialist, intellectual, and future foreign minister of Germany Walter Rathenau (1867–1922) wrote advocating such change.[135] Despite his being deeply acculturated, Rathenau's urgent demand, entitled "Höre, Israel!" (Hear, O Israel!), was presented as a religious proclamation, a new *Shema* for modern Jews: "Look at yourselves in the mirror! This is the first step toward self-criticism. . . . As soon as you have recognized your unathletic build, your narrow shoulders, your clumsy feet, your sloppy roundish shape, you will resolve to dedicate a few generations to the renewal of your outer appearance."[136] The harsh and disturbing nature of Rathenau's description notwithstanding, his critique was suffused with the sentiment that improvement was necessary, difficult, but ultimately possible.

In his important 1930 study of Jewish self-hatred, the philosopher and Zionist Theodor Lessing (1872–1933), who had himself suffered from feelings of inferiority, converted to Protestantism, and then returned to Judaism, wrote rhetorically to remind Ashkenazic Jews: "Who *are* you? The son of the slovenly Jewish peddlar, Nathan, would you think, and of lazy Sarah whom he had accidentally slept with because she had brought enough money into their marriage? No! Judah Maccabee was your father, Queen Esther was your mother. From you, and you alone, the chain goes back—via defective links to be sure—to Saul and David and Moses. They are present in every one of you. They have been there all the time and tomorrow their spirit could be revived."[137] The Jews were, he believed, an Asiatic people, stranded in exile in a Europe that was not their real home. Whether the transformation of the Jewish body was to take place in Berlin or Be'er Sheva was immaterial. Whether committed to remaining in the Diaspora or just as determined to leave it, social critics such as Rathenau and Lessing, however much their politics might have differed, agreed on the most fundamental point—the Jewish body was sick, and it was time to restore it to good health and exhibit pride in its appearance.

One of the cornerstones of race science and romantic Sephardism was its elevation of subjective notions of beauty and ugliness to legitimate scientific categories of classification. Let us return to Fishberg and his description of Sephardic beauty, but now as he introduces gender into the equation. He noted that the Sephardim

> have generally black or brown hair, occasionally red and rarely blonde; large black or brown eyes, seldom grey, and rarely blue. In addition to their dark complexion, they are short of stature and either dolichocephalic or mesocephalic. The face is oval, the forehead receding, the eyes almond-shaped with the outer extremity very pointed, while the dark eyebrows are very bushy at the inner end, where they tend to unite over the root of the nose. The traditional Semitic beauty, which in women often assumes exquisite nobility, is generally found among these Jews, and when encountered among Jews in Eastern or Central Europe is always of this type. Indeed, it is hard to imagine a beautiful Jewess, who looks like a Jewess, presenting any other physical type. It appears that in addition to the delicacy and the striking symmetry of the features which are often met with, it is also the brilliant, radiant eyes which give these Sephardim their reputation for bewitching elegance and charm. The Spanish and Andalusian women are said by some to owe their charms to these beautiful eyes, which are alleged to have their origin in the small quantities of Semitic blood which flows in their veins.[138]

Fishberg's semierotic descriptions of Sephardic women reveal an attraction and fascination that seem to stem from the cultural and physiological distance that he as a Russian-born Jew felt from these people. Most telling, in the picture of Jewish beauty he has drawn, is that he denies the Ashkenazic Jew any inherent attractiveness, claiming that if an Ashkenazic female were

Fig. 104.—Jewess in Constantine.

2.15. "Jewess in Constantine." Maurice Fishberg, *The Jews*, 142.

to ever display beautiful features, she would inevitably turn out to be of Sephardic origin. In fact, the existence of Semitic characteristics, according to Fishberg, even lies at the root of Spanish female beauty. Fishberg here suggests that Sephardic Jews bore within them Semitic "blood," thus affirming the archaeological record and notions of the untainted lineage connecting the Sephardic Jews to the ancient Hebrews. He then goes further to suggest that sexual relations between Jews and Spaniards bequeathed a legacy of Israelite beauty to the Christians of modern-day Spain.

Fishberg's *The Jews: A Study of Race and Environment* was the most important and influential text of its kind. An important source of its influence was its contribution to the visualization of Sephardic aesthetic superiority. Fishberg's study was not only replete with many comparative charts and tables, it was also lavishly illustrated with 142 portraits of Jewish types. Beyond Sephardim and Ashkenazim, rare images of Bokharan, Indian, Chinese, Yemenite, Ethiopian, and Caucasian Mountain Jews provided readers with vivid evidence of Jewish anthropological diversity. It would be easy to dismiss many of the photographs as examples of the orientalized objectification of Near Eastern and Sephardic Jews. The women, whether from Algiers, Tunis, Tangiers, or Jerusalem, tend to be young and vivacious, and are always in national dress. With their proud looks, the men from these places are likewise pictured in traditional clothing. However, these are highly stylized studio portraits, so we cannot know with any certainty whether the people in the photographs owned these clothes, or whether they took them from the abundant costume racks that studio photographers the world over had at their disposal.[139] It is reasonable to assume that many of these people, perhaps especially the women, attended the schools of the Alliance Israélite Universelle and would normally have worn Western clothing. Their appearance in traditional costumes may well have been an act of self-expression, an attempt to reclaim an aspect of their own lost or disappearing worlds.[140] Fishberg's captions do not give us any clues on that score.

While the photographs that appear in the book are his choice, they reflect not only his personal prejudices but, I would suggest, those of Ashkenazic social and scientific commentators more generally. With few exceptions, the Sephardic Jews are exotic, beautiful, and indeed sensual, and Fishberg has juxtaposed these with images of what are often coarse and physically unappealing Ashkenazim. Most of the Eastern European Jews he depicts are noticeably older than the Sephardim, if not very advanced in years. The men are frequently Hasidic and thus bearded and quite wizened. In keeping with his negative descriptions of Ashkenazic aesthetics, Fishberg also reproduces a drawing of a religious Jew by the German painter Ismael Gentz. The subject, draped in a frock coat reaching to the ground, has his back to the viewer. Fishberg has provided the illustration with caption "The Ghetto Bend," making it sound as if the man has a diagnosable, clinical condition, one with a technical name. It is Fishberg, the Ashkenazic physician, and not Gentz, the Christian artist, who has diagnosed the Jew. He is the antithesis of everything acculturated Western, as well as noble Sephardic, Jews represent:

> Next to dress and deportment the Jew in Eastern Europe has often a peculiar attitude of the body which is distinctly characteristic. The inferior hygienic, economic, and social conditions under which he was compelled to live in the Ghettoes have left their mark on his body; he is old prematurely, stunted, decrepit; he withers at an early age. He is emaciated, his muscles are flabby, and he is unable to hold his spinal column erect. That this peculiar attitude of the body has a great influence on the type of the Jew can be seen from the

drawing by Ismael Gentz, . . . which shows graphically that it is not always the face that betrays the religious belief in the case of the Eastern European. The decrepit condition of the body is one of the most important stigmata of the Jew's long confinement in the Ghetto.[141]

However, Fishberg hastens to inform the reader that this is not a permanent condition. It is merely an acquired characteristic, the result of the adverse social and economic conditions under which the Jews have historically lived. With the unshakable faith of an environmental determinist, Fishberg reminds us that "in Europe it can be seen that the Jew's spine becomes more erect, his muscles more developed, and his gait more elastic, as one proceeds from east to west, and when France, Belgium, and especially England, is reached." Even in the United States, "on the East Side of New

Fig. 2.—JEW IN TUNIS.

2.16. "Jew in Tunis." Maurice Fishberg, *The Jews*, 9.

Fig. 48.   Fig. 49.

Fig. 50.   Fig. 51.

Figs. 48-51.—Ashkenazi Types of Jews, Eastern Europe.

2.17. "Ashkenazi Types of Jews, Eastern Europe." Maurice Fishberg, *The Jews*, 112.

2.18. Ismael Gentz, "The Ghetto Bend."
Maurice Fishberg, *The Jews*, 164.

Fig. 112.—THE GHETTO BEND.
[*Drawing by Ismael Gentz.*]

York City it can be seen that a fair proportion of the older immigrant Jews are stunted and more or less hunched. But their children, who have had the benefit of Western education, walk erect and cannot be distinguished by the attitude of their bodies."[142]

From the middle of the nineteenth century the increasingly wide distribution of the kinds of photographs of Sephardim to be found in works such as Fishberg's, as well as the frequent depiction of Oriental Jews in the formalist works of European painters—among them Eugène Delacroix, Théodore Chassériau, Princess Mathilde Bonaparte, daughter of Jérôme and cousin of Napoléon III—further cemented an image of non-Western Jews that conferred upon these subjects, at the very least, custodianship of Jewish physical beauty. To be sure, the non-Jewish French painters often portrayed their Jewish subjects in highly sensual, alluring ways, their faces and deportment revealing the mysteries, erotic and otherwise, of the Orient.[143] However, for Jewish artists such as Simeon Solomon, Maurycy Gottlieb, and Édouard Moyse, the Jews, especially those portrayed in biblical scenes, conformed to images that fed into and reaffirmed popular Jewish conceptions of heroic, dignified, biblical (read non-Ashkenazic) figures.

No artist better depicted Fishberg's "old prematurely, stunted, [and] decrepit" ghetto Jew, juxtaposing him with the new, vibrant, beautiful, and healthy Hebrew, than the *Jugendstil* artist Ephraim Moses Lilien (1874–1925). Born in the Galician city of Drohobycz, Lilien was an illustrator, photographer, and Zionist, and produced many of the movement's most classic and widely disseminated images, in what has been referred to by historian Michael Stanislawski as an "extraordinary mélange of decadence and Jewishness."[144] In addition to his illustrated Bible, with its heroic and attractive Israelites, Lilien is best known for Zionist graphic art. In this genre he most frequently employed his trademark pen-and-ink drawings, creating orientalist sensuality through the use of delicate androgynous figures, strikingly beautiful women, as well as chiseled males meant to represent new Jewish heroes whose settlement in the Land of Israel brought with it a restoration of their ancient Judean beauty. These figures are also intended to point the way to a Jewish future.[145] In a significant number of drawings one sees an elderly, religious Jew often sitting forlorn, and sometimes enveloped in thorns, a symbol of his diasporic imprisonment. Juxtaposed with this Eastern European Jew there is the new Jew, muscular, angular, walking behind a plow, both physically and presumably mentally rejuvenated by performing agricultural labor in the land of his ancestors. It matters not that Lilien did not intend his "new Jew" to be an explicit model of robust Sephardic manhood. What he did intend was that such figures not be the traditional Ashkenazic Jew of the ghetto, most frequently depicted as bent, enervated, and aged.

Fig. 74.—POLISH JEW IN JERUSALEM.

2.19. "Polish Jew in Jerusalem" (photographed by Ephraim Moses Lilien). Maurice Fishberg, *The Jews*, 123.

Lilien often depicted Herzl, and he also took the iconic photograph of him on the balcony of the Drei Könige Hotel in Zurich at the Fifth Zionist Congress of 1901.[146] In the scores of imitations of this iconic photograph, which Lilien actually staged, Zionism's most charismatic leader is statuesque, his deep black eyes and thick, long black beard making him resemble less a Central European Jew than an Assyrian ruler who has stepped off an ancient bas-relief. Photography was an important medium for Lilien, and Herzl was by no means his only subject. Upon returning to Germany after a trip to Palestine in 1906, Lilien penned an article, accompanied by twelve photographs, entitled "A Journey to Jerusalem." Describing the locals, Lilien noted that they were "a delight to the eyes of all artists . . . their brows are high and wide. Their gaze proud and free. Their noses are not long and hooked, as one might expect among Jews, but wide and straight. As a general rule, the Asiatic Jew is marked, like his Levantine counterpart, by great physical beauty, a proud and feather-light gait and nimble, graceful movements."[147] While Lilien was a Zionist artist, and the physician Fishberg a staunch opponent of Jewish nationalism, both parties concurred that the ideal type to represent the Jewish people in the future must be someone who bore no resemblance to the diasporic Ashkenazi of popular imagination and visual culture.[148] Whether depicting Sephardim or, as contemporary culture posited, their ancient ancestors from the Near East, all commentators agreed that they exemplified Jewish beauty.

The late nineteenth century's multifaceted denigration of the Ashkenazic body and simultaneous celebration of Sephardic corporeality grew out of the traditional, late eighteenth-century maskilic critique, the kind with which we began this chapter. The Jew of Central or Eastern Europe was presented as a debased or degraded figure who only stood to benefit from emulating his Sephardic coreligionists by blending in with the non-Jewish world around them. This is what situates many of the Jewish race scientists like Auerbach, Ruppin, and Fishberg or artists like Lilien in a long tradition of Ashkenazic self-criticism. To be sure, the methodology of the anthropologists, peppered with detailed anthropometric descriptions, differs greatly from that of social and political critics, while the photography and artistic representations of Jews were unique products of their times. However, the Jewish social commentary they all produced was informed by a narrative and a set of prejudices whose origins can be traced back to Berlin and Königsberg of the late eighteenth century.

It is clear that in the scientific discourse about Jewish racial types at the fin de siècle, a discourse bolstered by widely disseminated artistic representations of Jews, the construction of an elaborate racial myth—that of the superiority of the Sephardic Jew over the Ashkenazic—afforded Jews, whether political activist, anthropologist, or artist, the possibility of refracting through the prism of their own historical experience a variation on contemporary European myths of racial and national origin. The historian Leon Poliakov has noted that "every society claims a genealogy, a point of origin. There is no culture, however old, which has not in this manner provided itself with a spontaneous anthropology."[149] This is precisely what was being done by those Ashkenazic Jews critiquing their own cultural and physical characteristics. In elevating the Sephardic over the Ashkenazic Jew, they found within Jewry a superior and, reciprocally, an inferior type. For all these men, irrespective of their politics or the communal positions they held, the promise of Jewish regeneration was predicated upon

2.20. Postcard in Russian, German, and Hebrew of Herzl looking out over the Rhine from his hotel-room balcony (photographed by Ephraim Moses Lilien).

2.21. The idealized "Jewish face" is that of the Sephardic, or Oriental, Jewish woman (drawing by Ephraim Moses Lilien). Fishberg, *The Jews*, 95.

the revitalization of the frail, Ashkenazic ghetto Jew in the image of the
physically robust, morally healthy, and beautiful Sephardi.

Whereas the two opening chapters of this study have focused on the sensory and corporeal dimension to representations and self-representations
of Sephardim and Ashkenazim, the story we are telling here also resides
in the inanimate realm. It was principally in the field of architecture, specifically with the building of orientalist and neo-Moorish-style synagogues
throughout Germany in the nineteenth century, that we see the most visible manifestation of an imagined Sephardic aesthetic. It is fair to say that
most non-Jews were unconcerned with differences between Sephardim and
Ashkenazim. In fact, most were completely unaware of them. Thus the de-

bates over Hebrew accents, deportment, and appearance were very much part of a dialogue conducted largely among Jews. Not so with architecture, which was, by its very nature, a public affair. Here, non-Jews joined with Jews in becoming deeply involved in the discourse of Jewish aesthetics. They also became major contributors to its practice, as the synagogues to which we will now turn became actual sites reflecting German ideas for a Jewish aesthetic. They also display German-Jewish notions of Sephardic beauty and the German-Jewish relationship to a past that was not theirs, and how the blending of the two could be marshaled to point the way to a new era, one in which the traditional German-Jewish aesthetic of the past could be cast aside in the quest for a more noble, more dignified, and more beautiful future.

CHAPTER THREE

◄❍►

Of Minarets and Menorahs

THE BUILDING OF ORIENTAL SYNAGOGUES

One measure of important art and architecture is the extent to which it can provoke discomfort, anxiety, and fear as well as wonderment, joy, and pride. If, as Ludwig Mies van der Rohe, one of the giants of modern architecture, once sagely quipped, "Architecture is the spatially apprehended will of the epoch," then the will of the client is an expression of that era's taste, economic well-being, and sense of self and community.[1] Architecture projects a host of values that reflect the self-perception of an entire epoch. The designs that are accepted, as well as those that are rejected—and those that are rejected yet nonetheless desired—all reflect a complex matrix of social, economic, and aesthetic concerns that manifest themselves at every phase of the building project. Ideally, the building itself represents an amicable resolution of those often conflicting pressures. But even when this turns out not to be the case, a building is far more than a mere structure. It is a repository of stories and is in itself a narrative.

The narrative that is synagogue architecture in nineteenth-century Germany is a story about the changing character of the Jewish community. It tells us about the slow but steady pace of Jewish urbanization, population growth, economic status, relations with non-Jews, and, most important in this context, how it was deemed best to project Jewishness in the public sphere. There were many styles of architecture used in synagogue design in nineteenth-century Germany, but among the most arresting and perhaps surprising were those that manifested various Oriental designs. Surprising, if not counterintuitive, because in this era German Jewry worked ceaselessly to shed a common image of Jews as a foreign, Oriental people. The synagogues ranged from those that were inspired by ancient Egyptian architecture, elegant yet monumental at one and the same time, to Romanesque synagogues with their soaring domes and rounded arches, to the most ornate of them all: the neo-Moorish synagogues, with their towering minarets, giant domes, polychrome exteriors, windows with Islamic-style arches, and stunningly ornate interiors.

All of these buildings, some of them truly spectacular houses of worship, represent precisely the intricate web of social, ideological, and aesthetic factors that characterize all complex and serious architecture. They also presented both a challenge and an opportunity for German Jews. On the one hand new synagogue building challenged Jews to find the best way to take the ideology and practices of self-fashioning and extend them from the private into the public realm. As an opportunity, new synagogue building prompted German Jews to seriously consider their relationship to the Jewish past. Which aspects of that history or its communities did they most admire? Were there particular periods, Jewish communities, and Jewish cultures with which they did not wish to identify? Examining synagogue architecture actually allows us to plot, in the most materially tangible way, the answers to some of these questions.

Traditional historiographical descriptions and interpretations of these synagogues have almost entirely focused on the synagogues themselves, without sufficient consideration to placing them within the larger context of European, especially German, architectural history, as well as Jewish urbanization and acculturation. All of these developments spurred the massive infrastructure project undertaken by German Jewry, and, of course, the advent of orientalist architecture. Failing to locate the history of these synagogues within those contexts has gone some way to creating a false, or at least incomplete, impression of the meaning of these synagogues, in particular what Jews themselves thought about such buildings, and how they understood them and their own relationship to them. It is the linkage of aesthetics, religious experience, and historical context that endows these structures with meaning beyond their use as sites of worship.[2]

To more fully exploit the interpretive potential of these synagogues, we must recognize that they did not stand alone, outside of the historical moment. Rather, they must be seen as part and parcel of the changing nature of modern German cityscapes, considered as contributions to German architecture, and as perhaps the most visible, yet anomalous, example of modern German Jewry's great nineteenth-century building project. When we look at orientalist or Sephardicized synagogues in light of contemporary German debates over the meaning of national architecture, and the concomitant Jewish version of that debate, a new picture emerges. Furthermore, by considering such synagogues in light of other Jewish construction projects in the nineteenth century, we may detect a historical and social dynamic at play that differs from what has hitherto been identified. Doing so allows us to more fully appreciate the special character of these synagogues, and, crucially, we will have identified another very important expression of the general Sephardicist dimension of German-Jewish culture.

Examining the history of this architectural moment provides the historian of orientalism with an important opportunity to escape simplistic binaries: Western versus Eastern, classical versus nonclassical, Orient versus Occident. Because of the sheer variety of orientalist building styles we are able to see how both Jews and non-Jews saw themselves. How did both parties understand Jewish origins, and how should they be interpreted, understood, and then memorialized through architecture? What will become apparent is that the recourse to Oriental motifs in Germany was not even always a Jewish expression of self. Sometimes these buildings were less the product of communal desire than they were the result of Christian imposition. Because of the many varieties of orientalist architecture, the decision to build in the Oriental style also occasioned discussions about which Orientals were called upon for inspiration. Strategic and more prosaic concerns and demands also had a role in making Germany the first site of such buildings. Local factors such as communal history, social structure, regionalism, the surrounding built environment, and—as ever with architecture—the extent of funding available all played a part in the type of building to be erected. Orientalist architecture did not mean just one thing and was as diverse as the communities who commissioned or had such projects foisted upon them. In other words, consideration of the architectural history of nineteenth-century German Jewry sheds further light upon the entangled relationship between orientalism and the Jews.

• • • • •

Nineteenth-century Europe experienced explosive population growth. In 1800 there were 187 million Europeans; by 1900 there were approximately 400 million.[3] The radical social changes attendant on such growth and the ever more complex nature of society generated a building boom. As travel became increasingly common, as industrialization kept expanding, as consumerism took hold, as criminality increased with urbanization, as local government grew in size, and as states offered improved social services such as education, health care, and housing, Europeans built at a frenzied pace. Thousands of railway stations, town halls, markets, arcades, department stores, offices, factories, hospitals, schools, prisons, cemeteries, exhibition and municipal buildings, and literally hundreds of thousands of houses, apartment blocks, and churches of all denominations sprang up across Western Europe.[4] In France alone 40,000 schools and 70,000 residential buildings were built in the nineteenth century, while in one single year, 1852, some 200 Gothic-style churches were under construction.[5]

The sheer scale of these building projects and the speed with which they were undertaken meant that European architecture of the nineteenth century was characterized by many success stories as well as many failures. Above all it was architecture of enormous diversity and novelty, aided and abetted by the advent of new building materials and construction techniques.[6] Cast iron, steel, and reinforced concrete all made their appearance for the first time in the history of architecture; such ancient building materials as glass were used in an entirely new way. The establishment of new institutions in the nineteenth century helped both professionalize architecture and spread and systematize knowledge about various styles and construction techniques. Innovation was the order of the day, as the founding of new technical colleges and art schools, the publication of myriad building journals and handbooks, as well as art periodicals, and the establishment of professional societies all served to make architectural knowledge and theory widely accessible and to facilitate the cross-fertilization of ideas.[7] The nineteenth century also brought with it the end of single patrons commissioning a single style. Now there were many patrons, among them municipal authorities, individual captains of industry and commerce, philanthropists, and religious bodies, all championing their own architectural visions according to their own diverse preferences.

There was much that was new and noteworthy and much that was new and crushingly utilitarian in this age. There were endless row houses, huge, impersonal blocks of flats, cavernous warehouses, and factories that dwarfed and confined those who toiled inside them. These were buildings for and of the age of industrialization. They provided no respite, no escape, and left nothing to the imagination. However, there were other buildings that were novel yet fanciful, buildings that elicited a smile and allowed the mind to wander to faraway times and places. European interpretations of Chinese pagodas, Indian palaces, and Islamic minarets jostled with modern adaptations of classical, Romanesque, and Gothic forms. But there was still more. Plans were drawn and models were built for Tudor, French Renaissance, Venetian Renaissance, rococo-classical, rococo-Gothic, and even "Indian Gothic" buildings. Describing the work of the English architect John Nash, the architectural historian Nikolaus Pevsner wrote that by the early nineteenth century "the fancy-dress ball of architecture is in full swing"; this felicitous phrase can well be used to sum up the whole era.[8]

In architectural terms the nineteenth century was the high point of historicism, the term denoting the use of building styles from the past and the reworking of those designs into "more or less new combinations."[9] It was an era of architectural referencing, citation, and acknowledgment, an age of undogmatic revivalism.[10] It was not imitative of past forms; rather, borrowing became the sincerest form of flattery. Different, often conflicting, styles were drawn together to form a hybridized whole. At other times loose interpretation of a single style was the architect's manner of citing the past, either his own or that of others. New gardens and parks, both manicured and untamed, rounded out changing landscapes, whether bucolic country estates or bustling urban centers. In an age of curiosity, of collecting, of rising historical consciousness, of empire, and of statism, Europeans built in a manner that reflected all of those impulses. It was indeed the case that "architecture [was] the spatially apprehended will of the epoch."

For Jews too the nineteenth century was a time of enormous population growth, urbanization, and, in Central and Western Europe, increasing embourgeoisement. In 1800 there were approximately 2.7 million Jews in

Europe. One hundred years later there were 8.7 million. They accounted for approximately 82 percent of all the world's Jews. So where the general European population doubled over the course of the nineteenth century, the number of Jews tripled.[11] Given that our concern in this study is with Germany, we can observe these developments with some precision. In 1816, the total number of Jews in German states, not including the Hapsburg Empire, was 260,000. By 1910 that number had risen to 615,000. During the same period the Christian population also grew significantly from 23.6 million to 64 million. While Germany's population became urbanized gradually over the first seven decades of the nineteenth century, the larger cities began to show a disproportionate increase in the Jewish population relative to the non-Jewish.[12]

After the 1870s the migration of Jews to big cities in almost every country in which they lived was so pronounced that one is justified in referring to the process not merely as urbanization but, more accurately, as "metropolitanization."[13] In German-speaking Europe, cities such as Frankfurt am Main, Hamburg, Berlin, and Vienna all experienced a significant rise in the number of Jewish residents. To take but a handful of examples, in 1871 Berlin had a Jewish population of 36,000. Owing to migration from the Prussian countryside and from Eastern Europe, in a mere forty years that number had risen nearly 300 percent, and so by 1910 Berlin had 144,000 Jewish residents. Vienna's Jewish population grew from 72,000 in 1880 to 175,000 in 1910, largely as a result of migration from Galicia. Over the same period, Frankfurt's Jewish population rose from 10,000 to 26,000, Cologne's from approximately 3,000 to 12,300, Munich's from almost 3,000 to 11,000, and Dresden's Jewish community rose from a mere 1,200 to 7,300.[14]

As was the case with the non-Jewish population, these massive demographic changes, plus the nationwide expansion and renovation of German cities, gave impetus to a building boom.[15] Naturally, Jews made use of most of the new apartment buildings, factories, shops, department stores, banks, bridges, parks, and gardens that sprouted up everywhere.[16] But they also had their own specific architectural needs. As such, from the end of the eighteenth century and throughout the nineteenth, Jewish communities all over Germany embarked upon a great infrastructure project, building schools, synagogues, ritual bathhouses, cemeteries, and hospitals, all for the purpose of meeting the needs of a rapidly growing and urbanizing Jewish population.[17]

• • • • •

In architectural terms, most of the new Jewish buildings were not constructed in a particular Jewish style. Rather, all of them were either completely integrated or, as was the case with cemeteries, made to blend in with the natural as well as built environment as much as possible. It is in this context that we can best appreciate the true significance and daring of the neo-Moorish synagogues of Germany. Unlike almost every other new Jewish construction, they were anything but unobtrusive, and as such were profound symbols of the ambiguous and sometimes contradictory status, both real and imagined, of the Jews—central yet marginal, European but Oriental, liberated yet constrained, tolerated more than accepted.

The same historical forces that prompted the building of new schools, hospitals, and cemeteries led to the construction of many new synagogues across Germany. Expanding Jewish communities required more and bigger houses of worship, and all of these building projects required that conscious architectural and aesthetic choices be made. The clients, in this case, the Jewish communities, had to decide in which style to build, which style best reflected their collective sense of self, and what kind of message a particular style of building sent to both Jews and non-Jews. Architecture not only fulfilled social needs but also served didactic purposes. Of course, other crucial factors—such as cost, the size and location of the lot upon which a synagogue was to be built, the surrounding architectural environment, and the views of the permission-granting authorities, among them city councils and town fathers—also played a determinative role.

Architecture is the intimate bond of pragmatism and desire, with social conditions and history animating and driving the relationship. In 1886, the American architect Henry Van Brunt wrote about contemporary architecture: "The architect, in the course of his career, is called upon to erect buildings for every conceivable purpose, most of them adapted to requirements which have never before arisen in history. . . . Out of [the] . . . eminently practical considerations of planning must grow elevations, of which the essential character, if they are honestly composed, can have no precedent in architectural history."[18]

The ahistoricity of which Van Brunt spoke can also serve as our guide, for the nineteenth century was an epoch of radical rupture in the history of the synagogue. Its visibility, prominence, and aura of permanence were features reflective of the Jews themselves, who, as a group, were on the cusp of or already in receipt of legal emancipation. Just as that monumental development completely reconfigured the relationship of Jews to the nation-state and to their non-Jewish neighbors, so too does the synagogue occupy in the nineteenth century a place relative to the landscape that it had never previously held.

In Europe, from at least since the promulgation of the Theodosian Code in 438 C.E., which, among other things, explicitly prohibited the building of new synagogues, until legal emancipation in the nineteenth century, Christian elites could and often did determine whether a new synagogue could be built, the number of such houses of worship, their dimensions, their location, and even their design.[19] In the Middle Ages and into the early modern period, synagogues, when permitted, were located on the margins of a town, often near the city walls, an echo of Jewish social marginality. Not only the location but also the height of synagogues was of great concern to the Christian authorities, and so they insisted that no synagogue be allowed to stand taller than a church. Jews sometimes skirted this regulation by building the ground floor at basement level.[20] So intrusive were Christian authorities that they also dictated the number of windows that could be installed, and whether a synagogue was permitted to sport a clock tower.

It was not just because of these regulations that synagogues were mostly modest buildings. For Jews it made sense not to invest too much in their construction. Because they did not own the land upon which the synagogues stood, Jews had to pay rent to a Christian landholder. Leases could be abruptly terminated, and synagogues could be confiscated. Under such conditions there was simply too much risk in building grandly, even had permission been granted.[21] The goal of all the restrictions was to limit the conspicuousness of synagogues and reinforce the idea that they stood as symbols of the subordination of Judaism to Christianity.

Until the modern period, synagogues in Western Europe were unassuming structures, with few genuinely distinguishing Jewish features. They tended to be built in styles similar to those of contemporary churches and secular buildings. Small and often located at the rear of a neighboring building, they were, one might say, hidden in plain sight. While all the townspeople would have known of the existence and location of the local synagogue, it would not have been considered to be anything but a Jewish house of worship. That is to say, the synagogue would not have been thought of as part of the city's built environment, let alone cultural patrimony.

This began to change slowly and somewhat randomly with the Enlightenment, for it is then that synagogues began to be built by both Christian rulers and an emerging Jewish haute bourgeoisie. Traditionally marginalized, synagogues began to be afforded greater prominence and were used for didactic purposes, to demonstrate either the tolerant benevolence of the non-Jewish rulers who commissioned them, or the integrationist impulse of Jewish elites. The enlightened monarch Leopold III, Duke of Anhalt-Dessau, built the great Garden Kingdom of Dessau-Wörlitz, the largest English-style park of its kind in continental Europe.[22] In what was an extraordinary act the duke commissioned his court architect, Friedrich Wilhelm von Erdmannsdorff, to build a synagogue and place it prominently in the park. Opened in 1790, and used by the local Jewish community, the Wörlitz synagogue, which was modeled after the Temple of Hercules Victor in Rome, was round in shape, with twelve pilasters striping the exterior, interspersed with rounded windows that sat just below the roofline.[23] Leopold's decision to build the synagogue was born of his genuinely tolerant worldview, and his decision to erect it in such a public place was driven by his

3.1. Wörlitz synagogue. Courtesy Yad Vashem, Jerusalem.

desire to openly express that tolerance and to have the synagogue serve as an adornment to his gardens.

In terms of design the Wörlitz synagogue, the late baroque synagogue of the small Bavarian city of Floss (1817), and the Seitenstettengasse synagogue in Vienna (1826) were notable for their shape: round, ovate, or, in the case of Floss, octagonal, something entirely novel in the history of synagogue design. This shape suited the shared tastes of Christian rulers and, in the case of Vienna, the wealthy, Reform-minded Jewish patriarchs who commissioned the synagogue. A critical article written on the occasion of the one hundredth anniversary of the deliberately hidden Seitenstettengasse synagogue described the oval-shaped structure: "The interior space was diaphanous, with inexact dimensions, very middle class (*sehr bürgerlich*), not at all romantic, neither religious nor Jewish." They who commissioned the building, according to one highly critical Jewish voice, "were not men of deep feelings (*Dämmergefühle*). They wanted a final break with the East and its mysticism. They wanted to build a Temple of rational humanism."[24] So here we have cases of newly constructed synagogues that broke with tradition, whether in terms of location, purpose, or design. What united them was that they were all built in a European style, bearing no reference to Jewish history.

That would change, however, with another design chosen by non-Jewish architects for synagogues that were intended to be easily visible and part of a general program of urban beautification. That style was Egyptian and was thus the first manifestation in Europe of the Oriental synagogue. The emergence in the mid-eighteenth century of travel literature about Egypt, and early nineteenth-century accounts of Napoleon's 1798 invasion of that land, inspired the Egyptian Revival movement in architecture, which was used in a wide variety of buildings in the United States, England, and, to a far lesser extent, on the Continent.[25] Synagogues were likewise built fully in this style or, as in the majority of cases, displayed Egyptian elements, particularly around the ark containing the scrolls of the Torah.[26]

Napoleon's campaign inspired a number of lavish architectural studies of ancient Egypt, which, when considered alongside the already long-standing tradition of speculating about the design of Solomon's Temple in Jerusalem, led some architects to believe that the original temple had been of Egyptian design.[27] It was thus but a short step to imagining that ancient Egyptian buildings could also serve the quest for an authentic style or decorative form for the modern synagogue.[28] Indeed many of the terms used to describe Jews during the debates over Jewish emancipation in the later eighteenth and early nineteenth centuries were also used in reference to Egyptian architecture: "antiquity," "permanence," "cohesiveness," "intensity."[29] But while this language was used in praise of Egyptian buildings, when applied to Jews, these terms were not always intended as compliments.

In Germany, a number of synagogues bore Egyptian design elements, two of the most historically significant examples being those that were constructed in Karlsruhe in 1798 and Munich in 1826. Even though the respective Jewish communities sought to build new synagogues, the construction of both houses of worship was actually initiated by the Christian authorities.[30] In the former, the Margrave of Baden, Karl Friedrich, had his royal architect, Friedrich Weinbrenner, design the synagogue, whose facade was composed of two wings containing apartments and administration offices, separated in the middle by two towering, flat-roofed Egyptian columns, between which was a single, large pointed arch, which served as a grand entranceway that led to a central courtyard. Joining the two columns together and hanging above the large arch was an arcade, with a further three, small, pointed arches. This upper arcade led to the women's gallery. Once inside the courtyard on its east side, the visitor came upon the synagogue itself, a rectangular, barrel-vaulted structure. The entire complex made it the most lavish synagogue of its time in Germany, and although the building betrays Weinbrenner's penchant for the eclecticism characteristic at this stage of his career, the variety of styles—in addition to the Egyptian there were some classical and Gothic elements as well—reflected the fact that synagogue architecture at this point had no developed history and thus no usable mod-

3.2. Karlsruhe synagogue.

els. Weinbrenner was thus free to let his imagination roam.[31] However, the Egyptian columns and what might be termed Oriental-Gothic arches only highlighted the fact that those making use of the building were Europeans, but of exotic, indeed Eastern origins.

In Munich, the Bavarian king Ludwig I had his architect, Jean-Baptiste Métivier, design the building. Ludwig's father, Maximilian I, had donated white marble, which was carved into the shape of palms for application to the exterior of the building. Less obviously Egyptian than the synagogue in Karlsruhe—it was for the most part neoclassical but bore Egyptian capitals atop red marble columns on the interior—the Munich synagogue seems, at least ideologically speaking if not in terms of its design, even more Egyptian than the synagogue in Karlsruhe. Métivier's immediate predecessor as chief royal architect was Leo von Klenze, perhaps Germany's foremost advocate of classical architecture. In his *Instructions for the Architecture of Christian Worship* (1822) he traced the religious history of the world prior to the advent of Jesus and wrote of the Jews that "at all times they were and still are a most malleable people, who outwardly adopt the customs of the lands and people among whom they live but inwardly never give up their own characteristics. They remained true to their religious laws and outwardly were influenced by Egyptian and, later, Phoenician [culture]."[32] This observation was reflected in the tenor of the city's new synagogue, which was Orthodox in orientation but whose congregation remained under the strict supervision and thus influence, cultural and otherwise, of Munich's authorities.[33]

Their elegant proportions and design notwithstanding, the synagogues in Karlsruhe and Munich, unlike the one at Wörlitz, reaffirmed the Jews' outsider status. These structures were located far outside the respective city centers and, in the case of Munich, situated in such a cramped street that the synagogue's entrance was placed on the side of the building; there was no room for steps at the front. These synagogues were not constructed in a completely Egyptian style but, rather, used Egyptian elements such as capitals, cornices, pillars, and aedicules (openings flanked by two columns); still, they went a step further than those at, say, Wörlitz and Vienna in displaying a style of architecture that exoticized the Jews by referencing their ancient Near Eastern roots. But more than this, both Margrave Karl Friedrich and King Ludwig were philhellenes and great proponents of neoclassical architecture. The choice of Egyptian elements for these two synagogues—both rulers and architects believed that Israelite buildings of biblical times were similar to those of ancient Egypt, and Weinbrunner referred to his design as an "Oriental fantasy"—was intended to convey the message that Egyptian and, by extension Hebrew, cultures were inferior to that of Greece; thus the Egyptian style, while unworthy of Christian emulation, was nonetheless well suited for Jewish purposes.[34]

By way of comparison, the first Reform synagogue in Frankfurt was erected in 1815 at the instigation not of the Christian authorities but of the Jewish community.[35] Because Napoleon had installed the city's ruler, Prince Karl von Dahlberg, a French imperial style of architecture was used for building design in Frankfurt. The political regime, which was under French influence, had liberated the Jews, whose response was to build a synagogue that would signal the congregation's gratitude and desire for rapid social and cultural integration. A preexisting structure was used for the exterior of the building, whose entrance portal was a rounded arch, flanked by two Egyptian columns, atop which sat a flat roof. On the inside, which was entirely renovated, pillars with Egyptian capitals were used to support the women's gallery. But while the synagogue may have reflected French "Egyptomania," to use the term coined by the noted architectural historian James Stevens Curl, it was unusual in two main respects. First, beyond a few monuments, headstones, and archways, "Egyptomania" did not really make its way into French and German architecture, and thus, as a building, especially as a house of worship, the synagogue was most atypical. Second, as it was in an area characterized by late medieval buildings, it stood out noticeably from its surroundings. Herein was the dilemma posed by all the orientalized synagogues of the nineteenth century. Did they highlight the Near Eastern origins of the Jews and thus their cultural incompatibility with Germans, or could the synagogues be made to be expressions of the Jewish willingness to conform to the majority and yet assert Jewish difference? The Frankfurt synagogue straddled both orientations, for as different as it was from its built surroundings, it was the first synagogue to be constructed outside the old ghetto, which ironically, had long been referred to as "Little Egypt."[36] The choice of this particular style was intended to remind non-Jews as well as Jews of the latter's roots. Moreover, those Jewish origins, so indelibly identified with slavery, could be juxtaposed with the condition of freedom in which the Jews of Frankfurt now found themselves. The synagogue could thus be said to teleologically encapsulate the Jewish march through history. Such historicization would come into starker relief as Jews as well as Germans began to seriously struggle with the idea of what it was that constituted an ideal national style of architecture.

In 1828, a young architect, Heinrich Hübsch, who had been a student of Friedrich Weinbrenner's, published a short book with a simple, yet thought-provoking title, *In What Style Should We Build?* In this fifty-four-page extended essay, Hübsch questioned the appropriateness and relevance of classical architecture for the current age. He identified four principal factors that determined style: materials, technical skills, climate, and present needs.[37] On the basis of these criteria he made the case for a Byzantine style of architecture, which opted for rounded arches and was thenceforth known in Germany by a term he coined, namely, *Rundbogenstil* (round-arch style). Hübsch represented a new generation of architects who had come of age during the proto-romantic Sturm und Drang era. They sought to break with the formal classicism of the previous generation, not wanting to be bound by architectural conventions and aesthetic dictates they found stifling. The contemporaneous emergence of new building techniques and materials also prompted calls for a break with the past.[38]

Heinrich Hübsch's essay sparked a robust, indeed heated debate that went on for decades. It was one that pitted, for the most part, advocates of neoclassicism, *Rundbogenstil*, and neo-Gothic designs against each other.[39] At the root of Hübsch's question about a German national style of architecture lay the larger problematic—who are the Germans? The various architectural styles that were discussed were freighted with far more than mere aesthetic considerations. Each style was considered a reflection of the people who built these structures. For some, classical architecture represented the rational and universal character of the Greeks, qualities to which modern Western culture was heir. Linking gender, virtue, political freedom, and architecture, the eighteenth-century French diplomat and scholar of ancient Greece Marie-Gabriel-Florent-Auguste de Choiseul-Gouffier combined notions of "male simplicity" and "republican simplicity" to take note of "the male character which the Greeks imprinted on the Doric Order during the splendid centuries of their liberty."[40] For others, Gothic architecture betrayed the deep, Christian religiosity associated with Germanness, while some even advocated for Gothic architecture on environmental grounds. In 1804, Friedrich von Schlegel, the poet, critic, and husband of Moses Mendelssohn's daughter, Dorothea, wrote: "The admired facade of the Louvre may be excellent in its kind but what can be more out of place than twenty or thirty Grecian or Italian columns in a strange land and climate? Gothic architecture is the style of building best adapted to a northern climate and a colder zone."[41] Those who favored the round-arched Byzantine style saw it as the first great postclassical innovation in the history of architecture, displacing the ancient form of trabeated construction, that is, the use of horizontal beams or lintels rather than arches. Those who opted for *Rundbogenstil* believed it could form the basis of a new style of building for a German nation that epitomized a creative, forward-looking spirit.

Just as contemporary philosophies of language, music, and aesthetics informed their own emerging sense of self, German Jews could not but be influenced by the general German architectural and self-fashioning debate taking place. This was because any discussion of a German national style was bound to shine a spotlight on Jews, their position in society, their architectural needs, and the question of whether their buildings could be subsumed within a German national style or whether a new and distinct approach had to be found for them. Hübsch's preferred Byzantine style actually became one of the more popular design options for building synagogues around 1840 and thereafter. In part this emerged out of a growing discomfort with the use of Egyptian style for synagogues; significantly, the position was most clearly articulated by Albert Rosengarten (1809–1893), Germany's first Jewish architect.

By the late eighteenth century, in the western German city of Kassel, the existing synagogue had become too small and too dilapidated to continue serving the growing Jewish community.[42] As had been the case elsewhere, the local landgrave proposed that a new synagogue be built. For about three decades, beginning in 1781, a series of designs were commissioned, most of which were rejected by the Jewish community. There were financial reasons for this, with the wealthier members fearing they would be made to bear the costs of the landgrave's extravagant tastes, and then there were aesthetic and social reasons, with many fearing that what the landgrave wanted would be too conspicuous, while religious sensibilities led more conservative members of the community to the opinion that a new synagogue would become a stronghold of Reform Jews.[43] Finally, there was the issue of style. Once a suitable plot of land was found, the Jewish community requested that the architectural commission be given to August Schuchardt, a government architect and supervisor of Albert Rosengarten. It is possible that the community sought out Schuchardt because they actually wanted to build the first synagogue in Germany designed by a Jewish architect, namely, Rosengarten. Meanwhile, Kassel's director of buildings, Johann Conrad Bromeis, proposed his own design, an Egyptian-style synagogue, one that was in keeping with the wishes of the officials who manned the government office in charge of religious buildings. Bromeis was only doing his masters' bidding; personally, he was opposed to the Egyptian style. In

1832 Schuchardt pointed out the problems with Bromeis's design, specifically that it lacked stylistic purity, and that the very solidity of the Egyptian style, which indicated permanency, belied the history of Jewish wandering and thus their collective saga of impermanency. Building in the preferred style of their slave ancestors' owners also constituted an affront, as did building a synagogue whose architecture was drawn from a polytheistic civilization. Other progressive architects and engineers weighed in, maintaining that enlightened times such as these demanded that similarities, not differences, between religions be emphasized. Thus synagogues and churches should be built to harmonize with each other, and both should be erected in the classical style, for it best represented progress and rationality. Still the landgrave insisted on an Egyptian style. In 1834, he had his court architect, Julius Eugen Ruhl, draw up another synagogue plan, and again the community dug its heels in and rejected his design, which highlighted Islamic decorative features.[44] That Judaism's origins were in the East was undeniable, but that did not justify building in an Eastern style. For if it did, they argued, then churches should also be built in Oriental forms because Christianity likewise emerged in the East.

The community wanted a Western design and wished for the synagogue to be built by Rosengarten. Their persistence paid off: on August 8, 1839, Kassel's new synagogue was dedicated.[45] A dogged opponent of the Egyptian style, Rosengarten claimed that the Egyptian and German climates were nothing alike, that the two forms of construction were utterly different, that Egyptian architecture, contrary to contemporary views, bore no resemblance to the Temple of Solomon, and that, in fact, the Jews never even had a temple in Egypt. The subject of what the Temple in Jerusalem looked like or how it was appointed aroused Rosengarten's greatest ire, leading him to declare that Solomon's Temple was as removed from a contemporary synagogue as "a pagan temple is from a Christian church." He demanded that "every Oriental style be rejected."[46]

At Kassel, Rosengarten built Germany's first Byzantine-style synagogue. It was a large barrel-vaulted basilica with a central nave, lined with pillars, atop which were rounded arches. These in turn were flanked by two aisles. The underside of the arches harmonized with the heavily decorated apse, containing the ark, which stood out in relief against an ornate wall. On top of the wall was a half shell, which bore the same decoration as was to be found on the arches along the central nave and the wall behind the ark that held the Torah scrolls.

The exterior was very solid, with three stories of round-arched windows. Only along the facade at the upper level were there five round windows. To avoid the block-like appearance of a large rectangle, the risalit facade extended beyond the width of the building behind it. Two towers on either side of the entrance portal housed the staircases leading up to the women's

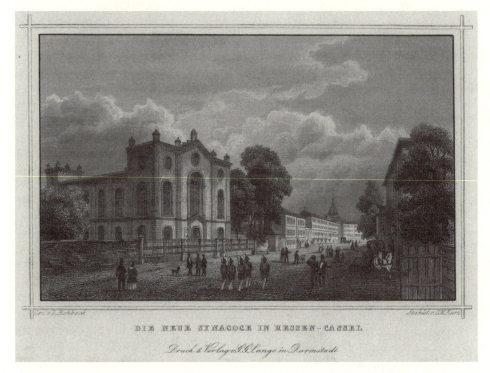

DIE NEUE SYNAGOGE IN HESSEN - CASSEL.

Druck & Verlag v. G. G. Lange in Darmstadt

3.3. Kassel synagogue (exterior). William A. Rosenthall Judaica Collection, Special Collections, College of Charleston.

gallery. The exterior of the building was also colorful, with yellow-hued walls offset with red stone borders around the openings.

The *Rundbogenstil* was adaptable for Jewish use because it satisfied the need to establish the Eastern or Oriental origins of the Jews, while, at the same time, the presence of Byzantine architecture beyond the eastern Mediterranean and into Southern Europe also allowed for the affirmation of the Jews' rootedness in Europe. Rosengarten had rejected neo-Moorish synagogue design as lacking appropriate motifs, as an exercise in mere decoration, while he considered neo-Gothic design to be appropriate only for churches. By contrast the historical suitability of *Rundbogenstil* design followed from the fact that "it approaches the style of the first Christian churches, which were probably based on synagogues built under Roman rule. Both find their ideal in the basilica."[47] Moreover, the similarity between Byzantine and Romanesque architecture—they shared features such as rounded arches, thick walls, massive pillars, and a central dome—meant that Byzantine architecture could be seen as an Eastern version of Western Europe's Romanesque, further cementing the Europeanness of both the style and the Jews.[48]

No agreement as to what constituted a proper German national style of architecture was ever fully reached in the great architectural debate inaugurated by Heinrich Hübsch; consensus, however—through an act of discursive omission—did lead to one seemingly unanimous resolution. Nowhere among the many ideas put forth was there a consideration of adopting Oriental designs. This was not so elsewhere. Europeans first became acquainted with the East through the proliferation of travel reports that began to circulate after 1500, but a deeper appreciation of Oriental art and architecture began with actual contact through commerce.[49] In England exposure to and appreciation of Oriental culture began as early as the sixteenth century, following on the heels of Elizabeth I's founding of the Levant Company in 1581, which was followed by the founding of the East India Company in 1600. In Holland, greater contact began with the establishment of the Dutch East India Company in 1602. In both Britain and the Netherlands it began modestly, with an expressed taste for Eastern silks, Turkish and Persian rugs, the opening of coffeehouses to purvey the new, exotic beverage, and the building of Turkish baths. In Holland, glazed tiles from Delft bore tulip patterns in the cobalt blue of the Turkish Iznik style, which the Dutch exported to Britain.[50] In France too there was a prevalence of Oriental themes in eighteenth- and nineteenth-century painting.[51] In the realm of building, the greatest architect of the seventeenth century, Sir Christopher Wren, was deeply taken with Ottoman domes, just at that time when he was putting the finishing touches on his designs for St. Paul's Cathedral.

To the interest in things Near Eastern was soon to be added the culture of the Indian subcontinent. By the middle of the eighteenth century the first complete structures in an orientalist style were built. A building known as the Alhambra was erected in London's Kew Gardens, as was a mosque and a Chinese pagoda. There soon followed Oriental structures commissioned by individual monarchs, such as King George IV, whose architect, John Nash, built the stunning, Mogul-style Royal Pavilion at Brighton between 1815 and 1822. Other members of the upper classes built Oriental-style summerhouses, garden pavilions, orangeries, and kiosks, and more modest interpretations of orientalist architecture were confined to the decoration of designated rooms in castles, palaces, and manor houses.[52]

In contrast to these developments, it was the absence of such colonial and commercial links between Germany and the East that served to reinforce the idea that the architecture of Muslim lands was strangely exotic, unfamiliar, and, in the context of the search for a German national style of building, wholly inappropriate. While there were some buildings erected in Germany that bore orientalist features, they were few and far between. With Germany groping for its own national style, Oriental architecture, when discussed at all in the great German architectural debates of the nineteenth century, was dismissed as frivolous, suitable only for entertainment and recreational purposes. Seen as decorative rather than decorous, profane rather than profound, Oriental architecture was deemed incapable of reflecting the German character traits of seriousness, piety, and solidity, if not masculinity. Writing in 1844, the staunch advocate of a Germanic, Christian national style, the architect Carl Albert Rosenthal, asserted that Oriental architecture, "apart from the absence of the Christian element[,] ... has one fault that prevents it from being recommended for general approval: an almost total disregard for the symbolic expression of structural forces; that is, the lack of architectonic character." Asserting that at the time of its advent, Islam had no architectural style of its own, Rosenthal claimed that Arab conquerors merely captured Byzantine churches and ornately decorated them to the extent that it seemed as if "the wonders of their own fairy tales have come alive." As such, "the Arabian style is confined to pure decoration, which looks all the more strange as their religion prohibits figurative work. The style is charming, although never more than a lively play of fancy."[53] A year later, in 1845, Johann Heinrich Wolff, a professor of architecture at Kassel and an advocate of a German building style based on classical architecture, addressed a meeting of architects in the city of Bamberg. Despite his disagreement with Rosenthal on what would best serve as a German national style of architecture, Wolff reiterated the former's views on Muslim architecture. Even when praising the innovative design of arches by Arab architects, Wolff noted that the latter "were evidently far advanced in technical skill [over their predecessors], and the squat heaviness of existing arches and columns seemed to them as superfluous as it was incompatible with their predilection for opulence and daintiness (*Reichthum und Zierlichkeit*)."[54]

As part of the building boom that took place all over Europe in the nineteenth century, hundreds of new synagogues were constructed. Aside from certain fundamental requirements, such as the building's facing eastward in the direction of Jerusalem and a separate section for women, there was no established design that had to be followed. This is a key reason why synagogues appear in such a fantastically wide array of styles.[55] But in Central Europe a significant number were built according to a neo-Moorish design. It is true that such synagogues were constructed all over the world, but they first appeared in Germany, and the orientalist dimension to the story is particular to that country in light of the local architecture and the social and legal position of the Jews there. It is no small paradox that in Britain and Holland, where an appreciation of Oriental architectural forms was strongest, no neo-Moorish synagogues were built. The historian Saskia Coenen Snyder has observed that in England such opulent designs would have been considered ostentatious, unseemly, and unnecessary because as an accepted and emancipated minority, British Jews sought only to blend in. In Holland, in addition to the freedom they enjoyed, the Jewish community was extremely poor; the cost of building the extravagant neo-Moorish synagogues was prohibitive for working-class Dutch Jews. Indeed, almost alone among major Jewish communities in the nineteenth century, the Jews of Amsterdam did not build any large, monumental synagogues, let alone opulent neo-Moorish ones.[56] By contrast, in Germany, a place where such designs were rejected by the guild of architects and by cultural critics, the trend toward building neo-Moorish synagogues was especially pronounced.

In fact, from the middle of the nineteenth century, neo-Moorish style architecture in Germany was associated almost exclusively with synagogues. We have thus far traced Egyptian and Byzantine-style synagogues as early manifestations of orientalizing architectural tendencies among German Jews. We focus now on the most overt and spectacular manifestations of Jewish orientalist building style—the neo-Moorish synagogues. Historians have only been able to conjecture why this phenomenon occurred; the documents do not reveal with any exactitude the reasons for the decisions taken to build in this fashion. Some have seen these synagogues as expressions of increasing Jewish self-assertion and self-confidence, whereas others detect a desire to link contemporary German Jews to the Jewish Golden Age in Muslim Spain; yet others have seen the neo-Moorish turn in German synagogue architecture as part of the larger European invention of a Moorish style. Some scholars have described the trend as an expression of European Jewry's "feeling of 'Semitic' or 'oriental' pride" (not necessarily Jewish pride), and finally, by contrast, according to one architectural historian, the synagogues were built because nineteenth-century Jews "had come to acknowledge and accept their non-European origins and to take pride in this aspect of Jewish history."[57] To varying degrees there is merit in these differing interpretations, but even those that are more valid than others work only for some places at some times.

Because such synagogues were built in both small towns and large cities, in Central and Eastern Europe, as well as the United States, it is difficult to generalize about the motives Jews had for building neo-Moorish synagogues. Local conditions dictated parochial concerns. What prompted Jews to build in this style in Berlin was different from that which motivated them in Leningrad, Budapest, or Cincinnati.[58] We must, therefore, be attentive to the particular circumstances confronted by the preemancipated Jews of Germany. Any analysis of these structures should situate the preference by some Jewish communities for orientalist synagogue design within the context of the rancorous debate over a German national style of architecture. Although almost as many Romanesque-style synagogues were built in Germany as Oriental ones after midcentury, the Byzantine style could not make a claim to Jewish architectural uniqueness, as many churches and secular buildings were also of *Rundbogenstil* design. By contrast, Christian claims to the neo-Gothic were almost absolute and incontestable. By a process of elimination, that left the lien on neo-Moorish architecture in Germany to Jews.

The story here is characterized by a calculated ambivalence, somewhat of an oddity given the costs and commitment entailed in building synagogues, and the grandness and seeming permanence of these edifices. The Moorish-style synagogues represent more than just a stylistic choice based upon competitive tenders by architectural firms. Rather, for the Jewish clients, and for what were for the most part Christian architects, the building of synagogues in the Moorish style was driven by two impulses:first, a Christian perception of Jews as foreign, and the need they felt to capture Jewish exoticness in architectural form; and second, a Jewish exploration of identity, the debates and anxieties over which became starkly manifest with the building of new, highly visible synagogues in German cities.

Almost counterintuitively, neo-Moorish synagogues afforded German Jews the opportunity to claim, perhaps reclaim, part of their Eastern heritage just at the time that they were becoming increasingly Western in both a secular and a religious sense. Most importantly, they represented historical and religious rupture. As such, they are, in architectural terms, analogous to the linguistic turn we have previously examined. If Sephardic-inflected Hebrew represented a rejection of anything that smacked of Yiddish, including Ashkenazic Hebrew, neo-Moorish synagogues represented a rejection of the traditional synagogue, the very buildings in which one would worship in Ashkenazic Hebrew. It was, perhaps in a majority of cases, Reform or moderately progressive congregations that built in this fashion. Moving furthest and most rapidly from Orthodox aesthetics, the synagogues of Reform congregations were built after a fashion that in a highly artificial way established the Oriental origins of the Jews, all while those congregations pursued the Westernization of Jewish liturgy, theology, and the service itself. This was a delicate balancing act, and in some cases the calculated ambivalence suggested that the outer form of a given temple might be drawn from an imagined Oriental origin but that there were clear limits to the extent that those origins would be celebrated. The form of these synagogues bestowed a sort of Jewish authenticity, albeit a manufactured one, on the congregations that built in this fashion. Above all, they offered Jewish congregations the opportunity to appear dignified and sensitive to the importance of aesthetics.

The instrumental use of the past, this time architectural and not intellectual, reflected a working through of issues of Jewish identity as Jews struggled to prove their Europeanness in order to win extended civic rights, if not full emancipation. The neo-Moorish synagogues suggest a compromise position: for some German architectural critics, it was Arabs who invented the pointed arch, and though they deemed that it remained unfulfilled in its potential, it was the inspiration and model for the pointed and perfected arch characteristic of Gothic architecture.[59] Here can be read religious su-persessionism in stone. Just as Christianity was seen as a fulfillment of Ju-daism, so too could the source for a Jewish architecture—Islamic style—be considered an incomplete execution of an idea perfected by later Christian architects and builders. In 1859, the German architect Oscar Mothes illus-trated this very point via the use of a gendered metaphor: "The Moorish way of building is the bride of the Gothic style."[60] Given gender relations in the nineteenth century, Mothes's choice of words still implies a position of Muslim and hence Jewish subordination. Still, Islamic architecture could be considered related to Gothic forms.

At the same time, Moorish architecture bestowed upon the Reform tem-ples, and hence the congregants, a link to an "Oriental" past, thus endow-ing their religious project of relatively recent origin with authenticity de-rived from antiquity. Where, however, that authentic link to the past was domesticated, as it were, was in the fact that the synagogues were neither replicas of Near Eastern synagogues nor Sephardic synagogues, built on designs derived from Muslim Spain. Rather, the choice to build Oriental synagogues was part of a much larger trend in nineteenth-century Euro-pean architecture—the neo-Moorish revival. Where the synagogues break off from that trend is that where Christians used neo-Moorish forms for theaters, parks, gardens, and other structures built for recreational purposes, Jews employed the neo-Moorish style for houses of worship, as focal points of Jewish communal and religious life.

In Germany, the earliest neo-Moorish synagogues built in the nine-teenth century were erected in small towns. The first of these was opened in 1832 in the Palatinate town of Ingenheim. Within this one provincial synagogue, designed by Friedrich von Gärtner (1791–1847), director of the Munich Academy of Arts and official architect of the Bavarian court, we see a mélange of orientalist designs. While no neo-Islamic decorations were employed on the interior—Renaissance-style arcades straddled the slender pillars that culminated in floral sculpture holding up the women's gallery—an Egyptian theme was employed for the Torah ark, and an aedi-cule was bedecked with a frieze of palm trees, a botanical feature strikingly out of place in this rural Bavarian landscape. The most noticeably Islamic feature to be found at Ingenheim appeared on the exterior in the form of horseshoe-arched windows, which were nearly identical to those dating from North Africa and Spain in the thirteenth and fourteenth centuries. Ingenheim was the model for other similarly designed regional synagogues, a number of them built by August von Voit, a pupil of von Gärtner's at the Munich Academy.[61]

The building of provincial synagogues in neo-Moorish design was short-lived, lasting only until the 1870s. A combination of high costs and shrink-ing regional communities, whose members were making their way to big

3.4. Ingenheim synagogue.

cities, is the most probable cause for the decline in such architecture. However, coterminous with their advent and decline in rural areas, the most spectacular manifestations of German neo-Moorish synagogue design began to appear in large cities. To undertake a comprehensive examination of all such synagogues is beyond the scope and goal of this chapter. Instead, we shall consider four of the most important examples—those at Dresden, Leipzig, Vienna, and Berlin. Not only did these monumental urban buildings constitute a high point in the evolution of orientalist synagogue design; the discourse about the national (and racial) identity of both Jews and Germans echoes from these structures with unique clarity.

When Albert Rosengarten designed the above-mentioned Romanesque synagogue in Kassel (1839), he not only established himself as Germany's first Jewish architect but also became Germany's first Jewish architecture critic and historian. In an article of 1840 on the new synagogue in Kassel he dismissed the Gothic style as inappropriate for the synagogue because it was both too costly and too Christian. He likewise rejected the Egyptian style as having no historical connection to the Temple in Jerusalem.[62] In the 1878 English translation of his magnum opus of 1857, *A Handbook of Architectural Styles*, Rosengarten added a lengthy excursus on contemporary synagogue architecture that did not appear in the original German. In the midst of a discussion about church architecture Rosengarten broke off to address a subject of intimate concern to him—the large number of neo-Moorish synagogues being built in Germany. His outline of Jewish history reveals his understanding of the relationship between Jewish identity and Jewish architecture, and deserves to be quoted in full:

> Whilst treating of the subject of modern churches, it may not be out of place to say a few words about the style in which the numerous new synagogues are constructed. The Moorish style is that in which they are generally erected, but there is no substantial ground for justifying this selection.
>
> The motives for the form of a building of this description may be historical, religious or constructive. Taking the historical aspect into consideration, it would seem natural that the Temple of Solomon at Jerusalem, described in the Bible, would be taken as the model for these buildings, in remembrance of the time when the Jews possessed an independent kingdom under their own kings. But the design of the old Jewish Temple was based upon a different order of things, and was calculated for religious sacrifices that were so intimately connected with their worship. But in point of fact, after the Jewish kingdom was subjugated by the Romans, and the Jews themselves were led into Roman captivity and subsequently scattered all over the world, no other principle has been followed in the design of their synagogues, than to adopt the prevalent architectural style at the time existent in the various countries in which they settled.
>
> Thus as synagogues were built in the Middle Ages in the Gothic style, as is still to be seen at Prague and elsewhere, and it may naturally be taken for granted that the Romanesque style was previously employed, as it was for Christian Churches: that is to say, when the permission to build synagogues was accorded to the Jews in the state of oppression in which they

lived. The case may also have been analogous in the earliest Christian times, and the basilica may also have been employed for Jewish worship; whilst in the East the Byzantine style was doubtless had recourse to till it was merged into the Moorish. Naturally after this change, synagogues, like all buildings in the East, were constructed in the Moorish style, which for a long time was prevalent throughout the whole country. This is, however, no reason that for the synagogues of the Jews in the West, who were mixed up with the Christian population in political and social questions, the Moorish style should be considered appropriate; and still less does this afford grounds for the pleasure palace of the Moorish kings of Spain, that is to say the Alhambra at Granada, being taken as a model for the interiors of modern synagogues, whilst externally Turkish domes and other Oriental and Arabic forms are introduced, so that the crescent alone is wanting at the summit to mark the buildings as intended not for the religious rites of the Jews but of the Mohammedans.

There is not the slightest justification for the Moorish style being adopted as normal for Jewish synagogues: it has been merely a question of partiality and perverted taste, and a vague and unauthorized notion of imparting an oriental aspect to the buildings; the Moorish style is as inconsistent with the purpose of the building on religious grounds as it is on historical. The chief endeavour in Jewish as in Christian worship is that, over and above the observances necessitated by worship itself, the very fact of entering and staying in the sacred edifice should have a solemn and elevating effect on the mind. This end is not attained by Moorish buildings in the same degree, as it is by other more completely developed styles, such as the Classical and Medieval. This desired impression must be brought about by architectural form, and cannot be satisfactorily conveyed by the mere splendour of gilding or colouring, which marks the Moorish style. But no further proof is required to show that no preference should be accorded to this style on constructive grounds, inasmuch as it is itself deficient in any real constructive element, just as it is wanting in stylistic signification when compared with the Classical as well as the Romanesque and Gothic styles.[63]

While Rosengarten rehearses some of the well-worn Christian critiques of Islamic architecture that had been heard since the 1830s, his tone is made more urgent by the fact that, unlike the Christian architects with whom he concurred, Rosengarten had to contend with the reality that his was a view that did not have wide support outside the Jewish community and had increasingly less within it. Between the building of the synagogue at Kassel and the 1850s, Christian architects and municipal authorities became firmly convinced that the neo-Moorish should be adopted as the Jewish "national style" of architecture. With the number of synagogues that were built in this style it is apparent that the Jewish communities likewise came to embrace an aesthetic at which they had previously balked.

There is no one single cause for the changed attitude among Jews. Rather, one might point to the cumulative impact of several developments from the 1840s to the 1860s that led German Jews to embrace orientalist designs. First, in 1840 the Damascus Affair, which led to the arrest, torture, and death of Jews on trumped-up charges that they had murdered a Capuchin monk in order to use his blood to bake matzah, was an event that deeply shocked world Jewry. The Damascus blood libel led Jews, unaccustomed to seeing themselves as members of a global nation, to a realization of the interconnectedness of all Jews and a sense of mutual responsibility. These sentiments were facilitated and strengthened by the founding of Jewish newspapers wherein reports on Jews in distant lands served to link European Jewish communities with those in the Near East. Jewish philanthropy on a global scale, aimed at alleviating the plight of poverty-stricken and imperiled Jews, many of whom were in the Near East, also dates from this time, further enhancing a sense of historic fraternity among all Jews.[64] Second, the 1840s also bore witness to significant growth of the Reform movement in Germany, and in practical political terms this meant that liberal forces gained control in community after community. Where accommodation with traditionalists could not be achieved, communities began to split, at first by holding separate Reform and Orthodox services. Increasingly, however, the Reformers set about building their own synagogues, and with increasing frequency they did so in the neo-Moorish style. The willingness of such Jews to call attention to themselves with this flamboyant style of architecture is no small thing given that it was these same Jews who were so dedicated to the process of deep acculturation.[65] A third factor that indirectly prompted a reconnection with the Oriental origins of the Jews was antisemitism. The conservative reaction that followed in the wake of the failed revolutions of 1848–1849 led to the rescinding of the emancipatory gains that had been made. Where Article 12 of the Prussian Constitution of 1850 noted that religious faith must not be a barrier to the enjoyment of civic rights, Article 14 asserted that, "notwithstanding the freedom of religion guaranteed in Article 12, the Christian religion shall form the basis of all institutions of the state."[66] While German Jews certainly redoubled their efforts at cultural integration at this time, they were also made painfully aware of where things stood. The reassertion of the state's Christian identity, a self-styled return to its roots, was met by a Jewish reassertion of their own historical origins. This did not mean an abandonment of the idea that they were Germans of the Jewish faith; rather, there was a willingness to more assertively celebrate, through the design of their houses of worship, a time and place where Jews and Judaism flourished. Fourth, the political battles also found their complement in the world of scholarship, where, as we will see in chapter 5, Jewish historians and orientalists, frustrated and embittered by contemporary antisemitism, responded by producing scholarship that glorified Jewish life under Islam, singing its praises, thereby placing it in stark relief to the miserable way Jews had been treated under Christianity. This turn to history, especially under the impact of romanticism and the concomitant quest for a German national style of architecture, also fed into the architectural choices made by and on behalf of Jews. Taken together all these developments account for changing Jewish sensibilities and the willingness of communities to invest in building synagogues that were bold, even ostentatious, and stylistically most un-German.

DRESDEN

On May 8, 1840, in the city of Dresden, a new synagogue was officially dedicated in an elaborate ceremony before a host of Jewish and Christian dignitaries.[67] The state of Saxony, in which Dresden lay, was a region with a long history of antisemitism. Jews had been expelled from the city in 1430 and had been allowed to return only around 1700. Well into the third decade of the nineteenth century there were still only about 3,000 Jews in all of Saxony, living under the weight of myriad laws that restricted them to petty trade and money lending.[68] Yet in 1834 the city's 634 Jews were granted permission to erect a new community synagogue after it had been determined that Dresden's four private synagogues were too small to accommodate the community. After protracted negotiations with city officials and the eventual purchase of a suitable block of land, the community asked the renowned Protestant architect Gottfried Semper to design their synagogue, for which he was paid 500 taler.[69] Semper was a liberal revolutionary in an otherwise conservative, if not reactionary, environment. The synagogue he designed would also show off his independent, progressive side. It was a massive structure, with 300 seats for men, 200 for women, and a further 500 standing-room places. It is ironic then, that while the synagogue, which was the largest in Germany at that time, sat in a relatively prominent place, the city fathers nonetheless envisioned a Jewish community that would blend in and become somewhat inconspicuous. Semper made sure that was not to be the case.

The building's exterior was composed of an eclectic mix of Christian, Byzantine, and Romanesque elements and was covered in white plaster, offset by red brickwork around the porthole and arched windows and doorways, creating a refined and most understated, yet eye-catching appearance. The synagogue's most distinctive external feature was its pyramidal roof, intended to recall the biblical tabernacle, and the twin, somewhat stunted towers that flanked the synagogue's entrance. On top of each one was a Star of David, with a third standing sentinel over the central cupola. It is with the interior, however, that Semper's synagogue in Dresden marked a milestone

3.5. Dresden synagogue (exterior).

in the history of synagogue architecture in that it was the first such building to have its interior decorated in neo-Moorish style. According to Semper, he borrowed decorative motifs from the medieval Alhambra palace in Granada. Pillars that recalled the ornate columns in the Court of the Lions held aloft the wooden entablature of the women's gallery. This superstructure of moldings that rested horizontally on the capitals was executed with an inlay pattern composed of light and dark wood. The ceiling of the dome was painted a brilliant blue with rays of light intended to recall "the seventh heaven of the Old Testament [*sic*]," while the walls were sumptuously painted in a dazzling array of colors, depicting floral and geometric designs, that left the observer in no doubt of the Jews' Oriental roots.[70] The Eternal Lamp, or *ner tamid*, that hung on three chains before the ark was of Moorish design. It is one of history's puzzling ironies that those two radical antisemites Richard and Cosima Wagner ordered, with the assistance of Friedrich Nietzsche, a replica of Semper's beautiful, evocative lamp for their house "Tribschen," which sat on Lake Lucerne.[71]

Semper's liberal use of color is directly related to the important role he played in the discovery of polychromy among the ancients. In the 1830s he had asserted that the Parthenon had been painted red, set off with hints of green, purple, and gold.[72] When one bears in mind that the Parthenon represented the focal point of classical architecture, his choice to lavishly apply color to the interior of the new synagogue in Dresden takes on a deeper meaning about the essential interconnectedness of human cultures. Applying Semper's theory that the polychromatic decoration of Greek temples should "precisely resemble the appearance of a fine day in an eastern climate," his subtle move to do for the interior of the synagogue what the Greeks had executed on the exterior of the Parthenon—Semper also designed the synagogue's chandeliers—should leave us in no doubt that his intention was to highlight the Eastern origins of the Jews and the luminous quality of their faith.

With his liberal and tolerant sensibilities, Semper captured the duality of Jewish identity. The exterior of the building was for all intents and purposes German. Its mixed elements and even its pyramidal roof, a feature of medieval German churches, was Semper's way of recognizing the Germanness of his Jewish clients. His choice of an Oriental interior was his way of acknowledging both the incompleteness of the emancipation project and what he considered the splendid Eastern origins of the Jews. Among those Jews who pushed for the building of the synagogue, the head of the Dresden Jewish community, Bernhard Beer, reflected on the salutary effects of the "new community synagogue, wherein uplifting sermons in the German language would be held regularly, and through the promotion of the religious-moral sensibility of the Israelites the whole population of Dresden will be enriched; [and] architecturally, the city will have gained a new adornment."[73]

LEIPZIG

While the New Temple in Dresden was not directly emulated elsewhere, Semper's innovation would be taken up more fully in other major cities, where both the exteriors and interiors of synagogues most spectacularly reflected the flowering of the orientalist turn in Jewish architecture. Where Semper was the master, it was his apprentice, Otto Simonson (1829–1914), who designed what was Germany's first fully neo-Moorish synagogue. It was located in Leipzig, the only other city in Saxony, besides Dresden, in which Jews were permitted to reside. The city's Reform congregation commissioned the Dresden native Simonson, one of the few Jewish architects at that time in Germany, to design their new synagogue. In 1853 he submitted his plans to the Leipzig city building inspector, C. Kanitz, and the art historian Ludwig Puttrich, for it was these two men who had the final say on all proposals. Simonson's submission was approved, and two years later, on September 10, 1855, the synagogue's dedication ceremony took place, with thousands in attendance.[74]

Because of the Leipzig fair, the city drew many Jews of widely differing cultural orientations. There were therefore many small synagogues in the city, and the goal of the community and municipal authorities alike was to build a central synagogue for the use of all Jews. It is for this reason that Simonson's house of worship was designed to accommodate 2,000 worshippers, with seating for 1,200.[75] Of the many features that made this synagogue so distinctive, its orientation was among the most striking, and it was made integral to the Oriental appearance of the building. Located at the spot where two streets met, the synagogue conformed in its design to the unusual layout of the block of land upon which it sat and thus was constructed in the shape of an isosceles triangle, a fact that enhanced the building's exotic character. The synagogue thus had two facades, one on the Zentralstrasse and the other on the Gottschedstrasse. At the very point of the building, where the two angles met, there was a wall, and against it stood a massive semicircular, silo-like structure, on top of which was a highly polished, fluted copper cupola, framed by a horseshoe arch, crowned with a Star of David. On the synagogue's interior, it was this exterior, cylindrical-shaped edifice that was home to the ark that held the Torah scrolls.[76] Resting directly upon the triangular outer walls was a massive rectangular gallery with a sloping roof; carved into the gable was a five-arched frieze, composed of Islamic horseshoe arches, which were in turn crowned with a representation of the two Tablets of the Law. The sides of the rooftop gallery were broken up by three sets of triple windows, each topped with trefoil arches. The synagogue's two massive facades were punctuated by four gigantic arch moldings, which stood out in relief against the plaster outer walls. They ran up from street level to just short of the roof, and above them sat a small rosette window. Inside the first and fourth arches there were single windows crowned with a horseshoe arch, while the second and third arches contained two sets of double windows, one at the first-floor level, illuminating the men's section, the other at the upper level, which allowed light into the women's gallery, all similarly crowned with horseshoe arches. Running along the top of the outer walls were crenellated parapets. Identical, unobtrusive street-level entrances were placed in the fourth arch on either facade. These entrances were housed in towers that contained the stairs leading up to the women's gallery. Likewise topped with battlements, the towers, together with the rampart-like facade, endowed the synagogue with the appearance of a fortress. Of all the synagogues in Germany at that date, Leipzig's most closely resembled a North African or Spanish mosque.[77]

The synagogue's spacious triple-aisled interior reflected a continuation of what Simonson called "Moorish" style, but with the consistent goal of adapting that form to meet contemporary Jewish needs, architecturally and in terms of identity politics. The focal point of the interior was the Torah shrine, an ornate structure, which resembled a mosque's *mihrab*. It was housed

Die Synagoge der israelitischen Gemeinde zu Leipzig, entworfen von dem Architecten Otto Simonson, in ihrer dereinstigen Vollendung.

3.6. Leipzig synagogue (exterior). William A. Rosenthall Judaica Collection, Special Collections, College of Charleston.

in the apse, in front of which hung a highly embroidered curtain, which, depending on the occasion, was easily substituted with another of different color and design. Immediately above the ark holding the Torah scrolls was a giant rose window, which drew light not directly from the outside but indirectly through a small aperture in the apse's calotte, or rounded cavity. With the decoration of the interior, the architect took great liberties, applying here Islamic elements and there Christian architectural features, such as the rose window and chandeliers—and he applied Islamic forms of decoration to these "Christian" elements. Simonson shared the predilection for polychromy so beloved by his teacher, Semper, and he rendered the apse a blaze of color. Yellow skirting boards formed the base for green walls, which rose to meet a stunning blue ceiling bedecked with stars and a giant sun. All of this was further illuminated by the bright light that streamed in through the colored rose window.

A monumentally large and highly decorated horseshoe arch framed the whole eastern end of the synagogue. Another small rosette sat immediately above the arch at its highest point, kissing the base of a series of five trefoil windows, thus continuing a feature that marked the synagogue's exterior. The giant arch that spanned the width of the central nave served a number of purposes: it formed the entrance to the gallery containing the ark; it created a dramatic distinction between the apse and the central nave; and, finally, the relatively short lateral extensions at the base of either side of the arch linked the upstairs women's galleries on either side of the nave. When congregants faced the great arch, to its left they saw the pulpit, an orientalized masterpiece that looked similar to a mosque's *minbar*, with marble stairs leading up to a platform from where the sermon was delivered, and where the preacher stood beneath a dome roof that hung, seemingly suspended in midair, above his head. The Oriental pattern was repeated along the length of the women's galleries as one large horseshoe arch after another formed an arcade along the front of the women's section. Stationed above each arch a triple trefoil window sat at the highest point in every clerestory and served to unite walls and ceiling. The latter, thatched with longitudinal beams and crossbeams, sporting stalactite carvings hanging from the joints, was highly ornate and paneled, decorated with rosettes, floral tendrils, and geometric designs.[78] The entire effect was a beautifully harmonious exercise in symmetry, ornamentation, and Jewish architectural and artistic innovation.

Simonson, whose father was the custodian of a Dresden synagogue, remained firmly fixed on designing a uniquely Jewish building, one that was simultaneously new and informed by Judaism's ancient history. While the Moorish design of the synagogue constituted the "modern" insofar as no other contemporary (or past) German buildings looked like it, thus making it uniquely new and Jewish, the overall design drew its legitimacy from Simonson's interpretation of where the synagogue stood in relation to Jewish architectural history. And here, he considered what he had built in Leipzig to be a descendant of the ancient Temple in Jerusalem. Tellingly, in all official publications, including his own, Simonson's house of worship was always referred to as a "temple," never as a synagogue. Beyond nomenclature there was architecture itself. Simonson imagined that the layout of the structure in Jerusalem consisted of an entrance hall, a main gallery, and the Holy of Holies. Somewhat cryptically, he considered his building in Leipzig to be a "completion of the tripartite division of [Solomon's] Temple."[79] By "completion" it would seem that Simonson was referring to Judaism's evolution from a religion based on sacrifice mediated by a ruling priestly class to a democratic, participatory faith, a transformation that is reflected in a religious architecture that now required a sanctuary in which the mass of worshippers could pray. The evolution was also a geographic and cultural one. While Judaism began in and remained inextricably tied to the East and later flourished under Islam, particularly that which took root in Spain, it

3.7. Leipzig synagogue (interior).

was now in Germany that Simonson invented a new Jewish national architecture to complement the new expression of religious piety—Reform Judaism:

> The Temple is built in the Moorish style, which appears to me to be the most characteristic. Judaism adheres with unshakable reverence to its history; its laws, its customs and practices, the organization of its ritual; in short, its entire essence lives in its reminiscences of its motherland, the Orient. It is those reminiscences that the architect must accommodate should he wish to impress upon the building a typical [Jewish] stamp. And yet he retains sufficient freedom only if he were to understand which Oriental flowers were the correct ones and skillfully pick them. [By doing so] he will not lapse into deadly imitation but rather he will judiciously capture the necessary motifs and work them harmoniously into something new. . . . Then he will have a work in which he can rejoice, one that is singular, different from others, that is separated off and yet finds amicable acceptance.[80]

For Simonson, the building became a metaphor for Leipzig's Jews. They were not to deny their Oriental heritage. Instead, they were to embrace it, all the while recognizing and celebrating the cultural distance they had traveled, the reward for which would be "amicable acceptance." Not long after completing his masterpiece, Simonson left Germany for Russia. The New Temple in Leipzig would be the last synagogue he ever built. Taking up residency in St. Petersburg, he soon thereafter converted to Christianity in order to wed the daughter of a Russian official.[81] Whether Simonson considered his new religion to merely be a decorative patina covering his indelible, Oriental Jewish core we will never know. What is certain is that the "amicable acceptance" he wished for his own Jewish community of Dresden would be accorded to him by his new family only on the condition that he renounce Judaism and become a Christian.

VIENNA

Just as the neo-Moorish architectural revival was an international movement, so too were orientalized synagogues to be found the world over. While Germany was home to the largest concentration of such buildings, our story gains an added dimension if we leave Germany but still remain in German-speaking Europe, training our sights on Vienna. It was there, on June 15, 1858, that one of the jewels of orientalized synagogue architecture, the Leopoldstädter Tempel, was formally dedicated.

As was the case elsewhere in German lands, there was a noticeable growth in the size of the Jewish population after midcentury. As migration from the hinterlands increased, the Jewish population of Vienna rose from a mere

6,000 to 7,000 on the eve of the 1848 revolutions, and to 52,350 by the late 1860s.[82] This explosive twenty-year growth led to calls for the building of new synagogues to accommodate the rising Jewish population, now including an ever-growing number of Orthodox Jews from Galicia. After the middle of the century, the majority of Vienna's Jews lived in the city's second district, the Leopoldstadt. Home to rich and poor, secular and Orthodox, it was a variegated, highly diverse and densely populated neighborhood. The existing Seitenstettengasse synagogue, an elegant, oval-shaped, Biedermeier structure built between 1825 and 1826, was simply too small for the growing population, and the municipal authorities were determined to close down the myriad unofficial Jewish prayer houses that dotted the area. For these reasons Emperor Franz Joseph acceded to the community's request and granted them permission to erect a new "nonsectarian" synagogue in the Leopoldstadt.[83]

Following a design competition, the city authorities selected the submission of Ludwig Förster (1797–1863), a German-born architect living in Vienna. A major figure in his profession, Förster was a politically well-connected professor at the Viennese Academy and a founder of the major Austrian journal for architecture, the *Allgemeine Bauzeitung* (General Journal for Construction). He was responsible for many of Vienna's finest buildings and was one of the key designers of Vienna's iconic Ringstrasse, a broad belt of land containing a mix of public and private buildings that encircled the old city, separating it from the new suburbs.[84] In 1836, the year Förster founded his journal, he observed that the "genius" of the nineteenth century was that it was an era without its own architectural style. It had, he wrote, "no decisive color."[85] An architect dedicated to innovation, Förster believed that history must serve as a guide to forging a contemporary style for differently purposed buildings. In the *Allgemeine Bauzeitung's* first issue, Förster laid out the editorial goals and intellectual program of the journal, informing readers that one section of his publication would be dedicated to news of the latest archaeological discoveries.[86] It is precisely this sensibility that he introduced into his design of one of the world's grandest orientalized synagogues.

The emphasis here is on the description of the synagogue as "orientalized," as opposed to neo-Moorish, for it was so much more than merely the latter. To be sure, the synagogue bore all the typical features of neo-Moorish urban synagogues, frequently referencing the Alhambra.[87] However, it was pathbreaking rather than imitative. In contrast to the Seitenstettengasse synagogue, which was deliberately tucked away behind a courtyard on a dingy side street, Förster's new temple was prominent and bathed in light on all sides. It had a tripartite facade with a central risalit, which housed a monumental Romanesque portal for the main entrance, and large round-arched windows on the flanks and sides of the building. Large quatrefoil windows

ANSICHT nach der NATUR.

BETHAUS
der israelitischen Cultusgemeinde
(in der Leopoldstadt)

Verlage Artaria & C. in Wien

3.8. Leopoldstädter Tempel. Vienna. William A. Rosenthall Judaica Collection, Special Collections, College of Charleston.

that encased a second, smaller, quatrefoil window sat above the arches, a feature that wrapped around the sides of the building. Running along the top of the synagogue on all sides was an ornate crenellated cornice; colorful linear and geometric patterns adorned the exterior, and the stucco work, with its predominantly yellow, red, and dark gray color scheme, took on the appearance of an ornate Oriental rug.[88]

The men entered through the central portal; woman entered through the north and south towers that flanked the central entrance, and they climbed the staircases housed in the towers up to the grand, split-level women's galleries. The pillars holding up the galleries and the balustrades were

JUDEN-TEMPEL

Wien, bei L. T. Neumann
Ausschliessendes Eigenthum des Verlegers.

3.9. Leopoldstädter Juden Tempel. Vienna.

made from delicate wrought iron work, which added a note of whimsy and airiness.[89] Synagogues were among the earliest and most frequent users of wrought iron when it appeared for the first time in the nineteenth century, thus making such houses of worship innovative not merely in an aesthetic sense but in a technical one as well.

The interior layout of this colossal synagogue, which seated two thousand worshippers, was built with a triple-aisled basilica floor plan, with the walls and ceiling a kaleidoscope of blazing colors and carved ornamentation, including lavish tile mosaics from the great English ceramic manufacturer Minton, and paintwork in gold, red, blue, yellow, and green. The most heavily decorated part of the interior and its centerpiece was the eastern wall, home to the ark, which was framed by a triple-layered arch and decorative pillars, on top of which sat the Tablets of the Law and, above it, a magnificent rose, all of which was further housed inside a monumental arch. The ceiling, suspended over the eastern end of the synagogue, was punctuated with a gigantic skylight, which, together with the side windows,

3.10. Leopoldstädter Tempel (interior; watercolor by
Emil Ranzenhofer).

allowed for as much sunlight to pour in as Vienna could provide. Förster
stated that in order to prevent worshippers from being disturbed by strong
sunlight, these leadlight windows were made of blue, red, and yellow glass,
which provided a "calming and solemn" color scheme. When natural day-
light was in short supply or services were held at night, the interior was
illuminated with chandeliers, which bore five hundred gaslights, all replicas
of wax candles.[90]

All of these features represent the synagogue's debt to Moorish building,
but in no way does this define the limits of Jewish orientalist architecture.

Förster's commitment to historicization led him to the belief that the guiding principle for contemporary synagogue design was to "select those architectonic forms that served those peoples related to the Israelites, in particular the Arabs, and admit only those modifications that are conditioned by climate and the discovery of new building techniques." In his address at the cornerstone-setting ceremony of the synagogue on March 15, 1858, Förster declared that the optimal way to arrive at the appropriate building style in this instance was to take into account the latest archaeological discoveries concerning "ancient Oriental building styles" in the region of the Tigris and the Euphrates. It was the findings from these digs, ones that he said corresponded to the biblical descriptions of Solomon's Temple, that were to inform the synagogue architect's choice of layout and motifs. For Förster, it was those decisions, based on sound historical and archaeological evidence, that would allow the new temple in Vienna to be in accord with its ancient forerunner in Jerusalem.[91]

According to Förster, the layout of his temple was modeled on that of Solomon's and was divided into three main sections: a vestibule, a main sanctuary, and the eastern end, where the ark was to be found.[92] But Vienna's synagogue was to be linked with more than just Solomon's Temple. It would be a multicultural mélange of many Oriental building styles, materials, and techniques—the application of all kinds of stones and bricks for the walls, Assyrian enameled tiles modeled on those used at Nineveh, Persian polygonal designs, cornices heavily decorated with overlapping, bejeweled niches, and round-arched arcades, and walls bedecked with designs composed of plaited plants, bands, lines, palms, and chains.[93] As such, the Leopoldstädter Temple was to serve as a most visible manifestation of an organic connection that bound the Jews of Vienna not merely to the Israelites but to all the peoples of the ancient Near East. Here was an expansive orientalist view of Jews, one that saw them not as an isolated, small, parochial tribe but as one component of a larger ethnic constellation of peoples, sharing space and culture. Moreover, could there be a better metaphor for the highly diverse Jews of the Austro-Hungarian Empire or the empire itself? One among many, the Jews were at home in this multinational environment, where they both partook of the culture of the majorities among whom they lived and simultaneously contributed to them. Förster hinted at this in his description of one crucial aspect of the synagogue's exterior. As he envisioned it, the right and left pillars on the facade's central risalit recalled those two columns on Solomon's Temple, the one named after Boaz on the left and the other after Jachin on the right. And then, Förster declared, "to erect such columns in front of temples has passed into Arabic architecture, and we find such in the form of minarets (light towers) among the Orientals in general."[94] Of course, the minarets were not light towers, and the architecture of the Arabs was not influenced by that of the Israelites.

That, however, is beside the point. Förster's claims about the Jewish people and their place in the world, their ability to both learn from and teach those among whom they lived, was as valid for the ancient Near East as it was for the Central Europe of his day. Rather than marginalize and segregate them, Förster, in his orientalizing of the Jews, provided a positive affirmation of both their assimilability and their right to celebrate their difference.

BERLIN

At the time of its building, the Neue Synagoge on the Oranienburgerstrasse was the biggest, costliest, and easily the most conspicuous synagogue in Europe, if not the world. It was designed in the 1850s and inaugurated in 1866; the time of its advent marks a challenge to those historical interpretations that see in the synagogue an expression of German-Jewish cultural and political self-confidence. Rather, the synagogue was, paradoxically, an expression of self-assertion born of uncertainty, of dashed political hopes, and of frustration with a Jewish cultural and economic status that was not matched by the security that came with full political and legal equality. Seen against the backdrop of the failure of the revolutions of 1848 to rectify the subordinate civic status of the Jews, and the continued conservative re-action against them, the Neue Synagoge was a raucous cry for emancipation and not a heady celebration in anticipation of it. This liberal community, one that favored moderate reforms, presented the synagogue to the city of Berlin as a fait accompli, one that betokened the permanent presence of the city's Jews. The imposing structure was meant to signal to the Prussian government that it could no longer avoid Jews as neighbors, nor could it ignore their political anomalousness. Whatever its internal purposes the new synagogue was also intended to awaken the German authorities to a new reality.[95]

Though it was opened in 1866, the Neue Synagoge's history actually began in 1846, when the Jewish community submitted a request to build a new synagogue in Berlin Mitte, the area of the city with the highest concentration of Jews. As was the case elsewhere in Germany, Berlin's Jewish community was growing rapidly, and a new synagogue was desperately needed. In 1840, approximately 6,500 Jews lived in Berlin, a number that rose to nearly 9,600 in 1848; by 1855 that number had risen to just over 12,500, and by 1861 the Jewish population had grown to just under 19,000. With continued migration to the city from Germany's eastern provinces, the Jewish population reached 28,000 in 1866, the year the Neue Synagoge was inaugurated, and climbed to 36,000 in 1871, the year of German unification, the founding of the Second Reich, and the formal emancipation of the Jews.[96]

When the congregation first petitioned for a new synagogue, its proposal
was vetoed by King Frederick William IV, who insisted instead that the synagogue be built on the outskirts of the city in the district of Kreuzberg.
There were several reasons for the veto: the king and city officials feared the
synagogue would draw even more Jews to central Berlin, that it would prove
a disturbance to those attending nearby church services, and that promoting an area at considerable distance from the city center would contribute
to the building up of undeveloped areas of the city.[97] However, these were
not the only reasons for the twenty-year time span between the submission
of the first request to build and the opening of the new synagogue. German
preoccupation with the midcentury revolutions and the threat they posed
to the existing order took precedence over all government activities. On
the Jewish side, anxieties over the impact of the ever-widening communal
split between Orthodox and Reform factions led the executive council of
the community to shelve the initial plans and instead renovate and expand
the existing synagogue on the Heidereutergasse. With this decision they
hoped that some form of harmonious coexistence might emerge; more importantly, they wished to prevent what would inevitably have become the
widening influence of the Reformers over the community at large once
they had attained their own synagogue.[98]

The architect they chose for this commission was the Eduard Knoblauch
(1801–1865). A student of the great Prussian architect and city planner Karl
Friedrich Schinkel and one of the most important German architects of
the nineteenth century, Knoblauch renovated the synagogue on the Heidereutergasse in a style that combined the classical and the Romanesque.[99]
Considered an aesthetic success, the building nevertheless failed to solve the
problem that had led to the renovation in the first place, namely, the lack of
space. The newly remodeled synagogue plus the temporary Notsynagoge,
also called the Interims Synagoge—which housed an astonishing 1,800
worshippers and had been renovated with private, as opposed to communal, funds—were still unable to accommodate the expanding Jewish community of Berlin.[100]

In 1856 the Reform congregation purchased a plot of land at Oranienburgerstrasse 30 even before they had received final permission to build.[101]
The congregation announced an international competition to choose an
architect for a "brightly lit" synagogue that was stipulated to hold a mini-
mum of 2,200 seats (1,200 for men and 800 for women), upstairs galleries
for the women, entrances separated according to sex, sufficient space for a
60-person choir, and an apartment for the rabbi, as well as administrative
offices and classrooms. The total cost was not to exceed 125,000 taler. The
judging panel, which was composed of members of the Berlin Association
of Architects, ultimately declared the winner to be Eduard Knoblauch, who,
coincidentally, also lived on the Oranienburgerstrasse.[102] The congregation's

haste in moving ahead in this fashion was indicative its desire to effect the course of events rather than wait passively for the government to make decisions on their behalf.

As with some of the other synagogues we have examined, the shape of the block of land on the Oranienburgerstrasse was not ideal for erecting a monumental synagogue—the frontage was narrow relative to the depth of the plot, and the land itself did not run along a straight, rectangular, East-West axis, but rather was crooked, with a sort of dogleg shape. While this fact posed considerable architectural problems, the location, on one of Berlin's main thoroughfares in the heart of a Jewish district, was optimal. The rather low two- and three-story homes that ran the course of the street guaranteed that the proposed synagogue would tower above everything in the vicinity.[103]

Knoblauch's designs for the synagogue evolved over time. The extant plans testify to his struggle to adequately fill the space by meeting both architectural requirements and the community's needs. What began as a relatively unadorned Schinkelsque design, with *Rundbogenstil* exterior features and a "baroque monumentality" on the interior, ended up a highly ornate neo-Moorish structure that was both an ornament to the city and a statement by the congregation that they intended to be seen. No longer would they accept synagogues that were hidden in backstreets or on the outskirts of town. Instead, as the call for tenders articulated, "the synagogue had to be visible from the street, and the building as well as the entrance had to correspond to the purpose of a dignified display."[104]

There was, of course, no better way to be seen than to build an opulent neo-Moorish house of worship in the middle of Berlin. When the synagogue was completed, its boldness and magnitude were apparent to all. For the exterior Knoblauch used yellow masonry through which he ran horizontal stripes of red brick. Cornices and plinths were made of hewn granite, while all doors and windows facing the exterior were framed in red sandstone surrounds. The height of the facade was 92 feet, while the depth of the synagogue was 308 feet. The great design problem that Knoblauch struggled with was the sharp turn the plot of land took, and how to construct a building that did not look crooked or askew when viewed from the street. His solution was to build, directly on the spot where the ground plan revealed its awkward angle, a dodecagonal vestibule that was invisible from the exterior. At the roof each face of the twelve-sided structure contained windows and Islamic decorative elements and served as the base for the synagogue's showpiece, the onion dome that soared majestically some 160 feet into the air. Wrapped in a blanket of zinc and swaddled in gold ribbing, crowned with a Star of David, the great dome was the brightest and most joyful architectural feature to be found anywhere in Berlin. The dome shone incandescently in the sunlight, its visibility enhanced by virtue of the fact that rather than occupying the space over the central intersection of the ground plan, as was the case in most houses of worship, irrespective of religion, this one sat perched at the front of the building. This is precisely what the clients demanded from their architect. The synagogue was intended to draw attention to itself, the Jewish community, and the city of Berlin.

The exterior was a mixture of Islamic and Romanesque elements, the combination of the two only heightening the Oriental appearance of the building. The facade was triple fronted, with the central section set back from the two structures flanking it, rather than protruding, as was the case with the Leopoldstädter Temple in Vienna. From the street level the portal that was the men's entrance consisted of three doors, which led into a vaulted vestibule and then onto a second hall, which in turn led into the small synagogue with a vaulted ceiling that was used for daily services. The three doors constituting the entranceway were encased in three very tall pointed-arched windows above which was a highly decorated relief, and above this a further three, round-arched windows composed of sixty-three panes of glass, in a neo-Gothic style. Each window section was topped with three porthole windows, two smaller ones on either side of a large rosette window. The three pointed arches of the portal sat atop four slender granite columns directly copied from the Alhambra. The capitals were coated in bronzed zinc. Running along the top of the entire building was a diamond-pattern crenellation. Just as was the case with the neo-Moorish masterpiece, the Dohányi synagogue in Budapest, designed by Ludwig Förster, the central section of the Neue Synagoge's facade was flanked by two towers, the one on the right housing the Jewish community administration and a library with 67,000 volumes. The tower on the left served as a Jewish museum. At street level, the towers, which were linked by an elaborate iron lattice grate, also served as the entrances to the staircases leading upstairs to the women's galleries. Above each of these towers were a further two octagonal structures that contained eight rectangular-paned windows topped with round-arched windows; a decorative horizontal band of masonry separated these windows from the six square windows that sat just below the magnificent onion domes crowning the octagonal towers. The tops of the cupolas stood approximately a hundred feet off the ground; they were smaller versions of the great central dome and helped unify the entire facade.

Though Europeanized, the exterior minarets borrowed heavily from North African mosques and from the Giralda, a late twelfth-century minaret in Seville, while the magnificent crenellations that adorned the top of the synagogue were typical of those found in Cairene mosques. In its general shape, the great dome revealed similarities to Persian domes such as that at Isfahan, although its decoration owes much to seventeenth-century Indian mosques, not to mention the more recently built Royal Pavilion at

3.11. Emil de Cauwer, *Synagoge in der Oranienburger Straße, 1865* (Berlin).

Brighton.[105] It was, in other words, a pan-Islamic-style building that drew on the finest Arab examples and European interpretations of mosque architecture.[106]

With seating for 3,200 worshippers, the triple-nave interior was a massive 188 feet long, 126 feet wide, and soared to a height of 87 feet.[107] The side galleries on the ground-floor level were divided into ten sections, each delineated by slender iron columns, which rose to support the women's galleries, formed by an arcade of five giant arches. At the eastern end of the sanctuary was the monumental apse, the back wall of which housed the choir in an arcaded niche composed of rounded arches. This was also where the organ, invisible to the public, was housed. In the center of the apse was a freestanding *aron ha-kodesh*, the holy shrine in which the Torah scrolls were housed. The shrine was a square multistory structure, with a giant rounded arch for an opening, and was crowned with a dome. Like the lectern and the pulpit, the shrine was made of shimmering white marble. A bronze grate and carpet-covered marble stairs that spanned the width of the apse separated this section of the synagogue from the main sanctuary. The entire interior was a dazzling kaleidoscope of color, light, and texture. With Moorish decorative patterns from the thirteenth and fourteenth centuries, the floors were inlaid with intricate mosaics; the walls were covered in richly colored stucco and then painted with stars and flora, while stalactite features hung from the ceiling, and geometric and honeycomb patterns were widely deployed, including on the elaborate friezes that accented the temple's interior. A technical breakthrough helped bathe the entire synagogue in a palette of many colors. The windows were double paned, with the outer windows made of clear glass and the inner windows of stained glass. An innovative system of gas lamps was installed in between the two panes throughout the synagogue. While the myriad windows allowed for abundant light to pour into the synagogue, the placement of the gas lamps and the way they illuminated the stained glass helped create what one attendee at the synagogue's dedication ceremony in 1866 called a "magical effect."[108]

Owing to illness Knoblauch stopped work on the building in 1859, and he was succeeded by August Stüler. Both men had passed away by the time the synagogue was dedicated on September 5, 1866. In the presence of an array of official dignitaries, including Otto von Bismarck, the architects' work was recognized in the encomiums. The Neue Synagoge was an immediate sensation. A contemporary newspaper account vividly described the synagogue as "a fairy-tale structure. . . . In the middle of a plain part of the city we are led into the fantastic wonder of the Alhambra, with graceful columns, sweeping arches, richly colored arabesques, abundant wood carvings, all with the thousandfold magic of the Moorish style."[109] A report of the dedication ceremony in another newspaper sought to explain what the

3.12. Torah ark. G. Knoblauch and F. Hollin, "Die Neue Synagoge in Berlin" (1867).

synagogue meant for Berlin's urban landscape: "The new house of worship is the pride of the Berlin Jewish community; but even more, it is an ornament to the city, one of the most remarkable creations of modern architecture in the Moorish style, and one of the finest construction projects that the northern German seat of royal power (*Residenzstadt*) has carried out in recent years."[110] There could be no more appropriate a reporter than Lewis Carroll, author of *Alice in Wonderland*, who, together with the English theologian, Henry Liddon, visited the Neue Synagoge on Friday, July 19, 1867. In Berlin on their way to Russia, Carroll noted in his diary that after a full day of sightseeing, "later in the evening we strolled out and looked at the Jewish Synagogue, said to be well worth the inspection." His first cursory visit was followed by a second the very next day:

> We began the day by visiting the Jewish Synagogue, where we found the service going on, and remained until it was over. The scene was perfectly novel to me, & most interesting. The building itself is most gorgeous, almost the whole interior surface being gilt or otherwise decorated—the arches were nearly all semi-circular, tho' there were a few instances of the shape sketched here—the east end was roofed with a circular dome, & contained a small dome on pillars, under which was a cupboard (concealed by a curtain) which contained the roll of the Law: in front of that again a small desk facing west—the latter was only once used. The rest of the building was fitted up with open seats. We followed the example of the congregation in keeping our hats on. Many men, on reaching their places, produced white silk shawls out of embroidered bags, & these they put on square fashion: the effect was most singular—the upper edge of the shawl had what looked like gold embroidery, but was probably a phylactery [*sic*]. These men went up from time to time & read portions of the lessons. What was read was all in German, but there was a great deal chanted in Hebrew, to beautiful music: some of the chants have come down from very early times, perhaps as far back as David. The chief Rabbi chanted a great deal by himself, without music. The congregation alternately stood & sat down: I did not notice anyone kneeling.[111]

What is curious and what makes the Neue Synagoge different from those at Dresden, Leipzig, and Vienna is that Knoblauch never articulated an ideological motive behind his decision to build in an Oriental manner. The sources reveal only that he chose a neo-Moorish design because it was appropriate for this "large, self-contained community."[112] To be sure, the neo-Moorish style had become almost exclusively identified in Germany with synagogue architecture, so on that score Knoblauch was operating on the basis of precedent and custom. There is no direct evidence, however, that Knoblauch set out to build an Oriental palace for an Oriental people. They did not seek to reconnect with their Oriental past; rather, what was being articulated by this particular congregation might be termed a *Prachtsideol-*

OPENING OF THE NEW JEWISH SYNAGOGUE, BERLIN.—SEE PAGE 277.

3.13. "Opening of the new Jewish synagogue, Berlin," *Illustrated London News*, 22 September 1866.

ogie, an ideology of splendor, a purely aesthetic imperative to create a stunning, monumental synagogue, one that demonstrated that Jews could be a people with an eye for the beautiful. Knoblauch's neo-Moorish design was an expression of grandeur and good taste, and the congregation happily accepted it because they believed it spoke loudest to those who continued to deny them their rights.

Knoblauch's choice was also governed by the project's structural demands and the opportunities they afforded him. He was a pioneer in the use of steel frames for the building of synagogues, and the use of such material, especially the graceful iron pillars, lent itself to building in the neo-Moorish style. This meant that the heavy masonry of the Romanesque style could be avoided.[113] What could easily be dismissed as an exercise in isolating and stigmatizing the community, by orientalizing it, would do a disservice to both Knoblauch's and his clients' intentions. In the choice of this design Knoblauch was able to provide them with a technically cutting-edge structure that critics and other professional architects unanimously considered a triumphant example of modern building construction. Indeed Knoblauch, one of the greatest architects of his era, considered the synagogue to be his "most successful" professional achievement.[114]

While many observers registered their astonishment at the beauty and technical proficiency manifested in Knoblauch's synagogue, there were many for whom such a building was either a source of embarrassment or a confirmation of everything that they had long believed, namely, that the Jews were aliens of different racial stock and the synagogue was proof that they could never become Germans. The greatest praise for the synagogue, indeed for most of the Oriental synagogues in Germany, came from well-intentioned Christian architects or newspaper reporters. It was they who promoted the idea that German Jews required their own Jewish national building style, and it was largely they who opted for Oriental designs.

For the few Jewish architects in Germany, such synagogues were an architectural and ideological error. The designer of the neo-Gothic synagogue in Hamburg, Edwin Oppler, had been a student and colleague of the great French exponent of Gothic Revival architecture Eugène-Emmanuel Viollet le Duc, and had worked with him on the restoration of Notre Dame in Paris. Oppler's preference for Romanesque and especially neo-Gothic sought to present Jews as being an integral part of the German past. Appealing to precedent, he noted that Jews had always built in the "German style," and pointed to those synagogues constructed in Germany from the ninth century to the fourteenth. A year prior to the opening of Berlin's Neue Synagoge, Oppler declared: "The German Jew wants above all to be German, he struggles and suffers for equality with his Christian brothers. Can and should he then isolate himself by means of his house of God without any ritual basis for doing so?" A shared history demanded a shared architecture; hence Oppler insisted that "a building, if it wants to make a claim to monumentality, must above all be national. The German Jew in a German state should therefore build in a German style." Railing against neo-Moorish synagogues, which, he claimed, "had not the slightest connection to Judaism," Oppler looked forward to the day when "no Jewish community would build in this style."[115]

Other Jews objected on different grounds. Concerns were expressed that though most Jews still lived in Berlin Mitte, many had begun to move out, and this new synagogue was at an inconvenient distance for those who had departed the old neighborhood. For others, it was about the expense of the synagogue on the Oranienburgerstrasse. Despite an initial budget of 125,000 taler, the final cost had ballooned to a staggering 750,000 taler.[116] And here is where Berlin's Neue Synagoge was fodder for the antisemites. It was criticized for its opulence, its decadence, and for being a symbol of imagined Jewish power. Bigger than any church in the city, the synagogue represented what enemies of the Jews called the *Verjudung* (Jewification) of Germany. When the German orientalist and notorious antisemite Paul de Lagarde asserted that Jews could never become Germans, he pointed to the Neue Synagoge as evidence: "Through the style of their synagogue, the Jews emphasize [their] alien nature every day in the most obvious manner, though they nevertheless wish to enjoy equality with the Germans. What does it mean to claim a right to the honorable title of a German, while building your most holy sites in the Moorish style, so that no one can forget that you are a Semite, an Asian, an alien?"[117] Here, the worst fears of Jewish architects such as Albert Rosengarten and Edwin Oppler, as well as anonymous members of the community, were confirmed. Oriental synagogues, whether Egyptianized or neo-Moorish, served only to reify Jewish difference. Lagarde, who developed a Germano-Christian theology and believed that Jews practiced ritual murder and were engaged in a conspiracy against Germany, maintained that because of their religion, the Jews were an utterly separate and distinct group. Not only could they therefore never become Germans; he stated that the danger they posed demanded that they be exterminated like bacilli.[118] Long after it had been built, the synagogue remained a lightning rod for antisemites. In 1879, the antisemitic historian Heinrich von Treitschke, whom we shall meet again later, asserted bitterly that the power the Jews held over Germany was evidenced by the fact that "the most beautiful and opulent house of prayer in the capital was a synagogue."[119]

All of the Oriental synagogues built in Germany between 1830 and 1870—and there are numerous others that could be added to those analyzed here—filled a specific purpose and thus constitute an arresting chapter in the history of orientalist thought and practice, as well as the creation of a new, specifically Ashkenazic aesthetic. Mostly designed by Christian architects but approved of and paid for by Jews, these synagogues constitute a partnership, one whose significance is enhanced by the sums of money involved: the Jewish clients had to be absolutely sure that this was indeed what they wanted and how they wished to be seen. When it came to architecture, the process of orientalization was thus more symbiotic than coercive. To be sure, after 1870 the claims about Jews as Orientals were not benign and were part of the stock charges of the antisemitic movement. And indeed, after this date, Jews ceased to build new synagogues in the Oriental style, opting for other designs that were more inconspicuous. The Oriental moment in the history of Jewish architecture in Germany had passed.

The malleability of orientalist culture meant that different constituencies could arrive at different interpretations of the synagogues built in those styles. While many Christians saw the synagogues as reflective of the Jews' Oriental origins, whether seen positively or negatively, others saw them as worthy exemplars of a Jewish national style of architecture. Indubitably, the implication that Gothic was inappropriate for Jews sent a clear message that Germans and Jews were different. (It should be noted that despite this, a considerable number of neo-Gothic synagogues were built, and thus the granting of permission from Christian authorities to build in this style was not uncommon.) From the Jewish side there was not one congregation commissioning these synagogues that would not have considered itself to be German. But let us not forget that Germans and Jews were different, and that while they came to occupy the same cultural universe, Jews continued to be bearers of another, quite un-German culture. In other words, they carried with them a second load, and did so willingly. The orientalist synagogues reflected this more honestly than did the Romanesque and neo-Gothic, which served only to unsuccessfully camouflage the differences. In the content and ceremonial of their services, and in the aesthetic of synagogue officials and attendees, the Oriental synagogues were clearly German houses of Jewish prayer. Yet at the same time, as the process of acculturation progressed over the course of the nineteenth century, these glorious Oriental synagogues were also one of the most effective and elegant means by which German Jews could assert their difference and halt the slide toward invisibility.

The neo-Moorish synagogues gave rise to flights of fancy, transporting worshippers to bygone days of Jewish glory in medieval Spain. They were not, however, the only means by which the Sephardic experience was brought home to German Jews. At the same time that the synagogues were built, an entirely new form of Jewish popular culture began to appear. The historical novel presented readers with melodramatic and gripping tales of cruel inquisitors, Jewish martyrs, and heroic Marranos steadfastly holding on to their faith. Hardly anything did more to stimulate the Ashkenazic imagination and its image of Sephardic Jewry than Jewish belles lettres. We turn now to these page-turners.

CHAPTER FOUR

———◄●►———

Pleasure Reading

SEPHARDIC JEWS AND THE GERMAN-JEWISH
LITERARY IMAGINATION

These [Spanish] Jews, resembling all others both physically and mentally but granted by the Arabs equality with Muslims, proceeded to plumb in concert all the known sciences of the day. . . . And they employed [in their writings] not Hebrew but Arabic. Indeed those Jews expelled from this land to France, Holland, Italy, and England, to the detriment of Spanish economic life, and their still living progeny have never formed the contrast to Christian society which was so striking in the other family of Jews [the Ashkenazim] kept intentionally apart. They are marked by less discrepancy in morality, purer speech, greater order in the synagogue, and in fact better taste.[1]

It is with these words written in 1820 that a young Jewish law student, Eduard Gans, petitioned the Prussian government to approve the name and activities of his fledgling society, the Verein für Cultur und Wissenschaft der Juden (Association for the Culture and Scholarship of the Jews). Ever fearful of the revolutionary potential of young men forming new associations, the Prussian authorities policed such groups closely. Gans's paean to Sephardic Jews was intended to allay the fears of government officials. By extolling the acculturated virtues of Spanish Jewry, Gans sought to suggest that his generation of German Jews was just as dedicated to cultural and social fraternity with Christians as the Sephardic Jews had been with their Muslim neighbors. The authorities, in other words, had nothing to fear. Feeling assured, they granted permission for the establishment of the association, and Gans went on to serve as its president from 1821 to 1823.

Gans's appeal should be read as more than a mere formal request to a government agency. It was also a declaration of self-perception and a programmatic statement for the association he was attempting to found. Gans asserted that in body and mind, physical appearance and modes of thinking, the Sephardic Jews were at one with their Arab neighbors. They shared their intellectual pursuits, with Gans suggesting that it was the investigation of secular knowledge that had brought them together. Religious separation did not have to mean social and cultural separation. The vast realms of philosophy, medicine, and poetry existed as a shared cultural patrimony. Along with their meager belongings, the banished refugees of 1492 took their worldview with them, forged, as it had been, during the *convivencia*. That inheritance, characterized by openness to the world around them, had left such a deep impression upon Iberian Jewry that it manifested itself wherever Sephardic Jews settled. Moreover, their worldliness took on the form of an acquired and hereditary characteristic, passed on to the descendants of those who had been expelled from Spain. Most notably, their suffering and torment during the Reconquista had not made them insular, parochial, or unnaturally suspicious of Christians. The overall impact of this inheritance was to make the Sephardim morally and aesthetically superior to Ashkenazim. In contrast to their Spanish coreligionists, the medieval Jews of Germany and Poland had been unable to resist the negative consequences of the persecutory and unenlightened environments in which they lived. In their speech, in their appearance, in their culture, and in their attitude toward outsiders they were children of the ghetto. This was the tragic bequest the Ashkenazim had made to their progeny.

Over the long course of European history none of this seemed to matter very much. Europe made no efforts toward social unity, and so, as Gans observed, "as long as numerous groups had not been integrated into a totality,—this one particularity—Jewry—hardly seemed to be exceptional."[2] But times were changing; now Europe was beginning to derive its strength and meaning from the way that the plurality of the social classes functioned as a whole. According to Gans in an address he delivered to his association in 1822, the differences between groups were such that "no social class, and no social condition, is divided from any of the others by sharply drawn lines, which bespeak difference and unity at one and the same time."[3] The practical consequence of this philosophy as it applied to Jews was the hope that—and here Gans quoted the German philosopher and literary critic Johann Gottfried Herder—"There will be a time when no one in Europe will ask any longer, who is a Jew and who is a Christian?" Gans then asserted that "to hasten the coming of this day. . . . this is the task, gentlemen, which we have set for ourselves in establishing our society." It would be an association dedicated to the study of "Jewish religion, history and philosophy," one whose findings "will be integrated into the whole of human knowledge."[4]

Gans had a Hegelian understanding of the unfolding of history—in 1837 he published the first edition of Hegel's *Lectures on the Philosophy of World History*—and he internalized Hegel's view that Judaism and all other non-Western cultures were necessary but incomplete steps on the path toward the consciousness and objectification of human freedom, which would find "realized expression [only] in the cultures of modern Western societies." All of this informed the programmatic dimension of Gans's appeal to the authorities and his subsequent address to members of the association.[5] Neither the Jews nor Judaism would perish, he said, but "in the larger movement of the whole they will have seemed to disappear, and yet they will live on as the river lives on in the ocean." In other words Gans predicted that the Jews would become an invisible presence, and perhaps this was even his preference. Their impact would, like an ocean current, be felt but not seen.

Those who took up Gans's challenge to establish an "unbiased and completely independent" body dedicated to Jewish scholarship were not as sanguine as Gans was about Judaism's or the Jews' plunge into obscurity. Some of them may have shared his pessimism about the Jewish future, but they were not as dismissive of its past. Where he declared that the "studies of ignorant, prejudiced rabbis . . . did not produce any faithful or credible results," those who would actually become the practitioners of the academic study of Judaism sought, contra Gans, to highlight the exceptional moments in the Jewish past, moments when Judaism was "part of the whole" and was not "exclusive and isolated from other branches of knowledge."[6] The moments they frequently focused upon were those encounters that took place in the Islamic orbit, especially in Spain.

In this chapter and in the one to follow, we will encounter two new kinds of Jewish intellectuals—novelists and historians, both of whom played an enormous, indeed decisive, role in fueling the Ashkenazic imagination as it pondered and celebrated Sephardic aesthetics. Emerging for the first time in the nineteenth century, these two groups introduced entirely new textual traditions and thus expanded the definition and boundaries of Jewish culture. In the first instance, according to literature scholar Nitsa Ben-Ari, the value of the Jewish historical novels that were written in Germany in the nineteenth century "did not lie in their literary value—they were not written by or for a literary-cultural elite"; it lay, rather, in the central role they played in the emergence of a Jewish "national consciousness."[7] This was achieved largely under the mighty influence of the historical novelist Sir Walter Scott, who enjoyed enormous popularity in Germany, to the extent that he was credited with having awakened German national consciousness among German authors.[8] Epic tales that bolstered nationalist sentiment with political messages that valued freedom over tyranny struck a receptive chord. With Scott's chivalric romance *Ivanhoe* (1820), and its leading Jewish character, the beautiful Rebecca, her father the moneylender, Isaac of York, and its positive representation of Jews and frequent references to the persecution they faced, the author also became a hero to the Jewish public. His Rebecca was a model for the Jewish damsel who refuses to abandon her people, a figure that appears with some frequency in the historical novels we will encounter below. More generally, Scott's oeuvre legitimized the writing of Jewish novels that promoted ethnic solidarity, a development further enhanced by other popular English novels with philosemitic themes that appeared later on in the nineteenth century, among them Grace Aguilar's *Cedar Valley* (1850), Benjamin Disraeli's *Alroy* (1860), and George Eliot's *Daniel Deronda* (1876).[9]

Jewish historical novels, especially those set in Spain, also served other ends. By the time they began to appear in the late 1830s, German Jewry had just emerged from what was called a *Taufepidemie*, an "epidemic of baptisms," which lasted from approximately 1770 to 1830.[10] The Hebrew-language journal *Ha-Me'assef* had folded owing to the lack of a significant Hebrew readership, and increasing numbers of Jews had defected, even if only informally, from Jewish culture. The historical novel, thought some, could help stem the tide of assimilation. This was the view of the Reform rabbi Abraham Kohn of Hohenems, Austria, who opined that reading highly entertaining literature was the quickest and most effective means to promote "true humanitarianism [and] cultivation of the spirit and heart." It had the power to "spread [new] ideas [and] awaken feelings and senti-ments." If this were "true in general then how much truer is it true for we Israelites? We do not yet have an entertaining, German-language, popular and youth literature for Jews."[11]

Ironically, increasing Jewish assimilation was coterminous with the rise of the German romantic movement, which, with its celebration of folk cul-ture, medievalism, and rugged individualism as expressive of the soul of the nation, tended to exclude Jews, even if not explicitly. Just as a Jewish architecture was needed that would both reflect the Jewish past and take its place within the German public sphere, so too was a Jewish style of lit-erature required to satisfy the emotional and intellectual needs of German Jews for a past to which they could relate, while being simultaneously com-patible with newly emerging German literary trends. In the case of both buildings and books, cultural artifacts could be turned out so as to satisfy the German-Jewish need and desire to remain distinctive and visible while neither offending nor alienating their German neighbors.

In chapter 5, focusing on the writing of history, I will document a more intensive Jewish scholarly engagement with Islam than had previously ex-isted. Jewish historians who, like Eduard Gans, extolled the virtues of the Sephardic Jews—by which they meant those Jews who lived in Muslim Spain—frequently reached further back to examine Islam itself, beginning with its Arabian origins. They did this in order to examine its affinity with and its debt to Judaism, as well as explore the social and cultural context that made for the propitious circumstances Jewish communities enjoyed in the Muslim orbit. They also focused on the tragic consequences for Jews when tolerance was replaced by tyranny. What links Jewish novelists and Jewish historians in the embryonic phase of their respective pursuits is a shared commitment to recording and commemorating the Jewish past via the creation of a multigenre, secular, Jewish literary canon. And in this Jewish national literature, the Sephardim occupy a central position.

• • • • •

As this chapter is concerned with the novelistic transmission of ideas about Sephardic history, an understanding of the secular Jewish reading and writing practices that emerged in nineteenth-century Germany will help us better understand how a set of ideas about Spanish Jews came to have a sort of canonical authority, one that was central to both Jewish intellectual and popular culture. Beginning in the 1830s the transmission of ideas and new knowledge about the Jewish past was institutionalized among German Jews with the establishment of Jewish reading societies. Originally intended to promote general knowledge, these bodies eventually became sites where Jewish history was studied and discussed by readers. The number of such bodies, which functioned as lending libraries too, proliferated; they were also venues for public talks on all aspects of Jewish history. For example, Abraham Geiger, who will be discussed at length in the following chapter, founded the Jewish Teaching and Reading Association (Jüdischen Lehr-und Leseverein) in Breslau in 1842. Here, Geiger delivered public lectures on all aspects of the Jewish past, including the glory days in Spain. Now it must be admitted that all the publications and public talks in the 1830s and 1840s attracted very few people. This is most likely because Geiger and his fellow practitioners of scholarly Jewish history writing were actually opposed to its popularization and did little to render their work readable for the masses.[12]

Indeed, the German-Jewish public did not have the appetite to wade through the kind of dry, even if pathbreaking, scholarship of the practitioners of *Wissenschaft des Judentums* (Academic Study of Judaism). Despairingly, one of the founders of the association, the historian Leopold Zunz (1794–1886), wrote in a letter of 1830 to the Jewish librarian and historian from Hamburg Meyer Isler that "it is a real misfortune to write for Jews! The rich Jews do not pay attention, the Jewish scholars cannot read it, and the fools review it."[13] Zunz's ire seems misplaced. Writing a century later, the Anglo-Jewish historian and master stylist Cecil Roth described the cause of the situation Zunz so lamented, seeing it as an ongoing problem: "In England, history is a branch of literature; in Germany, it is a branch of science. It is perhaps not unfair to add that while in England scientific accuracy is regarded as essential, in Germany literary charm is considered a superfluous luxury." After the great historian Heinrich Graetz (1817–1891), who he conceded wrote in an "easy and graphic style," there wasn't one Jewish historian, according to Roth, save, perhaps, David Kaufmann in Budapest, "who was able to make real contributions to Jewish scholarship in a thoroughly readable form." Learned articles in scholarly journals and *Festschriften*, complained Roth, could not "be studied, even by the professional, with real pleasure." The same held true for popularized Jewish histories, for "they inspire in the intelligent reader a sense of revolt rather than of enthusiasm."[14]

Zunz underestimated his fellow Jews. The popular Jewish revolt against reading professional history did not mean that Jews were not interested in their collective past. Quite the contrary was true. One man who intuitively sensed that Jews might be moved, indeed enthralled, by Jewish history was Ludwig Philippson (1811–1899). The founder in 1837 of what would soon become Germany's major Jewish newspaper, the *Allgemeine Zeitung des Judentums*, Philippson believed that the answer to the Jewish public's apparent lack of interest in genuine historical scholarship was the publication of historical novels.[15] Holding to the view that they could instruct as well as capture the Jewish imagination, he declared belles lettres to be "a marriage between scholarship and poetry."[16] Moreover, Philippson believed in the power of popular literature to elevate the spiritual and cultural level of German Jewry; to that end he turned his paper into a venue for the publication of serialized works of Jewish historical fiction.[17]

Philippson's instincts were correct. As a newspaper publisher he read the spirit of the times better than the closeted historians. The first half of the nineteenth century saw a significant expansion of the German reading public, and among Jews, just as for contemporary Germans, the historical novel became an especially popular, indeed beloved, literary genre.[18] It has been estimated that approximately half of all German novels published in the nineteenth century were works of historical fiction.[19] Not content to merely publish fiction in the *Allgemeine Zeitung des Judentums*, Philippson started a literary supplement to the paper, the *Jüdische Volksblatt*, where he likewise promoted new Jewish fiction. In 1855 he went yet a step further and founded a Jewish book club, the Institut zur Förderung der israelitischen Literatur (Institute for the Promotion of Jewish Literature). During its first year of existence the institute had an impressive 2,500 subscribers, a number that had grown to 3,600 by its third year of existence, with at least a third of them from abroad. With its books mostly going to lending libraries, reading clubs, and private individuals, the institute, which published works of fiction, also published historical works, even by those historians who had once expressed disdain for popularization.[20] Philippson and others successfully convinced them that only the sale of popular literature could subsidize and thus support their scholarship. A major undertaking that helped bring about an important transformation in Jewish popular culture, the institute put out some 200,000 copies of the eighty-seven titles it published before it shut down after eighteen years of operation in 1873. The institute and its literary selection had a very broad impact beyond Germany in that many of its titles were published in Russian, English, Hebrew, Yiddish, Polish, and Danish.[21]

So popular was literature, especially on Jewish themes, that it became the liturgy of secular Jews. And while Orthodox Jews may not have considered belles lettres a substitute for Holy Writ, even Marcus Lehmann's neo-Orthodox newspaper, *Der Israelit*, regularly published historical fiction, much of it his own, which was avidly read by the paper's religious subscribers.[22] Even so, the Orthodox publishers strongly preferred presentist literary fiction over the historical novels that the Jewish public demanded, for the former did not demand any critical historical research, which might in turn see the traditional canon, including the Bible, reduced to being source material for "trivial literature." This could only lead to what the founding father of neo-Orthodoxy, Samson Raphael Hirsch (1808–1888), called "a profanation of the Most Holy" (*Entweihung des Heiligsten*). By contrast, Philippson and the Reform camp saw a critical approach to religious sources as perfectly compatible with the production of edifying historical novels.[23] Indeed it stood to give them greater substance and reaffirm rather than challenge faith.

These ideological disputes about the peril and promise of literature notwithstanding, it was historical fiction that the people wanted most. Recently, the historian Amos Bitzan has alerted us to the importance of what he has termed "pleasure reading," which he defines as "the practice of reading primarily for the purpose of providing immediate delight to the self." In the Jewish world, this started among literate women and "gradually overtook the idealized practices of learned men's textual study known as 'Talmud Torah.'"[24] Such pleasure reading, having begun in Jewish society among women in the big cities in the eighteenth century, later saw men, even those from small towns and villages, take up the practice. Indeed it can be claimed that what had begun as this most feminine of Jewish practices—the reading of profane literature—came to replace normative male reading practices, leaving the traditional Jewish male engagement with texts in Germany in the hands of an ever-shrinking but tenacious Orthodox community.

This Jewish "reading revolution," as Bitzan has termed it, also provoked anxiety and ambivalence among Jewish modernizers in the nineteenth century. Their goal was to refashion Jewish culture and harmonize it with German culture. They did not want to promote change just for its own sake but saw it as part of a process of Jewish modernization that laid as much stress on the modifier as on the noun. They wanted modernization in a Jewish key. Since reading was very much a solitary and individual practice, they feared the unintended consequences of a focus on the self, which they envisioned as coming at the expense of maintaining and strengthening the bonds of community. In light of this, Jewish modernizers adopted a shrewd tactic. Rather than fight a rearguard action against the reading revolution, they sought to co-opt it by encouraging secular reading habits but endowing the undertaking with a higher purpose, one that took it beyond the personalized pleasure principle. The turn to history, in both its novelistic and academic forms, was a means by which pleasure reading was brought under control and used for a higher end than mere personal satisfaction.

Most recently, the literary scholar Jonathan Skolnik has summed up the role of historical fiction among nineteenth-century German Jews, claiming that "it was a literary vehicle for dissimilation, a site where Jewish authors sought to write Jewish history into German history and into new notions of universal history, while at the same time redefining their cultural-religious heritage in modernity."[25] In this light we can better appreciate Philippson's crusade. Alarmed at German Jewry's rapid secularization, especially in urban centers after midcentury, he declared that his goal in publishing "depictions of the rich history of Israel in novella form" was to "deepen religious feeling."[26] It should be added that many other newspapers, journals, and novels beyond those owned or promoted by Philippson were likewise put before the Jewish public in the hope that they would achieve similar ends. To inculcate religiosity may have been what Philippson and others intended, but what happened in reality is that among Jews historical novels and history writing created ethnic solidarity and sympathy, and provided German Jews, in the formulation of the literature scholar Florian Krobb, with a "collective autobiography."[27] So while these novels did not promote piety, they certainly enlarged a sense of the Jewish collective self and strengthened Jewish feeling and affect across time, space, and community.

It is of greatest interest to us that novels that dealt in one way or another with Sephardic Jewry were especially popular, but they were novels of a particular stripe. While there were stories, works of historical fiction, and poetry that focused on Golden Age figures like Maimonides or Judah Halevi, their personal real-life tragedies notwithstanding, these were encomiums to exceptional men, whose lives might engender the admiration and sympathy of readers but not foster identification with them in a collective or even proto-national sense. For that, an entire community had to be the protagonist, and so it is little wonder that many of the most popular and influential works of historical fiction focus on the twilight years of Sephardic Jewry and the tragic fate of a Jewish community that had been destroyed. There is also the simple fact that bad news captures people's attention in ways that good news does not. The destruction of Spanish Jewry was a catastrophe on a historic scale, so great that even nineteenth-century Germany Jewry, with no historic connection to the Sephardim, could be swept up in their plight as it was depicted to them in belles lettres. In promoting literature on Spanish Jewry, Philippson was blunt in declaring his intention. He wanted German Jews to have a positive image of Jews from the past: "The Jew was not only the degenerate inhabitant of German and Slavic ghettos: he was also the noble Andalusian, the wealthy business magnate, the inquisitive rabbi."[28] Historical fiction promised to paint vivid portraits of such figures for Germany's rising Jewish middle class.[29]

In their quest to both instruct and entertain readers, German-Jewish authors most frequently chose to portray Sephardic Jewry through the lens of the Marrano experience.[30] Just as the Marranos themselves were a highly differentiated group, so too did German-Jewish authors portray them in a variety of ways. "Marrano" was a word that carried as much metaphorical as it did literal meaning.[31] In the writings of some nineteenth-century German Jews, such as Philippson, the term "Marranos" was used in a most unspecific way and was made to stand for persecuted Spanish Jewry as a whole, and not just those New Christians who continued to practice Judaism in secret. Especially in the hands of Reform-minded authors and readers, such as those who subscribed to the *Allgemeine Zeitung des Judentums*, the history of the Sephardim was interpreted as the story of Jewish history writ large: persecution, expulsion, exile, displacement, faith, and tenacity.

By contrast, for Orthodox authors, the Marranos were at times to be looked upon not with pity but with contempt. In Marcus Lehmann's serialized novel *Eine Seder-Nacht in Madrid* (A Seder Night in Madrid; 1868), the Marranos, by which he really meant Jewish converts who had become faithful Catholics, were renegades. They were, in Lehmann's words, "those fifteenth-century Spanish Jews who were too weak to sacrifice their Fatherland, their property, and the sweet habits of their homeland for their faith." However, the term "Marrano" also had another, very different meaning for nineteenth-century German Jews, and Lehmann gives expression to this as well. In *A Seder Night in Madrid*, which takes place on the eve of Passover in the year 1570, the Marrano Perez Morteira receives word of his impending arrest by the Inquisition and flees his native Toledo to hide out in Madrid. Once there he sees a well-dressed Spaniard, Don Antonio del Banco, in the marketplace buying "parsley, lettuce, and horseradish," which immediately arouses Morteira's suspicion. "Could this man be a secret Jew?" he asks himself. Perez follows the man and reveals to him that he knows that Don Antonio is preparing for tomorrow night's Passover seder. After first denying it, Don Antonio confesses that he is indeed a Marrano. Because of the courage involved in secretly practicing Judaism—we are given a vivid description of the seder enhanced by a twenty-four-line Hebrew reworking of the *ma nishtana* (the Four Questions) in which the seder night is singled out as being different from and sadder than all other nights because of the surreptitious way it had to be celebrated in Spain—Lehmann also offers a sympathetic, if not heroic reading of the word "Marrano": he declares that the word described those Jews who had been forcibly converted but now bravely "carried on the religion of their fathers in arched-roofed, underground, hidden cellars."[32]

In the case of genuine Marranos, readers were expected to see in them Jews whose inner conviction was of greater worth and substance than their outer appearance. For German Jews committed to acculturation but still wishing to remain Jewish, the Marrano could be a prototype of a modern Jew, his conversion under duress notwithstanding. The Marrano possessed the qualities of devotion to Judaism and, once away from the Iberian Peninsula, commitment to social and cultural integration, and, of course, courage. Other Marranos were lauded precisely because they did not or could not remain true to their ancestral faith but also chose not to formally leave it. Important nineteenth-century novels and plays focused on iconic Sephardic figures such as Baruch Spinoza and Uriel da Costa. In such works, both men were presented as Jewish seekers of truth, religious nonconformists who did not become apostates. Other authors saw these two Sephardic mavericks as revolutionary freedom fighters and brave political martyrs, men who refused to surrender to the intolerance of religious leaders and their arbitrary exercise of power.[33]

The Marrano was not always a victim in German-Jewish belles lettres. In *Donna Clara* (1823), a poem by Heinrich Heine (1797–1856), the dramatic final stanza highlights the dignity and pride of the *converso* as well as his joy in exacting revenge against those who hated Jews. As the literature scholar Jeffrey Sammons has said of Heine, "His Jewish persona was militant, aggressive, rudely polemical toward Christian religion and gentile structures of oppression."[34] The noblewoman Donna Clara has fallen for an unnamed knight, who is the mouthpiece for Heine's fantasies of retribution. When he asks her why she is blushing, she responds:

"Gnats were stinging me, my beloved,
And in summer I hate these gnats,
As if they were a pack,
Of long-nosed Jews."

The knight seeks to reassure her: "Heed not gnats nor Jews, beloved." In the course of their dialogue she utters a string of antisemitic sentiments. Neither knows who the other is, not even so much as each other's name. Tentatively they seek to find out. Again, without divulging too much, the woman we know as Clara assures the knight:

"Nothing is false in me, my beloved,
Just as in my breast,
There is not a drop of Moorish blood,
Nor that of the filthy Jews."

Their mutual anonymity is no hindrance to their attraction to each other and, in fact, serves only to heighten the erotic tension. After they make love,

Clara again asks the knight his "precious name." And with this the hero humiliates Clara as he delivers his exquisite coup de grâce:

"I, Señora, your beloved,
Am the son of the acclaimed,
Great, learned Rabbi,
Israel of Saragossa!"[35]

It is little wonder that Heine proudly wrote to his friend Moses Moser on either November 5 or 6, 1823 (unusually the letter is dated thus), describing the poem as "a scene from my own life."[36] Heine's fantasy extended beyond the desire for mere revenge against antisemitism and entailed the assumption of an elegant Sephardic identity of highborn origins. In executing this, Heine adopts a rejectionist strategy in two registers. First, there is the rebuff of the Christian bigot; second, there is his personal desire to do so not through an Ashkenazic character but through the Sephardic knight.

In terms of representation, some of these Sephardicist works were melodramatic and gory renderings of the suffering of Spanish Jewry, while others were stories of triumph, which traced the adventures and achievements of the Sephardic refugees after they had settled elsewhere and become prominent in lands far from the Iberian Peninsula. In still other novels, gender plays a prominent role as the female protagonists are valorized as paragons of middle-class virtue, piety, and domesticity—characteristics that the bourgeois German-Jewish readers would have readily recognized and applauded.[37] The Jewish damsel in these stories also frequently rejected Christian suitors, even at the cost of personal happiness, in order to remain true to her faith and her people.

The first Sephardic-themed novel appeared in 1837. Entitled *The Marranos* (*Die Marranen*), it was a phenomenal success. The author was Phöbus Philippson, a country doctor and the brother of Ludwig, who promoted and published his sibling's novels in serialized form in his newspaper. This made Phöbus a household name throughout Jewish Germany and then well beyond Central Europe when *The Marranos* was translated into Yiddish, Hebrew, English, and Russian. All told, the book appeared in print eight times between 1837 and 1870. For these reasons, *The Marranos*, according to Ludwig, was "the beginning of the entirety of modern Jewish *belles lettres*." While he was hardly an objective commentator, the book was certainly important. According to the literary scholar Jonathan Hess, it was successful because it "both fulfilled and ignited the demands of the readership of this new paper for literary texts that would allow them to indulge in the pleasures of reading."[38]

Just what did the German-Jewish readership demand, and what gave them pleasure? On the one hand it would seem that they shared with non-Jewish Germans the general taste in such matters. There were many nineteenth-century German historical novels set in Spain during the Inquisition, and most offered the following ingredients: an exotic setting, sometimes a beautiful heroine, violence, intrigue, corruption, innocents engulfed by the flames of autos-da-fé, cruel monarchs, and a Catholic Church at once vicious and efficient at torturing and disposing of its enemies. In these works of fiction, Spain appears as a land of religious fanaticism and medieval superstition, a stark contrast to the rational, civilized, and moderate Protestant north.[39]

However, Jewish versions of these Christian novels were not identical. If they had been, there would have been no need for them. They needed to be made specifically Jewish, and this was done largely in three ways. First, Jewish novelists made sure to portray Jews as the Inquisition's principal victims, with the various grand inquisitors in these stories taking particular delight in torturing and extracting confessions from Jews. Second, there was another theme rarely found in the novels of Christian authors—a lament over the Reconquista and the sad fact that, as reported by the narrator in Philippson's *The Marranos*, "the brilliance of the Crescent had in recent days been dimmed by the Cross of the Christians."[40] Finally, there were times when German-Jewish authors corrected and thus contradicted depictions of Spanish literary heroes drawn in German fiction because they offended Jewish sensibilities. In Jonathan Skolnik's sensitive reading of German-Jewish historical fiction, he points out that certain Jewish authors openly channeled German literary giants such as Goethe and Schiller but sometimes challenged them as well. This was the case, for example, with Marcus Lehmann's novel *Die Familie Y Aguilar* (The Family Y Aguilar; 1873). In this work, the protagonist, Diego d'Aguilar, is being driven in a coach on a blisteringly hot day and asks the driver if they are far from their intended destination, the royal castle of Aranjuez. When the driver points it out to him in the near distance, the narrator declares: "Aranjuez! Made famous by Schiller's play *Don Carlos*. Don Carlos, however, the son of Philipp II, was not the hero of freedom and virtue which the fantasy of the German poet made him out to be. The real Don Carlos is of interest to Jewish history because of his presence at the Valladolid auto-da-fé. . . . He lit the pyre with his own hands, upon which fourteen persons were burned alive, and many others, too, after they had been strangled."[41] Given Gershom Scholem's claim about Schiller's importance to German Jews, it was no small thing for a Jewish author such as Lehmann to so boldly correct the revered poet and philosopher. The fictionalized accounts of Sephardic history offered numerous possibilities for engaging both the Jewish and the German pasts, while simultaneously trying to form a new, secular, Jewish textual canon that was in dialogue with or at least compatible with its German equivalent.

Above all, the Jewish reader expected a particular Jewish kind of pathos and sentimentality, an expectation that was fulfilled. Such Jewish novels may have been a new medium and form of secular Jewish culture, but their portrayal of Jewish suffering was in keeping with the ancient traditions of Lamentations. "How lonely sits the city that was full of people! She has become like a widow who was once great among the nations!" bemoans the poet over the destruction of Jerusalem. Spain was the new Jerusalem. In *The Marranos*, Philippson introduces us to Nissa, an elderly, forlorn Jew, originally from Germany but now residing in the besieged city of Granada. He turns to his bewitching eighteen-year-old daughter Dinah, who is reclining on a red velour divan and begins to recount his life's story. After having been driven from Germany, where for Jews "every step was fraught with peril, for the common people were but the prey for which the nobles contended," Nissa made an unsuccessful attempt to go to the Land of Israel. Again he returned to what Philippson anachronistically called the "Fatherland," where, he informs Dinah, "I met your mother." Following Dinah's birth Nissa and his family set off again:

> At that time the flower of our schools had been transplanted from the banks of the Tigris and Euphrates into this blessed country of the West. Here our thirst for knowledge might be satisfied; here it was said, we might give our undisturbed attention to the study of the Law, and to researches into the divine works. I left my home with you and your mother and went to Sepharad. I have been here sixteen years. The wild dove has its nest; the fox has its den; and man has his Fatherland. The only resting place for Israel is the grave. The wrath of the Lord knows no respite. And now also here, just as soon as the Cross is victorious, this land as a place of our honor and rest is finished.[42]

Here we have the Jews knowing good times in only two places since being exiled from the Land of Israel—Babylonia and Muslim Spain. By contrast, in pre-Reformation Germany and now in newly Catholic Spain, torment and suffering has been their lot. The novel is set in the cataclysmic year of 1492: with the Moorish armies vanquished, mosques closed, and the remaining Muslims fleeing to Africa, a dread falls over the land as Torquemada seeks license from King Ferdinand and Queen Isabella to mercilessly root out heresy. In this climate of fear and destruction the king's Jewish privy councillor, Don Isaak Abravanel, sends his son Jehuda to offer assistance to Dinah. Bereft at her father's death, she explains to the visitor: "During the siege I lost my father. A consumptive fever overcame his powerful constitution—he died in my arms; he who had sought in this country a peaceful home found only a grave. An old Moor, who during my father's life, often came to converse with him on astronomy (*Sternwissenschaft*), organized his burial, and supported me as far as his means allowed. But he, too, did not survive the downfall of his nation. I am now alone, quite alone, without a friend or relation in the world."[43] Just as her parents had suffered in the "Fatherland," so too does Dinah now experience anguish in what had become their new "Fatherland," Spain. And in a reprise of her parents' experience, Roman Catholic fanaticism had again shattered their lives; only this time it also destroyed the friendly relations that had existed between Muslims and Jews.

When Jehuda returns to report to his father on his visit to Dinah, it is immediately apparent to Don Isaak that his son is besotted with her, and he expresses his dismay. It is at this point that Philippson justifies or at least displays understanding for the Sephardic grandee's displeasure:

> Abravanel was not free from a certain pride, characteristic of the Spanish Jews and their descendants, which caused them to look down with a degree of contempt upon their coreligionists in France and Germany. In truth, they had, to a certain extent, earned this contempt. As a result of the eternal chain of misfortune meted out by their enemies, great and small, they fell into physical and spiritual decay and in them was fulfilled the word of Holy Writ: "And upon them that are left alive of you I will send a faintness into their hearts in the land of their enemies, and the sound of a shaken leaf shall chase them, and they shall flee as falling from a sword, and they shall fall when none pursueth." Thus living in constant fear, deprived of a means of earning a living through noble pursuits, and maintaining their lives by filthy usury with the clergy and the nobility, they did not follow those better and more elevating literary pursuits that distinguished the Spanish Jews. Abravanel therefore perceived with displeasure the impression that a German Jewess made upon his son.[44]

Whatever other messages the story contains for readers, *The Marranos* serves to affirm both the superior social and intellectual position of medieval Spanish Jewry under Islam and the way that their good fortune shaped the Sephardic sense of self, as well as their low opinion of Ashkenazim. However, both Philippson brothers were great patriots and were committed to the development of a modern German variety of Judaism. Phöbus's novel thus also made clear to readers that Spain was a chapter of Jewish history that had closed, and that nineteenth-century Germany represented its antithesis, for it was now the place where Jewish industry and talent would be rewarded and social acceptance granted.

In fact the lives of contemporary German Jews provided yet another way in which they could distinguish themselves from Spanish Jewry in its twilight years. By the 1840s, though not yet emancipated, German Jewry had no need to hide. They were most definitely not latter-day Marranos praying in "underground cellars." On the contrary, they enjoyed religious freedom, and their synagogues, no longer all tucked away in dimly lit side streets, were increasingly becoming the most identifiable of public edifices. With ghettos like the one in Frankfurt now demolished, Jews became a visible social presence outside the circumscribed areas they had previously inhabited. Moreover, as they became ever more voracious consumers of German culture, Jews were seen in disproportionately large numbers in new venues such as theaters, concert halls, and opera houses. The Marranos about whom they read might have elicited admiration for their courage, but the society in which they lived and that had forced them into hiding was a horror; the bleakness of their existence stood in marked contrast to the bright future that lay ahead for German Jewry.

In addition to the role Heine assigned to the Marrano in *Donna Clara*, Spanish history provided the great author and lyric poet with inspiration for reflecting on the contemporary politics of Jewish emancipation, assimilation, and the role of religion in the state.[45] Through the figure of the hidden Spanish Jew, Heine explored the impact of radical assimilation, its liberating effect as well as its limitations. In his unfinished novella *The Rabbi of Bacherach* (1840), the starkness of the contradictory emotions the figure of the hidden Jew elicits appears most clearly when Don Isaak, a Spaniard of Jewish extraction, is juxtaposed with traditional Ashkenazim. With his inimitable style, Heine's depiction of the encounter, set in the Middle Ages, is replete with evocative and surprising forays into Jewish aesthetics.[46] The link between modern Jewish historical fiction and modern Jewish historiography is keenly apparent in *The Rabbi of Bacherach* in that Heine repeatedly turned to Leopold Zunz, with whom he was on very friendly terms, for information about the history of Spanish Jewry. Once it appeared in print, Heine sent Zunz a copy of the book for him to place in the library of the Verein für Cultur und Wissenschaft der Juden and in the accompanying letter noted, "The major part of this book is source material and it is therefore indispensible for the history of our Jews."[47] Heine thus conceived of *The Rabbi of Bacherach* as reliable, fact-based fiction.

Heine's novella is set in Germany in the late 1480s, and of course while his characters are unaware of what the future holds, his readers are most certainly alert to the catastrophe that lies ahead for Spanish Jewry. The story takes place on Passover: the protagonists, Rabbi Abraham and his wife Sara, abruptly leave the seder after Rabbi Abraham becomes aware that the two "Jewish" strangers who knocked at his door asking to join the festive meal were in fact Christians who had surreptitiously planted the body of a dead child under the table. Fleeing their hometown of Bacherach in order to escape a false charge of ritual murder, they take refuge in the Frankfurt ghetto. That the story was published in 1840 was no accident. Heine was incensed by the trumped-up ritual murder charge leveled at Jews in Damascus that year, and repeatedly spoke out and wrote in protest.[48]

Despite the considerable historical research that went into this work, which is duly famous for its fine-grained and loving description of the seder and medieval German-Jewish life, Heine suddenly dispenses with historical accuracy at the incongruous conclusion, when a Spaniard suddenly appears in Frankfurt's ghetto.[49] Standing in the synagogue courtyard one day, Abraham and Sara are detected by the Spaniard. He wishes to speak with Sara, and after some hesitation the cavalier summons up the courage and approaches her. With his foppish manner and an ingratiating form of address he declares:

> Señora, I swear! Listen to me Señora! I swear by the roses of both the kingdoms of Castile, by the hyacinths of Aragon and the pomegranate blossoms of Andalusia, by the sun which illumines all Spain, with all its flowers, onions, pea-soups, forests, mountains, mules, he-goats, and Old Christians; by the canopy of heaven, on which this sun is nothing but a golden tassel; and by the God who sits on the canopy of heaven and contemplates day and night the creation of lovely women in ever-new forms ... I swear, Señora, that you are the most beautiful woman I have seen in all of Germany.[50]

Heine has turned the tables on almost all of the Sephardicist representations we have thus far encountered. Here we have the beautiful Ashkenazi being praised by none other than a noble Spaniard. However, one must hasten to add that this was unusual even for Heine, for he, like many of his German-Jewish contemporaries, held conventional and at times extraordinarily vicious opinions of Polish Jews, who, for example, he once said, would be better off if they were baptized, "not with common or garden water but with eau de cologne."[51]

Heine, however, is notoriously impossible to pin down. In 1822 he journeyed through the Prussian part of Poland. His report, *Über Polen* (On Poland), must be read as a rejoinder to David Friedländer's *On the Improvement of the Israelites in the Kingdom of Poland* (*Über die Verbesserung der Israeliten im Königreich Polen*; 1819), which we looked at in chapter 2, and which Heine recommends to his readers who seek more details about Polish Jews than he is prepared to give. After acknowledging the productivity and centrality of Jews to the Polish economy, Heine launches into a savage description of the sound, smell, and appearance of Polish Jews that is reminiscent of Friedländer's; however, typical of Heine, there is a surprising twist: "Despite the barbaric fur hat [*shtreiml*] that covers his head, and the even more barbaric ideas that fill it, I value the Polish Jews far more than many German Jews, who have a Bolivar on their heads and Jean Paul in their heads." The title of Friedländer's report recalls that of Christian Wilhelm Dohm's *On the Civic Improvement of the Jews* (*Ueber die bürgerliche Verbesserung der Juden*). Published in 1781, Dohm's tract recommended a cultural and behavioral path for German Jews to follow in order to attain emancipation. Accepting of the advice, Friedländer, writing in 1819, was of the opinion that German Jewry had made the recommended cultural transformation; his goal now was to promote among Polish Jews what Dohm had once recommended for German Jews.

Heine, while no friend of Polish-Jewish culture, was, however, not as self-satisfied as Friedländer was about the culture of Germany's assimilated Jews. The character of the Polish Jews, Heine tells us, was "whole and by breathing in the tolerant air [of Poland] bore the stamp of freedom."[52] This was a stark contrast to his perception of the slavish aping of German culture by Jews such as Friedländer and perhaps himself, notorious self-castigator that he was. In 1843 Heine observed: "I said somewhere that Judaism was not a religion but a misfortune; I should have said German Judaism."[53]

As ever, in the discourse on modern Jewish aesthetics language is the focus. In his report, Heine noted how his ears were "martyred" by the sound of Yiddish. Yet in that same year, 1822, Heine wrote to his friend Christian Sethe: "Everything that is German is odious to me.... German speech splits my eardrums. At times my own poems nauseate me, when I see they are written in German. Even ... German script irritates my nerves."[54] Even if only a passing sentiment or one made entirely in jest, it is a statement that Moses Mendelssohn, David Friedländer, indeed Heine's entire generation of Jews could never have expressed. And here is where Sephardim provided Heine with a way to relieve his discomfort with his own German-Jewish identity. At times he chose to fashion a Sephardic identity for himself, wherein he claimed that his family hailed from Holland, having fled there seeking refuge.[55] This rendered Heine a sort of latter-day Marrano, heroically holding fast to being Jewish, despite his various disaffections and his religious conversion. When he told a friend, Ludwig Kalisch, in 1850, that he made no secret of his Jewishness, "to which I have not returned because I have never left it," he was expressing a heartfelt personal sentiment but also placing himself in a class of Jews and literary characters of his own invention whose liminality, ambiguity, perseverance, and heritage he so admired.

Let us return to the Frankfurt ghetto: our visiting Spaniard wears a feathered cap and golden spurs, and his speech, like his appearance, is florid. His encomium to Sara is but a prelude to his asking her if she will accept him into her service, but Heine's extravagant Don Juan character succeeds only in offending the pious *rebbetzin*, who repels him with her "piercing glance." The manner and deportment of the haughty Spaniard, who possesses "a somewhat affected, dainty grace," holds no allure for the "beautiful Sara." Fearing he has offended her, the Spaniard declares that he too stems from the "House of Israel," and that his grandfather was a Jew, and most likely his father as well. As with his advances, his pedigree too fails to impress her.

Rabbi Abraham then recognizes the visitor from his own sojourn in Spain; he had once pulled him from a river in which he was drowning. Heine is sure to tell us that when in Spain, Abraham "became imbued with a freethinking mentality, exactly like Spanish Jews."[56] The rabbi of Bacherach

4.1. Max Liebermann, illustration for Heinrich Heine, *Der Rabbi von Bacherach* (Berlin: Propyläen-Verlag, 1923). Yale Collection of German Literature, Beinecke Rare Book and Manuscript Library, Yale University.

"outs" the Spaniard, who has not yet recognized Abraham, declaring that he knows him to be the *converso* scion of the Abravanel family. The visitor turns out to be named Don Isaak Abravanel, whose demeanor changes at this point as he threatens Abraham: "Señor Rabbi! You know me then. That means you also know what I am. And once the fox knows that I belong to the brood of the lion, he will beware, will he not . . . ?" The rabbi does not back down and instead goes on the offensive: "I understand very well that the lion, out of sheer pride, casts off his royal fur and disguises himself in the motley, scaly armor of the crocodile—just because it is the fashion to be a whining, sly, voracious crocodile!" And now Abraham, really speaking as Heine, with reference to his own baptism, says: "But beware, Don Isaak, you were not made for the crocodile's element. Water (you well know what I am talking about) is your misfortune, and you will go under."[57] Heine portrays the apostate as a vicious predator, a creature of not just physical but moral ugliness as well. His punishment will be that he drowns in his own baptismal water. Under the impress of recent history, Sephardic culture, once so beautiful, was no more (at least in Spain), and in its stead there was something hideous and no longer Jewish. It was the apostate.[58]

Abraham wins this round as Don Isaak, now recognizing Abraham, breaks into laughter and hugs and kisses his sparring partner. However, the battle is not yet over. And now Heine speaks through the mouth of Don Isaak. When Abraham asks him why he is in the ghetto, the Spanish cavalier responds as if he wishes to carve out a nonreligious definition of Jewishness: "Associating with God's own people is generally not one of my pastimes; in truth, I do not visit the Jewish quarter in order to pray but to eat." "You never loved us, Don Isaak," replies Abraham, to which the Spaniard retorts, "I love your cuisine better than your religion, which lacks the right sauce."[59]

Though he wrote it in the 1820s, Heine published *The Rabbi of Bacherach* in 1840—that is, long after his conversion to Protestantism in 1825; his formal defection from Judaism was a decision he forever regretted.[60] The reference to food, therefore, carries with it a special meaning. Throughout his works Heine frequently used culinary allusions, and in *The Rabbi of Bacherach* as well as in his poem, *The Princess Sabbath*, he specifically declared his love of Ashkenazic food. Far from observant before his conversion, Heine loved to eat, and there was a time when pig's trotters was his favorite dish.[61] However, his discussions of Jewish food are pregnant with meaning beyond being mere expressions of gustatory preference. Food was the one area of Judaism about which he was totally unconflicted, and it may well be one of the few areas in all Sephardicist writing where Ashkenazic taste, here meant in its gastronomic sense, trumps the Sephardic.

Don Isaak, a mouthpiece for Heine himself, goes on to reveal his bitter rejection of his own Jewishness: "Even when you had your best times, in the reign of my ancestor King David who ruled over Judah and Israel, I could not have stood living amongst you." Rabbi Abraham accuses Don Isaak of being worse than a Christian—he considers him a pagan, a charge the Spaniard gladly accepts: "Yes, I am a pagan, who declares his allegiance to 'Our Blessed Lady of Sidon, sacred Astarte,'" referring to the Semitic goddess of sexuality and pleasure and known among the Greeks as Aphrodite. "The cheerless self-tormenting Nazarenes are as little to my taste as the arid, joyless Hebrews."[62] The description of Judaism as desiccated brings to mind Hegel's idea of Judaism as "a religion of fearing," an entirely "non-spiritual entity," whose essence was the enslavement of Jews to the Law.[63] Heine may even have heard this charge with his own ears, as he attended Hegel's lectures between 1821 and 1823.[64]

With charges of heresy and apostasy and countercharges of Judaism's death making the atmosphere uncomfortable, Heine releases the tension by shifting the subject back to food—quintessentially Ashkenazic food. Perhaps seeking an element of reconciliation between the two men, Don Isaak proudly declares:

> Do not look at me with disdain. My nose has not become a renegade. When once by chance I came into this street at dinnertime, and the well-known savory odors of Jewish cuisine rose to my nose, I was seized with the same yearning that our fathers felt for the fleshpots of Egypt—pleasant-tasting memories of youth came back to me. In my imagination I saw again the carp with brown raisin sauce that my aunt prepared so edifyingly for Friday eve; I saw once more the steamed mutton with garlic and horseradish, which might tempt the dead back to life, and the soup in which dumplings swam about dreamily—and my soul melted like the notes of an enamored nightingale.[65]

Through poetic license Heine endows Don Isaak with a cultivated Ashkenazic palate and "pleasant-tasting memories of youth." In terms of Jewish identity, such recollections are all that remain for Don Isaak. In his culinary visits to the ghetto, this Gentile, descended from the house of King David, was expressing the desire to enjoy and retain at least one, elemental aspect of Jewish culture. This was no small thing for Heine, for just as his food allusions permitted him, the apostate poet, to recall and enjoy this important expression of Jewish authenticity, so too did it function in this way for Don Isaak.

What could the average German-Jewish reader of Heine's novella take from it? Perhaps that the world is not safe for Jews, or that no matter how seemingly comfortable they may have been, whether surrounded by family joyously celebrating Passover, as Rabbi Abraham and his wife Sara had been doing, or as a community fully at home in their land and culture, as had been the case with Spain's Jews, they were vulnerable. This was not a matter of recalling the distant past. Just as the novella appeared, the innocent Jews of Damascus were in the throes of an agony that had hit them like a thunderbolt. While Heine had Rabbi Abraham become educated and refined in Toledo, thus celebrating Spanish-Jewish institutions and culture, there is at the same time a pessimistic strain that runs through the story. All stood to be lost in an instant. Had it not happened throughout Jewish history?

Whether it was Jerusalem under the Romans, the Rhineland Jewish communities under the Crusaders, Spain under Ferdinand and Isabella, or even conservative Germany, whose regime of censorship forced Heine into Parisian exile, the Jews could find no rest. Beginning with the family seder where the opening scene of the novella sees the family recounting the story of the Exodus from Egypt, *The Rabbi of Bacherach* is the story of Jewish exile and wandering. It is also a story that with all its ambivalence about Jewish tradition—yet another reflection of Heine's personal attitude—Jews turn to each other in times of crisis. For Rabbi Abraham the crisis was the danger of being charged with ritual murder, for Don Isaak an existential crisis of longing; both men find refuge in the ghetto. While intellectually narrow and a place of material deprivation, it was nonetheless a haven of safety and respite. Heine did not want the Jews of his age to return to the ghetto, but he also did not want his readers to forget where they had come from. Just as Rabbi Abraham had returned to Germany from his Spanish sojourn, and just as Don Isaak, though now Christian, was nonetheless proud of his Jewish *yichus* (heritage), so too did Heine's Jewish audience have cause to be proud of their origins, however humble. This may have been the other lesson he sought to impart.

Heine's frequent invocation of the Marrano reflected his sense that their partial authenticity was what made Marranos such ideal exemplars of modern Jews. Their multiple identities, their straddling Jewish and non-Jewish cultures, certainly more sure-footedly with the latter, even their pride mixed with shame, typified not just postexpulsion *conversos* but in some respects modern German Jewry, which, through a mixture of voluntarism and external pressure, was also in the process of moving Judaism and Jewishness to realms more private than ever before. With Jewish identities that were elusive and fluid, disguised and revealed, Heine's Marranos were not merely Iberian historical figures but self-portraits expressive of a new form of Ashkenazic identity that Heine's Jewish readers might find familiar or even recognize in themselves.

Ludwig Philippson most definitely did not recognize himself in Heine's rendering. He loathed *The Rabbi of Bacherach* and wrote a scathing review of it in his newspaper. Seeing the novella as little more than the confessions of a renegade, Philippson mocked Heine's detailed descriptions of the Passover seder and the service in the Frankfurt synagogue, wherein the author "has forgotten [to include] nothing, up to and including the chatter in the women's gallery." The upshot is that "for the Jewish reader it is boring and for the Christian reader it is, in the end, incomprehensible."[66] Aside from Heine's ambivalence about Judaism, which Philippson found nauseating, he considered the novella a failure because it was of no didactic worth. There was nothing of value to learn from it, nor was it morally uplifting. It did nothing to bolster, reinvigorate, or contribute to the formation of a positive German-Jewish identity, and this, after all, was the point of Jewish historical fiction, as far as Philippson was concerned.

Nonetheless, Jewish readers lapped up these melodramas. Part of what made these stories so exciting and simultaneously so trite was the dramatic revelation of a character's secret identity, a plotline that was a mainstay of this literary tradition. In Lehmann's *A Seder Night in Madrid*, none other than the inquisitor himself turns out be a Jew of faith, the great-grandson of Rabbi Moshe del Medigo. Secretly given instruction in Judaism by his father, the latter appealed to the future inquisitor when he turned thirteen years of age, asking him to undertake an activity that would require "strength and courage." He wanted his son, whose real name is Diego del Medigo, to become a "guardian angel" to his "unfortunate [Jewish] brothers." The youth agreed, and at his father's direction Diego studied Catholic theology. He excelled and entered the priesthood, where he worked his way up the church hierarchy. Eventually he was in a position to become a bishop but chose instead to join the Inquisitional tribunal, where, in his position as chief judge (*Oberrichter*), he uses his office to undermine the Inquisition and set Jews free.[67]

The above-mentioned Diego d'Aguilar, whose Jewish name was Moses Lopes Pereira, had been a real-life *converso* and was the subject of many fictional accounts in both German and Ladino.[68] He was most likely born in Spain, lived in Lisbon, and then in 1722 departed for London and later Vienna, where he became a financier to and favorite of Empress Maria Theresa. A professing Jew, he was also the founder and benefactor of the Sephardic Jewish community of Vienna.[69] In 1854, Ludwig August Frankl—physician, celebrated author and poet, director of the Viennese Music Association, where he also held the title of Professor of Aesthetics, and secretary and archivist of the Jewish community in Vienna—published his serialized story "History of Diego d'Aguilar" in Ludwig Philippson's *Allgemeine Zeitung des Judentums*.[70] The scene is the inquisitor's palace in Madrid. One night there is a heavy knock at the door. The visitor, a woman, demands of the porter that she be taken to the inquisitor. She is denied entry, but the inquisitor is nonetheless awakened by the commotion, throws a purple cloak over his shoulders, and approaches the woman, demanding to know what she wants. Overcome with emotion, her lips trembling, she summons up the courage to say, "You condemned a young woman to death today." The inquisitor responds, "She lived as a Christian but belonged to the Jews." The woman asks that the condemned be set free; in response the inquisitor angrily demands that she leave his residence. As he turns to depart, she looks around the room, sees they are alone, and says, "She, whom you have condemned to the flames, is your sister." And with that the woman tears open her low-cut dress and, revealing more than just her bosom, tells the inquisitor, "You yourself [along with your sister] suckled milk from this breast." As childhood memories flood back to him, his mother whispers a Hebrew prayer and calls him by his real name, "Moshe." He and his mother escape the palace and conspire to flee Spain. Unable to save the sister, mother and son board a ship, set sail for London, and thereafter make their way to Vienna. There they meet Empress Maria Theresa and go on to enjoy a new life of power and privilege.[71]

Hackneyed and corny, most certainly, but nothing better illustrates the syncretistic relationship between Jewish historical fiction and history writing than this story, insofar as Frankl presents it as an authentic and reliable account, and establishes its veracity at the outset by detailing the chain of transmission; he claims to have been told the story of d'Aguilar by the haham (head) of the Turkish, that is, Sephardic community in Vienna, Ruben Baruch. He had in turn heard it from his father, the haham Juda, and his grandfather Abraham, son of Chaim Jehuda Baruch, money changer to the last vizier of Constantinople. Furthermore, the melodramatic rendering notwithstanding, the second and final installment of this serialized story is a remarkably detailed and sober historical account of d'Aguilar's triumphant return to the fold, his commercial success, and the honorable reputation he enjoyed in both Austrian and Jewish circles. Readers of the "History of Diego d'Aguilar" were thus treated to the legend and the real life of the man. With its literary flair and historical veracity it was a feel-good story that explicated a genuine link between the tragedy of the Sephardic experience and the hopefulness of Jewish life in nineteenth-century Central Europe.

Some Jewish authors who penned Sephardic historical fiction were sensitive not only to the practice of history but to the lived Sephardic experience, as is demonstrated in the unusual case of Adolf Zemlinsky (1845–1900), the Viennese author and father of the famous composer Alexander Zemlinsky. In the case of the Zemlinskys there was, as there had been with d'Aguilar, a genuine Sephardic–Central European connection. The Zemlinsky family had originally been Catholic, but when, in 1870, Adolf met and fell in love with Clara Semo, a Sephardic Jew from Sarajevo, he officially renounced Catholicism and converted to Judaism, taking the name Aharon ben Avraham and undergoing ritual circumcision. Out of religious conviction, the rest of the family also converted to Judaism. Adolf and Clara were married in Vienna's Sephardic synagogue on January 8, 1871, and thereafter Adolf became secretary of the Sephardic community. Clara's family had moved to Vienna in the 1860s, published a Ladino monthly, *El Correo de Viena*, and were promoters of the Haskalah. It was into this Viennese Sephardic milieu that Adolf Zemlinsky was ushered. So steeped in it was he that he is best remembered today for having authored a history of the Turkish-Israelite community of Vienna, in which considerable due is accorded Moses Pereira for his role in founding the community.[72]

Adolf Zemlinsky's understanding of Sephardic history and his sympathy for and total acceptance of its culture (he became editor of *El Correo*, and he sent his son, the young musical prodigy Alexander, to Vienna's Sephardic school), plus the fact that he had come from a devout Catholic family, informed his literary efforts, which included short stories on Judah Halevi and the false messiah Shlomo Molcho.[73] In 1874, Jewish readers of Marcus Lehmann's Orthodox-oriented newspaper, *Der Israelit*, were treated to Zemlinsky's literary account of the tribulations of Sephardic Jewry. *The Jew's Revenge: A Historical Tale from the Middle Ages* (*Die Rache des Juden: Historische Erzählung aus dem Mittelalter*) is one of those melodramatic fantasies wherein we see a merging of such themes as the intolerance of the Catholic Church, the barbarism of the Inquisition, and a secret identity revealed, which brings with it retribution for Jewish suffering.

In *The Jew's Revenge* we meet Benjamin Juda Levi, whose entire family was burned at stake in 1493 by the inquisitor Alfonso de la Puerta. At the time Benjamin witnessed this, he was only eight years old, and he swore revenge. Ten years later the orphan Benjamin returns to Spain from exile and exacts his retribution by kidnapping Alfonso's son and returning with him to Frankfurt am Main, where he raises him as a Jew, naming him Aron. Some time elapses, and Benjamin and Aron find themselves in Alfonso's torture chamber. In agony, Benjamin nonetheless takes exquisite pleasure in revealing Aron's real identity. The coup de grâce comes when Aron professes his love for Judaism and rejects his father. Alfonso is then overcome with remorse and is rendered incapable of persecuting Jews. He spends the rest of his days in prison, while Aron and Benjamin return to Frankfurt and live happily ever after.[74]

Ludwig Philippson did not much approve of such plotlines. Stories of revenge were presentist, providing only momentary enjoyment and catharsis; they did not illuminate a path to the future, a characteristic Philippson also considered essential if literature was to serve a higher function than mere entertainment. In his novella *Die drei Brüder* (The Three Brothers), first published in 1854, Philippson follows the fate of the siblings Don Abraham, Don José, and Sanzo. It is 1504 and the three have surreptitiously returned to Spain to meet up and commemorate the tenth anniversary of their father's death. Upon their reunion they regale each other with tales of the lives they have led since fleeing Spain. Abraham, a learned rabbi, influenced by the rationalist philosophy of Maimonides, found himself among the Ashkenazim of France, among whom "there was no trace of culture and education, but only squalor, both physically and spiritually. . . . A deep gulf cuts them off from the rest of humanity. Oh, how different it was in Spain." Abraham then strikes what is for us a familiar chord when he addresses the sounds of Ashkenazic Hebrew he heard in France: "Their pronunciation of the Holy Tongue was a great assemblage of incomprehensible prayers."[75] Abraham continues to tell his story about an encounter he had with a French Jew, raising yet another theme so central to our own story—that of his physical deportment. "When I arrived I found a shrunken little gray-haired man . . . [and] there I stood with the respectable height and breadth that the Lord gave me, in my stately Spanish dress. Here was this little man—the representative of French Jewry—jumping back and forth in front of me, and he spoke in the same fashion. He mixed a word from Scripture and then a saying from the Talmud."[76] Then, reprising a theme we have already encountered, where the Ashkenazic men in these novels are portrayed as misshapen and unappealing, Philippson describes Dina, the daughter of the "shrunken little gray-haired man," as "slim and sublime . . . her exquisite face was glowing and her brown eyes were shining brightly."[77] As luck would have it, the two fell madly in love, and "her parents were pleased." Bliss did not last long, however: Abraham's father-in-law—jealous of the community's warm embrace of the Sephardic scholar, who had built up a loyal following with his lectures on Rambam, Judah Halevi, Yosef Albo, and other Sephardic giants—drove the young couple apart, and Abraham from the city of Nîmes. Happily, a man from Holland, who had heard one of Abraham's lectures and was deeply impressed, invited him to Amsterdam, where Abraham soon became the "associate rabbi in this, the greatest congregation of the Western world." He is, he declares, "next in line to succeed the honorable old man who is the pride of Spanish Jewry."[78]

The middle brother, José, made his way to Turkey, where he became extraordinarily wealthy and powerful. Recognizing his dependency on royal patronage, he declares, "I thus pray to the Lord that He keep my noble lord Sultan Selim II in his good graces."[79] Along the way he had stopped in Antwerp, and it was there that he began to use the family's real name. José, in fact, turns out to be the great (real-life) Sephardic financier and statesman Don Joseph Nasi, Duke of Naxos, a man who used his power and privilege on behalf of his Ottoman coreligionists. In the economic realm, he had the sultan grant him permission to set up textile plants in the Land of Israel, intended to provide linen for the empire's subjects and work for the Jewish refugees from Spain, while in the political realm Don Joseph encouraged the sultan to form an alliance with the Netherlands so that together they could wage war on Spain.

The youngest brother is Sanzo, a man imbued more with the values of a Spanish knight than with those of a pious and knowledgeable Jew. Yet he combined his swashbuckling ways and love for his people, and became leader of the Beni Yehud, a tribe of Jewish Bedouins in the Sahara. They lived isolated and alone but were free and answered to no one. When Sanzo first came upon them and told them his story, and that of Jews everywhere, they expressed astonishment that there were Jews who chose to live among non-Jews who persecuted them, and were incredulous that those oppressed people would not prefer to join this tribe of free desert Jews. The group then reciprocated, telling Sanzo their history. As it turned out, they were descendants of the handful of survivors from the Banu Qurayza, the Medinan Jewish tribe almost totally wiped out by Muhammad. Sanzo observed how the tribe, cut off from the rest of world Jewry, now followed Jewish laws and performed rituals that they barely understood. He tells his brothers that they are "gallant, honest, and God-fearing" but also "crude, ignorant, and full of superstition."[80] Nonetheless, they are proud Jews. In this way Philippson portrayed them as being like Marranos. Though not in hiding or fearful, they too cling to the faith, sincerely, but imperfectly. The plight of the Beni Yehud might also be said to reflect that of those German Jews who, through increasing assimilation, were left with mere memories of the pious practices of previous generations. We must recall that Philippson was motivated to produce and promote these novels by his alarm about the increasing religious laxness and ignorance of German Jews.

Each of the tales in *The Three Brothers* is a story of triumph and hope. Despite their suffering and tribulations, these were three Sephardic boys who made good. The Jewish community of Spain may be no more, but the brilliance of Sephardic Jewry was not to be denied: the three brothers reestablished themselves elsewhere, became leading lights in their respective communities, and in so doing carried forth the grand legacy of Spanish Jewry.[81]

The German-Jewish consumers of this literature were deeply fond of stories of overcoming and success against all odds. The tragedy of Sephardic-Jewish history provided authors with ample opportunity to tell uplifting tales of Jewish perseverance and triumph. More than this, however, such stories also served as a rebuff to Eduard Gans's prediction, or hope, that the Jews would be rendered as invisible as a river's waters within the ocean. In the literary depictions of German-Jewish authors, Sephardic Jewry was living proof that the death of the community did not mean the death of the spirit, genius, or ambition of that community.

Ludwig Philippson, as has been noted by a number of scholars, was extremely cavalier with his historical facts, overreliant and uncritical in accepting the scholarly judgments of his father-in-law, the prominent historian of Sephardic Jewry Meyer Kayserling. For example, in his 1867 novel *Jakob Tirado*, the hero, after whom the book is titled, flees to Brussels in the 1590s so as to cease living the life of a *converso* and begin to live openly as a Jew. However, when the Inquisition arrives there under the sponsorship of the ruling Spanish branch of the Habsburgs, Tirado becomes involved in a plot to assassinate the grand inquisitor, the Duke of Alba. He flees Brussels and returns to Portugal to rescue a group of Marranos and spirit them away to Amsterdam, where they found the first Sephardic synagogue in the city.

Tirado, like Diego d'Aguilar, was indeed a real historical character, and in communal lore he plays a central role in what the historian of Sephardic Amsterdam Miriam Bodian has called the "restoration myth." Tirado was identified as a community founder by Daniel Levi de Barrios, a former *converso*, who became a member of the Amsterdam community in 1662 and was one of the chief promoters of the restoration myth through his *Triumph of Popular Government*, published in 1683. The restoration myth was a triumphalist narrative designed to give shape, coherency, and purpose to the story of the emergence of a Sephardic community in Amsterdam. Having dedicated his book in ingratiating fashion to the elders of the community —he was apparently desperate for their patronage—de Barrios did not, according to Bodian, write a "candid" work but instead "creat[ed] a shared, idealized past in order to perpetuate the community as a meaningful entity and project its destiny into the future." His restoration myth "suggested a harmonious, unconflicted, natural transition from the Iberian Catholic experience to normative Jewish life in Amsterdam."[82]

Philippson was overly reliant on *Sephardim* (1859), Kayserling's study of the romance poetry of Spanish and Portuguese Jews, blithely accepting his father-in-law's account of de Barrios's somewhat shaky history of the community's founding, which revolved around the exploits of Tirado, his *conversa* companion and niece who left Portugal with him, Maria Nunes, and the poet Jacob Belmonte.[83] Accuracy, however, was not Philippson's goal. Rather, he sought to generate interest in the Jewish past and respect for Judaism, to impart the lessons of history, not history itself. As he observed, "By representing the teachings, the history, and the entire spirit of Judaism in poetic form, in aesthetic garb, *belles lettres* gains tremendously in validity and brings lost souls back to Judaism."[84] It is safe to say that belles lettres probably did not bring that many lost Jewish souls back to Judaism. Those who had been lost were probably not subscribers to the *Allgemeine Zeitung des Judentums* and were most likely not members of Jewish book clubs. But many Jews were, and untold numbers read these and scores of other stories of Jewish suffering and heroism, tragedy and triumph, looking forward to each new installment with eager anticipation.

Beyond offering edification via heart-stopping entertainment, these stories generally concluded by providing readers with a sense of satisfaction and comfort via an oft-used theme—the seamless transition back to Judaism that was experienced by the returning *conversos*. Here, literature was especially unfaithful to history. Spiritually unconflicted, overjoyed at being free of the Inquisition, and free to practice Judaism, few if any literary protagonists who fled to places like Amsterdam between the sixteenth and eighteenth centuries were plagued by doubts, and hardly a one returned to Catholicism. Yet as we know, reintegration was extremely difficult for many of the Spanish exiles, and was a very delicate, emotional, and complex process in both practical and psychological terms.[85] According to the distinguished Jewish historian Yosef Hayim Yerushalmi, while thousands who fled the Iberian Peninsula came to established Jewish communities and took up the open practice of Judaism, "some found the adjustment difficult, and out of the ensuing intellectual ferment emerged those currents which formed the background of a Spinoza. But there were many other Marranos who, for various reasons, continued the double life of crypto-Jews even after leaving Spain and Portugal, and who formed a dispersion all their own."[86] There was also significant internal friction between the returning *conversos* and communal leadership, and even among the ex-Marranos themselves, over issues of belief and practice.

Just as the foundational restoration myths of the seventeenth century sought to present courageous Marranos fleeing Spain and returning to Judaism united and happy, the historical novels of the nineteenth century replicated this narrative. This story of a serene return to the faith, of remaining true to Judaism and the Jewish community, would have resonated deeply with readers. To be sure, German Jews were not Marranos, and nothing they had experienced was analogous to the history of the Sephardim. Yet had not they too undergone a great religious and cultural metamorphosis? While theirs was the same faith that their ancestors had practiced, it bore next to none of the aesthetic hallmarks of traditional Judaism. Whether the readers of these novels were allied to the Reformist or modern Orthodox camps, or sat somewhere in between, the new forms Judaism took in Germany in the nineteenth century would have barely been recognizable to previous generations. In this respect they too were radically changed Jews; yet, like the returning Sephardim they so eagerly read about, they could also claim that their transformation had not compromised their loyalty to Judaism and to their fellow Jews.

Finally, one other theme seems to permeate most of the Jewish historical novels dealing with the Sephardic experience. Whether this is overtly stated or merely implied, the expulsion of the Jews is represented not only as one of the greatest calamities in Jewish history but as a cause of Spain's irrevocable decline. Her glory, her power, her influence, once so manifest, no longer exist. The message of such literature is that no society and no state can afford to consider its Jews expendable, for to do so is to incur the grave consequences that such injustice will bring in its wake. Preaching the didactic role that historical novels and history had to play, writers like Ludwig Philippson were optimistic that forward-thinking states had learned the lesson of the past, and the tragedy that befell the Sephardim, and by extension, Spain, would not be repeated elsewhere. Both the Germany of the nineteenth century and its emergent Jewish community stood poised to fill the breach created by medieval Spain's bigoted folly.

In *Zakhor*, his poignant meditation on Jewish history and memory, Yosef Hayim Yerushalmi astutely observed: "The Holocaust has already engendered more historical research than any single event in Jewish history, but I have no doubt whatever that its image is being shaped, not at the historian's anvil, but in the novelist's crucible. Much has changed since the sixteenth century [which saw the first attempt at writing Jewish history]; one thing curiously remains. Now, as then, it would appear that even where Jews do not reject history out of hand, they are not prepared to confront it directly, but seem to await a new, metahistorical myth, for which the novel provides at least a temporary modern surrogate."[87] The popularity of the nineteenth-century German-Jewish historical novel is evidence of the keenness of Yerushalmi's observation, but while the novel was (and remains) a surrogate for history among Jews, in truth history and historical fiction were not entirely separate realms, because for the writers of both genres, their respective approaches to the past were mutually fructifying. Sometimes historical prose overtly betrayed the influence of the novel. At other times, fiction seemed to leave its influence not on scholarly prose but, rather, on the self-formation of the Jewish historian, the novel having been his first substantive exposure to non-Jewish culture. It was, in part, the enticing allure of that encounter that helped create the mind-set that enabled him to take up the secular craft of history.[88]

It is to the practitioners of Jewish historiography that we now turn, for they had an influence far beyond the paltry numbers who attended their lectures or read their dense scholarship. Their representations of Jewish life under Islam in general and in Muslim Spain in particular did not so much compete with popular Jewish conceptions about the Golden Age of Spanish Jewry as reinforce them, thanks to the weight of their authority.

CHAPTER FIVE

——————◄❂►——————

Writing Jewish History

THE CONSTRUCTION OF A GLORIOUS SEPHARDIC PAST

Along with the rise of the modern Jewish historical novelist, the nineteenth century saw the emergence of Jewish historians. They were scholars who were dedicated to casting a reflective and introspective eye on the Jewish past, seeking to apply critical methods of scholarly analysis to texts, where once such texts had been principally the focus of religious devotion and exegesis. Inspired, first and foremost, by the birth of historicism, the inner intellectual and institutional impetus for the critical and secular study of Jewish history came with the rise of *Wissenschaft des Judentums* (Academic Study of Judaism), an undertaking that began in Germany in the second decade of the nineteenth century.

The turn to history among Jewish intellectuals also saw many of them direct their attention to the pasts of other peoples and religious traditions. Such a development, for example, saw the birth of Jewish orientalist scholarship, whose principal focus was the world of Islam.[1] Among other subjects, Jewish historians concentrated on Islamic history and theology, as well as the connection between Judaism and Islam. They also addressed Jewish life in the Muslim world; the cultural and intellectual achievements of Jews in Muslim Spain especially attracted the attention and indeed admiration of nineteenth-century Jewish scholars. As testament to the interest in Iberian Jewish culture, the first half of the nineteenth century saw many new German translations of important Sephardic religious, ethical, and poetic texts. That in turn made such cultural riches accessible to increasing numbers of Jews, creating a demand for abridged and popular versions of such texts.[2] Jewish newspapers and journals also serialized Sephardic poetry and liturgical traditions and consistently profiled leading Sephardic figures. Finally, many works of Jewish historical scholarship were issued in popular versions, some of them specifically for children. *Wissenschaft des Judentums* was thus not a closeted intellectual enterprise, as the fruits of its scholarly research were put into the public domain and thus became a constituent dimension of German-Jewish vernacular culture.[3]

Whether young or old, intellectuals or the merely curious, what were Jewish readers treated to when they read Sephardic history? For the most part, Jewish historians were not all that interested in ordinary members of the community, focusing instead on the social and intellectual elites. Power, poetry, and philosophy attracted their attention, while the quotidian lives of the rank and file did not. To be sure, the nineteenth century was the era of nationalist historiography, which saw the spotlight shine upon "great men." In this respect, the scholars of *Wissenschaft des Judentums* were very much products of their age, tending to emphasize the achievements of Jewish statesmen, as well as those of rabbis, Hebrew poets, and grammarians, for they exemplified successful, dignified Jews, who were attentive to beauty in its visual, written, and aural forms. Indeed most historians privileged language as being one of the keys to Sephardic genius. In his study of medieval Hebrew poetry, Leopold Zunz noted that exposure to the grammatical studies and poetry of Arab scholars opened an entirely new world of creative possibilities for the Spanish-Jewish poets: the firm grasp of the rules of grammar that they had acquired endowed their language with "correctness," which in turn inspired their exegetical studies and opened up to them the "linguistic treasure trove of the Holy Scriptures."[4] In other words it was Jewish intimacy with the modalities of Arab intellectual life that provided them with access to the deeper recesses of Jewish culture. When Jewish historians turned to medieval Jewish philosophy and exegesis, their analysis was essentially a celebration of rationalist thought, which they presented as typical of the clear and luminous thinking of Sephardic intellectuals, who were in turn products of the Arab philosophical tradition.

Whether the subject was statecraft, poetry, or philosophy, the depictions of this world meant acknowledging the Arabs and their positive influence on Jewish intellectual life, as well as the beneficent social arrangements and interactions that were made possible for Jews under Islam. Jewish readers thus gleaned from their history books not only glowing images of high-achieving Sephardim but also a positive vision of Islam.[5] Finally, these sentiments and images were further enhanced when readers juxtaposed the representations of Sephardic Jewry with those of Eastern European Jews, who were frequently depicted as undignified, brutish, and superstitious. Historians not only made sure to express their cultural preference for the Sephardim; with their vivid powers of description they created lasting impressions of both communities and rendered indelible the image that there existed a wide aesthetic gulf separating the two groups.

The picture drawn by Jewish historians was a totalizing one, as Sephardic courtiers and intellectuals were taken as representative of the Sephardim as a whole. The poor, the marginal, the unlearned, those who were not poetically inclined, and those whose Hebrew was poor or nonexistent—one would assume that such Jews constituted the vast majority in Spain—were rarely depicted. By contrast, the poverty-stricken, the nonphilosophical, the pious Yiddish-speakers of Poland were cast as pitiable and quintessentially representative, while their leading intellectual lights were presented as exceptional, almost aberrant figures relative to the majority. So powerful were these depictions that with the growth of historical consciousness among Jews and the increasingly important role that Jewish historians came to possess in the nineteenth century, their representations of the Jewish past became authoritative and helped shape popular and very long-lasting opinions about the Sephardic and Eastern European Jewish pasts.

Beyond being seduced by the rich philosophical and poetical traditions of Spanish Jews, German-Jewish historians sensed the social implications of such lives led at the intellectual vanguard. For the earliest generations of Jewish historians, the lives of medieval Jewish poets and philosophers under Islam bespoke the promise that modern Jews could give full expression to their Jewishness while participating in the dominant culture. Thus they depicted the relationship between Islam and Judaism as one of mutual compatibility and cultural exchange.

Of the many Jewish historians who recognized the harmony of Jewish and Muslim culture, three in particular are the focus of this inquiry: Abraham Geiger, Heinrich Graetz, and Ignaz Goldziher. The three are linked in several ways. All three were from Central Europe—Geiger and Graetz from Germany and Goldziher from Hungary; all three were deeply committed Jews; they all made towering historiographical contributions and shared similar intellectual inspirations: Hegel's philosophy of history, the so-called higher biblical criticism, and a dedication to the critical study of the Jewish past.

Our three principals were also orientalists; within the context of this study, orientalism plays its most predominant role in this chapter. The story of the Jewish scholarly encounter with Islamic culture and the Jews of Islam underscores the inadequacy of Edward Said's dismissive claims about the practice of orientalism. Geiger, Graetz, and Goldziher serve as significant counterexamples to that interpretation. In his influential *Orientalism*, Said asserted that orientalism is mainly a "British and French cultural enterprise."[6] This claim was based on his belief that the determining motive behind orientalist scholarship was imperialism. Said observed that orientalism was an expression of fascination with the Muslim Near East mixed with unalloyed condescension. Notwithstanding considerable criticism, Said's position attained a sort of hegemony within the academy. One of the most salient effects this has had is to foster the exclusion from contemporary discourse and scholarship about orientalism of those scholars who did not fit the orientalist-as-imperialist mold. Nineteenth-century Jewish orientalists are just such a category, and they are so because their unique position in European society precludes their being squeezed into a scholarly paradigm that is informed by a neat Manichaean divide running along an East-West axis with room for only Christians and Muslims.

In exploring an alternative form of orientalism, we will see how fascination and contempt can coexist without being the product of state-sponsored imperialism. Rather, what will become apparent is that the orientalism of the Jewish scholars to be examined below exhibits a kind of inner dynamic, one where there are good and bad Jews, advanced and primitive Jewish communities, and the larger goal behind this scholarship is not an expanded European state but a more tolerant and progressive one, one in which Jews and a revivified and respected Judaism would find a welcome place.

As a consequence of their own rather marginal status vis-à-vis the Christian majority, Jewish historians expressed a particular kind of empathy for Islam and the positive environment it helped create for Jews living under its aegis. "Reversing the gaze," to borrow from Susannah Heschel, Jewish scholars were especially well disposed toward a faith whose outward trappings revealed its historical affinity with Judaism.[7] In fact, German-Jewish intellectuals had already suggested the possibility that Jews, as Orientals, were in a special position to turn to the study of the past in order to "improve" a Europe that stood to learn much from them. Heinrich Heine, himself a member of the Verein für Cultur- und Wissenschaft der Juden, pointed to just such a possibility.[8] In an essay of 1838 entitled "Jessica" that appeared in his *Shakespeare's Girls and Women*, Heine mischievously "orientalized" Germany, proudly remarking: "It is not only Germany that bears the physiognomy of Palestine: the rest of Europe, too, is rising to the Jews' level. I say 'rising,' for the Jews have always borne within them the modern principle that is only now unfolding visibly among the European nations."[9]

I would argue that the earliest Jewish scholars of Islam or Jews in the Muslim world were inspired by the "modern principle" of which Heine writes. He defined this principle as attachment "to the Law [Torah], to the abstract idea," and, above all, to "cosmopolitanism." Thus informed by Heine, we can begin to read orientalism against the grain. Indeed, we can commence by asking some questions: Was the knowledge produced by these Jewish orientalists the same as that produced by representatives of nations with imperial holdings in the Near East? How did it differ from the orientalism of those of different faiths, or from that of those who professed no religious faith at all? Why was the rhetoric of Central European Jewish orientalists sometimes so virulently anti-Western? As Europeans why did they not build their orientalist project on the foundations of a European triumphalism? Indeed, what of an orientalism that was shorn of the state-building project altogether? Since orientalism was often the intellectual handmaiden to colonialism, and colonialism was often fortified and abetted by Christian missionary activity, why were Jewish orientalists so uncompromisingly hostile to Christianity?[10] And finally, what does Jewish orientalist knowledge look like when it was predicated on a raging sense of the inferiority, not of the culture of the Muslim Other, but of the orientalist's own?

As a means of approaching these questions, with the aim of understanding Central European Jewish orientalism's inner logic and particular

motivations, I wish to suggest that we can best understand the phenomenon by recognizing that it was colored by at least four determining factors,
characteristic to it alone: (1) the desire of Jewish orientalists for Jewish civil
equality through emancipation; (2) their rejection (often virulent) of Orthodox, especially Eastern European, Jews and Judaism; (3) their antipathy
to Christianity; and (4) their Islamophilia, which saw them tirelessly promote the idea of a genuine Muslim-Jewish symbiosis, especially in Spain.
From this, it should be clear that Jewish orientalists generally approached
the Muslim world with a different set of sectarian assumptions and prejudices from those held by Gentile orientalists. Specific national, religious,
and political traditions all played a role in the production of orientalist
knowledge and, just as crucially, mind-set, as Jewish scholars expressed both
private and public sentiments about Muslims, Oriental Jews of both past
and present, and contemporary Ashkenazic Jews that were informed by
their status as Central European intellectuals with distinguished academic
credentials, while at the same time they remained part of Europe's marginalized Jewish minority. We will also see how the deeply personal aesthetic
sensibilities of these Jewish historians runs like a red thread through their
published scholarship, and in their private diaries and letters, to reveal the
various emotional fault lines that formed the jagged terrain of Central European Jewish identity in the age of emancipation.

ABRAHAM GEIGER

Abraham Geiger (1810–1874), known as the "founding father of the Reform movement" in Judaism, was the product of a traditionally observant
home and a thorough Jewish education.[11] Considered an *illui*, or child
prodigy, Geiger spent his formative years steeped in classical Jewish literature, to which he would later apply the critical methods of *Wissenschaft des
Judentums*. In 1829, he was admitted to the University of Heidelberg and
then later moved on to the University of Bonn, where he studied Near Eastern languages and general philosophy. There, at twenty-three years of age,
Geiger entered an essay contest sponsored by the philosophy faculty. The
question, posed by his teacher, the distinguished orientalist B. F. Freytag,
was designed to examine the Jewish sources of certain themes in the Koran.
Geiger's prize-winning Latin response was later expanded and translated
into German as *Was hat Muhammad aus dem Judenthume aufgenommen?*
(What Did Muhammad Adopt from Judaism?). It was the work for which
he was awarded the doctorate at the University of Marburg in 1834.[12] From
its first appearance, the book was hailed as a significant contribution to the
emerging field of scholarship on Islam. Although later scholars pointed to
its limitations, shortcomings that only expanded over time as the discipline

developed, it nevertheless continued to be hailed as a classic, even by those whose work superseded it.[13]

In the 1830s, Geiger began the serious study of historical and theological questions, a deep passion that remained with him throughout his life. In essence, Geiger sought to establish definitively the foundational role played by Judaism in the advent of Christianity and Islam. Such a goal was part of the larger political quest: the attainment of civic emancipation, and the winning of greater respect in Germany for Jews and Judaism. As Susannah Heschel has argued, this led Geiger to undertake "the proper assessment of Western civilization's role for Judaism, its texts and history, which had been neglected, misinterpreted, or deliberately falsified by Christian scholars."[14] Indeed, Geiger sought to undermine the privileged status that Christianity accorded itself in claiming to be the basis of Western civilization, an honor that he believed belonged to Judaism.

Geiger's contribution to the writing of religious history, including Islamic studies, was novel in a number of ways. Between 1820 and 1870, with the establishment of new institutions, associations, scholarly journals, and fields of academic specialization, Germany became the world leader in orientalist studies. According to Suzanne Marchand, the subject's preeminent historian, rather than imperialism, the field was rooted "in the traditions of Christian humanism and informed evangelism."[15] As such, orientalism in Germany was almost entirely dominated by Protestant men of faith. Being a Jewish orientalist in Germany at this time made Geiger a trailblazer, and it also meant that his approach would differ markedly from that of Christian scholars. Methodologically, Geiger was a comparativist and made a genuine attempt to historicize religious origins. In particular, he sought to accord the previously ignored or belittled textual sources of rabbinic Judaism their due in the development of Christianity and Islam. In Geiger's estimation, both the Gospels and the Koran bore the unmistakable stamp of midrashic and Talmudic wisdom. Yet most likely owing to the explosive nature of his methodology and argumentation, Geiger began his scholarly quest to establish the foundational nature of Judaism with his attempt to trace the theological debt Islam owed Judaism. He had wanted to begin his career by making a similar argument for Christianity, but anticipating what would surely have been a hostile response, he began with Islam and waited for three decades before he published this thesis as it applied to Christianity.

Another of Geiger's innovations, one that bespeaks a particular German-Jewish orientalism, is the way he characterized both Muhammad and Islam. While the Enlightenment saw the beginnings of a more positive representation of Islam and its founder, many scholars continued to dismiss Muhammad as a hypocrite and deceiver, as Voltaire had done, or they concurred with Herder, who called the prophet a "fanatic," while still others agreed with the great nineteenth-century Semiticist Theodor Nöldeke, who diagnosed him as "hysterical."[16] However, one should also add, because Said conveniently omitted it, that men such as Voltaire, Diderot, and Michaelis had equally negative things to say about postexilic Judaism and contemporary Jews.[17] Whether anti-Christian encyclopedist or Protestant Hebrew Bible scholar, these men were ecumenical in their prejudices toward contemporary cultures and peoples they considered Oriental, identifying religion either with fanaticism *tout court* or, for those scholars of religious faith, with cultural decline in the case of the post-Christian Orient.[18] Even more revealing because it should caution against the simplistic urge to string together decontextualized negative quotations about the Other in order to determine orientalist "guilt," is—as we have seen and will see further—the fact that in the eighteenth century, Jews too began to offer harsh critiques of Judaism. They focused on such things as the laws of Leviticus, arguing for their irrelevancy for the modern world, or derided what they considered the superstition and irrationality of Hasidism, or they offered bitter critiques of the Jewish educational system, or they decried, as did Moses Mendelssohn, the coercive power of the rabbis.[19] And as harsh as those internal Jewish critiques were, they paled in comparison with post-Reformation Protestant and Catholic judgments of each other, opinions that went beyond the page and the pulpit and onto the battlefield. Deeply held religious positions informed German orientalism to a far greater degree than was the case elsewhere in Europe, and provided a far stronger impetus to it than imperialism ever did. Contemporary scholarship that fails to recognize that eighteenth- and nineteenth-century European criticism of Arabs and Islam was part of a larger discourse—one that saw invective poured out upon Christianity and Judaism as well—does a disservice to the historical record.

To return to Geiger, he declared the negative Enlightenment-era opinions of Muhammad to be the product of "outright bias and misunderstanding of the human heart" (*einseitigkeit und gänzlicher Verkennung des menschlichen Herzens*). By contrast, Geiger saw Muhammad as a "genuine enthusiast (*wirklicher Schwärmer*) who was himself convinced of his divine mission, and to whom the union of all religions appeared necessary for the welfare of mankind."[20] This is not to say that Geiger was soft on Muhammad and Islam. Although contemporary reviewers found Geiger to be too generous,[21] he was highly critical of the "traces of hate" (*Spuren von Hass*) that he detected in Muhammad, charging him with misrepresenting Judaism. Part of Muhammad's misrepresentation was willful, but part of it was the result of the misunderstanding of Judaism by the Arabian Jews who transmitted erroneous religious ideas to Muhammad. This was because "the Jews of that region were amongst the most ignorant, as is shown by the silence of the Talmud concerning them" (9–10). Key to the problem is that Jews passed their knowledge of Judaism on to Muhammad orally. It did not derive from a serious textual engagement with Scripture (24). In many ways his later opposition to Orthodox Judaism, which was so crucial to his orientalism and his celebration of Sephardic Jewry, reprised this critique, namely, that Orthodoxy had given itself over to spurious rabbinic interpretations, while in the East Hasidism further corrupted Judaism by its embrace of legends and superstitious beliefs all transmitted orally to the faithful. In fact, Geiger confided to his diary that he found Islam's history fascinating "because everywhere echoes of Judaism can be found, namely, the Judaism that was formed by the rabbis and the fairy-tale whimsicalness of oriental Jews."[22] This kind of Jewish self-critique was foundational for Jewish orientalism and the German-Jewish idealization of Sephardic culture.

Geiger also recognized that Muhammad's vacillating attitude toward the Jews—initial optimism gave way to later frustration with their refusal to convert—reflected ever-changing historical circumstances. Above all though, for Geiger, evidence of the historicity of religions (a central doctrine of Reform Judaism) was manifest in the special affinity that existed between Judaism and Islam. As an example, Geiger argued that Muhammad's relatively beneficent evaluation of Judaism was characterized primarily by his liberal borrowing from it and his fairly benign treatment of Jews. Geiger also suggested that there were practical considerations that went into Muhammad's thinking. He was of the opinion that Muhammad's decision to leave the Jews alone was due to his fear of engaging them in theological disputation because of their "intellectual superiority" and their "power to shake the faith of others in the religion revealed to him" (10–11). Geiger seemed to appreciate Muhammad's respect for Jews.

However, Geiger's critique of Muhammad went further. Because he sought to assert the foundational nature of Judaism for Islam, Geiger denied that Muhammad had created a new religion. Rather, he "was in favor of borrowing from earlier religions. He desired no peculiarity, no new religion that should oppose all that had gone before" (30). Decades later Geiger described the Koran as "intellectually barren, ethically scant, and poetically arid."[23] This should not surprise us when we consider that, as an orientalist in the German tradition, Geiger was engaged in religious polemics, not imperialist politics. German Christian orientalists, even if they spoke of Islam in negative terms, were inclined to supersessionism vis-à-vis Judaism and, as adherents of the higher biblical criticism, advanced foundation-shaking challenges to traditional Christianity. German Jewish orientalists like Geiger were fighting a rearguard action against Christian triumphalism, German social discrimination, and Orthodox Judaism, all of which they considered an impediment to both Jews and the states in which they lived.

In his critique of Islam, Geiger was unwilling to attribute to Muhammad the status of divinely inspired prophet, for to have done so would have meant acknowledging the divine origin of Islam, a belief that would have run counter to Geiger's conviction that Judaism alone should be accorded that particular honor. Similarly, Geiger astutely noted that Muhammad could not accept Judaism in its entirety because doing so would have been tantamount to accepting the divine provenance of Jewish law. Islam's founder "could not maintain with the Jews that their Law was immutable (*Unabänderbarkeit*), for that would have been fatal to his system of religious syncretism (*Verschmeltzungssysteme*)" (34). Nor, according to Geiger, could Muhammad accept the Jewish proposition that the Messiah was yet to come, for that would have undermined his own claims to be the last prophet. So although a new religion did emerge, that was not, according to Geiger, Muhammad's initial intent; rather, it was to incorporate Jews into "his kingdom of the faithful (*Glaubensreich*) upon earth" (29).

Geiger's assessment was not the product of a Eurocentric, colonialist worldview so much as it was determined by his commitment to a comparative and source-critical religious history—albeit one that privileged Judaism. And even this observation about the religious imperative behind German orientalism can be brought into sharper focus when we recognize that Geiger belonged to the earliest generation of Islamicists, men who mastered the Koran for scholarly purposes, as contrasted with the long tradition of Christians who studied the Hebrew Bible, kabbalah, Hebrew, and Yiddish with the intention of missionizing.[24] Geiger's scholarly purpose, however, was not benign; it was driven by a politico-cultural agenda that was characteristic of *Wissenschaft des Judentums* more generally, its "competitive historicism." Its aim was to counter claims of Christian supersessionism by asserting that Judaism was the original and most genuinely universal religion.[25]

His criticism of Muhammad and Islam notwithstanding, for Geiger the links that bound Judaism and Islam together stood in marked contrast to the breach that characterized relations between Christianity and Judaism. Echoing the dictum of a German-Jewish contemporary, the novelist Berthold Auerbach, who claimed that the barometer of a country's morality was the way it treated its Jews, Geiger spoke highly of Arabia, for "it was very favorable to the Jews, who had fled to that country in large numbers after the destruction of Jerusalem, inasmuch as it enabled them to gather together and maintain their independence" (7). In fact, thirty years later, in the summer semester of 1872, in a lecture that he gave at Berlin's Hochschule für die Wissenschaft des Judentums, Geiger expanded upon the idea that Judaism flourished under Islam, claiming that it "survived and took root in those countries that long before had produced the first fruits of civilization: Egypt, Phoenicia, Syria, Assyria, and Babylonia." While it was also later influenced by Parsiism and Hellenism, Judaism "*developed its own fullest potential in closest union with Arab civilization.*"[26]

Geiger noted that Judaism principally flourished among the Arabs, for there it did not stand in religious contention with the majority. As with most scholars of the *Wissenschaft des Judentums* school, Geiger looked beyond Arabia to Jewish life in Muslim Spain as an example of Jewish communal and cultural efflorescence and integration into the larger society. In 1851, Geiger published a comprehensive study of the Spanish Hebrew poet Judah Halevi wherein he noted that it was language that allowed Jews to play so prominent a role in the general culture. It was in Spain, according to Geiger, that Arab and Jewish culture, inherently and intimately related as they were, became intertwined as Hebrew became Arabized, Arabic aesthetics became Judaized, and even the deepest of Jewish religious writings were produced in Arabic. Only among the poets, he notes, was Hebrew preferred. Scholars and the people, by contrast, preferred Arabic.[27] Belonging to a generation of German Jews a great many of whom lived in rural areas and still spoke Yiddish, Geiger saw the acquisition of an unaccented command of the vernacular as fundamental to the attainment of *Kultur* and social integration.[28]

Because Geiger was committed to comparative historical and philological scholarship, his positive evaluation of Islam was to a great extent conditioned by his attitude toward Christianity, an attitude that hardened over time. In a letter of 1865 to a friend of his, the Göttingen mathematician Moritz Stern, Geiger bitterly declared, "I may be mistaken about many things but I am not mistaken when I view Christianity as the adversary of great cultural endeavor. Christianity takes great pains to reveal the full extent of its intolerance; the papal encyclicals and the spoutings of the High Consistories, the synods and the Church Days truly contribute their fair share in this effort."[29] Geiger did not merely confine these sentiments to his private correspondence. With considerable courage he put them into print at this time. In a volume entitled *Judaism and Its History* (1864–1865) Geiger dedicated an entire chapter to Christianity as an ecclesiastical world power. After listing the Christian religion's positive achievements, such as its attempt to unify humanity, Geiger passed judgment: "But that which was, and still is, its power, is at the same time its weakness. It made the assertion, 'I am the new world, all that existed before is nothing,' and accordingly smashed and destroyed everything humane, beautiful, and noble that earlier times had produced." Christianity was gripped by a "lust for destruction" (*Zerstörungswuth*) and obliterated not only that which was "idolatrous and pagan as such, but all the intellectual treasures of antiquity too—all was adjudged to be the work of the devil, all must be destroyed."[30]

With his unvarnished views of Christianity there for all to see, it was inevitable that he would compare Jewish life under Islam with that in Christian Europe. In the summer of 1868 he wrote to Theodor Nöldeke, comparing the tolerance of the Muslim state that "admitted both Jews and Christians" with the exclusionary practices of Europe, claiming that not only were Catholic and Protestant clergy guilty of fomenting Jew hatred; "even the non-believers cannot refrain from spouting invective against Jews and Judaism, simply because this hatred has been inculcated into their hearts by Christianity."[31]

In the 1860s, approximately three decades after the appearance of his study of Islam, Geiger wrote a series of historical essays in which he again compared the state of Jews under the two dominant monotheistic faiths. He indicted Christianity yet again because "from the very beginning [it] saw itself as the fulfillment of Judaism's promise," and thus it was inherently unable to accommodate itself to peaceful coexistence with Judaism, for the latter's "tenacious longevity was a crushing blow (*niederschmetternder Schlag*) at Christianity and each individual Jew was an opposing witness to the truth of Christianity."[32] Thus did Christianity engage Judaism in an eternal struggle, with conversion of the Jews its ultimate goal. This was not just the analysis of a dispassionate historian; it was also the expressed fear of a committed Jew. Geiger's personal relationship with the Protestant theologian Franz Delitzsch, who, while sympathetic to Judaism, was nonetheless an active missionary, exacerbated Geiger's dismay and increasing bitterness at Christianity's ongoing conversionist impulse.[33]

Despite the fact that Geiger embarked on a lifelong quest that saw him try to tailor Judaism to conform to the aesthetic sensibilities of German middle-class life, he was not a slavish assimilationist. On the contrary, he was an ardent defender of Jewish rights, an intellectual who repeatedly took a public stand to defend his coreligionists by asserting, like Moses Mendelssohn before him, that the attainment of German citizenship should not have to entail the abandonment of Judaism.[34]

In the wake of intensifying antisemitism after the Jews were emancipated in 1871, Geiger spoke out against his detractors, and his scholarship became even more stridently anti-Christian. As a historian, he was especially stung by German biblical scholarship, which was replete with antisemitism and bolstered by a sincere belief in Christian supersessionism.[35] In 1872, he again wrote to Theodor Nöldeke, complaining of the treatment of Jewish sources at the hands of Christian Bible scholars. He assured Nöldeke that Jewish scholars were not trying to dictate the research agenda or methodological approach of Christians, but "we do have the right to denounce the ignorance of those who, despite such ignorance, and with boundless arrogance and spite, air their derogatory opinions on such matters; and we are justified in banning such persons from the company of fair and honest scholars."[36]

More than once Geiger was condemned as having denigrated Jesus, and indeed he was deeply engaged in polemics and intellectual combat with contemporary Protestant New Testament scholars who sought to tear asunder the historical and theological links between Judaism and Christianity. They also challenged his provocative interpretation that Christianity was a derivative of Pharisaic Judaism, and that Judaism, not Christianity, was the universal religion par excellence. Pharisaism was not a particular branch of ancient Judaism for Geiger, but rather "a tendency in world history, marked by rebellion against oppression, an ethical maturity, and adult conscious-ness (*erwachsenes Volksbewusstsein*)."[37]

And finally, this leads us to the extent to which Geiger's rejection of Orthodoxy—which began in earnest with his secular university studies, then peaked with the Titkin affair of 1838, and matured as he developed a theology of Reform Judaism—also influenced his more generous inter-pretation of Islam when compared with that of Christianity, thus reflecting a particular Jewish brand of orientalism.[38] For Geiger, a Judaism character-ized by ethical maturity, namely, Reform Judaism, stood in opposition to the "absolutism of the *Shulkhan Arukh*," which derived its legitimacy, and therefore its oppressive character, merely by virtue of having been written down. He objected to both a Christian critique that saw Judaism as ossi-fied and an Orthodox Jewish one that misunderstood what it called "tra-dition." This did not mean permanency from time immemorial; rather, Geiger interpreted the essence of Talmudic and rabbinic tradition to be its ever-dynamic striving for perfection, via its sensitivity to changing histori-cal circumstances and currents. In their hostile reaction to any innovation, Orthodoxy and Catholicism were comparable, in Geiger's view, in the way both sought hegemony.[39]

By contrast, Geiger considered the connection between the varieties of Judaism and Islam, asserting that the Judaism from which Islam emerged had been the purest form of the Jewish religion and that which most closely corresponded to Reform Judaism, for it was monotheistic, unencumbered by orthopractic detail, bound to biblical prophecy, and based on divine reve-lation. Moreover, he detected in the medieval Jewish culture that flourished under Islam in the Iberian Peninsula an admirable form of Judaism, one that differed markedly from that which emerged in Central and Eastern Eu-rope. While he saw both Eastern Europe and the Orient as "culturally defi-cient," Geiger was especially disapproving of the state of Judaism in Poland, which was characterized by "the new growth and further degeneration that is Hasidism," a religious expression he dismissed as "nothing more than ig-norance and slothful thinking" (*Unwissenheit und Denkfaulheit*).[40]

At the root of what Geiger considered to be this cultural degeneration was kabbalah.[41] He believed it was responsible for giving birth to Hasidism and, indeed, the entire psychology and culture of Polish Jewry. The irration-ality of the latter manifested itself even in the appearance of the Hasidim. Geiger was especially perturbed by their style of dress, which for him was a most visible sign of their irrationality. What so agitated Geiger was an arti-cle he read in a north German newspaper, the *Hamburger Nachrichten*. With a dateline of Warsaw, July 28, 1853, the report noted that in the Middle Ages, as Jews from neighboring lands fled to Poland in the wake of persecutions, they were guaranteed the right to "maintain their traditional Talmudic garb." With justification, Geiger scoffed at the idea that Hasidic dress was prescribed by the Talmud, and he was especially outraged by the article's implication that those medieval Jewish asylum seekers, most of whom were from Germany, had worn such clothes in that country before their flight east. "I am," he concluded, "repulsed by such parasites and Thersitians"—a reference to Thersites, a Greek soldier in the Trojan War, whom Homer depicted as physically misshapen, bandy-legged, lame, hunch-shouldered, coarse, and abusive, a man who spoke incessantly, and in a confused and jumbled way at that.[42] The learned Geiger may have been the only one to ever compare the Hasidim to one of Homer's characters, but the comparison aptly served his purpose in seeking to distinguish German from Eastern European Jews and rational Reform Judaism from superstitious Hasidism. Just as Homer made Thersites repulsive and set him in stark contrast to his social betters, King Agamemnon, Achilles, and Odysseus, Geiger resorts to a stock-standard German-Jewish description of the physically deformed, loquacious Eastern European Jew with his garbled speech. As we saw in chapters 1 and 2, the physical appearance and sonic qualities of Polish Jews were frequently portrayed as the antithesis of those Jews Abraham Geiger considered aesthetically, intellectually, and socially superior—medieval Spanish Jews and contemporary German Jewry.

Geiger clearly recognized the negative impact of persecution in medieval France and Germany on Jewish cultural life, the intellectual achievements of the biblical exegete Rashi notwithstanding. He also sharply indicted the generally anti-intellectual climate fostered by Christianity for what he regarded as the low level of early modern Polish Jewish culture (from which he exempted, among others, distinguished rabbis such as Shalom Shakhna, Moses Isserles, and Solomon Luria).[43] We can recall here Naphtali Herz Wessely's charge that deficiencies in the languages and culture of Polish Jews were in great part attributable to the uncultured environment in which they lived. In contrast, Islamic Spain gave rise to Jews whom Geiger described as "heroes of *Wissenschaft*." Their worldly poets, authors, and religious thinkers, especially those who wrote in Arabic (perhaps an oblique reference to his stance that German and not Hebrew should be the language of Jewish liturgy), were as close to ideal as any premodern Jewish community could ever hope to have become. In fact, long past the Golden Age of Spanish Jewry, the Sephardim continued to produce figures who served as excellent role models for modern Jews. In his search for Iberian Jewish precursors to various modern Germans whom he admired, Geiger referred to Isaac Abravanel (1437–1508) as the Wilhelm von Humboldt of his day.[44]

Heinrich Graetz

Heinrich Graetz (1817–1891), the greatest and most influential Jewish historian of the nineteenth century, shaped the way generations of students and the general Jewish public thought about the Jewish past. In his comprehensive history of the Jews, he addressed at considerable length the rise of Islam, Jewish influences on Islamic belief and practice, and the subsequent history of the Jews in the Islamic orbit. Graetz was the principal, or at least initial, source of knowledge about this subject for many European Jews, among them many future Jewish orientalists. He was also one of the chief architects of the popular image of Sephardic Jewry's Golden Age under Islam.

Graetz was born into humble circumstances in the small town of Xions in eastern Prussia. The town was located in the province of Posen, today part of Poland, and a large portion of this territory came under Prussian control following the partitions of Poland in the eighteenth century. Until that time, the Jews of this region had essentially been Polish, but after the Congress of Vienna in 1815, when even more of the area came under Prussian control, the Jews of Posen became increasingly attached to German culture.[45] Nevertheless, when Graetz was growing up, his neighbors were still Polish Jews. It was a group he came to loathe, and his feelings toward Polish Jewry came to play a decisive role in the formation of his worldview, and the history he wrote, including his assessments of Islam, Christianity, Orthodox Judaism, and the aesthetics of the latter—and, by contrast, his positive depictions of Sephardic Jewry.[46]

After pursuing his rabbinical studies from 1831 to 1836 in Wolstein, near Posen, Graetz experienced a spiritual crisis, one that was assuaged by his reading of Samson Raphael Hirsch's *Nineteen Letters on Judaism* (1836), an invented epistolary exchange between two young Jews, one committed to his faith, the other considering conversion to Christianity. Graetz's encounter with Hirsch, the father of German neo-Orthodoxy, developed into a personal relationship when Graetz was invited to live and study with Hirsch in Oldenburg. After a stint as a private tutor, Graetz entered the University of Breslau in 1842, prior to which he had had no formal secular education.[47] He eventually earned his PhD at the University of Jena in 1845, having written a dissertation entitled *Gnosticism and Judaism*.[48]

Although Graetz had begun as a champion of Orthodoxy, the influence of Hirsch began to wane when he became convinced that Hirsch's antihistoricism and Orthodoxy in general constituted a barrier to modernization and emancipation. However, he was also alarmed by what he perceived to be the extremism of the Reformist camp and its use of *Wissenschaft des Judentums* for political ends. Therefore, in the 1840s, Graetz joined a conservative bloc, allying himself with, among others, Zacharias Frankel, founder of Positive-Historical Judaism (what would later be called Conservative Judaism in the United States), a middle position between the Reform and Orthodox camps.[49] In particular, Graetz supported Frankel for having walked out in protest from the second Rabbinical Conference held in Frankfurt in 1845, after the majority decided against the necessity of reciting prayers in Hebrew. Thereafter, Graetz became a contributor to Frankel's *Zeitschrift für die religiösen Interessen des Judentums* (Journal for the Religious Interests of the Jews), a publication critical of Reform Judaism. In 1854, Graetz was appointed lecturer in Jewish history and Bible at the newly founded Jewish Theological Seminary of Breslau, where he taught until his death in 1891. In 1869 he was made honorary professor at the University of Breslau, an appointment that did not require his baptism. His disqualification, because he was Jewish, for a professorship at a German university also shaped the way he saw and depicted Islam and Christianity, and the differences in the respective ways they treated their Jews.

Graetz's greatest scholarly achievement was his comprehensive eleven-volume *History of the Jews*, published between 1853 and 1876.[50] It was offered to the public through Ludwig Philippson's Institute for the Promotion of Jewish Literature, as was Graetz's three-volume abridged version, *Popular History of the Jews*, which appeared between 1888 and 1891. The link between Graetz's approach to writing history and Philippson's program to make it available to the Jewish public was no mere accident. Like Philippson, Graetz also wished to inculcate pride in the Jewish past through an edifying depiction of it, and to strengthen bonds among Jews in the present. He was the first historian to write a comprehensive history of the Jews from a nationalist standpoint.[51] In contrast to Geiger and Zunz, Graetz fully understood the tenor of the literary times. He had been an eager participant in Germany's reading revolution and had also become a changed man because of it, for fiction allowed for his metaphorical escape from his provincial surroundings. The first non-Jewish books he ever read were adventure stories set in the Middle Ages, and what he gleaned from the style of such works never left him.[52] Understanding literature's power and capacity to effect change, Graetz made greater strides than anyone before him in combining serious scholarship with a novelist's sensibility. Replete with heroes, villains, and martyrs, his prose is passionate, and his powers of description are deeply evocative. Graetz's *History of the Jews* was a page-turner.

What concerns us here is how, in this work, he represented Islam and the Islamic world for Jews. In short, after proclaiming that "rising Islam was as intolerant as Christianity," Graetz saw each subsequent premodern encounter between Jews and Muslims as a story of liberation for Jews.[53] Crucially, however, his depiction of Jewish life under the Muslims was to a great extent determined by his negative conceptions of Christianity and Orthodox

Judaism, features that, as stated above, also seem to have helped determine Geiger's response to the Islamic world—and, as we shall see shortly, that of Ignaz Goldziher as well.[54]

To better appreciate Graetz's view of the Islamic environment for Jews, we must recognize that his description of Islam's rise came hard on the heels of his lament over the Christianization of Palestine. In the fifth volume of his *History of the Jews*, he writes: "Churches and monasteries arose in the Holy Land whose former masters were subjected to all sorts of persecution whenever they attempted to repair a dilapidated synagogue. Bishops, abbots, and monks lorded it over Palestine, and turned it into a playground of dogmatic wranglings (*Tummelplatz dogmatischen Gezänkes*) over the simple or dual nature of Christ."[55]

After the triumphant Christianization of the Holy Land, Graetz reports that there remained only one Jewish intellectual center—the academy of Mar Zutra III in Tiberias. Yet interestingly, while he laments the loss of their academic institutions, he boasts that the Jews still retained the aesthetic upper hand, noting that "Nazareth, the cradle of Christianity, where the most beautiful women in all Palestine were to be found, seems to have been mostly populated by Jews."[56] After its definitive separation from Judaism, Christianity, which made the "senseless believable and the unbelievable necessary," was indeed repugnant to Graetz, but here he betrays the belief that Christians themselves were not as beautiful as Jews, even, perhaps especially, in the birthplace of their religion. In fact, after he visited Nazareth, Graetz's enduring impression of the city was that he "and other tourists found its narrow streets [to be] full of refuse."[57] Theodor Herzl would echo Graetz's observation during his visit to Jerusalem in 1898, complaining in a diary entry that "the musty deposits of two thousand years of inhumanity, intolerance, and foulness lie in your reeking alleys." And again like Graetz, Herzl declared mockingly, "The one man who has been present here all this while, the lovable dreamer of Nazareth, had done nothing but help increase the hate."[58]

For Graetz beauty was not only physical; as it had been for an earlier generation of German maskilim, it was also aural, and his account of Jesus's ministry is particularly revealing. Praising him for his teachings, Graetz focused on the way he believed Jesus must have sounded when preaching. He saw the Galileans as victims of superstition, a consequence of their living among "heathen Syrians," and their dialect "had also become corrupted by their Syrian neighbors, through the intermixture of Aramaic elements." Worst of all for Graetz, "the Galileans could not pronounce Hebrew with purity, often mixing up or omitting the guttural sounds, and thus often incurred the ridicule of the Judeans who adhere to correct pronunciation." For Graetz, the ludicrousness of the Galileans' language was matched by the irrationality of their religious behavior insofar as they did not display the moderate and sensible customs of the Judeans and were instead "infamously splenetic and dogmatic."[59] It is uncanny just how much Graetz's screed about the Galileans' poor speech, poor manners, ignorance, superstition, and religious excess reads exactly the same as his critique of Eastern European Jewry, and especially Hasidism. For Graetz, both Christianity and Hasidism were perversions of authentic Judaism, and both Christians and Eastern European Jews had degenerated in both physical and moral terms from those Jews who lived before the advent of both movements.

Pre-Christian Judaism leads us to the Sephardim, because many scholars, Graetz included, believed that the Jews of Spain were directly descended from the Judeans. Those origins led Graetz to conclude that "Jewish Spain contributed almost as much to the development of Judaism as Judea and Babylonia." All over Spain, Judaism had acquired a "new vigor," and in large part this was due to its Judean bloodlines. Granada and Toledo were the new Jerusalem and Tiberias, and according to Graetz had become more familiar to the Jews than the Babylonian cities of Nehardea and Sura. Graetz noted that the Sephardim shared with other Spaniards the sentiment of "pride of ancestry"; in the Jewish case, he observed that the Spanish Jews themselves believed that they had been taken to Spain after the destruction of the Temple in 586 B.C.E. by the Babylonian conqueror Nebuchadnezzar.[60]

Jerusalem and Spain were linked in another way for Graetz. Emanating from the former was monotheism, the gift Judaism gave the world; it was a bequest of universal appeal. Like those of the Israelites, the history and culture of the Sephardim was of "universal importance." This made the Sephardim distinct, for according to Graetz's judgment the Jews of Byzantium, Italy, and France were really of "interest [only] for specialist students" (of Jewish history). Graetz would later go on to identify other parochial communities barely even worthy of consideration by the historian, Polish Jewry chief among them. He would also single out German Jewry, with the advent of Moses Mendelssohn, as the only Jewish community since that of the Spanish "Golden Age" to have produced a culture of universal significance.

Not only was Graetz inclined to compare and contrast one Jewish community with another; he frequently compared the larger environments in which Jews lived. This meant weighing Christianity against Islam, and the former was always found to have been a curse. Graetz was not the only Jewish intellectual to lament the destructive power wielded by Christianity, while extolling the comparatively benign nature of Islam. Heinrich Heine had said as much in his pro-Islamic and, to many, anti-Christian diatribe of 1821, *Almansor*.[61] Heine, who took the culture of the Near East seriously and on its own terms, and had read nearly all the Arabic and Persian classics that had been translated into German, scathingly wrote, "On the tower where the muezzin called to prayer, the faithful sang the words of the Prophet, tonsured monks are acting out their lugubrious charades." To stay with Heine a moment longer, because he symbolizes and indeed represents a deeply respectful German-Jewish orientalism of the early nineteenth century, it is worth recalling that his most famous and prophetic lines about Christian intolerance are to be found in this play that extols the culture of the Orient. In an interchange between Almansor and his servant, Hassan, the former remarks, "We heard that Ximenes the Terrible in Granada, in the middle of the marketplace—my tongue refuses to say it!—cast the Koran into the flames of a burning pyre!" And to this, the wise Hassan retorts with a warning: "That was only a prelude; where they burn books they will, in the end, burn human beings too."[62]

Repeatedly in his published work and private correspondence, Graetz expressed his unbridled yet ecumenical hatred for those who hated Jews. These included entire peoples, such as the Romans, the Christians, and the Germans, as well as individual antagonists like Luther and Voltaire, and Hellenized Jews such as Herod and Josephus, apostates, the false Messiah Shabbtai Zvi and his followers, and even contemporary adherents of Reform Judaism.[63] All set out to destroy the Jews. By and large Graetz's characterization of Jewish life under Christianity was an unremitting *Leidensgeschichte*, a history of suffering. Unable and unwilling to conceal his rage, Graetz held Christian anti-Judaism to be a congenital condition: "the first utterance of Christianity on the very day of its victory [at the Council of Nicaea in 325] betrayed its hostile attitude toward the Jews, and from it flowed those hostile decrees of Constantine and his successors, which laid the foundation of the bloody persecutions of subsequent centuries."[64]

Even under Islam, Graetz detected the recurrent theme of Judaism's progeny turning on the parent faith after a period of cordiality.[65] Still, nothing in the historical record of Jewish-Muslim relations could compare with the discrimination meted out by Christianity. By contrast, and especially from the perspective of nineteenth-century German Jewry, Islam had been good to the Jews. The contemplation of Jewish life under Muslim rule also provided comfort for the historian so traumatized by having to write the story of Christian persecution. In a remarkably self-reflective passage, Graetz observes, "Wearied with contemplating the lamentable plight of the Jews in their ancient home (*Urheimat*) and in the countries of Europe, and from the fanatical oppression of Christianity, the eyes of the observer rest with gladness upon their situation in the Arabian peninsula." This was because "here the sons of Judah were free to raise their heads, and did not need to look out with fear and humiliation. Unhindered, they were allowed to develop their powers in the midst of a free, simple, and talented people." It is true that Graetz assumed the "intellectual superiority" of the Jews over the

Arabian tribes, but the period he was referring to was prior to Muhammad's appearance and the subsequent creation of a new, Islamic civilization. In sum, he refers to this later age as a "glorious page in the annals of the Jews."[66]

As a consequence of their shared "Semitic descent" and high rate of intermarriage, the Jewish tribes of Arabia became "so thoroughly Arabic that they were distinguished from the natives only by their religious belief." Here, to paraphrase the term used in Graetz's day, the Jews were "Arabs of the Mosaic persuasion."·In terms of temperament, courage, and a shared love of poetry and language, Graetz saw Jews and Arabs as akin, and extolled the truly symbiotic nature of the relationship of the two peoples.[67] In fact, he declared in a positive and extremely generous vein that Islam "has exercised an immense influence on the course of Jewish history and on the evolution of Judaism."[68] And this is crucial because for Graetz, Jewish history was of significance only when considered from the vantage of the extent to which it was integrated into non-Jewish life.[69]

The theme of Jewish integration into the larger society, its successes and failures, permeates the eleventh and final volume of Graetz's *Geschichte der Juden*, which covered the period 1750–1848. What he had to say was significant in two ways: first was his portrayal of Moses Mendelssohn as acting in the spirit of his namesake by leading Jewish youth out of the desert of insularity and into the promised land of European culture; second was his bitter condemnation of the persistence of antisemitism in Germany. The two issues were connected insofar as the depth of Jewish acculturation elicited a virulent and organized backlash.

In the first instance Graetz identified the onset of the modern period in Jewish history with Moses Mendelssohn. Mendelssohn was, according to Graetz, the embodiment of the Jewish people: "crooked, awkward, dense, stuttering, ugly and repulsive in outward appearance." However, once exposed to the wider world and allowed to expand his intellectual horizons, he was ennobled. Mendelssohn's story was the story of the Jewish people in the modern period, for like him they had succeeded in "raising themselves from lowliness and contempt to greatness and self-consciousness."[70]

The journey from his birthplace, Dessau, to Berlin was more than just a mere trip. It was a transformative experience that saw Mendelssohn evolve from parochial Jew to cosmopolitan Jew. Graetz closely identified with Mendelssohn because his own metamorphosis from provincial yeshivah student to world-famous historian so strikingly resembled Mendelssohn's story at its core. Graetz saw Mendelssohn's historic significance in the way that he blazed a trail for all future generations of young German-Jewish men like himself, leaving home in search of *Bildung*, or self-cultivation.

Bildung was acquired through imbibing general culture and secular knowledge, and with its attainment someone like Mendelssohn underwent an aesthetic makeover. His facial features remained unchanged, and of course his humpback was as prominent as ever, but in spite of that deformity, as Graetz depicted him, Mendelssohn now carried himself with dignity and grace. He also became a different man sonically. According to Graetz, Mendelssohn did this by abandoning Yiddish—he of course did not—in favor of German. He learned a number of other languages as well. And relative to concerns about the sound of Hebrew in the Berlin Haskalah, Mendelssohn "abandoned the ossified, distorted, overembellished Hebrew style of his contemporaries, which had been reduced to a hideous, stuttering, decrepit tongue. Mendelssohn's Hebrew gushed forth as fresh and clear as a mountain stream."[71]

Yet to Graetz's way of thinking, non-Jewish culture was only partly responsible for the new Mendelssohn. Equally crucial for his radically new appearance, for his emergence as a new kind of Jew, were the writings of Maimonides, the Sephardic Jew par excellence. The latter was a man likewise depicted by Graetz as representative of his branch of the Jewish people. Like Mendelssohn, Maimonides was an exceptional figure, but he too inspired Jews to emulate him. Held in esteem by Jewish communities in the East and the West, he was, for Graetz, the "spiritual king of the Jews."[72] Mendelssohn, by comparison, "divined that he was called upon to purify the morals and aesthetics of his brethren."[73]

Graetz's close identification with Mendelssohn derived from one other similarity in their respective transformations. Struggling to emerge from the closeted world of the yeshivah, Graetz likewise incorporated Maimonides and Judah Halevi into his reading curriculum, gaining from the experience pleasure as well as moral and aesthetic profit.[74] It was these giant figures of Sephardic civilization whom Mendelssohn adopted as sure-footed guides; Graetz and other Jews who sought to remain deeply rooted in the Jewish world, but wanted to be equally at home in the surrounding culture, did likewise.

For Graetz, German Jewry, led by Mendelssohn, was poised to don the mantle previously worn by Spanish Jewry. Indeed, the language Graetz used to describe Mendelssohn's transformation after his introduction to the writings of Maimonides bears a striking similarity to his description of Spanish-Jewish leadership during the Golden Age under Islam. When Mendelssohn arrived in Berlin, we read that he was "violent and hot-tempered by nature." But by drinking in the words of Maimonides, "he taught himself such complete self-control that, like a second Hillel, he became distinguished for gentleness and placidity."[75] The behavioral traits of Sephardic elites are striking similar: "The prominent men, who, through either their political position or their other merits stood at the head of Spanish Jewry or as leaders of individual communities, were for the most part ethical characters imbued with the noblest dispositions and most tender sentiments. They were as chivalrous as the Andalusian Arabs, and excelled them in honesty and nobleness, a characteristic that they retained long after the Arabs became degenerate." Like Isaak Abravanel in Phöbus Philippson's novel *The Marranos*, Graetz thought the Sephardim were justified in seeing themselves as superior to the Ashkenazim: "Like their neighbors [the Arabs], they were self-consciously proud, which expressed itself in a long string of names, but this self-esteem rested on a firm moral basis."[76]

Neglecting the quotidian dimensions of life, nineteenth-century historians painted a picture of a community committed to the production of poetry, the arts, the study of Hebrew grammar, and Torah. It was one where particularistic identity was retained, and full participation in the social and cultural life of the nation was enjoyed. Invoking the image of a Jewish mission, Graetz saw the Sephardim as a model for German Jews as well as for others to emulate. Recapturing the spirit of Heine's remarks in his essay "Jessica," Graetz wrote that "the height of culture that the nations of modern times are striving to attain was reached by the Jews of Spain in their most flourishing period." This was because "many-sided knowledge was considered among the Spanish Jews, as well as among the Andalusian Muslims, as man's most beautiful ornament."[77]

In Spain, "Jews were equally active in Bible exegesis and grammar, in the study of Talmud, in philosophy, and in poetry. The bearers of such knowledge were not closed off from one another . . . [and] they were as removed from stifling gullibility (*dumpfer Stockgläubigkeit*) as they were from senseless mysticism (*hirnloser Schwärmerrei*)."[78] The negative reference here is to the traditional Jewish culture of Eastern Europe, a culture to which Graetz was uncompromisingly hostile. His sensibilities on this score were shaped perhaps by many things, not the least of which were his own humble beginnings in a village in the eastern reaches of Germany and his later abandonment of Orthodoxy. Together, they led him to express a kind of contempt for Eastern European Jews that was surely bred by familiarity and fear that German Jews, on the eve of emancipation, would be deemed as incorrigible as their Russo-Polish coreligionists.

In contrast to the "many-sided knowledge" that prevailed among Spanish Jews, among those in early modern Poland "the cultivation of a single faculty, that of hair-splitting judgment, at the cost of the rest, narrowed the imagination. . . . Twisting, distorting, judicial trickery (*Advokatenkniffigkeit*), mockery, and a foregone judgment against that which did not lie within their field of vision constituted the essential character of the Polish Jews."[79] Graetz's views were typical of his generation of German Jews. His contemporary the Austrian Jewish novelist Karl Emil Franzos (1848–1904), who wrote fictionalized accounts of Galician Jewry, observed in his novel *The Jews of Barnow*, "Every country has the Jews it deserves—and it is not the fault of the Polish Jews that they are less civilized than their brethren in the faith in England, Germany, and France. At least, it is not entirely their fault."[80]

Marginally less forgiving than Franzos, Graetz granted Polish Jews agency. Yet, appalled by what he imagined they did with it, he claimed that they could not "freely employ cunning against their coreligionists because all Polish Jews were in possession of equally sharp wits." Thus "it was the non-Jews who discovered to their disadvantage the superiority of the Talmudic spirit of the Polish Jews."[81] For Graetz, in religious terms nothing typified Polish-Jewish inferiority as much as Hasidism: "It seems strange that at the same time that Mendelssohn declared that rational thinking was the essence of Judaism, a banner was set out that announced the crassest madness as the basic character of Judaism." In contrast to the beauty of soul that he ascribed to Mendelssohn, Graetz said of Hasidim's founding figure, Israel ben Eliezer—known as the Ba'al Shem Tov—that he was a man who did not recognize the difference between "deception and self-deception." And whereas Mendelssohn left the ghetto behind when he moved to Berlin and frequented beautiful salons, ben Eliezer was born and remained in the Carpathian foothills, where "he learned what he would not have learned in dark, narrow, filthy holes that are called schools in Poland."[82] And nothing had caused the degeneration of Ashkenazic Jewry as much as Yiddish, Graetz's blind hatred of which recurs frequently in his *History of the Jews.* It was because of this "babbling pidgin" that "German and Polish Jews all over the globe had lost all sense of form, taste for artistic beauty, and aesthetic feeling."[83] He dismissed the language of his parents, the lingua franca of the home in which he grew up, by calling it a *halb tierische Sprache* (a half-animal language), thereby betraying his own narrow-mindedness and vulgarity.[84]

Graetz was far from alone among Jewish historians in holding such a view. In our previous discussion of Hebrew pronunciation, eighteenth-century critics lamented the destructive impact of Exile on the Jewish people, and how among its many consequences were the impoverishment of Hebrew and the fact that most Jews had little facility with the language. The historian Leopold Zunz, a leading voice among *Wissenschaft des Judentums* scholars, took a slightly different tack, making an argument that was profoundly influential for Graetz and other Jewish historians. It is worthy of consideration. For Zunz, exile had compromised most but not all Jews. As an example, he pointed to Spain, where Hebrew thrived and the Jews led culturally enriched lives. In his historical study entitled *The Religious Sermons of the Jews* (1832), Zunz relates how the expulsion of the Jews and the Inquisition led to the dispersal of the most "noble Jews" while the "bad ones" remained behind as New Christians. The refugees settled mostly in the Ottoman Empire but also in Italy, France, Holland, and the German states, bringing with them "*Bildung*, secular knowledge, literary treasures, and an active Jewish intellectual life."[85] Since Zunz's brief was to write the history of the Jewish sermon, he was primarily concerned with Jewish oral culture; he noted with admiration that the Spanish and Portuguese Jews preached in their native tongues but were also fluent in the languages of the countries in which they lived. In general, their "speech was correct" and they had mastered the "art of oratory."[86]

By contrast, the oral culture of German and Polish Jews could not have been more different from that of their Sephardic brethren. According to Zunz, at the beginning of the sixteenth century religious persecution and social isolation shaped their world. Beyond baptism, he wryly noted, no ruler had so much as even thought of instituting measures to improve the Jews. For their part, the Jews responded by retreating into isolation, looking upon the "German alphabet with horror, European science as foreign, and Christianity with abhorrence."[87] With their community shut off from German culture, Jewish backwardness was especially noticeable in two principal areas, both interlinked: language and institutions, by which he mean the rabbinate and schools.

Uncharacteristically for a practitioner of *Wissenschaft des Judentums*, Zunz looked upon the early German Middle Ages with a certain fondness, for it was then that Jews, with "the exception of a few isolated expressions and forms of pronunciation here and there," spoke the exact same language as their Christian neighbors. More startling, however, was Zunz's claim that at the end of the fourteenth century, when Jewish settlement began in Poland, the influx of German Jews who formed this new community continued to speak a "correct" German for some three hundred years. However, in the sixteenth century and increasingly in the following two centuries, the Jews in Poland began to speak Yiddish.[88] Many of those Jews moved west, and Zunz claimed that "rabbinical posts in most Jewish communities in Germany were occupied by Polish Talmudists, who were also employed as teachers in private homes." This, Zunz claimed, "contributed not a little to the linguistic confusion (*Sprachverwirrung*) of the German Jews." Indeed, "in many Jewish communities in Germany, the oral word was dispensed with" altogether.[89] Zunz portrayed the Polish rabbis as carriers of linguistic contagion who, once having arrived in Germany, infected the native-born and hitherto German-speaking Jews with Yiddish. Committed to the threefold task of celebrating Sephardic oral culture, denigrating Polish Jewry, and prying it apart from German Jewry, Zunz asserted that German Jewry's downfall was almost exclusively attributable to their transition to speaking Yiddish.

For Zunz, the consequence of speaking *Judendeutsch* (Judeo-German) was that the bonds of "social confraternity were broken, knowledge was uprooted, and the culture that these Jews had previously possessed [that is, dating to the time when they spoke German] could not be passed on."[90]

Zunz, who was an orphan and had not read a book in German before he was eleven years of age, was perhaps describing his own stultifying education at the Samson Talmud School in Wolfenbüttel. Exposed to a very narrow curriculum and instruction in Yiddish, Zunz was educated in an insular culture with little or nothing to recommend it to future generations.[91] The great cultural and social damage Polish Jewry had inflicted upon German Jews was made most manifest in Jewish schools. In contrast to the students in Sephardic schools, who used books in Spanish and Portuguese, children in Germany and Poland had to suffer with flawed textbooks in Yiddish and study with teachers who were unable to so much as even speak.[92] Even if Zunz's somewhat monocausal historical reconstruction and interpretation were implausible, he drew what was, among nineteenth-century German Jews, a widely accepted social portrait of Ashkenazic Jewry, and he was especially influential in shaping the ideological position of *Wissenschaft des Judentums* toward the history of Yiddish and its relationship to German, as well as the larger relationship of German to Polish Jewry.[93]

In Zunz's history of the first iteration of the modern Jewish *Sprachenkampf* (language war), the heroes of the story are Mendelssohn and Wessely, and the weapon with which they vanquished their foe, the Yiddish language, was the former's Bible translation:

> Finally, in 1778, a sample of Mendelssohn's Bible translation appeared, in which the genius of Hebrew and of the German language joined forces to deal a deathblow (*Todesstreich*) to Judeo-German [Yiddish]. It never occurred to rational people to allocate to the Jews a special Jewish German [language] as a kind of inheritance or preference (*Erbtheil oder Vorzug*). . . . The inspirational Wessely poured the cup of wrath over the ignorant young teachers, full of pain about the language of the German and Polish Jews, which appeared to him as an incurable disease (*die ihm eine fast unheilbare Krankheit erschien*). . . . With Mendelssohn's Bible translation and Emperor Joseph's Edict of Toleration . . . there was the complete improvement of education, the adoption of good textbooks, the spread of German reading with the exposure of Jews to bourgeois society, and the civilizing impact of the German language. [With these developments] Judeo-German was completely displaced as the vernacular, as the language of school instruction, and as the language of teachers and rabbis, literature and religious services. With this essential progress there was a greater expansion of science, concern for education and with educational institutions. In the first instance, Hebrew grammar and poetry were once again transplanted onto German soil. Just as Judeo-German retreated before German, so too did bad Hebrew style give way to correct language.[94]

At the center of Zunz's Whiggish interpretation of German-Jewish history stood the salutary metamorphosis of German Jews. It was, again, a transformation born of personal experience. In 1807, Samuel Meyer Ehrenberg, himself a graduate of the Samson Talmud School, became its director at the age of thirty-four and promptly modernized the curriculum and the method of pedagogy. The impact was immediate and direct, with Zunz later recalling that with "the incredible changes that have occurred both within us and outside us . . . we have traversed, or better still, flown through, a thousand-year history."[95] Thanks to the heroic efforts of individual maskilim, the once-benighted Yiddish speakers of Germany had abandoned the principal cause of their social, intellectual, and economic marginalization, and, with the (re)adoption of the German language, they had emerged separate from and superior to Polish Jewry.

This view was also reinforced in German-Jewish popular culture, in that we see a similar claim made in a curious work by the Jewish orientalist, translator of the Koran into Hebrew, and professor of Semitic languages at Heidelberg University Hermann Reckendorf (1825–1875). Between 1856 and 1857, Reckendorf published a five-volume historical novel, complete with footnotes, entitled *Mysteries of the Jews*. It was a collection of sketches from Jewish history that extended from 586 B.C.E., when Nebuchadnezzar exiled the Jews from Jerusalem, up to Reckendorf's own day. Told as a family chronicle of the Abravanels and narrated by successive generations of the family's leading figures, Reckendorf's novel sought, among other things, to show that the line of King David never disappeared but persisted all the way through to the Abravanels in Spain and beyond, with their descendants in post-1492 exile. In the rhapsodic section on Moses Mendelssohn, who was identified as an intellectual heir to Maimonides and Isaac Abravanel, Reckendorf stresses the young man's heroic ascent from the limited intellectual atmosphere of his youth in Dessau into the European intelligentsia. There, in a reprise of Zunz, Reckendorf claims, "teaching positions in Israelite schools were exclusively occupied by Polish Jews. . . . [where] they studied the Bible in Yiddish and strove with all their power to enlarge the divide between the Jewish nation and non-Jews as much as possible, for they saw the social harmonization of the two as a danger to their religion." Inspired by Spanish Jewry, Mendelssohn was both example and symbol of the successful breach between German and Polish Jewry, a process further fortified by the maskilim who followed in his wake.[96]

With Mendelssohn as a role model, both Zunz and Graetz embodied the larger transformation German Jewry underwent over the course of the nineteenth century. From religiously Orthodox, Yiddish-speaking backgrounds, they evolved into a very different kind of committed Jew—the modern German Jew.[97] By the time German Jewry was emancipated in 1871, the cultural and economic strides this community had taken since Mendelssohn's day were remarkable. Their strenuous and largely successful efforts to become German elicited praise and acceptance in some circles but a negative backlash in others. Graetz, ever combative, did not shirk from condemning the antisemitism that was so deeply entrenched in Germany and was, in fact, intensifying in the 1870s. In volume 11 of his *History of the Jews*, Graetz dwelt on what he called "Teutomania," and in 1879 he became deeply mired in an ugly public dispute with the Prussian nationalist historian Heinrich von Treitschke, who had just read the volume in preparation for the multivolume history of Germany that he was writing. Enraged by what he read, von Treitschke went on the attack, accusing Graetz of hating Christianity, being hostile to Germany, and promoting Jewish nationalism. However, von Treitschke did not confine his vitriol to his diatribe against Graetz; he used the incident to further stoke the flames of antisemitism then sweeping the country.[98] He declared that Jews, who were "growing in number and growing in arrogance," had a nefarious impact on the nation and stood poised to commandeer Germany for their own advantage. Graetz rightly noted in one of his responses to von Treitschke that the latter's attacks were not really restricted to German Jews but amounted to "a denunciation of the entire Jewish people."[99] Tellingly, von Treitschke declared that "Herr Graetz is a stranger (*Fremdling*) in the land in which it was his accident to be born; he is an Oriental who neither understands nor wishes to understand our people." Quite simply, he declared, there was "no room on the soil of Germany for two nations."[100] Jews had to become Germans, not German Jews, with what he called a *Mischcultur*. In fact, von Treitschke noted how, by contrast, Spanish Jews in the west and south of Europe "blended in" and made "good Frenchmen, Englishmen, and Italians." But Germany, he said, was dealing with the immigration of "swarms" of Polish Jews pouring across the border, and they were "foreign, unequal, and the essential opposite of Europeans, especially Germans."[101] Soon, however, the fine distinctions were set aside, and von Treitschke joined with the whole pan-European antisemitic movement, opposing what they called "international Jewry." Graetz saw in all of this the rejection of everything Moses Mendelssohn and the Jews of his own generation had striven for. Modern Christian Europe simply refused to offer the same kind of open acceptance that medieval Islam had afforded Jews.

Graetz's passions and prejudices determined his historical judgments. The material and cultural poverty of Polish Jewry—ironically he echoed von Treitschke here—stood in sharp contrast to the middle-class, cultured, Jews of Germany. Hasidism's superstition stood in sharp contrast to Mendelssohn's rational Judaism. Christianity's mistreatment of Jews stood in sharp contrast to Islam's acceptance of them. As a result of this, Sephardic Jewry had historically enjoyed aesthetic, cultural, and moral superiority over the Ashkenazim. With the expulsion of 1492, however, not only did Sephardic Jewry go into a state of decline; so too did Spain. For Graetz, there was an object lesson here. If German-Jewish acculturation and success led to a backlash and the contemporary antisemitic movement went unchecked, it would be a disaster not only for the Jews; Germany, like Spain and Portugal before it, would fall prey to its own blind hatred.[102]

IGNAZ GOLDZIHER

Ignaz Goldziher (1850–1921) was one of the nineteenth century's greatest scholars of Islam, a Hungarian Jew who made towering contributions to the field of Semitic studies.[103] In turning to Goldziher we will shift focus away from Sephardic Jewry, as such, and onto Islam itself. Goldziher's orientalist scholarship was far more than field defining, for his consideration of Islam sparked within him intense personal sentiments about Judaism. What was for Goldziher the beauty of Islam's unadorned worship and the simple piety of the *ummah*, or community of the faithful, stood in sharp contrast to the indecorous bourgeois Judaism of Budapest. More broadly, however, *Islamwissenschaft* (academic study of Islam) was also a means for Goldziher to understand the relationship among Judaism, Christianity, and Islam, which in turn led him to deeper reflections upon Jewish history and contemporary Jewish culture and identity in Central Europe.

Ignaz Goldziher was born in the small central Hungarian town of Székesfehérvár, approximately forty miles from the capital, Budapest. An ancient settlement, whose origins can be traced back to Roman times, Székesfehérvár was where all of Hungary's kings were crowned until the early eighteenth century. Thereafter, it went into steady decline, and by the time Goldziher was born, in 1850, Székesfehérvár had been reduced to an economically struggling provincial town of little importance. Nonetheless, the Goldziher family stayed in this community of about four hundred Jews until 1865, when, with little in the way of future opportunity, the family moved to Budapest.[104] As with Heinrich Graetz, Goldziher's provincial roots shaped his negative attitude toward traditional Jews. In his diary, Goldziher recalls an event that occurred when he was just eight years old, leaving a lasting impression on him. He decried the fact that a foreigner, Rabbi Joseph Guggenheimer—the son-in-law of Samson Raphael Hirsch, founder of modern Orthodoxy—took up a position in Székesfehérvár and "imposed petty rituals." The small community was split in two between the Orthodox and more liberal elements. Although Goldziher's father was with the progressive forces, he hired the Orthodox rabbi Moses Wolf Freudenberger to be his young son's private tutor, and it was under his teacher's influence that Goldziher seems to have considered both sides in the dispute with "equal contempt" and opted for a middle course.[105] For now, however, he held the Orthodox faction principally at fault. This small-town dispute was, in microcosm, a reflection of the overall tripartite religious split that emerged within nineteenth-century Hungarian Jewry. Later, in Budapest, his negative sentiments about the Jewish community were exacerbated by his encounter with the capital's acculturated middle-class Jewish community. In their own way, they were no better than the Orthodox as far as Goldziher was concerned. These factors colored his Jewish scholarship, his Jewish identity, and his *Islamwissenschaft*. Also like Graetz, he was unable to really break with Orthodox Judaism, and, though an advocate of reforms in principle, he saw no personal need for them.[106]

In the all-important question of language, Goldziher was very much a Jewish child of that age and place, and that too was reflected in his scholarship. Between the 1860s and the outbreak of World War I, Jews in Hungary underwent an intensive regime of cultural change. According to the historian Daniel Viragh, this process, known in Hungarian as *magyarosodás*, means "becoming Hungarian," or "Hungarianization"; even more pointedly, the cognate word *magyarosítás* denotes "becoming *like the* Hungarians."[107] Goldziher embodied this transformation. In a letter of 1905, the orientalist Theodor Nöldeke upbraided him for the unfortunate "Austrianisms" in his German. Goldziher defended himself by accepting the charge but claimed that he spoke this way because "he only began to learn German when he turned twelve years old."[108] This raises the question of what language he spoke at home before he became Bar Mitzvah in 1863. The "Austrianisms" that Nöldeke thought he heard and that Goldziher disingenuously acknowledged were, in fact, something else. It would appear from recent research that, as much as he would deny and decry it, he spoke *Judendeutsch*, which, as its name suggests, was a form of Judeo-German and was spoken by nearly all the Jews in the great central plain of Hungary when Goldziher was born. It was certainly not the eastern Yiddish Graetz grew up with, but neither was it High German, especially given that in its written form it used Hebrew letters.

Outside of the home one can assume that Goldziher spoke Hungarian. Later, when he became a scholar, he wrote in German, reserving Hungarian for his work on Jewish subjects and for the more intimate parts of his diary. By contrast, Goldziher associated Yiddish with the uncultured, the Orthodox, and Polish Jewry, while they, in turn, dismissed European languages as pathways to assimilation. These were not just private sentiments. The issue of language split Hungarian Jewry and came to a head in the 1860s. Just as German was the language middle-class Jews used and Hungarian was slowly being adopted, a synod of ultra-Orthodox Jews held in 1856 in northeast Hungary passed a resolution that "it is forbidden to preach in any other language but *Jargon* [Yiddish]. . . . Any Jew hearing a rabbi or anyone preaching in an alien language is obliged to leave the synagogue at once and go out into the street."[109] A similar resolution was passed at another congress in 1868–1869, where it was decided that the use of "alien languages"

(German and Hungarian) should not be permitted in synagogues and religious schools.[110] One of the places where the language struggle was especially acute was the town of Székesfehérvár.[111] Goldziher's formative years there, the disputes over language, and the split between reformers and the Orthodox would all play a determinative role in his personal and intellectual makeup.[112]

Goldziher's principal scholarly achievements were his critical history of Islamic oral tradition, the hadith, and a comprehensive study of the various sects of Islam, making him the first scholar to undertake such studies according to the methods of critical historiography.[113] Goldziher was a broad-ranging scholar, and his oeuvre included important studies on pre-Islamic and Islamic culture, the religious and legal history of the Arabs, and even critical analyses of Arabic poetry and language.[114] Finally, Goldziher produced a considerable corpus of writings on the history of Judaism, which he studied on its own terms and also comparatively with Islam. His main contributions in this area include his study of myths among the ancient Hebrews, comparative studies of medieval Arab and Jewish philosophy, Muslim and Jewish mnemonics, as well as a study of modern Hebrew poetry and a general summation of Judaism entitled *Essence and Evolution of Judaism*.[115] With the exception of a handful of writings in Hebrew (later edited by another distinguished German-Jewish orientalist, Shlomo Dov Goitein), and many works that appeared in Hungarian, the lion's share of Goldziher's scholarly work was produced in German. Since he also studied in Germany, absorbing that country's scholarly traditions, he is appropriately included in this study of German-Jewish orientalists.

One further feature establishes Goldziher in the camp of German-Jewish orientalist scholarship: the intellectual debt he owed Abraham Geiger. From Goldziher's earliest works he clearly demonstrated the extent to which he was sympathetic to Geiger's fundamental position regarding sacred texts, namely, that they were of human origin, and that it was the scholar's task to unravel the evolution of such writings, analyzing the succeeding social and intellectual contexts in which they were produced, and unearthing any changes that took place over time. As he said in his *Lectures on Islam* (1910), "[religion] never appears as an abstraction free from specific historical conditions. Advanced or primitive, religion exists in concrete forms that vary with social conditions." According to Geiger—a position Goldziher entirely supported—to continually strip away the layers of additions, emendations, and interpretations would eventually reveal core and pristine religious ideas and ideals. Goldziher described religious formation as follows: "At its earliest stage of development the character of a religion is already defined by the predominance of a particular motif, and that motif retains its ascendancy over all others as the religion evolves and passes through its historical existence. This is equally true of religions born of illumination experienced by an individual."[116] Speaking of the Koran but in terms applicable to the Hebrew Bible as well, Goldziher noted that "no religious community has dogmatically recognized canonical books, either revealed or inspired, that do not show, from the earliest stage of their execution, ancient variations."[117]

As a counter to viewing orientalism as a homogenous Christian cultural enterprise, it is instructive to note that Goldziher's views on Islam and cultural transmission in general were profoundly shaped by his Jewishness and, as Lawrence Conrad has demonstrated, his intense disagreement with Ernest Renan, the most significant nineteenth-century scholar of the French school of orientalism. Typically for the time, Renan, given to racism and antisemitism, delineated between Aryan and Semitic peoples, claiming that the latter were creatively and imaginatively barren compared to the former. The assertion drew a formal response from Goldziher.[118]

In 1876 Goldziher published *Der Mythos bei den Hebräern* (Mythology among the Hebrews), in which he argued for the adaptability of ancient Hebrew culture and the extent to which ancient Israelites borrowed elements of culture from surrounding peoples to create something entirely new and vibrant. Nomadic Hebrew tribes settled on the right bank of the Jordan River, an event that, according to Goldziher, marks "the true beginning of the history of the Hebrews." From the Canaanites and Phoenicians they borrowed those institutions that helped make them a sedentary people, a historical transition he referred to as "that remarkable turning-point in the life of the Hebrew people." Among the ideas and institutions they borrowed were legal and monarchical principles and a priesthood that governed a central temple. In time, according to Goldziher, "the religious and political centralization, which forms the program of David and Solomon, was the first and most forcible expression of the roused national spirit." Later on, in exile, Jews borrowed various Babylonian myths, such as those of the Creation story, the Fall, the Flood, and the Tower of Babel, incorporating them into a foundational story of Jewish origins.[119] The knowledge of such syncretism and cultural borrowing lay behind Goldziher's rejection of Renan's racial determinism and fixed religious and cultural categories, and he expressed as much in a letter he wrote to the German orientalist Martin Hartmann: "The spiritual life of a people is grounded not in its race, but in its historical destiny."[120]

Such a fluid view of the historical development of Judaism permitted Goldziher to make three crucial claims. The first was that no religion—not even the original monotheistic faith—was the product of a sudden religious revolution; rather, religion evolved by borrowing and rejecting from surrounding cultures. In other words, no faith could claim to hold the lien on doctrinal truth born of divine revelation. The study of history would demonstrate this and promised to unveil the secrets of the development of religious traditions. In "The Progress of Islamwissenschaft in the Last Thirty

Years," a lecture that Goldziher delivered at the St. Louis World's Fair in 1904, he declared, "The rise and development of Islam are subject to the same historical method of observation that modern science has taught us to apply, for instance, to the literary evidence of Ur-Christianity or to the oldest products of Rabbinical Judaism."[121] This claim serves as a vigorous rebuttal of Edward Said's assertions about the static, decontextualized representation of Islam by European orientalists. The Saidean view is especially difficult to sustain when applied to Jewish scholars of Islam and may well explain why Said all but ignored them, even one as distinguished as Ignaz Goldziher, whose application of the critical tools of *Wissenschaft des Judentums* to the study of Islam was undertaken precisely so as to avoid any superficial reading and depiction of that religious tradition—something, of course, that Geiger, Graetz, and other Jewish historians complained of bitterly when it came to the study of Judaism by Christian scholars.[122]

Second, at the heart of Renan's distinction between Aryan and Semitic cultures was the charge that the simplicity and primitive nature of Semitic languages mirrored the simplicity of the cognitive capacities of the "Semitic" peoples. As such, their incapacity for abstract thought left them bereft of mythology. The monotheism of ancient Israel and later of the Arabs was not a great achievement but was rather the product of the Semitic character, and the religious forms it took were as arid as the desert from which they had sprung. "The desert," declared Renan, "was monotheistic."[123] While he acknowledged that the great contribution to civilization of these people was in the religious realm, the issue for Renan was not religious invention but religious truth. Semitic monotheism was a primitive stage in the evolution of religion. However, Christian monotheism, which he held to be the truest faith, also emerged from a Semitic people, the Jews. How to account for this? How was Christianity not also an expression of primitive, Semitic religion? For Renan, Christianity came into its own by overcoming its original Semitism. It did this through Jesus, who was exemplary in that he rose beyond his Jewishness and rejected Judaism. Through him, Christianity became a universal religion, a condition it could never have achieved had it remained the provenance of Jews. Like the Hebrew language, which was God-given at the dawn of history and remained frozen in its infancy for all time, so too was Judaism a form of monotheism that was archaic, childlike, and immutable.[124] By contrast, Goldziher considered the development of religion to be an evolutionary process, whereby all humanity passed through the following four stages: mythology, polytheism, traditional monotheism, and finally critical monotheism, which was prophetic and universal.[125] Where Renan tirelessly reiterated that there is "an abyss between Semite and Arian,"[126] Goldziher not only rejected the whole idea of race; he believed deeply that passing through the various stages of religious evolution was predicated on the fact that all peoples were, in the most fundamental sense, possessed of a shared and original mental structure.[127] He arrived at this conclusion via his belief in a universal religion based on prophetic monotheism, whereas universalism for Renan meant Christianity and supersessionism. There could not be a more profound abyss between two orientalists. It is a cleavage that Said refused to recognize and countenance; he thereby shared Renan's penchant for unsubstantiated generalizing.

Third, there was a contemporaneity to Goldziher's argument about ancient Israel's open culture, and it had to do with the antisemitic canard that the Jews formed a tight-knit cabal. He was arguing that the Jews did not form a "state within a state," as the philosopher Fichte and a subsequent legion of antisemites claimed. They were neither misanthropic nor insular, two other ancient charges preferred against Jews. Modern Jews, according to Goldziher, as distinct from Orthodox ones, were primed for acculturation precisely because they were the real bearers of what had originally been an open, adaptable, and evolving religious tradition. According to historian David Moshfegh, where Geiger celebrated Judaism as universalist, Goldziher took this notion further by claiming that the Jewish people's great contribution to civilization was not Judaism per se but monotheism, for the latter was truly universal.[128]

Yet the Jews were not merely borrowers and adapters. In a direct refutation of Renan's thesis, Goldziher recognized the real innovations of Judaism, or what were referred to in his day as "Jewish contributions to civilization." They came about as a result of the fact that "the Hebrew nation was preserved from the state of intellectual passivity by the aroused consciousness of national individuality. The consciousness of individuality awoke, and as soon as it was fully aroused, there began that section of the life of the nation which was distinguished by a peculiar productiveness on the domain of ideas."[129] Not all parts of the nation were equally productive or open to cultural adaptation—only the most forward-looking elements.

This belief influenced Goldziher's orientalism, which, in other words, was conditioned by his rejection of Orthodox Judaism. Like Geiger and Graetz, he had been raised in precisely that tradition and later recalled that he had mastered the Bible in Hebrew by the time he was five. When he turned seven, he began preaching sermons at services that he and his friends had organized, while at age eight he began the study of Talmud, to which he wholly devoted himself for the better part of each day for years to come. By the age of twelve he was reading medieval Jewish philosophy in Hebrew, and in that same year, 1862, he wrote and published a short book on the history of Jewish liturgy, which he boldly called *Sikhat Yitzhak* (Isaac's Discourse). Notably, Goldziher, whose first name in Hebrew was Yitzhak, later referred to this text as "the first cornerstone of my bad reputation as a freethinker."[130]

By the time Goldziher was a teenager, he had come to long for secular study. A precocious child, he enrolled at the University of Budapest at the age of fifteen, in 1865. There he studied classical languages, philosophy, and German literature. Most significantly, however, he studied Turkish and Persian with Arminius Vámbéry, a Jewish convert, first to Islam and thereafter to Protestantism, and one of Europe's most famous orientalists.[131] Goldziher later testified that it was then that he "acquired [his] sincere love for Oriental studies."[132] This did not mean an end to his Jewish scholarship, his daily Talmud study, or his sentimental feelings for Judaism, which he declared at the age of seventeen was "the beating pulse of my life" (*der Pulsschlag meines Lebens*).[133]

Goldziher earned his doctorate at the University of Leipzig in 1869, at the age of nineteen, having written his dissertation on Tanhum ben Yosef ha-Yerushalmi, a thirteenth-century biblical exegete, philologist, and poet, who was probably born in Jerusalem but lived in Cairo, where he was court poet in the household of Maimonides's grandson. As a poet, Yerushalmi followed the Spanish school in terms of technique and genre and was among the greatest of thirteenth-century Hebrew poets outside of Spain.[134] Goldziher remained in Germany for a while and then went on to Leiden and Vienna for further study, returning to the University of Budapest in 1871–1872 as a *Privatdozent*, the equivalent of an unsalaried university lecturer. In addition to the fact that being Jewish prevented him from becoming a full professor, Goldziher was, as he states in his diary, the victim of religious, political, and academic intrigue. As a result of pressure to unseat Péter Hatala, a Catholic clergyman who publicly rejected the doctrine of papal infallibility, and professor of Arabic at the University of Budapest, the Vatican insisted on placing Hatala in a more cloistered setting, one where his views would not be so accessible to the public. Hatala was awarded the chair in Oriental studies at Budapest, a position that should have gone to Goldziher, who had all but been promised it. Goldziher felt deeply betrayed, becoming filled with resentment and bitterness for his stymied progress and its practical consequences, more of which will be discussed below.[135]

At this time, he was saved from total despair by embarking on a great journey of discovery to the Orient in 1873–1874.[136] His sojourn, which he referred to as his "Muhammadan year," was paid for courtesy of a stipend from the minister of culture, August Trefort, whom Goldziher later accused of trying to get him out of Budapest during the Hatala affair. The reason Trefort gave for sending the young Goldziher abroad was so that he could learn colloquial Arabic as well as the official Arabic used in consulates. Such a prosaic task did not coincide with Goldziher's greater ambitions. Instead, he sought to become "acquainted with Islam and its science, to be a member of a Muhammadan scholars' republic (*Gelehrtenrepublik*), and to learn the means by which, over the course of centuries, Islam became a world religion out of the judaized rite of Mecca. Next I wanted to study the influence of this system on the society and its morals. This double goal can be achieved only through contact with scholars and ordinary people, in mosques, bazaars, and hovels."[137] In other words, Goldziher's goal was to immerse himself thoroughly in Muslim life and culture. And indeed his body of scholarship, which amounts to a "thick description" par excellence, debunks Said's gross misrepresentation that "Goldziher [et al.] saw Islam ... as a 'cultural synthesis' ... that could be studied apart from the economics, sociology, and politics of the Islamic peoples."[138]

Goldziher was deeply moved by his encounter with the Muslim world, achieving a level of affinity with Islamic culture that went beyond the mere academic, as had been the case with Geiger and Graetz. And it certainly outstripped what he dismissed as the "one-sided rationalism of Christian scholars who, while safeguarding the sacrosanct character of their own scriptures and beliefs, subject those of Muslims to rigorous and even captious criticism."[139] Instead, Goldziher's scholarship displayed an unparalleled degree of compassion, respect, and admiration for the Muslim world. In 1890 he wrote that his stay in Damascus was "the most beautiful time of my life ... I truly entered in those weeks into the spirit of Islam to such an extent that ultimately I became inwardly convinced that I myself was Muslim and judiciously discovered that this was the only religion that, even in its doctrinal and official formulation, can satisfy philosophical minds." And never far from his scholarly and personal appraisal of Islam was his critical view of Judaism: "My ideal was to elevate Judaism to a similar rational level."[140]

Goldziher saw in Islam a pure essence—a religious characteristic so valued by nineteenth-century Jews dedicated to a reformist religious agenda. To his mind, that essence was the living embodiment of prophetic Judaism. Like Geiger and Graetz, Goldziher also rejected fundamentalist Orthodoxy and considered it an impediment to modernity and an affront to reason. In *The Essence and Evolution of Judaism*, a series of poorly attended community lectures he delivered in Budapest in the winter of 1887–1888, he argued energetically for the reform of Judaism along the lines laid out by Abraham Geiger, although he was not personally an adherent of Reform Judaism. He also worked fruitlessly for many years on reforming the Jewish educational curriculum in Budapest and sought to also reform the training of rabbis. He was rebuffed in both endeavors.[141] However, unlike Geiger and Graetz, Goldziher did not take a public stand on antisemitism, despite its role in his own professional setbacks. Like Geiger, Goldziher remained aloof from Jewish national concerns, repeatedly declining requests from Zionists that he intercede on their behalf with Ottoman authorities. Religiously speaking, he was a man unto himself. Despite all of his reticence and his reservations, Goldziher remained an observant Jew his entire life, although of a most unusual kind.[142] In truth, his religious beliefs are an enigma. Ironically, his hopes for his own Jewish identity lay in Islam, his love of which saw him become a Muslim in all but name. He testified, "Although I never pretended to be a Muslim, I termed my monotheism Islam, and I did not lie when I said I believed the prophecies of Muhammad."[143] Not only was he convinced of this; he was convincing, enrolling as a student—the first non-Muslim to do so—in Cairo's al-Azhar, the most venerable theological institution in Egypt. There, to the astonishment of his teachers, he engaged the great scholars of Islam in profound theological and jurisprudential debates.[144] The simplicity of the faith and its adherents stood in marked contrast to the qualities he saw among his contemporary Hungarian Jews, irrespective of whether they belonged to the reform-minded Neolog or Orthodox communities.[145]

Goldziher admired what he saw as the rational nature of Islam and, by comparison, detested the irrationality that seemed to characterize Orthodox Judaism, a tradition with which he was intimately familiar. He also became especially contemptuous of the social dimensions of Hungarian Jewish life, which he dismissed as shallow. Between 1867, when the Jews were emancipated, and the outbreak of World War I, Hungarian Jewry attained a remarkable level of material and professional success. By 1910, of the country's 900,000 Jews, some 203,000 were concentrated in Budapest, Europe's second-largest Jewish city after Warsaw. In the Hungarian capital, where Jews formed 20 percent of the city's total population, they owned some 60 percent of businesses; they were 63 percent of the city's physicians and 50 percent of its lawyers. Culturally, the Jews strongly identified with the Magyar majority, a feature best exemplified by the high level of linguistic assimilation, with Hungarian spoken across the broad spectrum of Jewish life from the deeply acculturated to the Hasidim. Hungarian Jewry was also marked by deep religious fissures between the Orthodox on the one hand and those advocating acculturation on the other. By the end of the nineteenth century, apostasy, especially among Budapest's upper-class Jews, was significant, as was intermarriage among the middle and upper classes.[146]

Cultural assimilation did not necessarily mean complete social acceptance. As a Jew, Goldziher, as noted above, was prohibited from taking up a full university appointment upon graduation. It would be decades before formal recognition of his talents came his way. In 1892 Goldziher became the first Jew elected to the Hungarian Academy of Sciences, and it was only in 1894 that the University of Budapest relented somewhat and made him an unsalaried honorary professor in the Faculty of Philosophy. However it was not until 1905, at the age of fifty-five, that he became a full professor with a salary. But with this we are running ahead of ourselves. Desperate for work, he turned to the senior rabbi at the Dohányi synagogue, Samuel Kohn, who, in 1876, appointed Goldziher secretary of the Israelite Congregation of Pest. It was a job he did under sufferance for the next thirty years. Despite the fact that his office was in this neo-Moorish jewel, one of the most beautiful synagogues in Europe, Goldziher hated both the job and people with whom he worked.[147] In particular, he writes with bitterness in his diary of the way he felt persecuted by the synagogue's president, Moritz Wahrmann. Goldziher claimed that Wahrmann publicly humiliated him and cruelly forced him to do senseless and mind-numbing clerical tasks. He was especially irked at having to take minutes at meetings presided over by Wahrmann and then produce several drafts of those minutes before they met with the president's satisfaction. With exasperation and fury, Goldziher wrote: "Great God! I am used to expressing my own thoughts; how should I be able to express that which goes on in the brain of a Polish Jew!"[148] (In truth, Wahrmann was, like Goldziher, a Hungarian.)[149] Like Graetz, Goldziher regarded Polish Jews with contempt, employing the expression *der Polak* as a generic term of opprobrium for all his Jewish "enemies." This stands in marked contrast to the tone of reverence he reserved for Islamic culture and society. His esteem was—no doubt gratifyingly—reciprocated: he was accorded profound respect by Arabs, who, as he says of the sheikhs of al-Azhar, treated him as if he "was one of their equals."[150]

One more episode accounts for the venom with which Goldziher wrote against his fellow Jews in his diary. As previously mentioned, in 1876 he published *Mythology among the Hebrews*. Because he relied on what was already the outmoded solar mythology theory of Max Müller—namely, that all Aryan myths were stories about natural phenomena—and applied it to the Hebrew Bible, Goldziher's work was harshly criticized by professional scholars. But he was especially stung by the way his "heresy" was received in Hungary. Hundreds of members of the Dohányi synagogue signed a petition demanding his ouster, claiming him unfit to work as the congregation's secretary. Among the Jews of Budapest, the mere application of such a methodology to sacred scripture was seen as blasphemous. As a result, when the Rabbinical Seminary of Budapest opened in 1877, Goldziher was shunned and not invited to join the faculty. Somewhat typically, Goldziher snidely commented that most of the professors were Moravian, "according to birth and character."[151] That is to say, they were, as far as he was concerned, Eastern European Jews.

Of Goldziher's work at the Israelite Congregation of Pest, the Hungarian Jewish anthropologist Raphael Patai asserted that "a man without Goldziher's intense scholarly drive, and, more important, with a thicker skin, could have found at least some measure of satisfaction in occupying the influential position of de facto manager of the largest Jewish congregation in the world."[152] But such was not the case. Goldziher came to despise the affluent yet Jewishly illiterate members of the synagogue. He resented them not only for their ignorance and materialism but for their failure to recognize the celebrated genius who was in their midst, a man forced to do a job that was beneath him. While the sheikhs at al-Azhar were in awe of his knowledge, he remained a prophet without honor among his Hungarian coreligionists. By contrast, Jewish colleagues and intellectuals outside of Hungary held Goldziher in great esteem; his European colleagues bestowed upon him a gold medal at the 1889 International Congress of Orientalists, that body's highest honor.[153] An irascible and somewhat tormented man, Goldziher experienced slights, both real and imagined, at the hands of Budapest Jews, which helped harden his negative opinion of the Jewish establishment.[154]

Despite his contempt for some of his fellow Jews, he was deeply moved by Judaism, and significantly some of his most intense Jewish experiences occurred in the Muslim environment. While he did not feel any closer to Oriental than he did to Hungarian Jews, loathing them both, it is still noteworthy that in Turkey he experienced almost ecstatic religious emotions. On Rosh Hashana, in 1873, Goldziher witnessed, opposite his living quarters, a group of Polish Jews celebrating the arrival of the New Year. "At my open window I listened to their divine service. Can this be called divine service? And still I hearkened from my window to every sound of their prayer, and when the sounds of the shofar, a rather hoarse instrument, hit my ear, I was at home with my dear, good parents.... Never before has the New Year holiday met me in such circumstances as this time; but believe me, never before was my heart filled with such sacred devotion as in these days, and never did I feel more sincere, more pious, more faithful."[155]

Sometime later, Goldziher returned to his diary to record his Yom Kippur experience:

> Today [October 1, 1873] was the Day of Atonement. . . . The Jewish house of prayer has always more disgusted than edified me. . . . And, nevertheless, it pulled me today to Hasköy [the Jewish neighborhood], to the house of prayer of the Sephardim . . . to appear in the community I detest, that I hate with all the fire and enthusiasm of my heart; and, still, I have never shed such hot tears as today in the midst of the community, in the Jewish synagogue. I cried bitterly, I lamented . . . I felt elevated as I kissed the Torah, whose legends and myths I mercilessly analyze, whose roster of authors I dare construe with certainty, whose formation as to year and day I make bold to fix with proud assurance. Am I weak or mad? A hypocrite I am not, for my tears flowed too endlessly salty against my will, this much I can say. Explain it, friends; I cannot.

He abruptly left the synagogue, claiming that the congregants were laughing at him, and made his way to the German synagogue. As he heard the shofar, he recalled, "I cry again, I tremble and shake, and again the laughter of the neighbors wounds me." Deeply hurt, he again took his leave of the services and went home. Finally alone: "Here I open up the second Isaiah and read in it his sermon about fasting. Here I am not ridiculed: Here is the Temple I seek."[156] In other words, his misanthropy made him the most unusual of modern Jews, committed to orthopraxy beyond the confines of community.[157]

It is of significance that on his yearlong sojourn in the Near East, Gold-ziher visited Jerusalem. As irascible as ever, he recorded his impressions, which reveal a deeply pious man utterly revolted by organized religion. Where he sought purity, he found defilement, in "the city of swindle, of the befooling of the people, the old city of the old ideals, the city of prophets, the center of the enthusiasm of my youth, the starting point of the con-tempt of my mature thought."[158]

It was not only his fellow Jews who incurred his wrath. Like Geiger and Graetz, he too reserved some of his most hateful denunciations for Chris-tianity. In November 1914, for example, he recorded in his diary that the war signified the "true bankruptcy of Christianity." "What," he asked, "has this system with its nineteen hundred year [history of] world conquest (*Weltbezwingung*) brought forth? Dogmas and pyres."[159] For Goldziher, Islam was not only a theological advance upon Christianity; it was surely a social one as well. After all, it had not discriminated against the Jews living in its orbit as Christianity had done. It had not enacted the autos-da-fé that had consumed so many Jews. While he never shied away from highlighting Mu-hammad's intolerance and even violence toward Jews, or the many "harsh words" spoken against them in the Koran, Goldziher was of the opinion that there existed a significant difference in the way Jews and Judaism were treated in Islamic doctrine and the social reality that prevailed after Mu-hammad's death, claiming that "after the foundation of the Muhammadan community a milder sentiment with respect to the Jews was introduced."[160]

Such generosity he would not afford Christianity. In a jeremiad he launched against the Christian missionaries he saw in Syria in 1874, he re-ferred to the fear that the Jews of Damascus had of them (and of Goldziher himself, whom they initially mistook for a convert and missionary). But at a deeper level, he must surely also have contemplated the necessity of his own conversion to Christianity if he wished to take up a professorial ap-pointment in Budapest. Echoing the passion and rage of Graetz, Goldziher recorded in his diary:

> In this abominable religion, which invented the wretched Christian blood libel, which puts its own best sons to the rack, they want to entice away the believers in the one and only Jehovah in Muslim lands. This is an insolence of which only Christianity, the most abominable of all religions, is capable. It has no forehead (*keine Stirne*) to become aware of the insolence that forms its historical character. The forehead of a whore (*die Stirn einer Hure*), that is the forehead of Christianity.[161]

The missionary goal of Christianity was closely allied to the colonial project of the European powers.[162] For this and other secular reasons, Goldziher was a bitter opponent of imperialism, an adventure that he regarded as corrosive and a distinct threat to the Muslim way of life. In Egypt, the opening of the Suez Canal in 1869 had been preceded by a period of Westernization. Goldziher stood in marked opposition to this trend, going so far as to agitate actively in the Cairo bazaars against the apparent advantages enjoyed by Europeans in Egypt. He even approached the anti-Western Arab nationalist Sayyid Salih Bey al-Magdi, furnishing this former minister of education with a developed set of historical theories about Egypt's Muslim culture and how its further propagation would be a valuable weapon against what he called the "dominant European plague." He went further. Bearing in mind that his sojourn in the Middle East had been financed by the Hungarian government, Goldziher boldly and publicly declared his unwillingness to attend any celebrations and receptions unless the sheikhs of al-Azhar had also been invited.[163]

Goldziher never waivered in his vehement opposition to European imperialism. In fact his antagonism went beyond public protest and made its way into his scholarship. In a subtle and prophetic interpretation of the impact of Westernization, Goldziher wrote in the epilogue to his *History of Classical Arabic Literature* (1908) that it had "evoked the resistance of religious orthodoxy and kindled the sentiment of nationalism." Foreign influences had led to "an Arab intellectual revival (*al-Nahda*, 'renaissance')." The "natural reaction to foreign ideas," he observed, led, in fact, to a "return to both the ideas and the types of classical Arabic literature." And just as he had intimated in reference to a pristine or reformed Judaism, "classical works from the Qur'ân to Ibn Khaldûn's *al-muqadimma* ... even in the light of Western intellectualism . . . were not contrary to human progress." In addition, though, Western ideas exerted a significant influence on Arab intellectuals and succeeded in drawing their attention to "political and social problems." The effect of this, in sum, was that "traditionalism and modernism run parallel to and not counter to each other."[164]

In conclusion, Jewish orientalists and historians of the nineteenth century—and there are many more who could be added to the scholars examined here—often functioned under a different set of assumptions from their Christian counterparts.[165] It is thus little wonder that they have generally been excluded from consideration in the literature on orientalism. For Geiger, Graetz, and Goldziher, the Jewish struggle against increasing antisemitism was a constant reminder that no matter how strong their own identification with Europe might have been, they could not approach Islam with the same Europeanist mind-set that Christian scholars brought to the subject. They could not be the intellectual vanguard of nations that, despite having emancipated Jews, continued to look upon them with suspicion and discriminate against them in practice. They shared little sense of a European *mission civilisatrice* when it came to Arabs. However, as Central European

Jews, they certainly felt superior to Eastern European Jews and believed that only Westernization could have a rehabilitative effect on them.

One further feature distinguished Jewish orientalists from their Gentile colleagues. Their own deep Jewish literacy made Islam and Arabic more intuitively familiar to them than it had been for Christian scholars.[166] Islam's jurisprudential culture and its tradition of commentary was in general outline immediately recognizable to scholars steeped in traditional Jewish culture. Edward Said's claim that orientalism sought "to cancel, or at least subdue and reduce, [the Orient's] strangeness and, in the case of Islam, its hostility," is an accusation more than it is a historical fact.[167] For Jewish orientalists it simply does not apply, for far from finding Islam strange and hostile, they found it entirely familiar and symbiotically linked to Judaism.[168] Rather, what they found peculiar and were hostile to—and were orientalist toward, in the Saidean sense—was Jewish ultra-Orthodoxy. Here, their inner neocolonialist mentality was on display. Yet, although perturbed by the "Polonization" of Judaism in the form of Hasidism, the Jewish orientalists examined here accepted as a badge of honor the Enlightenment's pejorative description of Judaism as "Oriental."[169] But in an ironic turn, they themselves desired Judaism in its "Oriental"—that is, its purely prophetic and not its European, rabbinic—guise. In an attempt to reify this claim, they turned respectfully to the study of Islam and the Jewish culture that flourished under its aegis, hoping that the grandeur and beauty of both could reinvigorate Judaism and weaken the "domination" and "hegemony" they themselves experienced at the hands of Europeans—both Gentile and Jewish.[170]

Epilogue

By the time our story ends, around the turn of the twentieth century, German Jewry had, with great energy, creativity, and rapidity, succeeded in building itself up into one of history's most productive and vibrant Jewish communities. In the span of about 120 years, what had begun as a socially and intellectually marginal group was now solidly bourgeois and had moved to the center of German high culture and toward the upper end of the economic scale. I have argued here that the constant invocation of a particular triumvirate—Sephardic Jews, the Golden Age, and Islam—by those who shaped Jewish opinion in Germany played a modest yet nonetheless important role in helping bring about the mind-set and attitudes that contributed to the great transformation and the advent of modern German Jewry.

With its repeated references to Spanish Jewry and its cultural and social achievements, the elite strata of German Jews in the eighteenth century hoped for similar success. It did not seek to imitate but rather to emulate Iberian Jewry, in accordance with the demands of its own time and place, and it desired that Christian Germany not imitate but rather emulate, within the confines of its own cultural particularity, the spirit of toleration exhibited by medieval Islam. Where this environment in Spain had once given rise to the *convivencia*, an optimistic patrician class of Jews hoped that radical Jewish cultural change as well as German tolerance would lead to the creation of a German version of the *convivencia*, a harmonious *Volksgemeinschaft* (national community), with Germans and Jews united in mutual respect, admiration, and service to the Fatherland.

Pursuing this goal, the Jewish elite succeeded in first definitively distinguishing German Jews from the larger Ashkenazic community of Poland and then, over the course of the nineteenth century, continued that task by consciously cultivating a new religious, linguistic, intellectual, and social path. As a result of this success, by around 1900, the Sephardim had somewhat lost their mystique for German Jews, or at least their utilitarian value as a foil for those who had sought to retune Ashkenazic culture in a uniquely German key. It is noteworthy, however, that after the Nazi rise to power, a brief and belated flowering of Sephardic-themed cultural productions took place, as German-Jewry, in the midst of its own hour of suffering, sought parallels in Jewish history.[1]

The overall success of the great cultural quest to harmonize Jewishness and Germanness bred a high degree of confidence and self-satisfaction among the first generation of Jews born after the founding of the Second Reich and the legal emancipation of the Jews in 1871. Even the coterminous rise of the antisemitic movement, which was in many ways a response to the rapid transformation and success of German Jewry, failed to mitigate the attachment Jews had to Germany, nor did it dampen Jewish confidence in the future. However, already prior to and especially during World War I misgivings began to be expressed by a select cadre of younger German Jews who, like that earlier generation of young Jews in the eighteenth century, became disaffected with the Jewish cultural legacy that their parents had bequeathed to them. Whether or not they or their parents realized it, what the new generation of rebels was rejecting was that mode of bourgeois Judaism that had been propelled in large part by the conscious quest for aesthetic transformation and the role the Sephardim played in that process.

Though smaller in scale than the first, and of shorter duration, the second aesthetic revolution was likewise radical but was more generationally confrontational and provocative because at its heart stood an embrace of the principal target of the first reaction—Eastern European Jewry. As with the previous embrace of the Sephardim, this valorization project appeared in a variety of settings and genres, both scholarly and vernacular. In 1898, a Viennese rabbi, Max Grunwald (1871–1953)—who, significantly, obtained his PhD in 1892 with a dissertation on Spinoza, as well as rabbinic ordination from the Jewish Theological Seminary in Breslau—began publication of a new journal, the *Mitteilungen der Gesellschaft für Jüdische Volkskunde* (Notes of the Society for Jewish Folkore). Grunwald remained the editor of the journal until its closure in 1929. For over three decades he presided over a new field of Jewish scholarship, wherein the customs and folkways of the people were, for the very first time, accorded their scholarly due.[2] While the journal was inclusive and global in its subject matter, from the inaugural issue the ethnography of Eastern European Jewry was particularly focal; within that, scholarship on the Yiddish language played an enormously important role. To this day, the journal remains one of the finest, archival repositories of Yiddish sayings and expressions, something the *Mitteilungen* was especially dedicated to collecting.

Almost coterminous with Grunwald's efforts came those of Leo Winz (1876–1952), a Ukrainian-born journalist, publisher, and Zionist. From 1901 to 1923, he published the journal *Ost und West* (East and West), which was committed to sparking a Jewish cultural and social renaissance, to help create a "self-conscious, inwardly strong, hallowed, true and fruitful Jewish life." The key to achieving this was, according to Winz, the breaking down of barriers, "the overcoming of estrangement within Jewry between individual groups and classes."[3] Winz believed that Western European (read German) Jewry needed the energizing impulse that could come only from Eastern European Jewry, and that Eastern Jews stood to learn much from their Western coreligionists—hence the journal's title, *Ost und West*. Not apart but together was the only way forward for German and Eastern European Jews.

Winz was dedicated to an utterly new, indeed revolutionary, presentation of Eastern European Jewish culture within a German context. His was not so much a romantic portrait of Eastern Jewry born of distance or ignorance—he was, after all, a product of that culture; rather, his intent was to demonstrate its ongoing relevance, creativity, and energy. Beautifully illustrated, the journal took a holistic view of Jewish culture and promoted Jewish art and artists such as the German expressionist Lesser Ury, translations of the great works of contemporary Hebrew and Yiddish fiction from Russia, and transliterated sheet music of Yiddish songs. *Ost und West* also published news stories and even racy articles, such as the one about Beethoven's love affair with a seventeen-year-old Viennese Jewish woman named Rahel Löwenstein. Despite the deep affection they felt for each other—the article is replete with the poetry the lovers exchanged—Winz also notes with pride that Rahel rejected Beethoven's hand in marriage because she refused to convert to Christianity.[4] One hears the not-so-dim echo of the heroine who rejects the Christian suitor in the Sephardic novels. In many ways this was the crux of the matter for Winz. Rahel was proud of being Jewish, as should be the readers of *Ost und West*. With a monthly circulation of about 62,000, the journal reached a wide audience with its message of Jewish multiculturalism, but with a clear appreciation for the beauty and depth of Eastern European Jewish culture. It was, Winz believed, a message that his generation of German Jews needed to hear. Frustrated because too few of them were paying attention, Winz changed tack; after its first three years, *Ost und West* spent less time promoting the glories of Eastern European Jewish culture and more time subtly berating the emptiness of German-Jewish bourgeois culture by adopting an anticapitalist and anti-Western line.[5]

The philosopher Martin Buber's 1906 German translation and adaptation of the Hasidic tales of Rabbi Nahman introduced, in domesticated and bowdlerized form, what may have been for German Jews the least well understood aspect of Eastern European Jewish culture, namely, Hasidism. The stories that Buber retold in his collection emphasized communal unity and mutual responsibility, as well as the dignity of work, even of the most mundane kind, and the need to live life in the presence of God. These were themes that in many ways echoed those promoted in *Ost und West*, though the journal was secular in orientation. The German readers of Buber's tales—they sold very well—were encouraged to see the grandeur and profundity of this religious tradition; even if they were unable to share and experience it for themselves, they were exhorted to celebrate this one piece of the larger mosaic that was Jewish culture as a whole. Hasidism's authenticity and vitality made it an important dimension of a grand cultural scheme—the promotion of what Buber called a "Jewish renaissance."[6]

In the aftermath of World War I the trends outlined above became even more pronounced. Unlike the first Jewish aesthetic revolt, whose leaders were maskilim and others who came from deep within traditional Judaism, those in the vanguard of the post–World War I rebellion were often young, assimilated German Jews, who looked upon the Jews of Eastern Europe with admiration, referring to them in the same hagiographic, celebratory language that German-Jewish intellectuals had previously showered upon the Sephardim.

Having encountered Polish Jews on the Eastern Front during World War I, some German-Jewish soldiers, mostly Zionists, depicted them not as a group to be shunned and ridiculed but instead as one to be admired, because they considered them to be authentic, real Jews, proud bearers of tradition, who had never allowed themselves to be seduced by Western ideals, had never abandoned their Yiddish vernacular, had never dispensed with their folk culture, had never practiced a "watered-down" Judaism, and were never embarrassed by their own aesthetic.[7] The author Arnold Zweig (1887–1968) served on the Eastern Front during the war and returned to write a rhapsodic appreciation of the Jews he encountered there: *The Countenance of Eastern European Jewry* (1920). With striking illustrations of these Jews drawn by the artist Hermann Struck (1876–1944), the book is the perfect exemplar of the genre; moreover, its focus is specifically on the aesthetic makeup of the Eastern European Jews, which Zweig frequently juxtaposed with that of the German Jews. The dignity and dignified appearance that German Jewry craved and sought to cultivate was, he claimed, to be authentically found in the visage of the Eastern Jew: "A noble and silent beauty of the evening lies upon his forehead. His deep-set eyes, resting softly, like dusky ponds, in the shadow of his chiseled cheekbones, know much wisdom. ... The tenderness of his mouth speaks in the words of the preacher about our vanity and about our chasing after the wind of our transitory existence."[8]

Of course this picture of Polish Jewry was as idealized, as romantic, and thus as distorted as had been the picture previous generations of German Jews had drawn of the Sephardim. However, as a critique of the bourgeois materialism and spiritual emptiness he felt had harmed German Jewry— between 1933 and 1948 Zweig lived in Haifa and thereafter moved to what became East Germany out of socialist convictions and disillusionment with Zionism—it is an important personal statement and one that reflects some of his generation's dissatisfaction with the Jewish cultural world they inhabited.

Zweig actually reprises the historical trajectory charted in this study. Acknowledging the common origins of German and Polish Jews, he then turns to the consequences of the fateful path that German Jewry chose— both its blessing and its curse. What a stark contrast between Zweig's depictions of Polish Jewry and the earlier ones that we have seen, and how unequivocally the earlier portraits of German Jewry have now turned into causes for shame and embarrassment:

> We know that our forefathers were relatives of the men we find today in the cities of Lithuania, Poland, and Galicia; no, we know that they lived in the Franconian hill regions and the German plains like us. Thus, today we speak different languages, think different thoughts, live a different kind of Judaism, eat different dishes, measure according to different standards, and we have traded part of our soul with Europe, giving up part of our Jewishness. For nearly five generations it has shaped us, this European fate and its freedom, its new air, its wonderful and artistic values, its integrating and liberating aura. And then it took the most explicit crisis of all to bring us to our senses: crisis of the heart, crisis of memory, crisis of countenance. For it is out of the stern, abstemious, forward-turned face of the [Eastern] Jew—witness to the helplessness of our times and to the indestructibility of a willfully chosen national substance—that the pompous, deliquescent, grotesque face of the Jewish trader on Nordic terrain is made, destined to disappear in the muck of eternal "newness" in all the big cities.[9]

The materialism and self-satisfaction of Zweig's urban German-Jewish merchant recalls Franz Kafka's wrenching letter to his father in which he excoriated him for bequeathing to him a Judaism that was likewise characterized by its materialism and spiritual emptiness. Writing in 1919, only one year before Zweig's work, Kafka bitterly rebuked his father, telling him: "You really had brought some traces of Judaism with you from the ghetto-like village community; it was not much and it dwindled a little more in the city and during your military service. . . . The whole thing is, of course, no isolated phenomenon. It was much the same with a large section of this transitional generation of Jews, which had migrated from the still comparatively devout countryside to the cities." Kafka then moves from this sociological observation to the personal, illustrating the generational friction that typified the second aesthetic rebellion of German-speaking Jewry: "It happened automatically; only, it added to our relationship, which certainly did not lack in acrimony, one more, sufficiently painful source for me."[10] Kafka, who out of intrinsic interest and perhaps spitefulness toward his father, who disapproved of nearly everything his son did, including his writing, undertook Hebrew lessons and began attending the Yiddish theater, and thus typified (as much as Franz Kafka can ever be called typical) the turn taken by the younger, disillusioned bourgeois Jewish youth of Central Europe toward the culture of Eastern European Jewry.

During the ill-fated Weimar Republic (1919–1933) there was a "renaissance of Jewish culture" in Germany, and an important component of that cultural flowering was the way large numbers of German Jews sought to acquaint themselves with the culture of Eastern European Jewry. This manifested itself in numerous ways: attending performances of traveling Yiddish and Hebrew theater troupes; reading Hasidic tales, as well as what was called "ghetto literature," novels set in *shtetlach*; learning Hebrew; becoming Zionist; or, as was the case with the scholar Gershom Scholem, self-consciously rejecting the biases of the scholars of the *Wissenschaft des Judentums*, in order to begin the systematic study of kabbalah. This was a scholarly journey upon which he had embarked even before his emigration from Berlin to Jerusalem in 1923.[11]

Although the objects of their attention and celebration had now changed, one thing remained constant for German Jews. Just as they never really assumed any manifestations of Sephardic culture, they also never attempted to adopt Eastern European Jewish culture. They did not begin speaking Yiddish, and very few became religiously Orthodox; while Zionism grew in strength in the Weimar years, it never achieved anywhere near the popularity it enjoyed at the same time in Poland. Just as had been the case in the nineteenth century, German Jewry still remained wedded to and enamored of German culture. Nothing had changed on that score.

However, when taken together, the two episodes of cultural infatuation, occurring at either end of our chronological spectrum, tell us something important about German Jewry. Its quest to become German was the result of hard work, much of it self-conscious. When Jews in Germany began their embrace of Sephardic culture in the eighteenth century, it came at a time when they were considered neither German nor even European. They were deemed Oriental, utterly different in mind, morality, and habits from the Christians among whom they lived. The forces that opposed Jewish emancipation never accepted the proposition that the Jews were capable of being anything other than Oriental, with all of the negative attributes that particular label connoted.[12] As such, the Jews would perpetually remain unwanted outsiders. There were indeed liberal Christians who thought otherwise, but even they were convinced that the Jews needed improving, for there was something defective about their cultural and moral universe.[13]

The Jewish elites of Moses Mendelssohn's era could not and would not accept the social marginalization of Jews and set about changing hearts and minds. In creating a narrative about the superiority of not just Sephardic culture but also the physical and moral character of the Sephardim themselves, maskilim and community leaders sought to impress upon Jews and non-Jews alike that change was possible, and that dignified bearing was contingent upon dignified treatment. In the nineteenth century the narrative became even more elaborate with the building of neo-Moorish synagogues, and the creation of a literary and scholarly canon that glorified the Sephardim. All of this was in turn made more concrete as the idealized era of Sephardic culture was given a seductive name—the "Golden Age" of Spanish Jewry.

The same ingredients that animated the first Jewish aesthetic revolution in Germany were to drive the second one as well. In both instances, the same internal Jewish dissatisfaction with Jewish culture was present, and likewise in both, there were serious external doubts as to whether the Jews could ever become German. The embrace of the Sephardim came at the time the first struggles were being waged for legal emancipation. The enchantment with Eastern European Jews after World War I came at a time when the cries that Jews were not real Germans were becoming increasingly shrill and insistent. It is true, as outlined above, that the Eastern European turn of German Jewry had begun in the decade before World War I. However, the brotherhood of the trenches in the early phase of hostilities soon gave way to a more fratricidal attitude as the war ground on. What began on the front came back to the home front after the war, as Jews were faced with ever-radicalizing antisemitism. It was only to escalate after the Weimar Republic collapsed in 1933. Finally, at the times of the respective romances, the backlash against Jews was, paradoxically, accompanied by greater Jewish social integration and success than had ever previously been seen. Yet in both moments this was insufficient for many Jews, and thus the nineteenth century and the Weimar years were witness to thoughtful and passionate attempts to define and refine what it meant to be Jewish and German.

In both eras—that of the Sephardic turn and that of the Eastern European Jewish turn, the former characterized by hope, the latter by anxiety—German Jewry's cultural and social development and aspirations manifested themselves in some form of dialogue, whether negative or positive, with Eastern European Jewry. The story told here reminds us that despite the genuine distinctiveness of German Jewry's modern history and culture, it remained deeply and inextricably intertwined with that of Eastern European Jewry. The character of German-Jewish self-fashioning made sure of that.

Notes

◄●►

INTRODUCTION

1. There were, of course, far more radical expressions of assimilation. See Deborah Hertz, *How Jews Became Germans: The History of Conversion and Assimilation in Berlin* (New Haven, CT: Yale University Press, 2007).

2. Delitzsch actually divided the five periods thus: the "Age of Development" (840–940); the "Golden Age" (940–1040); the "Silver Age" (1040–1140); the "Age of the Rose among Thorns" (the rose being Judah Halevi); and finally "the Age of Ruin." See Franz Delitzsch, *Zur Geschichte der jüdischen Poësie vom abschluss der Heiligen Schriften alten Bundes bis auf die neueste Zeit* (Leipzig: K. Tauchnitz, 1836), 44–45. See also Ismar Schorsch, *From Text to Context: The Turn to History in Modern Judaism* (Hanover, NH: University Press of New England, 1994), 83.

3. Ilan Eldar, "The Grammatical Literature of Medieval Ashkenazic Jewry," in *Hebrew in Ashkenaz*, ed. Lewis Glinert (New York: Oxford University Press, 1993), 245–266.

4. Jane Gerber, "Towards an Understanding of the Term: 'The Golden Age' as an Historical Reality," in *The Heritage of the Jews of Spain*, ed. Aviva Doron (Tel Aviv: Levinsky College of Education Publishing House, 1994), 21. See also the trenchant critique of Ivan G. Marcus, "Beyond the Sephardic Mystique," *Orim* 1 (1985): 35–53, where he observes that "we should be critical of this [nineteenth-century German Jewish] reading of pre-modern Jewish [Sephardic] history because it is both distorted and dysfunctional" (37). Marcus also argues against various historiographical treatments that would proffer an "Ashkenazic mystique," something, he says, is observable in studies written after the Holocaust that seek to romanticize the devastated civilization of Eastern European Jewry. He also cautions against those studies that argue that the rupture that separates premodern and modern Jews was so total that nothing in the way of continuity or "mechanisms for fashioning and refashioning Jewish memory" remained (44). Both approaches, he claims, distort the Jewish historical record.

5. Among nineteenth-century scholars, Leopold Zunz is, of course, a notable exception. In his pathbreaking *Die synagogale Poesie des Mittelalters* (Berlin: Julius Springer, 1855), he did study the poetry of Ashkenaz.

6. Moshe Perlmann, "The Medieval Polemics between Islam and Judaism," in *Religion in a Religious Age*, ed. Shlomo Dov Goitein (Cambridge, MA: Association for Jewish Studies, 1974), 103–138; David Nirenberg, *Communities of Violence: Persecution of Minorities in the Middle Ages* (Princeton, NJ: Princeton University Press, 1996), 166–199; and Sarah Stroumsa, "Jewish Polemics against Islam and Christianity in the Light of Judaeo-Arabic Texts," in *Judaeo-Arabic Studies*, ed. Norman Golb (Amsterdam: Harwood Academic Publishers, 1997), 241–250.

7. Moritz Steinschneider, *Polemische und apologetische Literatur in arabischer Sprache zwischen Muslimen, Christen und Juden* (Hildesheim: Georg Olms, 1877), 244–388.

8. Richard Harker, Cheleen Mahar, and Chris Wilkes, eds., *An Introduction to the Work of Pierre Bourdieu: The Practice of Theory* (London: Palgrave Macmillan, 1990), 13.

9. Pierre Bourdieu, *Distinction: A Social Critique of the Judgment of Taste* (Cambridge, MA: Harvard University Press, 1984), 2.

10. Terry Eagleton, *The Ideology of the Aesthetic* (Oxford: Blackwell, 2000), 14.

11. Martin Jay, *Force Fields: Between Intellectual History and Cultural Critique* (Routledge: New York, 1993), 75.

12. Eagleton, *The Ideology of the Aesthetic*. 4.

13. Of course all sumptuary legislation that Jews followed was socially contingent and negotiated. These rules were grounded in social reality, necessity, and circumstance. Gershon Hundert has gone so far as to suggest that "regulations on dress were a matter of foreign policy, while alimentary regulation was largely an internal matter." See his *Jews in Poland-Lithuania in the Eighteenth Century: A Genealogy of Modernity* (Berkeley: University of California Press, 2004), 87–88. See also Salo Wittmayer Baron, *The Jewish Community, Its History and Structure to the American Revolution* (Philadelphia: Jewish Publication Society of America, 1942), 301–307; Jacob Rader Marcus, *The Jew in the Medieval World: A Sourcebook, 315–1791* (Philadelphia: Jewish Publication Society, 1960), 193–197; "Sumptuary Laws," in *Encyclopedia Judaica* (Jerusalem: Keter, 1971), 15:515–516; and David Biale, "Jewish Consumer Culture in Historical and Contemporary Perspective," in *Longing, Belonging, and the Making of Jewish Consumer Culture*, ed. Gideon Reuveni and Nils Roemer (Leiden: Brill, 2010), 23–38.

14. Dror Wahrman, *The Making of the Modern Self: Identity and Culture in Eighteenth-Century England* (New Haven, CT: Yale University Press, 2004), 205.

15. Hannah Lotte Lund, *Der Berliner "jüdische Salon" um 1800: Emanzipation in der Debatte* (Berlin: De Gruyter, 2012); and Deborah Hertz, *Jewish High Society in Old Regime Berlin* (New Haven, CT: Yale University Press, 1988).

16. Warren Breckman, *European Romanticism: A Brief History with Documents* (Boston: Bedford/St. Martins, 2008), 9.

17. W.E.B. Du Bois, *Souls of Black Folk* (Oxford: Oxford University Press, 2007), 8.

18. Ibid., 9.

19. Steven Lowenstein, "The Shifting Boundary between Eastern and Western Jewry," *Jewish Social Studies* 4, no. 1 (Autumn 1997): 68.

20. Recent studies of Jewish pietistic movements in the eighteenth century have drawn links between those in Germany and Poland, insisting that they be considered as part of a single development. However, whatever phenomenological features and kabbalistically inspired theological principles they may have shared, the social reality of Hasidism as a long-lived, mass movement in Eastern Europe finds no analogue in Central Europe. See Rachel Elior, "Rabbi Nathan Adler and the Frankfurt Pietists: Pietist Groups in Eastern and Central Europe during the Eighteenth Century," in *Jüdische Kultur in Frankfurt am Main, von den Anfangen bis zur Gegenwart*, ed. Karl Erich Grozinger (Wiesbaden: Harrassowitz Verlag, 1997), 135–177, esp. 142.

21. See Steven Aschheim, *Brothers and Strangers: The East European Jew in German and German Jewish Consciousness, 1800–1923* (Madison: University of Wisconsin Press, 1982).

22. Breckman, *European Romanticism*, 5.

23. Michael Ferber, *Romanticism: A Very Short Introduction* (New York: Oxford University Press, 2010), 15.

24. Ibid., 1–13.

25. Isaiah Berlin, *The Roots of Romanticism* (Princeton, NJ: Princeton University Press, 2001), 20–21.

26. Olga Litvak, *Haskalah: The Romantic Movement in Judaism* (New Brunswick, NJ: Rutgers University Press, 2012), 25–26.

27. Yael Halevi-Wise, ed., *Sephardism: Spanish Jewish History and the Modern Literary Imagination* (Stanford, CA: Stanford University Press, 2012).

28. E. M. Butler, *The Tyranny of Greece over Germany: A Study of the Influence Exercised by Greek Art and Poetry over the Great German Writers of the Eighteenth, Nineteenth and Twentieth Centuries* (Cambridge: Cambridge University Press, 1935).

29. Frederick C. Beiser, *The Romantic Imperative: The Concept of Early German Romanticism* (Cambridge, MA: Harvard University Press, 2003), 89.

30. David Sorkin, "Wilhelm von Humboldt: The Theory and Practice of Self-Formation (*Bildung*), 1791–1810," *Journal of the History of Ideas* 44, no. 1 (1983): 55–73.

31. In the same passage Scholem also witheringly remarked, "For many Jews the encounter with Friedrich Schiller was more real than their encounter with actual Germans." Gershom Scholem, *On Jews and Judaism in Crisis: Selected Essays* (Philadelphia: Paul Dry Books, 2012), 79. Schiller's observation appears in the twenty-seventh letter of his work of 1794, *On the Aesthetic Education of Man. The Project Gutenberg EBook of The Aesthetical Essays*, http://www.gutenberg.org/files/6798/6798-h/6798-h .htm#link2H_4_0031.

32. George L. Mosse, *German Jews beyond Judaism* (Bloomington: Indiana University Press, 1985), 3.

33. See for example, Ismar Schorsch, *Jewish Reactions to German Anti-Semitism, 1870–1914* (New York: Columbia University Press, 1972).

34. Jacques Kornberg, *Theodor Herzl: From Assimilation to Zionism* (Bloomington: Indiana University Press, 1993), 76–77.

35. David Ben-Gurion, *Recollections* (London: MacDonald, 1970), 34; and quoted in Robert S. Wistrich, "Theodor Herzl: Between Myth and Messianism," in *Theodor Herzl: From Europe to Zion*, ed. Mark H. Gelber and Vivian Liska (Tübingen: Niemeyer, 2007), 13.

36. Lest one think that Herzl's invention reflects a decidedly nineteenth-century sentiment, in the course of writing this book, I had conversations with a surprising number of Ashkenazic Jews who declared to me that their families had originally come from Spain. This was invariably followed up with the proud declaration that their families did not speak Yiddish. Even taking into account the rather small sample size, one could be forgiven for wondering about this unusually large number of Polish and Ukrainian Jews who seem not to have spoken the language of their friends, families, and neighbors. Beyond this, these Ashkenazic Jews seem, by their declarations, to suggest that though they do not manifest in any way whatsoever an Iberian cultural or religious sensibility, they nonetheless bear traces of a Sephardic heritage that mysteriously does not require any performative quality to be real.

37. Edward W. Said, *Orientalism* (New York: Vintage, 1979), 3.

38. Said modified his earlier views in *Culture and Imperialism* (New York: Knopf, 1993).

39. Suzanne L. Marchand, *German Orientalism in the Age of Empire: Religion, Race, and Scholarship* (New York: Cambridge University Press, 2009).

40. For a literary-critical perspective that "ultimately challenges [Said's] work ... [and] assumption that orientalism *monolithically* constructs the Orient as the Other of the Occident" by recognizing "that orientalism is not a single developmental tradition but is profoundly heterogeneous," see Lisa Lowe, *Critical Terrains: French and British Orientalisms* (Ithaca, NY: Cornell University Press, 1991), preface and 190–200. See also Russell A. Berman, *Enlightenment or Empire: Colonial Discourse in German Culture* (Lincoln: University of Nebraska Press, 1998); Todd Kontje, *German Orientalisms* (Ann Arbor: University of Michigan Press, 2004); and James Hodkinson and John Walker, eds., *Deploying Orientalism in Culture and History: From Germany to Central and Eastern Europe* (Rochester, NY: Camden House, 2013).

41. Kenneth Baxter Wolf, "*Convivencia* in Medieval Spain: A Brief History," *Religion Compass* 3, no. 1 (2009): 72–85; Jonathan Ray, "Beyond Tolerance and Persecution: Reassessing Our Approach to Medieval Convivencia," *Jewish Social Studies* 11, no. 2 (2005): 1–18; David Nirenberg, "What Can Medieval Spain Teach Us about Muslim-Jewish Relations?" *CCAR Journal: A Reform Jewish Quarterly* (Spring/Summer 2002): 17–36.

42. Ismar Schorsch, "The Myth of Sephardic Superiority," *Leo Baeck Institute Year Book* 34 (1989): 47–66; Marcus, "Beyond the Sephardic Mystique"; Harold Hammer-Schenk, *Synagogen in Deutschland: Geschichte einer Baugattung im 19. und 20. Jahrhundert, 1780–1933*, 2 vols. (Hamburg: H. Christians, 1981); Hannelore Künzl, *Islamische Stilelemente in Synagogenbau des 19. und frühen 20. Jahrhunderts* (Frankfurt am Main: Peter Lang, 1984); Florian Krobb, *Kollektivautobiographien, Wunschautobiographien: Marannenschicksal im deutsch-jüdischen historischen Roman* (Würzburg: Königshausen & Neumann, 2000); Jonathan M. Hess, *Middlebrow Literature and the Making of German-Jewish Identity* (Stanford, CA: Stanford University Press, 2010); and Jonathan Skolnik, *Jewish Pasts, German Fictions: History, Memory, and Minority Culture in Germany, 1824–1955* (Stanford, CA: Stanford University Press, 2014).

CHAPTER ONE
THE SOUND OF JEWISH MODERNITY:
SEPHARDIC HEBREW AND THE BERLIN HASKALAH

1. Shmuel Feiner, *The Jewish Enlightenment* (Philadelphia: University of Pennsylvania Press, 2004), 2. The literature on the Berlin Haskalah is huge. In addition to the many references scattered throughout the notes, see David Sorkin, *The Religious Enlightenment: Protestants, Jews, and Catholics from London to Vienna* (Princeton, NJ: Princeton University Press, 2008); idem, *The Berlin Haskalah and German Religious Thought: Orphans of Knowledge* (London: Vallentine Mitchell, 2000); idem, *The Transformation of German Jewry, 1780–1840* (New York: Oxford University Press, 1987); Shmuel Feiner and David Sorkin, eds., *New Perspectives on the Haskalah* (London: Littman Library of Jewish Civilization, 2001); Michael A. Meyer, *The Origins of the Modern Jew: Jewish Identity and European Culture in Germany, 1749–1824* (Detroit: Wayne State University Press, 1967).

2. Naturally, this was a belief that was considered universally applicable, but it carried particular resonance for German Jews during the Haskalah and beyond. See, for example, Emmanuel Wohlwill, "Bemerkungen über Sprache und Sprachunterricht, als Beförderungsmittel der allgemeinen Bildung," *Sulamith* 7, no. 1 (1825): 25–

42, 79–100. Wohlwill was a teacher at the Israelite Free School in Hamburg. In the same issue, see the article by the non-Jewish Dr. Heß, "Über den Einfluß der Sprache auf's Denken und die Methode des Unterrichts in der Muttersprache," 232–261.

3. Shmuel Feiner, "From Renaissance to Revolution: The Eighteenth Century in Jewish History," in *Sepharad in Ashkenaz: Medieval Knowledge and Eighteenth-Century Enlightened Jewish Discourse*, ed. Resianne Fontaine, Andrea Schatz, and Irene E. Zwiep (Amsterdam: 2007 Royal Netherlands Academy of Arts and Sciences, 2007), 3.

4. Among those who either resisted or were indifferent to this ideological strain were religious traditionalists, as well as those advocating deeper acculturation into European society and those Jews whose path to modernity was not driven by a conscious ideological impulse. For a new interpretation of the path to modernity taken by the Lithuanian rabbinic elite, see Eliyahu Stern, *The Genius: Elijah of Vilna and the Making of Modern Judaism* (New Haven, CT: Yale University Press, 2013). Otherwise, see Michael Goldfarb, *Emancipation* (New York: Simon and Schuster, 2009); David Ruderman, *Jewish Enlightenment in an English Key: Anglo-Jewry's Construction of Modern Jewish Thought* (Princeton, NJ: Princeton University Press, 2000); Yosef Kaplan, *An Alternative Path to Modernity: The Sephardi Diaspora in Western Europe* (Leiden: Brill, 2000); Todd Endelman, *The Jews of Georgian England, 1714–1830: Tradition and Change in a Liberal Society* (Philadelphia: Jewish Publication Society of America, 1979).

5. Nearly all maskilic texts criticize the Jewish educational system and the rabbis. See Feiner, *The Jewish Enlightenment*. On Moses Mendelssohn's critique of Jews' not sufficiently appreciating nature, see Alexander Altmann, *Moses Mendelssohn: A Biographical Study* (n.p.: University of Alabama Press, 1973), 87. On appearance, see Elliott Horowitz, "The Early Eighteenth Century Confronts the Beard: Kabbalah and Jewish Self-Fashioning," *Jewish History* 8, nos. 1–2 (1994): 95–115. On diet and Ashkenazic culture's supposedly deleterious impact on the health of the Jews, see John M. Efron, *Medicine and the German Jews: A History* (New Haven, CT: Yale University Press, 2001), 69–77 and 83–88.

6. Ángel Sáenz-Badillos, *A History of the Hebrew Language* (Cambridge: Cambridge University Press, 1993), 255.

7. Andrea Schatz, *Sprache in der Zerstreuung: Zur Säkularisierung des Hebräischen im 18. Jahrhundert* (Göttingen, Ruprecht & Vandenhoeck, 2007), 115–116.

8. The maskil from Poland Isaac Satanow (1733–1805) who resided in Berlin suggested there were two Hebrew languages. See Schatz, *Sprache in der Zerstreuung*, 273; Isaac Barzilay, "From Purism to Expansionism: A Chapter in the Early History of Modern Hebrew," *JANES* 11 (1979): 3–15.

9. *Ha-Me'assef* 1 (1788): 84.

10. Richard Shusterman, *Surface and Depth: Dialectics of Criticism and Culture* (Ithaca, NY: Cornell University Press, 2002), 166. Shusterman claims that a more dialectical relationship exists in the concept or call for aesthetic purity insofar as while such purity can suggest homogeneity, it can also refer to such a perfect blend and composition of different elements that their seamlessness suggests purity. While this may be true, the point to be made is that art and, in the case before us, language, was considered "pure," even if demonstrably made up of different elements, so long as the beholder or listener, respectively, believed such productions to be unmixed.

11. This passage was reprinted in *Ha-Me'assef* 1 (1783–1784): 185. See also Barzilay, "From Purism to Expansionism," 5.

12. See Cordula Neis, *Anthropologie im Sprachdenken des 18. Jahrhunderts. Die Berliner Preisfrage nach dem Ursprung der Sprache* (Berlin: De Gruyter, 2003); Hans Aarsleff, "The Tradition of Condillac: The Problem of the Origin of Language in the Eighteenth Century and the Debate in the Berlin Academy before Herder," in *Studies in the History of Linguistics: Traditions and Paradigms*, ed. Dell Hymes (Bloomington: Indiana University Press, 1974), 93–156; Allan Megill, "The Enlightenment Debate on the Origin of Language and Its Historical Background," (PhD diss., Columbia University, 1975); and Avi S. Lifschitz, "From the Corruption of French to the Cultural Distinctiveness of German: The Controversy over Prémontval's *Préservatif* (1759)," *Studies on Voltaire and the Eighteenth Century* (2007:06): 265–290.

13. Léon Poliakov, *The Aryan Myth: A History of Racist and Nationalist Ideas in Europe* (New York: Meridian, 1977), esp. 71–105.

14. Among non-Jews in the eighteenth century, Hebrew's prestige waned, supplanted by Sanskrit and the study of the Vedas. Maurice Olender, *The Languages of Paradise: Race, Religion, and Philology in the Nineteenth Century* (Cambridge, MA: Harvard University Press, 1992), 6.

15. Yaakov Shavit, "A Duty Too Heavy to Bear: Hebrew in the Berlin Haskalah, 1783–1819: Between Classic, Modern, and Romantic" in *Hebrew in Ashkenaz*, ed. Lewis Glinert (New York: Oxford University Press, 1993), 111–128.

16. Moshe Pelli, *The Age of Haskalah: Studies in Hebrew Literature of the Enlightenment in Germany* (Leiden: E. J. Brill, 1979), 85.

17. Barzilay, "From Purism to Expansionism," 6.

18. Schatz, *Sprache in der Zerstreuung*, 133–170.

19. Johann Gottfried Herder, *The Spirit of Hebrew Poetry*, trans. James Marsh (Burlington, VT: Edward Smith, 1833), 28. On Herder's views of both ancient Israel and modern Jews, see Frederick M. Barnard, "The Hebrews and Herder's Political Creed," *Modern Language Review* 54, no. 4 (1959): 533–546; and idem, "Herder and Israel," *Jewish Social Studies* 28, no. 1 (1966): 25–33. On how Herder was seen by early German maskilim, see Moshe Pelli, "'These are the words of the great pundit, scholar and poet, Herder' . . . : Herder and the Hebrew Haskalah," in *Hebräische Poesie und jüdischer Volksgeist: Die Wirkungsgeschichte von Johann Gottfried Herder im Judentum Mittel- und Osteuropas*, ed. Christoph Schulte (Hildesheim: Olms, 2003), 107–124.

20. Judah Halevi, *Book of the Kuzari*, trans. Hartwig Hirschfeld (New York: Pardes Publishing House, 1946), 109–118. The citations are to be found on p. 109. For a fuller explication, see Wilhelm Bacher, "The Views of Jehuda Halevi concerning the Hebrew Language," *Hebraica* 8, nos. 3–4 (April–July 1892): 136–149.

21. Andrea Schatz, "'Peoples of Pure Speech': The Religious, the Secular and the Jewish Beginnings of Modernity," in *Early Modern Culture and Haskalah: Reconsidering the Borderlines of Modern Jewish History*, ed. David B. Ruderman and Shmuel Feiner (Göttingen: Vandenhoek & Ruprecht, 2007), 183.

22. Barzilay, "From Purism to Expansionism," 10. See Schatz, *Sprache in der Zerstreuung*, 197–223.

23. Moses Mendelssohn, "On the Question: What does 'to enlighten' mean?" in *Moses Mendelssohn: Philosophical Writings*, ed. Daniel O. Dahlstrom (Cambridge: Cambridge University Press, 1997), 314.

24. Justus Georg Schottel, *Ausführlich Arbeit von der Teutschen Haubt-Sprache* (C. F. Zilligern: Braunschweig, 1663; repr. Niemeyer: Tübingen, 1967), 60, 144 and 146.

25. Hans Aarsleff, *From Locke to Saussure: Essays on the Study of Language and Intellectual History* (Minneapolis: University of Minnesota Press, 1982), 47–48.

26. The Leibniz quotation appears in Olender, *Languages of Paradise*, 5.

27. Cited in Peter Fenves, "Imagining an Inundation of Australians, or, Leibniz on the Principles of Grace and Race," in *Race and Racism in Modern Philosophy*, ed. Andrew Valls (Ithaca, NY: Cornell University Press, 2005), 80.

28. Tracy Chevalier, ed., *Encyclopedia of the Essay* (Chicago: Fitzroy Dearborn Publishers, 1997), 526. For more on baroque German language theory and Leibniz's goal of creating a universal system of notation—which would allow for the detection and recording of errors of thought, reducing them to purely grammatical or syntactical errors and establishing such errors with mathematical certainty—see Jan C. Westerhoff, "*Poeta Calculans*: Harsdörffer, Leibniz, and the *mathesis universalis*," *Journal of the History of Ideas* 60, no. 3 (1999): 449–467; and Markus Hundt, *Spracharbeit im 17. Jahrhundert: Studien zu Georg Philipp Harsdörffer, Justus Georg Schottelius und Christian Gueintz*, Studia Linguistica Germanica, 57 (Berlin: De Gruyter, 2000).

29. See Avi Lifschitz, *Language and Enlightenment: The Berlin Debates of the Eighteenth Century* (Oxford: Oxford University Press, 2012), 95–142; Raoul N. Smith, "The Sociology of Language in Johann David Michaelis's Dissertation of 1760," *Journal of the History of the Behavioral Sciences* 12, no. 4 (1976): 338–346. Michaelis had also made a contribution to the question of Hebrew phonology when he published a treatise on Hebrew pronunciation, *Anfangs-Gründe der hebräischen Accentuation: nebst einer kurtzen Abhandlung von dem Alterthum der Accente und hebräischen Puncte überhaupt: auch einem Anhange, in welchem einige Schrifft-Oerter nach den Regeln der Accentuation untersuchet werden* (Halle: In Verlegung des Wäysenhauses, 1741).

30. Altmann, *Moses Mendelssohn*, 112–113.

31. More generally on Mendelssohn's philosophy of language, see Anne Pollok, *Facetten des Menschen: Zur Anthropologie Moses Mendessohns* (Hamburg: Feliz Meiner, 2010), 355–389.

32. There is a vast literature on eighteenth-century language politics and issues of dialect and pronunciation. A sample of those texts that have informed parts of this chapter include Joan C. Beal, *English Pronunciation in the Eighteenth Century: Thomas Spence's Grand Repository of the English Language* (Oxford: Oxford University Press, 1999); Charles Jones, *English Pronunciation in the Eighteenth and Nineteenth Centuries* (Basingstoke: Palgrave Macmillan, 2006); Ingrid Tieken-Boon van Ostade, ed., *Grammars, Grammarians, and Grammar-Writing in Eighteenth-Century England* (Berlin: Mouton de Gruyter, 2008); Peter Rickard, *The Embarrassments of Irregularity: The French Language in the Eighteenth Century* (London: Cambridge University Press, 1981); Lois C. Dubin, *The Port Jews of Habsburg Trieste: Absolutist Politics and Enlightenment Culture* (Stanford, CA: Stanford University Press, 1999), esp. chap. 4; Wilfried M. Voge, *The Pronunciation of German in the 18th Century* (Hamburg: Buske, 1978).

33. See Gerhard Oestreich, *Geist und Gestalt des frühmodernen Staates. Ausgewählte Aufsätze* (Berlin: Duncker and Humblot 1969); Norbert Elias, *The Civilizing Process*, vol. 2 (New York: Pantheon Books, 1982); Manfred Heinemann, *Schule im Vorfeld der Verwaltung: Die Entwicklung der preussischen Unterrichtsverwaltung von 1771–1800* (Göttingen: Vandenhoeck und Ruprecht, 1974); Susanne Godefroid,

Bürgerliche Ideologie und Bildungspolitik das Bildungswesen in Preußen vom Ausgang des 18. Jahrhunderts bis zur bürgerlichen Revolution 1848/49. Eine historisch-materialistische Analyse seiner Entstehungsbedingungen (Giessen: Achenbach, 1974); and Joachim Gessinger, *Sprache und Bürgertum: Zur Sozialgeschichte sprachlicher Verkehrsformen im Deutschland des 18. Jahrhunderts* (Stuttgart: Metzler, 1980).

34. Andreas Gardt, *Nation und Sprache: Die Diskussion ihres Verhältnisses in Geschichte und Gegenwart* (Berlin: De Gruyter, 2000), 169–170.

35. Heinrich Löffler, *Probleme der Dialektologie. Eine Einfuhrung* (Darmstadt: WBG, 1990).

36. Jeffrey A. Grossman, *The Discourse on Yiddish in Germany: From the Enlightenment to the Second Empire* (Rochester, NY: Camden House, 2000).

37. Mendelssohn detected a cause-and-effect relationship between the lowly status of the Jews and their vernacular. In 1782 Ernst Ferdinand Klein, assistant counselor-at-law at Breslau and later Berlin, had been charged with drafting a new oath for use by Jews in the courts. Klein turned to Mendelssohn for advice, presumably querying as to whether Yiddish might be a suitable language for the oath. "I am afraid," responded Mendelssohn, "this jargon has contributed more than a little to the uncivilized bearing of the common man. In contrast, it seems to me that the recent usage of pure German among my brethren promises to have a most salutary effect on them." Mendelssohn suggested an alternative option, namely, that the oath be rendered into "pure Hebrew so that it could be read in either pure German or pure Hebrew, or possibly both. . . . Anything at all rather than a mishmash of languages!" *Moses Mendelssohn: Selections from His Writings*, ed. and trans. Eva Jospe (New York: Viking Press, 1975), 106. David Sorkin argues strenuously that Mendelssohn's opposition to Yiddish was "an invention of a subsequent age," and that the above quotation is generally taken out of context. It was his devotees who claimed Mendelssohn as the authority for their own hatred of the language. While that may well be true, Mendelssohn certainly gave them plenty of ammunition, and contempt of Yiddish was an already well-established position in his day and among many with whom he consorted. Even if they attributed to him a sentiment that was not as fully developed as they claimed it was, he legitimated or was used to legitimate a widespread and deeply held German-Jewish aversion to Yiddish. See David Sorkin, *Moses Mendelssohn* (London: Peter Halban, 1996), 175n3.

38. On Mendelssohn and the extant Yiddish translations that he sought to render redundant with his own German translation, see Grit Schorch, *Moses Mendelssohns Sprachpolitik* (Berlin: Walter de Gruyter, 2012), 85–89. On the link between language and aesthetics in the German context, see Adrian Aebi Farahmand, *Die Sprache und das Schöne: Karl Philipp Moritz' Sprachreflexionen in Verbindung mit seiner Ästhetik* (Berlin: De Gruyter, 2012).

39. Benjamin Bennett, *Beyond Theory: Eighteenth-Century German Literature and the Poetics of Irony* (Ithaca, NY: Cornell University Press, 1993), 155.

40. Paul Guyer, "18th Century German Aesthetics," *The Stanford Encyclopedia of Philosophy* (Fall 2008 Edition), http://plato.stanford.edu/archives/fall2008/entries/aesthetics-18th-german/.

41. Alexander Gottlieb Baumgarten, *Theoretische Aesthetik: Die Grundlegenden Abschnitte aus der "Aesthetica" (1750/1758)*, ed. and trans. Hans Rudolf Schweitzer (Hamburg: Meiner, 1983), 3.

42. Kai Hammermeister, *The German Aesthetic Tradition* (Cambridge: Cambridge University Press, 2002), 7.

43. Hans Rudolf Schweizer, *Ästhetik als Philosophie der sinnlichen Erkenntnis: Eine Interpretation der "Aesthetica" A. G. Baumgartens mit teilweiser Wiedergabe der lateinischen Textes und deutscher Übersetzung* (Basel: Schwabe, 1973), 116–117.

44. Guyer, "18th Century German Aesthetics."

45. This was the position, for example, of Aaron Halle-Wolfsohn, who wrote in Hebrew, Yiddish, and German. With regard to the former he called for a return to the use of pure biblical Hebrew, shorn of rabbinic influence. See Jutta Straus, "Aaron Halle-Wolfson: Ein Leben in drei Sprachen," in *Musik und Ästhetik im Berlin Moses Mendelssohns*, ed. Anselm Gerhard (Tübingen: Max Neimeyer Verlag, 1999), 70.

46. Language was a subject Mendelssohn addressed early in his career with his rejection of Rousseau's view that the capacity for language was something that humans and animals shared; he chastised Rousseau for his neglect of the role played by Providence in the development of language.

47. Moses Mendelssohn, *Gesammelte Schriften. Jubiläumsausgabe*, ed. Alexander Altmann and Fritz Bamberger (Stuttgart-Bad Cannstatt: F. Frommann, 1971), 8:160 and 168.

48. Sorkin, *Moses Mendelssohn*, 66–67. The quotation appears on p. 66.

49. *Or la-Netiva*, *JubA* 14, 232.

50. For a good introduction to the German literature on language, see Hermann J. Cloeren, *Language and Thought: German Approaches to Analytic Philosophy in the 18th and 19th Centuries* (Berlin: Walter de Gruyter, 1988), esp. 1–77.

51. Shmuel Feiner, *Moses Mendelssohn: Sage of Modernity* (New Haven, CT: Yale University Press, 2010), 154.

52. *Moses Mendelssohn: Ästhetische Schriften*, ed. Anne Pollok (Hamburg: Felix Meiner Verlag, 2006).

53. On Winckelmann, see Klaus-Werner Haupt, *Johann Winckelmann. Begründer der klassischen Archäologie und modernen Kunstwissenschaften* (Wiesbaden: Marixverlag, 2014); and Katherine Harloe, *Winckelmann and the Invention of Antiquity: History and Aesthetics in the Age of Altertumswissenschaft* (Oxford: Oxford University Press, 2013).

54. Altmann, *Moses Mendelssohn*, 70.

55. Leigh Eric Schmidt, *Hearing Things: Religion, Illusion, and the American Enlightenment* (Cambridge, MA: Harvard University Press, 2000), 15–28; Alain Corbin, *Time, Desire, and Horror: Towards a History of the Senses* (Cambridge, UK: Polity Press, 1995); idem, *Village Bells: Sound and Meaning in the Nineteenth-Century French Countryside* (New York: Columbia University Press, 1998).

56. Hans-Joachim Neubauer, *Judenfiguren: Drama und Theater im frühen 19. Jahrhundert* (Frankfurt: Campus, 1994); idem, "Auf Begehr: Unser Verkehr: Über eine judenfeindliche Theaterposse im Jahre 1815," in *Antisemitismus und jüdische Geschichte. Studien zu Ehren von Herbert A. Strauss*, ed. Rainer Erb and Michael Schmidt (Berlin: Wissenschaftlicher Autorenverlag, 1987), 313–327; and idem, "Stimme und Tabu: Was das Theater erfindet und was es vermeidet," in *Judenfeindschaft as Paradigma: Studien zur Vorurteilsforschung*, ed. Wolfgang Benz and Angelika Königseder (Berlin: Metropol, 2002), 70–78.

57. Ruth HaCohen, *The Music Libel against the Jews* (New Haven, CT: Yale University Press, 2011), 2.

58. Anselm Gerhard, ed., *Musik und Ästhetik im Berlin Moses Mendelssohns* (Tübingen: Max Neimeyer Verlag, 1999), 11.

59. "Musikblatt," *Sulamith* 3, no. 1 (1810): 72. The music for piano was by the Jewish actor and composer Julius Miller from Dresden. See also the Hebrew song composed by Joseph Wolf, an editor of *Sulamith*, in honor of the seventieth birthday of His Highness Prince Leopold Friedrich Franz. It was sung in the Dresden synagogue. *Sulamith* 3, no. 1 (1810): 267–272. And see the song written for the Israelite School in Westphalia in *Sulamith* 3, no. 1 (1810): 289–294. For more, see the brief and thus all the more noteworthy report on the audience's enthusiastic reception of Julius Miller's operetta *Julie or the Flower Basket* in *Sulamith* 4, no. 1 (1812): 205–206.

60. Peter Wollny, "'Ein förmlicher Sebastian und Philipp Emanuel Bach-Kultus': Sara Levy, geb. Itzig und ihr musikalisch-literarisher Salon," in Gerhard, *Musik und Ästhetik*, 220–221. All of Daniel Itzig's daughters were in close contact with court musicians, and Sara Itzig Levy, great-aunt to Felix Mendelssohn-Bartholdy, even studied harpsichord with J. S. Bach's son Wilhelm Friedemann Bach. She also became the leading collector of early eighteenth-century music, amassing a giant library that she donated to the Berlin Singakademie.

61. Celia Applegate, *Bach in Berlin: Nation and Culture in Mendelssohn's Revival of the St. Matthew Passion* (Ithaca, NY: Cornell University Press, 2005), 10–18. It is noteworthy that, in 1794, the Berlin Singakademie's founder, Carl Friedrich Christian Fasch, composed a work entitled *Mendelssohniana: 6 mehrstimmige Gesänge* for two to six voices, with organ accompaniment. The work was based on Moses Mendelssohn's German translation of Psalm 30. Mendelssohn's translation of the book of Psalms and Song of Songs was published posthumously in 1788. See Edwin Seroussi, "Beautifying Worship: Music in Early Reform Synagogues of Northern-Germany (ca. 1810–1840)," in *Fasch und die Musik im Europa des 18. Jahrhunderts*, ed. Guido Bimberg and Rüdiger Pfeiffer (Weimar: Böhlau, 1995), 241–252.

62. Almut Spalding, *Elise Reimarus (1735–1805), the Muse of Hamburg: A Woman of the German Enlightenment* (Wurzburg: Konigshausen & Neumann, 2005), 259–279.

63. The title of the piece was *Sulamith und Eusebia. Eine Trauerkantate auf den Tod Moses Mendelssohns*. Gerhard, *Musik und Ästhetik*, 14.

64. On Friedländer, see Meyer, *The Origins of the Modern Jew*, 57–84.

65. The Rousseau quotation appears in Downing A. Thomas, *Music and the Origins of Language: Theories from the French Enlightenment* (Cambridge: Cambridge University Press, 1995), 5.

66. David Friedländer, *Ueber die Verbesserung der Israeliten im Konigreich Pohlen: Ein von der Regierung daselbst im Jahr 1816 abgefordertes Gutachten* (Berlin: Nicolaische Buchhandlung, 1819), 48–54.

67. Friedländer even published Mendelssohn's Hebrew treatise on the immortality of the soul, *Sefer Ha-nefesh* (Book of the Soul) in 1787, the year after Mendelssohn's death, and had worked together with Mendelssohn on his Bible translation. See Sorkin, *Moses Mendelssohn*, 22.

68. Altmann, *Moses Mendelssohn*, 66–67. On Mendelsohn as music theorist, see Harmut Grimm, "Moses Mendelssohns Beitrag zur Musikästhetik und Carl Phillip Emanuel Bachs Fantasie-Prinzip," in Gerhard, *Musik und Ästhetik*, 165–186; Wolf-

gang Suppan, "Moses Mendelssohn und die Musikästhetik des 18. Jahrhunderts," *Die Musikforschung* 17 (1964): 22–33.

69. Feiner, *Moses Mendelssohn*, 28–29.

70. Ibid., 40.

71. Laurenz Lütteken, "Mendelssohn und der musikästhetische Diskurs der Aufklärung," in *Moses Mendelssohn im Spannungsfeld der Aufklärung*, ed. Michael Albrecht and Eva J. Engel (Stuttgart-Bad: Friedrich Fromann, 2000), 160–161 and 170–172. On the eighteenth-century philosophical discourse on music in France, see Thomas, *Music and the Origins of Language*.

72. Grimm, "Moses Mendelssohns Beitrag zur Musikästhetik," 149. On Mendelssohn and Kirberger, see Laurenz Lütteken, "Zwischen Ohr und Verstand: Moses Mendelssohn und Johan Philipp Kirnberger und die Begründung des 'reinen Satzes' in der Musik," in Gerhard, *Musik und Ästhetik*, 135–163.

73. Lütteken, "Mendelssohn und der musikästhetische Diskurs der Aufklärung," 172–174. On Mendelssohn's thirteen-year-long project of translating the psalms, see Sorkin, *Moses Mendelssohn*, 46–52.

74. Both quotations are to be found in Altmann, *Moses Mendelssohn*, 410–411.

75. Sorkin, *Moses Mendelssohn*, 68–69.

76. Leon Botstein, "The Aesthetics of Assimilation and Affirmation: Reconstructing the Career of Felix Mendelssohn," in *Mendelssohn and His World*, ed. R. Larry Todd (Princeton, NJ: Princeton University Press, 1991), 5–42.

77. Jonathan Karp, "The Aesthetic Difference: Moses Mendelssohn's *Kohelet musar* and the Inception of the Berlin Haskalah," in *Renewing the Past: Reconfiguring Jewish Culture from al-Andalus to the Haskalah*, ed. Ross Brann and Adam Sutcliff (Philadelphia: University of Pennsylvania Press, 2004), 93–120.

78. *Kohelet musar, JubA* 14, 4.

79. Altmann, *Moses Mendelssohn*, 85.

80. Hannah Ginsborg, "Kant's Aesthetics and Teleology," *The Stanford Encyclopedia of Philosophy* (Fall 2008 Edition). http://plato.stanford.edu/archives/fall2008/entries/kant-aesthetics/.

81. Henoch Yalon, *Kuntresim le-inyanei ha-lashon ha-ivrit*, vols. 1 and 2 (1937): 116n6 and 316n4.

82. Quoted in H. J. Zimmels, *Ashkenazim and Sephardim: Their Relations, Differences, and Problems as Reflected in the Rabbinical Responsa* (London: Oxford University Press, 1958), 85.

83. Ibid., 86.

84. Abraham Schwartz, *Sefer Derekh ha-Nesher ve-Torat ha-Emet*, vol. 1 (Satumare: M. L. Hirsh, 1928), 43–44. My thanks to Eliyahu Stern for bringing this source to my attention. Also see Rachel Elior, "Rabbi Nathan Adler and the Frankfurt Pietists: Pietist Groups in Eastern and Central Europe during the Eighteenth Century," in *Jüdische Kultur in Frankfurt am Main, von den Anfangen bis zur Gegenwart*, ed. Karl Erich Grozinger (Wiesbaden: Harrassowitz Verlag, 1997), 165fn 67.

85. Andrea Schatz, "Returning to Sepharad: Maskilic Reflections on Hebrew in the Diaspora," in Fontaine, Schatz, and Zwiep,, *Sepharad in Ashkenaz*, 263–277.

86. Edward Breuer, "Naphtali Herz Wessely and the Cultural Dislocations of an Eighteenth-Century Maskil," in Feiner and Sorkin, *New Perspectives on the Haskalah*, 27–47.

87. M. Bondi, "Beitrag zur Geschichte der Herkunft des Gelehrten Hartwig Wessely," *Sulamith* 15, no. 1 (1817): 94–99. The author states that "before Wessely, no one in Germany put any care into a Hebrew lecture."

88. Naphtali Herz Wessely, *Worte der Wahrheit und des Friedens an die gesammte jüdische Nation. Vorzüglich an diejenigen, so unter dem Schutze des glorreichen und großmächtigsten Kaysers Josephs II. wohnen*, trans. David Friedländer (Berlin: n.p., 1782).

89. Naphtali Herz Wessely, "Words of Peace and Truth (1782)," in *The Jew in the Modern World*, ed. Paul Mendes-Flohr and Jehuda Reinharz (New York: Oxford University Press, 1995), 71.

90. Naphtali Herz Wessely, *Divrei shalom ve-emet* (Berlin: n.p., 1782), 28a.

91. Both quotations appear in ibid., 29a.

92. Ibid., 28a–28b.

93. Pelli, *The Age of Haskalah*, 113–130, and Feiner, *Moses Mendelssohn*, 153–159. *Words of Peace and Truth* was put to the flames in many communities, especially in Eastern Europe. According to Wessely's harshest critic, the Polish rabbi David ben Nathan Tevele of Lissa, "in Vilna, the great city of God, they have burned Wessely's book in the streets. Before doing so they hung his book from an iron chain in the courtyard of the synagogue." In a sermon, he decried Wessely as "a sycophant, an evil man, a man poor in understanding, the most mediocre of mediocre men," and described *Words of Peace and Truth* as nothing more than "eight chapters of bootlicking." Mendes-Flohr and Reinharz, *The Jew in the Modern World*, 74–76.

94. Wessely, *Divrei shalom ve-emet*, 29a–b.

95. Ibid., 59b. Wessely had lived in Amsterdam and Hamburg, where in both cities he frequently heard the Sephardic pronunciation of Hebrew. Altmann, *Moses Mendelssohn*, 189 and 357. In Amsterdam he formed a close relationship with the Sephardic community courtesy of his friendship with the poet David Franco-Mendes. Israel Zinberg, *History of Jewish Literature*, vol. 8 (Cincinnati: Hebrew Union College Press, 1976), 61.

96. Wessely, *Divrei shalom ve-emet*, 60a–b and partially quoted in Zimmels, *Ashkenazim and Sephardim*, 87. Twenty-four years later, in 1806, David Fränkel, one of Wessely's ideological heirs and coeditor of *Sulamith*, was less pessimistic than Wessely. Although it is clear that much still needed to be done to effect the aesthetic improvement of German and Polish Jewry, Fränkel doesn't despair. With an optimism so characteristic of his journal's editorial line, he suggests that if Sephardic practices are used as a model, then change is possible. Praising Sephardic synagogue services, he says that "their preachers are excellent; their schoolteachers are praiseworthy and their schools, such as the one in Livorno, earn the highest praise. Their speech is unmixed and pure and their behavior was not noticeably flamboyant." David Fränkel, "Gallerie schädlicher Mißbräuche, unanständiger Convenienzen und absurder Ceremonien unter den Juden. Ein paar Worte über Denk- und Pressefreihet," *Sulamith* 1, no. 1 (1806): 319–331.

97. Wessely, *Divrei shalom ve-emet*, 60b.

98. Ibid., 60b–61a.

99. Ibid., 61a.

100. Feiner, "From Renaissance to Revolution," 1.

101. Martin Jay, *Songs of Experience: Modern American and European Variations on a Universal Theme* (Berkeley: University of California Press, 2004), 140.

102. Michael A. Meyer, *Response to Modernity: A History of the Reform Movement in Judaism* (New York: Oxford University Press, 1988), 7 and 49. See also the responsa on whether to pray in Sephardic or Ashkenazic Hebrew in Zimmels, *Ashkenazim and Sephardim*, 308–314.

103. In Germany, following the discovery of the link between Sanskrit and European languages, the two figures most responsible for promoting the view that language is a manifestation of national character were the linguist Franz Bopp (1791–1867) and the philosopher Wilhelm von Humboldt (1767–1835).

104. Jacob Petuchowski, *Prayerbook Reform in Europe: The Liturgy of European Liberal and Reform Judaism* (New York: World Union for Progressive Judaism 1968), 105 and 109.

105. The latter prohibitions appear in the Synagogenordnung of the Principality of Birkenfeld in 1843. See Petuchowski, *Prayerbook Reform in Europe*, 115.

106. Abraham Z. Idelsohn, *Jewish Music: Its Historical Development* (New York: Dover, 1992), 235–236.

107. Wilhelm Gesenius, *Gesenius' Hebrew Grammar* (Oxford: Clarendon Press, 1910), 32.

108. David Leimdörfer, ed., *Festschrift zum hundertjährigen Bestehen des Israelitischen Tempels in Hamburg 1818–1918* (Hamburg: M. Glogau, 1918), 68–70.

109. Seroussi, "Beautifying Worship," 251.

110. Meyer, *Response to Modernity*, 57.

111. See Meyer Kayserling, "Rabbi Santob de Carrion," *Jershurun* 9 (1856): 484–492. The quotation appears on p. 485. More generally, see Carsten Schapkow, *Vorbild und Gegenbild: Das iberische Judentum in der deutsch-jüdischen Erinnerungskultur 1779–1939* (Cologne: Böhlau, 2011), 80–135.

112. Tudor Parfitt, "The Use of Hebrew in Palestine, 1800–1882," *Journal of Semitic Studies* 17 (1972): 237–252; and idem, "The Contribution of the Old Yishuv to the Revival of Hebrew," *Journal of Semitic Studies* 29, no. 2 (1984): 255–265. Shlomo Haramati is in basic accord with Parfitt. See his *Ivrit safa meduberet* (Tel Aviv: Misrad ha-bitakhon, 2000). Benjamin Harshav strongly disagrees with this claim, suggesting it is a gross exaggeration. According to him, it was only with the second aliyah that a significant social and culturally dedicated stratum of settlers emerged to make Hebrew the lingua franca. See Benjamin Harshav, *Language in Time of Revolution* (Berkeley: University of California Press, 1993), 85–86 and 101–112. Even historico-statistical analyses of how many Hebrew speakers there were in Palestine fail to clarify the matter because it is unclear how much and what kinds of Hebrew were being employed. See Nathan Efrati, *Mi leshon Yehudim li leshon uma: Ha-dibur ha-Ivri be-Eretz Yisra'el be-shanim 1882–1922* (Jerusalem: Akademyah la-lashon ha-'Ivrit, 2004), esp. 1–31 and 108–126. The debate is well summarized in Arieh B. Saposnik, *Becoming Hebrew: The Creation of a Jewish National Culture in Ottoman Palestine* (New York: Oxford University Press, 2008), 65–67.

113. Ron Kuzar, *Hebrew and Zionism: A Discourse Analytic Cultural Study* (Berlin: Mouton de Gruyter, 2001), 259–260.

114. Harshav, *Language in Time of Revolution*, 155.

115. Eliezer Ben-Yehuda, *Ha-khalom ve-shivro*, ed. Reuven Sivan (Jerusalem: Mossad Bialik, 1978), 71–72.

116. Ibid., 97. See also Harshav, *Language in Time of Revolution*, 158.

117. Ben-Yehuda, *Ha-khalom ve-shivro*, 106.

118. Rathenau, a wealthy industrialist and the first-ever Jewish foreign minister of Germany—he served a mere four months in 1922 before being gunned down by right-wing radicals—employed this description in an article in which he advocated the assimilation of German Jews. See "Höre Israel!" *Die Zukunft* 18 (March 6, 1898): 452–462. A partial translation is to be found in Mendes-Flohr and Reinharz, *The Jew in the Modern World*, 814–817.

119. On Safa Brura, see Efrati, *Mi leshon Yehudim li leshon uma*, 7–11.

120. See *Leket teudot: le-toldot va'ad ha-lashon ve-ha-akademiyah la-lashon ha-ivrit, 1890–1970* (Jerusalem: Academy of Hebrew Language, 1970), 31 and 92–93, and Harshav, *Language in Time of Revolution*, 159–160.

121. Harshav, *Language in Time of Revolution*, 159.

122. *Leket teudot*, 161.

123. Miryam Segal, *A New Sound in Hebrew Poetry: Poetics, Politics, Accent* (Bloomington: Indiana University Press, 2010), 49–72; and Efrati, *Mi leshon Yehudim li leshon uma*, 36–42.

124. *Leket teudot*, 31.

125. This was a view expressed, for example, by the Russian maskil Yitzhak Ber Levinzon in his *Te'udah be-Yisrael* (1828). In a diatribe against Yiddish, Levinzon claimed that "the man who lacks a pure and lucid language and script is a man despised." Quoted in Israel Bartal, "From Traditional Bilingualism to National Monolingualism" in Glinert, *Hebrew in Ashkenaz*, 143.

126. *Leket teudot*, 159.

127. Arieh Saposnik has keenly observed the paradox here: "The children were expected to be shaped into rooted, whole Hebrews by educators who themselves were not." Saposnik, *Becoming Hebrew*, 83.

128. Harshav, *Language in Time of Revolution*, 162. See also Segal, *A New Sound in Hebrew Poetry*, 73–99, who, in discussing the newly accented Hebrew poetry in the generation after Bialik, introduces the category of gender and the role it played in the sound of modern Hebrew.

129. Shelomo Morag refers to the Hebrew that emerged in Israel as "Ashkenized-Sephardi." See his "The Emergence of Modern Hebrew: Some Sociolinguistic Perspectives" in Glinert, *Hebrew in Ashkenaz*, 213–214; Ghil'ad Zuckermann, "'Abba, why was Professor Higgins trying to teach Eliza to speak like our cleaning lady?': Mizrahim, Ashkenazim, Prescriptivism and the Real Sounds of the Israeli Language," *Australian Journal of Jewish Studies* 19 (2005): 210–231.

Chapter Two
"Castilian Pride and Oriental Dignity":
Sephardic Beauty in the Eye of the Ashkenazic Beholder

1. Known in antiquity but then forgotten in the Middle Ages, physiognomy was revived and made popular by the Swiss theologian and interlocutor of Moses Mendelssohn Johann Caspar Lavater. Lavater, who challenged Mendelssohn to ei-

ther refute the truth of Christianity or accept it, published his first essays on physiognomy in 1772, maintaining that a proper reading of an individual's face was a
window onto inner character. Phrenology, which was related to physiognomy and
became wildly popular, was the science of reading the outer bumps of the skull, with
a similar view to determining a person's inner character. Phrenology was invented
by the German physicians Franz Josef Gall and Johann Gaspar Spurzheim in the
early nineteenth century. See Johan Caspar Lavater, *Essays on Physiognomy* (London:
D. Blake, 1840); and Johan Gaspar Spurzheim, *The Physiognomical System of Drs. Gall
and Spurzheim* (London: Baldwin, Cradock and Joy, 1815).

2. See Christian Wilhelm Dohm, *Ueber die bürgerliche Verbesserung der Juden*
(Berlin: F. Nicolai, 1781); and Henri Jean-Baptiste Grégoire, *Essai sur la régénération
physique, morale et politique des Juifs* (Metz: Impr. de C. Lamort, 1789).

3. Shmuel Feiner, *The Origins of Jewish Secularization in Eighteenth-Century Europe* (Philadelphia: University of Pennsylvania Press, 2010); idem, *The Jewish Enlightenment* (Philadelphia: University of Pennsylvania Press, 2004).

4. Todd M. Endelman, *Jewish Apostasy in the Modern World* (New York: Holmes
& Meier, 1987).

5. Miriam Bodian, *Hebrews of the Portuguese Nation: Conversos and Community
in Early Modern Amsterdam* (Bloomington: Indiana University Press, 1999); Yosef
Kaplan, Richard H. Popkin, and Henry Méchoulan, eds., *Menasseh Ben Israel and His
World* (Leiden: Brill, 1989), 45–62. The quotation appears in Kaplan, Popkin, and
Méchoulan on p. 53.

6. On notions of the purity of blood among Iberian Jews, see Yosef Hayim Yerushalmi, *From Spanish Court to Italian Ghetto; Isaac Cardoso: A Study in Seventeenth-
Century Marranism and Jewish Apologetics* (New York: Columbia University Press,
1971); and idem, *Assimilation and Racial Anti-Semitism: The Iberian and the German
Models* (New York: Leo Baeck Institute, 1982).

7. See José Luis Cardoso and António de Vasconcelos Noqueira, "Isaac de Pinto
(1717–1787) and the Jewish Problems: Apologetic Letters to Voltaire and Diderot,"
History of European Ideas 33, no. 4 (2007): 476–487; Adam Sutcliffe. "Can a Jew Be a
Philosophe? Isaac de Pinto, Voltaire and Jewish Participation in the European Enlightenment," *Jewish Social Studies*, 6, no. 3 (2000): 31–51; and Richard H. Popkin,
"Hume and Isaac de Pinto," *Texas Studies in Literature and Language* 12, no. 3 (1970):
417–430.

8. Philip Le Fanu, trans., *Letters of Certain Jews to Monsieur Voltaire, Containing
an Apology for Their Own People, and for the Old Testament* (Philadelphia: H. Hooker;
Cincinnati, G. G. Jones, 1848), 33–34 and 37.

9. Ibid., 37–38.

10. Ibid., 42.

11. David Friedländer, *Aktenstücke, die Reform der Jüdischen Kolonieen in den
Preussischen Staaten betreffend* (Berlin: Voß, 1793), 5.

12. Ibid., 9–13. In fact the singular importance of the Jews to the local econo-
mies was also recognized in Galicia. See the article by the philosopher and writer
Ignaz Jeitteles, "Bemerkungen eines Reisenden über den Charakter der Einwohner
in Galizien. (Eine Rapsodie)," *Sulamith* 1, no. 2 (1807): 182–188. The article is, in fact,
a commentary on and translation of a report written in French by Dr. Schultes, a
professor of chemistry and botany at the University of Krakow. Jeitteles has inserted

passages from Friedländer on the difference between Galician peasants and the Jews that essentially accord with Schultes's observations. On Schultes's take on the role of Jews in fostering local industry, see esp. pp. 185–186.

13. Friedländer, *Aktenstücke*, 152–153.

14. Quoted in Dovid Katz, *Words on Fire: The Unfinished Story of Yiddish* (New York: Basic Books, 2004), 181.

15. Steven M. Lowenstein, "The Yiddish Written Word in Nineteenth-Century Germany," *Leo Baeck Institute Year Book* 24 (1979): 179–192; Steven E. Aschheim, *Brothers and Strangers: The East European Jew in German and German Jewish Consciousness, 1800–1923* (Madison: University of Wisconsin Press, 1982).

16. Glenn Dynner, *Men of Silk: The Hasidic Conquest of Polish Jewish Society* (Oxford: Oxford University Press, 2006); and Marcin Wodziński, *Hasidism and Politics: The Kingdom of Poland, 1815–1864* (Oxford: Littman Library of Jewish Civilization, 2013).

17. Michael A. Meyer, *Response to Modernity: A History of the Reform Movement in Judaism* (New York: Oxford University Press, 1988), 44–45.

18. On the particular character of the Enlightenment's impact on Jews in Poland, see Nancy Sinkoff, *Out of the Shtetl: Making Jews Modern in the Polish Borderlands* (Providence, RI: Brown Judaic Studies, 2004); and David E. Fishman, *Russia's First Modern Jews: The Jews of Shklov* (New York: New York University Press, 1996).

19. Ernst Frankel, "David Friedländer und seine Zeit," *Zeitschrift für die Geschichte der Juden in Deutschland* 6 (1935): 65–77.

20. For an analysis of Herz's activities in these two areas, see Martin L. Davies, *Identity or History? Marcus Herz and the End of the Enlightenment* (Detroit: Wayne State University Press, 1995); Brigitte Ibing, "Markus Herz, a Biographical Study," *Koroth* 9, nos. 1–2 (1985): 113–121; and Wolfram Kaiser and Arina Völker, "Berolina iubilans: Berliner Ärzte als hallesche Doktoranden (V). Markus Herz (1747–1803) und die Berliner jüdischen Ärzte," *Zeitschrift für die gesamte innere Medizin* 42 (1987): 618–623.

21. With this formulation I have paraphrased Martin Davies. See Davies, *Identity or History?*, 70–71.

22. Ibid., 7.

23. Quoted in Deborah Hertz, *Jewish High Society in Old Regime Berlin* (New Haven, CT: Yale University Press, 1988), 100.

24. "Biographie des Herrn Marcus Herz," *Sulamith* 3 (1811): 77–97 (an anonymous work).

25. "ein sanfter, höchst lieblicher Ausdruck [. . .] den schönsten Fuß und Hand, edle Haltung [. . .] seine Sprache war rein, wie denn die portugiesischen Israeliten überhaupt den jüdischen Jargon un Ton nicht haben." Henriette de Lemos Herz, *Henriette Herz in Erinnerungen Briefen und Zeugnissen*, ed. Rainer Schmitz (Frankfurt am Main: Insel Verlag, 1984), 14. I am grateful to Amos Bitzan for bringing this source to my attention.

26. Raphael Patai, *The Jewish Mind* (Detroit: Wayne State University Press, 1996), 249.

27. On Herz's physical beauty and its portrayal within the larger context of Berlin high society, see Liliane Weissberg, "Weibliche Körperschaften: Bild und Wort bei Henriette Herz," in *Von einer Welt in die andere: Jüdinnen im 19. und 20. Jahrhundert*, ed. Jutta Dick and Barbara Hahn (Vienna: Brandstätter, 1993), 71–92; and Marjanne E.

Gootzé, "Posing for Posterity: The Representations and Portrayals of Henriette Herz as the 'Beautiful Jewess,'" in *Body Dialectics in the Age of Goethe*, ed. Marianne Henn and Holger A. Pausch (Amsterdam: Rodopi, 2003), 67–96.

28. Michael A. Meyer, *The Origins of the Modern Jew: Jewish Identity and European Culture in Germany, 1749–1824* (Detroit: Wayne State University Press, 1967), 26.

29. James H. Lehmann, "Maimonides, Mendelssohn and the Me'asfim: Philosophy and the Biographical Imagination in the Early Haskalah," *Leo Baeck Institute Year Book* 20 (1975): 87–108. See also the extensive bibliography on the subject of Maimonides and the Haskalah in Moshe Pelli, *The Age of Haskalah: Studies in Hebrew Literature of the Enlightenment in Germany* (Leiden: E. J. Brill, 1979), 133.

30. *Ha-Me'assef* 2 (1785): 45 and 192. Quoted in Lehmann, "Maimonides, Mendelssohn and the Me'asfim," 95.

31. *Ha-Me'assef* 2 (1785): 81. Quoted in Lehmann, "Maimonides, Mendelssohn and the Me'asfim," 88.

32. For a fascinating look at the changing legacy of Moses Mendelssohn and the increasingly critical view of him in the two hundred years after his death, see Michael Brenner, "The Construction and Deconstruction of a Hero: Moses Mendelssohn's Afterlife in Early-Twentieth-Century Germany," in *Mediating Modernity: Challenges and Trends in the Jewish Encounter with the Modern World. Essays in Honor of Michael A. Meyer*, ed. Lauren B. Strauss and Michael Brenner (Detroit: Wayne State University Press, 2008), 274–289.

33. "Toledot ha-Rav Yitzhak Abravanel," *Ha-Me'assef* 1 (1784): 57–61.

34. Quoted in Lehmann, "Maimonides, Mendelssohn and the Me'asfim," 105–106.

35. Alfred Klee, Rahel Wischnitzer-Bernstein, and Josef Fried, *Gedenkausstellung Don Jizchaq Abrabanel: Seine Welt, Sein Werk* (Berlin: M. Lessmann, 1937); and Hermann Simon, *Das Berliner Jüdische Museum in der Oranienburger Strasse: Geschichte einer zerstörten Kultustätte* (Berlin: Union, 1988), 63–71.

36. Jean-Christophe Attias and Jane Marie Todd, "Isaac Abravanel: Between Ethnic Memory and National Memory," *Jewish Social Studies* 2, no. 3 (1996): 137–155.

37. Jonathan Skolnik, "The Strange Career of the Abarbanels from Heine to the Holocaust," in *Sephardism: Spanish Jewish History and the Modern Literary Imagination*, ed. Yael Halevi-Wise (Stanford, CA: Stanford University Press, 2012), 114–126.

38. This was how Abraham Joshua Heschel depicted him in his study *Don Jizchak Abravanel* (Berlin: E. Reiss, 1937). Of course not all German Jews felt similarly about Abravanel. In 1936, living under Nazi rule, the German-Jewish Zionist historian Yitzhak Fritz Baer published his *Galut*, in which he dedicated an entire chapter to Abravanel. Baer's analysis is a critical one, in which he concludes that despite his station in life, Abravanel had no answer to the vicissitudes of Jewish history, and with the expulsion from Spain he met the same fate as his coreligionists. In Baer's Zionist reading of Jewish history, Abravanel had no political solution to the problem of Exile. Yitzhak F. Baer, *Galut* (New York: Schocken Books, 1947), 60–68.

39. See the programmatic statement in the first issue by the coeditor, Joseph Wolf, "Zweck und Titel dieser Zeitschrift," *Sulamith* 1, no. 1 (1806): 1–11. In the same issue see the reference to "Mendelssohn's undying spirit" in David Fränkel, "Gallerie schädlicher Mißbräuche, unanständiger Convenienzen und absurder Ceremonien unter den Juden. Ein paar Worte über Denk- und Pressefreiheit," 329.

40. Wolf, "Zweck und Titel," 6–7.

41. Ibid., 6.

42. Schapkow, *Vorbild und Gegenbild*, 123–124.

43. Wolf, "Zweck und Titel," 4.

44. Joseph Löwisohn, "Menasse ben Israel, der glückliche Sachwalter seiner Glaubensgenossen," *Sulamith* 4, no. 2 (1812): 1–5.

45. Gotthold Salomon, "Rabbi Moses ben Maimon," *Sulamith* 2, no. 2 (1809): 376 and 378.

46. See Isaac Euchel "Forward," *Ha-Me'assef* 2 (1784).

47. See George L. Mosse, *German Jews beyond Judaism* (Bloomington: Indiana University Press, 1985).

48. On spas, see Mirjam Zadoff, *Next Year in Marienbad: The Lost Worlds of Jewish Spa Culture* (Philadelphia: University of Pennsylvania Press, 2012); and on sports, see Michael Brenner and Gideon Reuveni, eds., *Emancipation through Muscles: Jews and Sports in Europe* (Lincoln: University of Nebraska Press, 2006); and Eugen Weber, "Gymnastics and Sports in Fin-de-Siècle France: Opium of the Classes?," *American Historical Review* 76, no. 1 (1971): 70–98. Weber notes that in France in particular, many advocates of sport also saw it as a means of inculcating a martial spirit among the youth of the nation. Among Jews, sport became so important that it gave rise to a genuine Jewish sporting culture, formalized as such with the advent of Jewish sports journals. See, for example, the following contemporary publications: *Jüdische Turn- und Sportzeitung*; *Mitteilungsblatt des Sportvereins Bar Kochba* (Dresden); *Nachrichtenblatt des Sportklub "Hakoah"*; *Nachrichtenblatt des Jüdische Box-Clubs Maccabi*; and the *Touristik und Wintersport im Sportklub Hakoah*.

49. Sander L. Gilman, *Making the Body Beautiful: A Cultural History of Aesthetic Surgery* (Princeton, NJ: Princeton University Press, 1999), 122. For a different interpretation, one that stresses the liberal tendencies of student nineteenth-century fraternities, see Lisa Featheringill Zwicker, *Dueling Students: Conflict, Masculinity, and Politics in German Universities, 1890–1914* (Ann Arbor: University of Michigan Press, 2011).

50. Michael Berkowitz, *The Jewish Self-Image: American and British Perspectives, 1881–1939* (London: Reaktion Books, 2000).

51. Sander L. Gilman, ed., *Der Schejne Jid: Das Bild des "jüdischen Körpers" in Mythos und Ritual* (Vienna: Picus, 1998).

52. There is an extensive literature on the subject of archaeology and nationalism. A good starting point for an overview is Philip L. Kohl, "Nationalism and Archaeology: On the Constructions of Nations and the Reconstructions of the Remote Past," *Annual Review of Anthropology* 27 (1998): 223–246. See also the volume edited by Philip L. Kohl and Clare Fawcett, *Nationalism, Politics, and the Practice of Archaeology* (Cambridge: Cambridge University Press, 1996), esp. the introduction and the essay by Bruce Trigger, "Romanticism, Nationalism and Archaeology," 263–279; and Suzanne L. Marchand, *Down from Olympus: Archaeology and Philhellenism in Germany, 1750–1970* (Princeton, NJ: Princeton University Press, 1996).

53. Susannah Heschel, *Abraham Geiger and the Jewish Jesus* (Chicago: University of Chicago Press, 1998).

54. According to Allan Sekula, between 1880 and 1910 photographic archives "were seen as central to a bewildering range of empirical disciplines, ranging from art history to military intelligence." See his "The Body and the Archive," *October* 39

(1986): 56. See also Helmut Gernsheim, *The History of Photography from the Camera Obscura to the Beginning of the Modern Era* (London: Thames & Hudson, 1969); Christopher Pinney and Nicolas Peterson, eds., *Photography's Other Histories (Objects/ Histories)* (Durham, NC: Duke University Press 2003); and Christopher Pinney, *Photography and Anthropology* (London: Reaktion Books, 2011). Particularly pertinent to this discussion is Elizabeth Edwards, ed., *Anthropology and Photography, 1860– 1920* (New Haven, CT: Yale University Press, 1992).

55. Mary Warner Marien, *Photography: A Cultural History* (Upper Saddle River, NJ: Pearson Prentice Hall, 2006), 50–64.

56. Mitchell Hart, "Picturing Jews: Iconography and Race Science," in *Studies in Contemporary Jewry*, vol. 11, ed. Peter Medding (Oxford: Oxford University Press, 1995), 159–175.

57. Joseph Jacobs, *Studies in Jewish Statistics, Social, Vital and Anthropometric* (London: D. Nutt, 1891), xvii.

58. Marien, *Photography*, 79.

59. Quoted in Sekula, "The Body and the Archive," 52.

60. Daniel Novak, "A Model Jew: 'Literary Photographs' and the Jewish Body in Daniel Deronda," *Representations*, 85, no. 1 (Winter 2004): 70.

61. On Jacobs, see my *Defenders of the Race: Jewish Doctors and Race Science in Fin-de-Siècle Europe* (New Haven, CT: Yale University Press, 1994), 58–90.

62. Judt maintained that contemporary Jews atavistically display the same features as those Jews appearing on the bas-reliefs of Lachish: "brown complexion, low forehead, curly hair, thick lips, and prognathism." J. M. Judt, *Die Juden als Rasse: Eine Analyse aus dem Gebiete der Anthropologie* (Berlin: Jüdischer Verlag, 1903), 141. This opinion was widespread. See, for example, J. C. Nott and G. R. Gliddon, *Types of Mankind: or, Ethnological Researches, Based upon the Ancient Monuments, Paintings, Sculptures, and Crania of Races, and upon Their Natural, Geographical, Philological and Biblical History* (Philadelphia: J. B. Lippincott, Grambo, 1854), 111–141.

63. Judt, *Die Juden als Rasse*, 220–221.

64. Elias Auerbach, "Die jüdische Rassenfrage," *Archiv für Rassen- und Gesellschaftsbiologie* 4, no. 3 (1907): 332–361.

65. Steven E. Aschheim, *At the Edges of Liberalism: Junctions of European, German, and Jewish History* (London: Palgrave Macmillan, 2012), 39–58.

66. Arthur Ruppin, *Briefe, Tagebücher, Errinerungen*, ed. Schlomo Krolik (Königstein: Jüdischer Verlag Athenäum, 1985), 348–349. The quotation appears on p. 351. See also Amos Morris-Reich, "Arthur Ruppin's Concept of Race," *Israel Studies* 11, no. 3 (2006): 1–30.

67. Arieh Bruce Saposnik, "Europe and Its Orients in Zionist Culture before the First World War," *Historical Journal* 49, no. 4 (2006): 1109. Such an insistence that Zionism not be the vehicle for a European *mission civilisatrice*, that it was not an agent of colonialism, was augmented by the claim that Judaism and Islam shared profound affinities born of their common Oriental origins. According to another observer writing before World War I, Meir Wilkansky, Jews and Arabs shared such a strong, almost metaphysical bond to the Land that it served to eradicate the differences between them. While some Zionists made claims for the physical likeness of Jews and Arabs, Wilkansky asserted that they also shared auditory and religious sensibilities. According to him, when the "songs of the Qur'an are sung, the Hebrew

trills attract the hearts of Israel, gather in the courtyards and ascend to the roofs. . . . The choir lowers its head and body . . . and responds, breathing '*Allah*,' or '*Eloheinu*'." Saposnik, "Europe and Its Orients," 1110. For a fuller discussion of the creative tensions between the orientalist and Occidentalist tendencies of Zionist culture, see Arieh Bruce Saposnik, *Becoming Hebrew: The Creation of a Jewish National Culture in Ottoman Palestine* (New York: Oxford University Press, 2008).

68. Arthur, comte de Gobineau, *The Inequality of the Human Races* (New York: G. P. Putnam's Sons, 1915), 122–123.

69. Nott and Gliddon, *Types of Mankind*, 116.

70. Houston Stewart Chamberlain, *Foundations of the Nineteenth Century* (London: John Lane, The Bodley Head, 1912), 336 and 353. On Chamberlain's political and racist worldview, see Geoffrey C. Field, *Evangelist of Race: The Germanic Vision of Houston Stewart Chamberlain* (New York: Columbia University Press, 1981), esp. 169–224.

71. Chamberlain, *Foundations*, 389.

72. Ibid., 394.

73. Ibid., 389.

74. Ibid., 329.

75. Ibid., 272–273.

76. Ibid., 396 and 398.

77. Etan Bloom, "Arthur Ruppin and the Production of the Modern Hebrew Culture" (PhD diss., University of Tel Aviv, 2008), 104–109.

78. Max Grunwald, "Durch Spanien und Portugal: Reiserrinerungen an das Frühjahr 1929," *Menorah* 9, nos. 3–4 (1931): 99–118.

79. Léon Poliakov, *The Aryan Myth: A History of Racist and Nationalist Ideas in Europe* (New York: Meridian, 1977), 1–8. For an example of the linkage of nationalism and archaeology, see Michael Dietler, "'Our Ancestors the Gauls': Archaeology, Ethnic Nationalism, and the Manipulation of Celtic Identity in Modern Europe," *American Anthropologist* 96, no. 3 (1994): 584–605.

80. Anatole Leroy-Beaulieu, *Israel among the Nations: A Study of Jews and Antisemitism* (London: William Heinemann, 1895), 184.

81. Samuel Weissenberg, "Die Spaniolen: Eine anthropometrische Skizze," *Mittheilung der Anthropologischen Gessellschaft in Wien* 39 (1909): 225–236. Max Grunwald said likewise, "The purity of the Semitic type is especially pronounced in the Sephardic Jews." See his "Durch Spanien und Portugal," 102.

82. The literature on late nineteenth-century antisemitism is vast. Among the best general histories are those of Leon Poliakov, *The History of Anti-Semitism*, 4 vols. (New York: Vanguard Press, 1965); Jacob Katz, *From Prejudice to Destruction: Anti-Semitism, 1700–1933* (Cambridge, MA: Harvard University Press, 1980); John Weiss, *The Politics of Hate: Anti-Semitism, History, and the Holocaust in Modern Europe* (Chicago: Ivan R. Dee, 2003); Robert S. Wistrich, *A Lethal Obsession: Anti-Semitism from Antiquity to the Global Jihad* (New York: Random House, 2010); and David Nirenberg, *Anti-Judaism: The Western Tradition* (New York: W. W. Norton & Company, 2013).

83. Peter Dittmar, *Die Darstellung der Juden in der populären Kunst zur Zeit der Emanzipation* (Munich: K. G. Sauer, 1992); Julius H. Schoeps and Joachim Schlör, eds., *Bilder der Judenfeindschaft: Antisemitismus Vorurteile und Mythen* (Augsburg: Bechtermünz, 1999); Fritz Backhaus, "'Hab'n Sie nicht den kleinen Cohn geseh'n?' Die

Bilderwelt antisemitischer Postkarten vom Kaiserreich bis in die NS-Zeit," *Jahrbuch für Antisemitismusforschung* 6 (1997): 313–323; and Julia Schäfer, "Verzeichnet. Über 'Judenbilder' in der Karikatur als historische Quelle," *Jahrbuch für Antisemitismusforschung* 10 (2001): 138–155.

84. Joshua Trachtenberg, *The Devil and the Jews: The Medieval Conception of the Jew and Its Relation to Modern Anti-Semitism* (Philadelphia: Jewish Publication Society, 1983), 27. As another example, the toothless, fleshy, old Jewish men who gather around the baby Jesus to circumcise him, in Jörg Ratgeb's Herrenberger Altarpiece of 1521, are certainly portrayed with depraved hideousness.

85. For example, the magnificent early sixteenth-century drawings of Prague Jews by Roelandt Savery and Paulus van Vianen, court artists to Holy Roman emperor Rudolf II, are remarkable for their accurate representations. Indeed, according to the Flemish Savery, he drew Jews as *naer het leven* (from life). Their faces are entirely natural, as are their poses, whether it is "Jews Praying in the Altneushul," or "Two Scholars" in discussion, or "Three Jews" in conversation. There is nothing grotesque, nothing hostile, and nothing intended to evoke feelings of revulsion in these works of art. See Joaneath Spicer, "The Star of David and Jewish Culture in Prague around 1600, Reflected in Drawings of Roelandt Savery and Paulus van Vianen," *Journal of the Walters Art Gallery* 54 (1996): 203–224.

86. On the representation of Jews in medieval and early modern art, see Bernhard Blumenkranz, *Juden und Judentum in der mittelalterlichen Kunst* (Stuttgart: W. Kohlhammer, 1965); Ruth Mellinkoff, *Antisemitic Hate Signs in Hebrew Illuminated Manuscripts from Medieval Germany* (Jerusalem: Center for Jewish Art, Hebrew University of Jerusalem, 1999); Petra Schöner, *Judenbilder im deutschen Einblattdruck der Renaissance: Ein Beitrag zur Imagologie* (Baden-Baden: V. Koerner, 2002); and Mitchell B. Merback, ed., *Beyond the Yellow Badge: Anti-Judaism and Antisemitism in Medieval and Early Modern Visual Culture* (Leiden: Brill, 2008). This is very different from deformity and ugliness. See also Stefan Rohrbacher and Michael Schmidt, *Judenbilder: Kulturgeschichte antijüdischer Mythen und antisemitischer Vorurteile* (Hamburg: Rowohlt, 1991).

87. Sara Lipton, *Images of Intolerance: The Representation of Jews and Judaism in the Bible moralisée* (Berkeley: University of California Press, 1999), 15.

88. Norman Roth, ed., *Medieval Jewish Civilization: An Encyclopedia* (New York: Routledge, 2003), 52–57; and Sara Lipton, *Dark Mirror: The Medieval Origins of Anti-Jewish Iconography* (New York: Metropolitan Books, 2014), 169–200.

89. Isaiah Shachar, *The Judensau: A Medieval Anti-Jewish Motif and Its History* (London: Warburg Institute, 1974).

90. Richard I. Cohen, *Jewish Icons: Art and Society in Modern Europe* (Berkeley: University of California Press, 1998), 16–25.

91. Michael Zell, *Reframing Rembrandt: Jews and the Christian Image in Seventeenth-Century Amsterdam* (Berkeley: University of California Press, 2002).

92. Cohen, *Jewish Icons*, 33 and 52–66.

93. Isaiah Shachar, "The Emergence of the Modern Pictorial Stereotype of 'The Jews' in England," in *Studies in the Cultural Life of the Jews in England*, ed. Dov Noy and Issachar Ben-Ami, Folklore Research Center Studies, vol. 5 (Jerusalem: Magnes Press, 1975), 331–365; Daniel M. Vyleta, *Crime, Jews and News: Vienna 1895–1914* (New York: Berghahn, 2007).

94. George L. Mosse, *The Crisis of German Ideology: Intellectual Origins of the Third Reich* (New York: Grosset & Dunlap, 1964).

95. Eduard Fuchs, *Die Juden in der Karitatur: Ein Beitrag zur Kulturgeschichte* (Munich: Albert Langen, 1921). On the theme of urbanism and antisemitism, see Hillel J. Kieval, "Antisemitism and the City: A Beginner's Guide," in *People of the City: Jews and the Urban Challenge*, ed. Ezra Mendelsohn, Studies in Contemporary Jewry, vol. 15 (Oxford: Oxford University Press, 1999), 3–18.

96. Falk Wiesemann, *Antijüdischer Nippes und populäre Judenbilder: Die Sammlung Finkelstein* (Essen: Klartext, 2005); and Isabel Enzenbach and Wolfgang Haney, eds., *Alltagskultur des Antisemitismus im Kleinformat. Vignetten der Sammlung Wolfgang Haney ab 1880* (Berlin: Metropol Verlag, 2012). See also Isabel Enzenbach, "Stamps, Stickers and Stigmata. A Social Practice of Antisemitism Presented in a Slide-Show," *Quest. Issues in Contemporary Jewish History. Journal of Fondazione CDEC*, no. 3 (July 2012), www.quest-cdecjournal.it/focus.php?id=307.

97. Sander L. Gilman, "'Die Rasse ist nicht schön—Nein, wir Juden sind keine hübsche Rasse!' Der schöne und der häßliche Rasse," in Gilman,, *Der Schejne Jid*, 57–74. Patricia Vertinsky, "Body Matters: Race, Gender, and Perceptions of Physical Ability from Goethe to Weininger," in *Identity and Intolerance: Nationalism, Racism, and Xenophobia in Germany and the United States*, ed. Norbert Finzsch and Dietmar Schirmer (Washington, DC: German Historical Institute; Cambridge: Cambridge University Press, 1998), 331–370. On Jews and obesity, see Sander L. Gilman, *Fat: A Cultural History of Obesity* (Cambridge, UK: Polity, 2008), 101–22; and George L. Mosse, *Nationalism and Sexuality: Respectability and Abnormal Sexuality in Modern Europe* (New York: Howard Fertig, 1985).

98. Michael Hau, *The Cult of Health and Beauty in Germany: A Social History, 1890–1930* (Chicago: University of Chicago Press, 2003); Karl Toepfer, *Empire of Ecstasy: Nudity and Movement in German Body Culture, 1910–1935* (Berkeley: University of California Press, 1997); Paul Weindling, *Health, Race and German Politics between National Unification and Nazism, 1870–1945* (Cambridge: Cambridge University Press, 1989); and Robert Nye, *Masculinity and Male Codes of Honor in France* (New York: Oxford University Press, 1993).

99. See George L. Mosse, *The Image of Man: The Creation of Modern Masculinity* (Oxford: Oxford University Press, 1996), 17–55; and Hans Jürgen Lutzhöft, *Der Nordische Gedanke in Deutschland 1920–1940* (Stuttgart: Ernst Klett Verlag, 1971).

100. See Esther Benbassa and Aron Rodrigue, *Sephardi Jewry: A History of the Judeo-Spanish Community, 14th–20th Centuries* (Berkeley: University of California Press, 2000); Veselina Kulenska, "The Antisemitic Press in Bulgaria at the End of the 19th Century," *Quest. Issues in Contemporary Jewish History. Journal of Fondazione CDEC*, no. 3 (July 2012), www.quest-cdecjournal.it/focus.php?id=296; Katherine Fleming, *Greece: A Jewish History* (Princeton, NJ: Princeton University Press, 2008).

101. Todd M. Endelman, "Benjamin Disraeli and the Myth of Sephardi Superiority," *Jewish History* 10, no. 2 (1996): 21–35.

102. Ivan Hannaford, *Race: A History of an Idea in the West* (Washington, DC: Woodrow Wilson Center Press, 1996).

103. See my *Defenders of the Race: Jewish Doctors and Race Science in Fin-de-Siècle Europe* (New Haven, CT: Yale University Press, 1994); and Veronika Lipphardt, *Biol-*

ogie der Juden: Jüdische Wissenschaftler über "Rasse" und Vererbung 1900–1935 (Göttingen: Vandenhoeck & Ruprecht, 2008).

104. John M. Efron, "Scientific Racism and the Mystique of Sephardic Racial Superiority," *Leo Baeck Institute Year Book* 38 (1993): 75–96.

105. Judt, *Die Juden als Rasse*, 3–18.

106. See Louis L. Snyder, *Race: A History of Modern Ethnic Theories* (New York: Longmans, Green and Co., Alliance Book Corporation, 1939), 90–225.

107. Richard Andree, *Zur Volkskunde der Juden* (Bielefeld: Velhagen & Klasing, 1881), 39. For similar remarks by Gentile anthropologists, see Carl Vogt, *Lectures on Man* (London: Longmans, 1864), 434; Friedrich Maurer, "Mitteilungen aus Bosnien," *Das Ausland* 49 (1869): 1161–1164 and 50 (1869): 1183–1185; Augustin Weisbach, "Körpermessungen verschiedener Menschenrassen," *Zeitschrift für Ethnologie* 9 (1877): 212–214; Bernhard Blechmann, *Ein Beitrag zur Anthropologie der Juden* (Dorpat: W. Just, 1882), 59; Ludwig Stieda, "Ein Beitrag zur Anthropologie der Juden," *Archiv für Anthropologie* 14 (1883): 61–71; and J. Kollmann, "Schädel und Skelettreste aus einem Judenfriedhof des 13. und 14. Jahrhundert zu Basel," *Verhandlungen der naturforschenden Gesellschaft zu Basel* 7 (1885): 648–656.

108. Adolf Neubauer, "Notes on the Race-Types of the Jews," *Journal of the Royal Anthropological Institute of Great Britain and Ireland* 15 (1885): 19.

109. Ibid., 20.

110. We will see in chapter 5, on the writing of Spanish-Jewish history, that two of our protagonists, Heinrich Graetz and Ignaz Goldziher—the former from eastern Prussia, the latter from a small town in Hungary—were raised in what were essentially traditional Eastern European Jewish environments. Their own rapturous views of Sephardic Jews and the Islamic environment that allowed for the flowering of Sephardic culture were very much a reaction to the forms of Judaism they saw in their early lives, and that they came to despise.

111. Meyer Kayserling, *Biblioteca Española-Portugueza-Judaica and Other Studies in Ibero-Jewish Bibliography* (New York: KTAV, 1971). On Kayserling, see the biographical essay in this volume by Yosef Hayim Yerushalmi (introduction).

112. Meyer Kayserling, "Sephardim," in *Jewish Encyclopaedia* (New York: Funk and Wagnalls, 1905), 11:197.

113. Chamberlain, *Foundations*, 275.

114. This situation was somewhat rectified with the development in Germany of the cult of the Eastern European Jew from the time of the First World War. See Aschheim, *Brothers and Strangers*, esp. 100–214.

115. Kayserling, "Sephardim," 197.

116. Ibid.

117. Ruth Benedict, "Race: What It Is Not," in *Theories of Race and Racism: A Reader*, ed. Les Back and John Solomos (London: Routledge, 2009), 113–118.

118. F. Max Müller, *Biographies of Words, and the Home of the Aryas* (London: Longmans, Green, and Co., 1888), 120.

119. Friedrich Hertz, *Race and Civilization* (New York: KTAV, 1971), 75–99.

120. On language, see Sander L. Gilman, *Jewish Self-Hatred: Anti-Semitism and the Hidden Language of the Jews* (Baltimore: Johns Hopkins University Press, 1986), 209–270.

121. The Geonic era extended from 589 C.E. to 1038 C.E. Kayserling, "Sephardim," 198.

122. See my *Medicine and the German Jews: A History* (New Haven, CT: Yale University Press, 2001).

123. To be sure, the encyclopedia is full of articles on all aspects and major personalities of Ashkenazic civilization as well as an entry on the derivation of the word "Ashkenaz." Nevertheless, it is noteworthy that a single entry under "Ashkenazim" was not regarded as a valid or necessary category for discussion.

124. George L. Mosse, *Toward the Final Solution: A History of European Racism* (New York: Harper & Row, 1980), 35–50.

125. On Auerbach's life, see his autobiography, *Pionier der Verwirklichung: Ein Arzt aus Deutschland erzählt vom Beginn der zionistischen Bewegung und seiner Niederlassung in Palästina kurz nach der Jahrhundertwende* (Stuttgart: Deutsche Verlags-Anstalt, 1969). Auerbach's most comprehensive treatment of the Jewish racial problem was his above-cited "Die jüdische Rassenfrage."

126. On the appropriation of *völkisch* ideology by Jews, see George L. Mosse, *Germans and Jews: The Right, the Left, and the Search for a "Third Force" in Pre-Nazi Germany* (Detroit: Wayne State University Press, 1987), 77–115.

127. Other Zionist assessments of intermarriage and the harm it brought to the "race" are Felix Theilhaber, *Der Untergang der deutschen Juden* (Berlin: Jüdischer Verlag, 1921), 124–137; and Arthur Ruppin, *Die Juden der Gegenwart* (Cologne: Jüdischer Verlag, 1911), 154–179.

128. For Auerbach, one of the laudable features of premodern Jewish society was that through *Halakha*, or Jewish law, the Jews instigated their own self-preservation based on a legal code characterized by its stringent proscriptions against intermarriage. Auerbach, "Die jüdische Rassenfrage," 335.

129. For Felix Theilhaber, the intermarriage rate in Germany meant that the community had to rely on Eastern European Jewry to prevent it from dying out.

130. Maurice Fishberg, *Die Rassenmerkmale der Juden: Eine Einführung in ihre Anthropologie* (Munich: Ernst Reinhardt, 1913).

131. Maurice Fishberg, *The Jews: A Study of Race and Environment* (New York: Walter Scott, 1911), 111–113.

132. See n97 above and, on theater, Hans-Peter Bayerdörfer and Jens Malte Fischer, *Judenrollen: Darstellungsformen im europäischen Theater von der Restauration bis zur Zwischenkriegszeit (Conditio Judaica)* (Niemeyer: Tübingen, 2008).

133. Judt, *Die Juden als Rasse*, 7–8.

134. Fishberg, *The Jews*, 110.

135. For more on Rathenau, see Shulamit Volkov, *Walter Rathenau: Weimar's Fallen Statesman* (New Haven, CT: Yale University Press, 2012).

136. Walter Rathenau, "Höre Israel!" in *The Jew in the Modern World*, ed. Paul Mendes-Flohr and Jehuda Reinharz (New York: Oxford University Press, 2011), 816.

137. Theodor Lessing, *Der Jüdischer Selbsthass* (Munich: Matthes & Seitz Verlag, 1984), 51.

138. Fishberg, *The Jews*, 108–110.

139. Sarah Graham-Brown, *Images of Women: The Portrayal of Women in Photography of the Middle East 1860–1950* (London: Quartet, 1988).

140. On the Alliance Israélite Universelle, see Aron Rodrigue, *Jews and Muslims: Images of Sephardi and Eastern Jewries in Modern Times* (Seattle: University of Washington Press, 2003), 80–93.

141. Fishberg, *The Jews*, 163–164.

142. Ibid., 165. See also G. M. Morant and Otto Samson, "An Examination of Investigations by Dr. Maurice Fishberg and Professor Franz Boas Dealing with Measurements of Jews in New York," *Biometrika* 28, nos. 1–2 (1936): 1–31.

143. Laurence Sigal-Klagsbald, ed., *Les Juifs dans L'orientalisme* (Paris: Skira Flammarion, 2012).

144. Michael Stanislawski, *Zionism and the Fin-de-Siècle: Cosmopolitanism and Nationalism from Nordau to Jabotinsky* (Berkeley: University of California Press, 2001), 100.

145. Along with these human forms as part of a new Jewish art, Lilien was also largely responsible for the popularization of symbols such as the menorah, the Star of David, and the olive branch, depicting them as quintessentially Jewish and Zionist.

146. More generally, see Gilya Gerda Schmidt, *The Art and Artists of the Fifth Zionist Congress, 1901: Heralds of a New Age* (Syracuse, NY: Syracuse University Press, 2003).

147. Micha and Orna Bar-Am, *Painting with Light: The Photographic Aspect in the Work of E. M. Lilien* (Tel Aviv: Tel Aviv Museum of Art, 1991), 37.

148. Maurice Fishberg, *Di gefar fun di idishe natsyonalistishe bevegung: In ireh farshidene formen vi di rassenfrage, Tsien-Tsienizm, teritorializm, Ahad-ha-'Am-kulturizm, natsyonal-kulturele-oytonomye* (New York: M. Mayzel, 1906).

149. Poliakov, *The Aryan Myth*, 3.

CHAPTER THREE
OF MINARETS AND MENORAHS:
THE BUILDING OF ORIENTAL SYNAGOGUES

1. The original reads, "Baukunst ist immer raumgefaßter Zeitwille, nichts anderes." Ludwig Mies van der Rohe, "Baukunst und Zeitwille," *Der Querschnitt* 4 (1924): 31–32. Mies generally eschewed the word "architecture" in favor of *Baukunst* or the "art of building." See Ransoo Kim, "The 'Art of Building' (*Baukunst*) of Mies van der Rohe" (PhD diss, Georgia Institute of Technology, 2006), 53.

2. Lindsay Jones, *The Hermeneutics of Sacred Architecture: Experience, Interpretation, Comparison*, vol. 1, *Monumental Occasions: Reflections on the Eventfulness of Religious Architecture* (Cambridge, MA: Harvard University Press, 2000), 29.

3. David I. Kertzer and Marzio Barbagli, eds., *The History of the European Family* (New Haven, CT: Yale University Press, 2001), x.

4. Nikolaus Pevsner, *A History of Building Types* (Princeton, NJ: Princeton University Press, 1976).

5. Claude Mignot, *Architecture of the Nineteenth Century in Europe* (New York: Rizzoli, 1984), 7–8.

6. James Stevens Curl, *Victorian Architecture: Diversity and Invention* (Reading, UK: Spire Books, 2007).

7. Spiro Kostoff, ed., *The Architect: Chapters in the History of the Profession* (Oxford: Oxford University Press, 1977). See also Dell Upton, "Pattern Books and

Professionalism: Aspects of the Transformation of Domestic American Architecture, 1800–1860," *Winterthur Portfolio* 19, nos. 2–3 (1984): 107–150. For but one concrete example of architectural influence through the publication of model books, see Karen David-Sirocko, "Anglo-German Interconnexions during the Gothic Revival: A Case Study from the Work of Georg Gottlob Ungewitter (1820–64)," *Architectural History* 41 (1998): 153–178.

8. Nikolaus Pevsner, *An Outline of European Architecture* (Baltimore: Penguin, 1960), 622.

9. Henry-Russell Hitchcock, *Architecture: Nineteenth and Twentieth Centuries* (Baltimore: Penguin, 1963), 469n1.

10. Peter Collins, *Changing Ideals in Modern Architecture, 1750–1850* (Montreal: McGill-Queen's University Press, 1998), 62.

11. Evyatar Friesel, *Atlas of Modern Jewish History* (Oxford: Oxford University Press, 1990), 15.

12. Stefi Jersch-Wenzel, "Population Shifts and Occupational Structure," in *German-Jewish History in Modern Times*, vol. 2, ed. Michael A. Meyer (New York: Columbia University Press, 1997), 50–59.

13. The term was coined by Salo Wittmayer Baron, *A Social and Religious History of the Jews* (New York: Columbia University Press, 1937), 2:266.

14. Monika Richarz, "Demographic Developments," in Meyer, *German-Jewish History in Modern Times*, 3:30–31.

15. Grote, Ludwig, ed. *Die deutsche Stadt im 19. Jahrhundert. Stadtplannung und Baugestaltung im industriellen Zeitalter* (Munich: Prestel Verlag, 1974).

16. Jews were also major patrons and architects, commissioning and designing many of these new architectural projects. According to Fredric Bedoire, in the development of "secular architecture and urban design, [the] Jewish entrepreneur class played a prominent part and tried to fashion a new, modern society." See his *The Jewish Contribution to Modern Architecture, 1830–1930* (Jersey City, NJ: KTAV, 2004), 8.

17. For a general discussion, see Aliza Cohen-Mushlin and Harmen H. Thies, eds., *Jewish Architecture in Europe* (Petersberg: Imhof, 2010); and Daniela Gauding and Aliza Cohen-Mushlin, *Beiträge zur jüdischen Architektur in Berlin* (Petersberg: Imhof, 2009). More specifically, on schools see, Mordechai Eliav, *Jüdische Erziehung in Deutschland im Zeitalter der Aufklärung und Emanzipation* (Münster: Waxmann, 2001). On ritual bathhouses see, Daniela Gauding, "Jüdische Ritualbäder in Berlin," in Gauding and Cohen-Mushlin, *Beiträge zur jüdischen Architektur in Berlin*, 33–45. On cemeteries, see Ulrich Knufinke, *Bauwerke jüdische Friedhöfe in Deutschland* (Petersberg: Imhof, 2007); and Michael Brocke and Christiane E. Müller, eds., *Haus des Lebens: Jüdische Friedhöfe in Deutschland* (Reclam: Leipzig, 2001). On hospitals, see Alexander Philipsborn, "The Jewish Hospitals in Germany," *Leo Baeck Institute Year Book* 4 (1959): 220–234.

18. Henry Van Brunt, "On the Present Condition and Prospects of Architecture," *Atlantic Monthly* 57, no. 341 (March 1886): 374–384.

19. There was an edict in 415 C.E. prohibiting the patriarch Gamaliel from building new synagogues, and a more sweeping one in 423 C.E. banning all new synagogue construction. See Amnon Linder, ed., *The Jews in Roman Imperial Legislation* (Detroit: Wayne State University Press, 1987), 287–288. See also Gregory A.

Dickenson and Aaron J. West, "Imperial Laws and Letters Involving Religion AD 311–364," http://www.fourthcentury.com/index.php/imperial-laws-chart.

20. In the modern period, this was the case, for example, on Berlin's Heidereutergasse. In the city's first community synagogue, known as the Great Synagogue, which was built between 1712 and 1714, the men's prayer room was placed nearly two meters underground. Karin Keßler, "Halakhic Rules in Synagogue Architecture," in Cohen-Mushlin and Thies, *Jewish Architecture in Europe*, 246.

21. Medieval synagogues were often just large rooms, located on the upper floors in private homes of the well-to-do. In Germany, stand-alone buildings constructed as synagogues were to be found in communities such as Frankfurt, Speyer, and Worms and were frequently built in the Gothic style of contemporary church architecture. Where some German synagogues' external features bore striking similarities to nearby cathedrals, as was the case at Worms, medieval Spanish synagogues tended to be extremely plain and nondescript on the outside while being highly ornate on the inside. In this they were similar to churches and mosques, both of which bore this general design. See Carol Herselle Krinsky, *Synagogues of Europe: Architecture, History, Meaning* (Mineola, NY: Dover, 1996), 38–47. On the early modern synagogue, see Barry Stiefel, "The Architectural Origins of the Great Early Modern Urban Synagogue," *Leo Baeck Institute Year Book* 56 (2011): 105–134.

22. Kaedan Gazdar, *Herrscher im Paradies: Fürst Franz und das Gartenreich Dessau-Wörlitz* (Berlin: Aufbau-Verlag, 2006); and Thomas Weiss, *Infinitely Beautiful: The Garden Realm of Dessau-Wörlitz* (Berlin: Nicolai, 2005).

23. Helen Rosenau, "German Synagogues in the Early Period of Emancipation," *Leo Baeck Institute Year Book* 8 (1963): 214–225; and Rachel Wischnitzer, *Architecture of the European Synagogue* (Philadelphia: Jewish Publication Society, 1964), 158–159.

24. It should also be noted that after the police rejected the initial plot of land proposed by the community because it lay too close to a church, the location on the Seitenstettengasse was accepted on the condition that the synagogue not be visible from the street, and so it was built behind a five-story apartment building. See Max Eisler, "Der Seitenstetten Tempel," *Menorah* 3 (1926): 149–157. The quotation appears on p. 157. By contrast, for a glowing contemporary report on the opening of the new temple, see "Einweihung des neuen Israelitischen Bethauses zu Wien. am 9. April 1826 (2 Nissan 5586)," *Sulamith* 7, no. 1 (1826): 267–276 and 290–297.

25. Alfred Grimm and Isabel Grimm-Stadelman, *Theatrum Hieroglyphicum: Ägyptisierende Bildwerke im Geiste des Barock* (Dettelbach: Röll, 2011); James Stevens Curl, *The Egyptian Revival: Ancient Egypt as the Inspiration for Design Motifs in the West* (New York: Routledge, 2005); Jean-Marcel Humbert and Clifford Price, eds., *Imhotep Today: Egyptianizing Architecture* (Portland, OR: Cavendish, 2003); Richard G. Carrott, *The Egyptian Revival: Its Sources, Monuments, and Meaning, 1808–1858* (Berkeley: University of California Press, 1978); and Hans Vogel, "Aegyptisierende Baukunst des Klassizismus," *Zeitschrift für Bildende Kunst* 62 (1928–1929): 160–165.

26. Rachel Wischnitzer, "The Egyptian Revival in Synagogue Architecture," in *The Synagogue: Studies in Origins, Archaeology, and Architecture*, ed. Joseph Gutmann (New York: KTAV, 1975), 334–350.

27. See, for example, Christian Ludwig Stieglitz, *Geschichte der Baukunst der Alten*, vol. 1 (Leipzig: Dykschen Buchhandlung, 1792), 43–58; Johann Georg Sulzer, *Allgemeine Theorie der schönen Künste*, vol. 1 (Leipzig: Weidmannschen Buchhandlung,

1792), 318; Harold Hammer-Schenk, *Synagogen in Deutschland: Geschichte einer Baugattung im 19. und 20. Jahrhundert, 1780–1933*, (Hamburg: H. Christians, 1981), 1:75–85; Alexander Roitman, *Envisioning the Temple* (Jerusalem: Israel Museum, 2003); Helen Rosenau, *Vision of the Temple: The Image of the Temple of Jerusalem in Judaism and Christianity* (London: Oresko Books, 1979).

28. Diana Muir Appelbaum, "Jewish Identity and Egyptian Revival Architecture," *Journal of Jewish Identities* 5, no. 2 (July 2012): 1–25.

29. Hammer-Schenk, *Synagogen in Deutschland*, 1:71–75. Of course, for those opposed to Jewish emancipation, the "antiquity" of the Jews could also be interpreted as antiquatedness, just as their status as "fathers of mankind" could also denote their primitiveness, while their "perseverance" in sticking to their customs reflected their lack of progress. Similarly, even when admired, Egyptian architecture, like the Jews, was seen as "incomplete" or an earlier form that found perfection later on with the advent of the Greeks. See Johann Sulzer, who asserted that the morality of a people was reflected in its architecture. For example, he maintained that after the fall of the emperors, Roman architecture reflected the "despotism" that came in their wake. See his *Allgemeine Theorie der schönen Künste*, 1:317–318.

30. In Bavaria, Jews had been forbidden to settle since the fifteenth century. In 1750 there were only 20 Jews in all of Munich, but with the expansion of Bavaria thanks to the Peace of Lunéville in 1801, the numbers steadily increased to 300 Jews by 1802, and 607 in 1825. Jacob Segall, *Die Entwicklung der judischen Bevölkerung in München 1875–1905* (Berlin: Verein für die Statistik der Juden, 1910), 2. Within the Jewish community it was thus recognized that there was an urgent need for a new synagogue. For the authorities, the growth in the number of Jews alarmed the police, who placed considerable pressure on the Munich Jewish community to expeditiously purchase a block of land and build a synagogue on it. There were two tendencies at work here. The first was driven by the Enlightenment idea of improving the Jews and making them useful. A police report of 1808 noted that "even now a secret police unit is occupied with a general plan to effect the civic and moral refinement of this hitherto neglected part of humanity." Stefan Schwarz, *Die Juden in Bayern im Wandel der Zeiten* (Munich: Günter Olzog, 1963), 128. Access to general education and the institution of a dignified prayer service in an appropriate house of worship were considered essential to that process. The other reason the police were so keen to have one large synagogue for the whole community was so that they could keep an eye on them and thus dissolve the scores of prayer services that were held in private homes.

31. David Wojtowicz and David B. Brownlee, "The New Imagery of Public Architecture," in *Friedrich Weinbrenner: Architect of Karlsruhe*, ed. David B. Brownlee (Philadelphia: Architectural Archives of the University of Pennsylvania, 1986), 24.

32. Leo von Klenze, *Anweisung zur Architektur des Christlichen Cultus* (Munich: n.p., 1822), 3. Also quoted in Hammer-Schenk, *Synagogen in Deutschland*, 1:54. Von Klenze is consistent, going on to observe that once Jews came into contact with Greek culture, they became Hellenized. It was this necessary step that made for the rise of Christianity, which, von Klenze believed, was derived from Greek culture. Von Klenze, *Anweisung*, 2.

33. For a description of the official opening of the synagogue, see "Einweihung der neuen Synagoge," *Sulamith* 7, no. 1 (1826): 210–216.

34. On the Westenriederstrasse Synagogue in Munich, see Selig, *Synagogen und Jüdische Friedhöfe in München*, 39–58; and Krinsky, *Synagogues of Europe*, 72–73.

35. There is actually some dispute over the year when the synagogue in the form described here was actually built. See Hammer-Schenk, *Synagogen in Deutschland*, 2:558n128.

36. Ibid., 1:58–62.

37. Heinrich Hübsch et al., *In What Style Should We Build?: The German Debate on Architectural Style*, trans. Wolfgang Herrmann (Santa Monica, CA: Getty Center for the History of Art and the Humanities, 1992), 4.

38. Mitchell Schwarzer, *German Architectural Theory and the Search for Modern Identity* (Cambridge: Cambridge University Press, 1995).

39. Silke Walter, "'In welchem Style sollen wir bauen ?'—Studien zu den Schriften und Bauten des Architekten Heinrich Hübsch (1795–1863)" (PhD diss., University of Stuttgart, 2004). For an older treatment, one that places the debate in the larger context of nineteenth-century German architecture, see Wolfgang Herrmann, *Deutsche Baukunst des XIX. und XX. Jahrhunderts*, vol. 1 (Breslau: Ferdinand Hirt, 1932). The most important essays published in the debate are to be found in Hübsch et al., *In What Style Should We Build?*; Klaus Döhmer, *"In welchem Style sollen wir bauen?" Architekturtheorie zwischen Klassizismus und Jugendstil* (Munich: Prestel-Verlag, 1976).

40. Collins, *Changing Ideals in Modern Architecture*, 90.

41. Ibid., 101. On Gothic revival architecture, see Georg Germann, *Gothic Revival in Europe and Britain: Sources, Influences and Ideas* (Cambridge, MA: MIT Press, 1973).

42. The most detailed account of what follows is to be found in Ludwig Horwitz, *Die Kasseler Synagoge und ihr Erbauer* (Kassel: Vietor, 1907).

43. Harold Hammer-Schenk, "Die Architektur der Synagoge von 1780 bis 1933," in *Die Architektur der Synagoge*, ed. Hans-Peter Schwarz (Frankfurt: DAM, 1988), 177.

44. Krinsky, *Synagogues of Europe*, 314.

45. For a detailed description of the synagogue and the inauguration ceremony, see Horwitz, *Die Kasseler Synagoge*, 17–24.

46. Albert Rosengarten, "Die neue Synagoge in Cassel," *Allgemeine Bauzeitung 5* (1840): 205.

47. Ibid., 205–206.

48. Krinsky, *Synagogues of Europe*, 80.

49. Hannelore Künzl, "Der Einfluß des alten Orients auf die europäische Kunst besonders im 19. und 20. Jh." (PhD diss., University of Cologne, 1973), 45–63.

50. Miles Danby, *Moorish Style* (London: Phaedon Press, 1995), 151–153.

51. See, for example, Donald A. Rosenthal, *Orientalism: The Near East in French Painting, 1800–1880* (Rochester, NY: Memorial Art Gallery of the University of Rochester, 1982); and Mary Anne Stevens, ed., *The Orientalists: Delacroix to Matisse. European Painters in North Africa and the Near East* (London: Royal Academy of Arts, 1984).

52. Patrick Conner, *Oriental Architecture in the West* (London: Thames and Hudson, 1979), esp. 131–153 on the Royal Pavilion; and Hannelore Künzl, *Islamische Stilelemente in Synagogenbau des 19. und frühen 20. Jahrhunderts* (Frankfurt am Main: Peter Lang, 1984), 100.

53. Hübsch et al., *In What Style Should We Build?*, 119. Rosenthal's original article appeared as "In welchem Style sollen wir bauen? (Eine Frage für Mitglieder des deutschen Architektenvereins)," *Zeitschrift für prakitsche Baukunst* 4 (1844): 23–27.

54. Hübsch et al., *In What Style Should We Build?*, 140. Wolff's original article appeared as "Einige Worte über die von Herrn Professor Stier bei der Architektenversammlung zu Bamberg zur Sprache gebrachten architektonishen Fragen," *Allgemeine Bauzeitung* 10 (1845), Literatur- und Anzeigeblatt für das Baufach. Beilage zur *Allgemeinen Bauzeitung* 2, no. 17: 255–270. The quotation appears on pp. 266–267.

55. Max Grunwald, "Wie baut man Synagogen?" *Allgemeine Zeitung des Judentums* (1901): 115–117. Grunwald makes the point that there had never been a "Jewish" architectural style, and that synagogues had always taken their lead from the surrounding built environment.

56. Saskia Coenen Snyder, *Building a Public Judaism: Synagogues and Jewish Identity in Nineteenth-Century Europe* (Cambridge, MA: Harvard University Press, 2013), 158–159 and 257. Coenen Snyder notes that a few Moorish-inspired synagogues were built in provincial cities: Eindhoven (1866), Tilburg (1873), Groningen (1906), and Nijmegen (1912), while in Amsterdam, Moorish elements were to be found only rarely, and when they appeared, it was more frequently in the interior than on the exterior of the synagogues.

57. Krinsky, *Synagogues of Europe*, 83; Ismar Schorsch, "The Myth of Sephardic Superiority," *Leo Baeck Institute Year Book* 34 (1989): 57; Danby, *Moorish Style*, 14; Ivan Kalmar, "Moorish Style: Orientalism, the Jews, and Synagogue Architecture," *Jewish Social Studies* 7, no. 3 (2001): 70; and Wischnitzer, *Architecture of the European Synagogue*, 217.

58. For other examples, see Olga Bush, "The Architecture of Jewish Identity: The Neo-Islamic Central Synagogue of New York," *Journal of the Society of Architectural Historians* 63, no. 2 (June 2004): 180–201; Lajos Kalmár, Gabor Deutsch, and Vera Farago, *The Dohány Street Synagogue and the Treasures of the Jewish Museum* (Pécs: Alexandra, 2005).

59. Hammer-Schenk, *Synagogen in Deutschland*, 1:251–255.

60. Quoted in ibid., 255.

61. Ibid., 259–265; and for a detailed description of these small synagogues, see Künzl, *Islamische Stilelemente*, 126–154.

62. Rosengarten, "Die neue Synagoge in Cassel," 205.

63. Albert Rosengarten, *A Handbook of Architectural Styles* (Boston: Longwood Press, 1977), 484–486.

64. See Jonathan Frankel, *The Damascus Affair: "Ritual Murder," Politics, and the Jews in 1840* (Cambridge: Cambridge University Press, 1997); and Derek J. Penslar, *Shylock's Children: Economics and Jewish Identity in Modern Europe* (Berkeley: University of California Press, 2001), 90–123.

65. Michael A. Meyer, *Response to Modernity: A History of the Reform Movement in Judaism* (New York: Oxford University Press, 1988), 183.

66. Werner E. Mosse, "From 'Schutzjuden' to 'Deutsche Staatsbürger jüdischen Glaubens': The Long and Bumpy Road of Jewish Emancipation in Germany," in *Paths of Emancipation: Jews, States, and Citizenship*, ed. Pierre Birnbaum and Ira Katznelson (Princeton, NJ: Princeton University Press, 1995), 84. For a fuller account, see Jacob

Toury, *Soziale und politische Geschichte der Juden in Deutschland, 1847–1871: Zwischen Revolution, Reaktion und Emanzipation* (Düsseldorf: Droste, 1977).

67. For a description of the inauguration, one that focuses on the musical repertoire, which was a crucial part of formulating a new German-Jewish aesthetic, see *Der Orient* 20 (May 16, 1840): 151–152.

68. Jersch-Wenzel, "Population Shifts and Occupational Structure," 54.

69. Hammer-Schenk, "Die Architektur der Synagoge," 186.

70. Gottfried Semper, "Die Synagoge zu Dresden," *Allgemeine Bauzeitung* 12 (1847): 127; Helen Rosenau, "Gottfried Semper and German Synagogue Architecture," *Leo Baeck Institute Year Book* 22 (1977): 237–244; and Brian de Breffny, *The Synagogue* (New York: Macmillan, 1978), 159. For more on Semper's use and understanding of history's role in the production of modern architecture, see Mari Hvattum, *Gottfried Semper and the Problem of Historicism* (Cambridge: Cambridge University Press, 2004).

71. Colin Eisler, "Wagner's Three Synagogues," *Artibus et Historiae* 25, no. 50 (2004): 9–15. Because they did not wish to be seen inquiring about the lamp, let alone purchasing one, the Wagners sent Nietzsche to procure from Semper a scale drawing of the lamp that he then took to the silversmiths, who used it in making the replica lamp.

72. David van Zanten, *The Architectural Polychromy of the 1830's* (New York: Garland, 1977), 63.

73. Emil Lehmann, *Ein Halbjahrhundert in der israelitischen Religionsgemeinde zu Dresden: Erlebtes und Erlesenes* (Dresden: Gustav Salomon, 1890), 22, and quoted in Hammer-Schenk, "Die Architektur der Synagoge," 186.

74. Hammer-Schenk, "Die Architektur der Synagoge," 202.

75. "Synagogen in Deutschland," http://www.cad.architektur.tu-darmstadt.de/ synagogen/inter/menu.html.

76. For excellent color reproductions of Simonson's drawings of the proposed synagogue, see Josef Reinhold, "Die verspätete Emanzipation der Juden in Sachsen als legislativer Rahmen. Die Konstituierung der Israelitischen Religionsgemeinde zu Leipzig und die ersten Jahrzehnte ihrer Entwicklung," *Journal Juden in Sachsen* (April 2010): 14.

77. Künzl, *Islamische Stilelemente*, 189–190.

78. For detailed descriptions of the temple, see Otto Simonson, *Der neue Tempel in Leipzig* (Berlin: F. Riegel, 1858); Künzl, *Islamische Stilelemente*, 187–203; Hammer-Schenk, *Synagogen in Deutschland*, 1:265–275. CAD drawings of the synagogue can be seen at "Synagogen in Deutschland" (Leipzig), http://www.cad.architektur .tu-darmstadt.de/synagogen/inter/menu.html.

79. Quoted in Hammer-Schenk, *Synagogen in Deutschland*, 1:270.

80. Simonson, *Der neue Tempel in Leipzig*, 3.

81. Reinhold, "Die verspätete Emanzipation der Juden," 13.

82. Of the 6,000 Jews only 1,800 were legally registered, the rest being technically illegal residents. Anson G. Rabinbach, "The Migration of Galician Jews to Vienna, 1857–1800," *Austrian History Year Book* 11 (1975): 43–54; William O. McCagg, *A History of Habsburg Jews, 1670–1918* (Bloomington: Indiana University Press, 1992), 145; Robert S. Wistrich, *The Jews of Vienna in the Age of Franz Joseph* (Oxford: Oxford University Press, 1990), 38–61. The best social history of Viennese Jewry remains

Marsha L. Rozenblit, *The Jews of Vienna, 1867–1914: Assimilation and Identity* (Albany: State University of New York Press, 1983).

83. Gerson Wolf, *Geschichte der Juden in Wien, 1156–1876* (Vienna: Alfred Hölder, 1876), 159. Rather than competing with each other, both temples were jointly administered by the same committee. See Gerson Wolf, *Vom ersten zum zweiten Tempel: Geschichte der israelitischen Cultusgemeinde in Wien, 1820–1860* (Vienna: Wilhelm Braumüller, 1861), 105–106.

84. Carl E. Schorske, *Fin-de-Siècle Vienna* (New York: Vintage Books, 1981), 24–115.

85. Bruno Grimschitz, *Die Wiener Ringstraße* (Berlin: Angelsachsen Verlag, 1938), 8.

86. Ludwig Förster, "Plan der Bauzeitung und Aufforderung an Männer vom Fache, dieselbe durch Mittheilungen zu bereichern," *Allgemeine Bauzeitung* 1 (1836): 1.

87. Künzl, *Islamische Stilelemente*, 221. For an excellent array of pictures of the temple, see Pierre Genée, *Wiener Synagogen, 1825–1938* (Vienna: Löcker Verlag, 1987), 53–59.

88. See Hammer-Schenck, *Synagogen in Deutschland*, 1:302–307; and Künzl, *Islamische Stilelemente*, 221–231.

89. Ludwig Förster, "Das israelitische Bethaus in Wien," *Allgemeine Bauzeitung* 24 (1859): 16.

90. Ludwig Förster, "Ueber Synagogenbau," *Allgemeine Zeitung des Judentums* 23 (1858): 315–316. The gaslights had an illumination capacity equal to that of three thousand wax candles.

91. All quotations in this paragraph appear in ibid., 314.

92. Ibid., 315. On Solomon's Temple and later attempts to re-create it, see Steven Weitzman, *Solomon: The Lure of Wisdom* (Stanford, CA: Stanford University Press, 2011), 98–112.

93. Förster, "Das israelitische Bethaus in Wien," 14.

94. Ibid.

95. On the halting process of emancipation at this time, see Hans Liebeschütz and Arnold Paucker, eds., *Das Judentum in der Deutschen Umwelt, 1800–1850: Studien zur Frühgeschichte der Emanzipation* (Tübingen: J.C.B. Mohr, 1977); Werner E. Mosse, Arnold Pauker, and Reinhard Rürup, eds., *Revolution and Evolution: 1848 in German-Jewish History* (Tübingen: J.C.B. Mohr, 1981); Peter G. J. Pulzer, *Jews and the German State: The Political History of a Minority, 1848–1933* (Oxford: Blackwell Publishers, 1992); Reinhard Rürup, "The Jewish Emancipation and Bourgeois Society," *Leo Baeck Institute Year Book* 14 (1969): 67–91; Reinhard Rürup, "Emancipation and Crisis: The 'Jewish Question' in Germany, 1850–1890," *Leo Baeck Institute Year Book* 20 (1975): 13–25.

96. *Encyclopaedia Judaica*, vol. 4 (Berlin: Eschkol Verlag, 1929), 251.

97. Kreuzberg is located in what is today central Berlin.

98. Hammer-Schenk, *Synagogen in Deutschland*, 1:284.

99. On Knoblauch, see Azra Charbonnier, *Carl Heinrich Eduard Knoblauch (1801–1865): Architekt des Bürgertums* (Munich: Deutscher Kunstverlag, 2007).

100. Coenen Snyder, *Building a Public Judaism*, 27.

101. Hermann Simon, *Die Neue Synagoge Berlin: Geschichte, Gegenwart, Zukunft* (Berlin: Stiftung Neue Synagoge Berlin—Centrum Judaicum, 1992), n.p.

102. See the competition announcement, for which the first-place winner received 500 taler, the runner-up 300 taler, and the third-place finisher, 200 taler.

"Concurrenz-Eröffnung für Pläne zu einer neuen Synagoge in Berlin," *Zeitschrift für Bauwesen* 7 (1857): 448–450.

103. Eduard Knoblauch, "Die neue Synagoge in Berlin," *Zeitschrift für Bauwesen* 16 (1866): 5.

104. "Concurrenz-Eröffnung für Pläne," 448–449. The term "baroque monumentality" appears in Hammer-Schenck, *Synagogen in Deutschland*, 1:210.

105. Künzl, *Islamische Stilelemente*, 316–317; and Hammer-Schenk, *Synagogen in Deutschland*, 1:292.

106. Emil Breslauer, "Die Einweihung der neuen Synagoge zu Berlin," *Allgemeine Zeitung des Judentums* 39 (1866): 622.

107. Along the southern wall Knoblauch actually found room for another aisle, so technically the synagogue was a quadruple-nave structure, but the heart of the main sanctuary was a traditional triple-nave floor plan.

108. Breslauer, "Die Einweihung," 623.

109. The description appeared in the *National Zeitung*, September 6, 1866, Supplement, p. 1, and quoted in Hammer-Schenk, *Synagogen in Deutschland*, 1:289.

110. *National Zeitung* (September 6, 1866), and quoted in Hammer-Schenk, "Die Architektur der Synagoge," 212.

111. Roger Lancelyn Green, ed., *The Works of Lewis Carroll* (London: Hamlyn, 1965), 972–973.

112. Ludwig Pietsch, "Carl Heinrich Eduard Knoblauch," *Zeitschrift für Praktische Baukunst* (1865): 301.

113. Künzl, *Islamische Stilelemente*, 321.

114. Knoblauch, "Die neue Synagoge in Berlin," 3.

115. See Harold Hammer-Schenk, "Edwin Oppler's Theorie des Synagogenbaus. Emanzipationsversuch durch Architektur," *Hannoversche Geschichtsblätter* (1979): 99–117. For more on Oppler, see Saskia Rohde, "Im Zeichen der Hannoverschen Architekturschule: Der Architekt Edwin Oppler (1831–1880) und seine schlesichen Bauten," *Hannoversche Zeitung* (2000): 67–86.

116. See Coenen Snyder, *Building a Public Judaism*, 62–64.

117. Paul Lagarde, "Die Stellung der Religionsgesellschaften im Staate" (February 1881), in Simon, *Die Neue Synagoge Berlin*, 10.

118. George L. Mosse, *The Crisis of German Ideology: Intellectual Origins of the Third Reich* (New York: Grosset & Dunlap, 1964), 31–39.

119. Heinrich von Treitschke, "Herr Graetz und sein Judenthum," in *Der Berliner Antisemitismusstreit*, ed. Walter Boehlich (Frankfurt am Main: Insel Verlag, 1988), 37.

CHAPTER FOUR
PLEASURE READING: SEPHARDIC JEWS AND THE GERMAN-JEWISH LITERARY IMAGINATION

1. Quoted in Ismar Schorsch, *From Text to Context: The Turn to History in Modern Judaism* (Hanover, NH: University Press of New England, 1994), 75.

2. Eduard Gans, "A Society to Further Jewish Integration," in *The Jew in the Modern World: A Documentary History*, ed. Paul Mendes-Flohr and Jehuda Reinharz (New York: Oxford University Press, 2011), 241.

3. Ibid., 240.

4. Ibid., 242.

5. Andrew Buchwalter, "Is Hegel's Philosophy of History Eurocentric?" in *Hegel and History*, ed. Will Dudley (Albany: State University of New York Press, 2009), 87.

6. Gans, "A Society to Further Jewish Integration," 242.

7. Nitsa Ben-Ari, *Romanze mit der Vergangenheit: Der deutsch-jüdische historische Roman des 19. Jahrhunderts und seine Bedeutung für die Entstehung einer jüdischen Nationalliteratur* (Tübingen: Max Niemeyer Verlag, 2006), 7. It is Ben-Ari's further contention that this literature in Hebrew translation played a key role in the spread and development of Jewish nationalism in Eastern Europe. While it can be argued that this tradition of historical fiction certainly played a role in the development of Jewish ethnic solidarity in Germany, to claim that in translation it was a key component in the development of Jewish nationalism in Eastern Europe overprivileges it to the exclusion of many other more important regional factors. The argument also exaggerates the existence of a Hebrew-reading public. If anything, it was the translation of German-Jewish historical novels into Yiddish—some of them were renderings of an earlier Hebrew translation—that would have had a far larger readership and thus greater impact. For a more expansive reading of the impact of these translations on Eastern European Jewry, see Shmuel Feiner, *Haskalah and History: The Emergence of a Modern Jewish Historical Consciousness* (Portland, OR: Littman Library of Jewish Civilization, 2002), 234–240.

8. Ben-Ari, *Romanze mit der Vergangenheit*, 25–26.

9. Ibid., 32–34.

10. See Steven M. Lowenstein *The Berlin Jewish Community: Enlightenment, Family, and Crisis, 1770–1830* (New York: Oxford University Press, 1994), 120–133; and Deborah Hertz, *How Jews Became Germans: The History of Conversion and Assimilation in Berlin* (New Haven, CT: Yale University Press, 2007).

11. Cited in Ben-Ari, *Romanze mit der Vergangenheit*, 40. On Kohn's tenure as rabbi in Lemberg and his murder, see Michael Stanislawski, *A Murder in Lemberg: Politics, Religion, and Violence in Modern Jewish History* (Princeton, NJ: Princeton University Press, 2007).

12. From the very beginning, the Verein für Cultur und Wissenschaft der Juden and its journal, the *Zeitschrift für die Wissenschaft des Judentums*, had great difficulty in attracting members to attend its meetings or read its publications. See Ismar Schorsch, "Breakthrough into the Past: The Verein für Cultur und Wissenschaft der Juden," *Leo Baeck Institute Year Book* 38 (1988): 3–29, esp. 6–9.

13. Nils Roemer, *Jewish Scholarship in Nineteenth-Century Germany: Between History and Faith* (Madison: University of Wisconsin Press, 2005), 38–40.

14. Cecil Roth, "Jewish History for Our Own Needs," *Menorah* 14, no. 5 (1928): 430–431.

15. On Philippson, see Johanna Philippson, "Ludwig Philippson und die *Allgemeine Zeitung des Judentums*," in *Das Judentum in der deutschen Umwelt, 1800–1850: Studien zur Frühgeschichte der Emanzipation*, ed. Hans Liebeschütz and Arnold Paucker (Tübingen: Mohr, 1977), 243–291.

16. Nitsa Ben-Ari, "1834: The Jewish Historical Novel Helps to Reshape the Historical Consciousness of German Jews," in *Yale Companion to Jewish Writing and Thought in German Culture, 1096–1966*, ed. Sander Gilman and Jack Zipes (New

Haven, CT: Yale University Press, 1997), 148. Ben-Ari translates *Wissenschaft as* "science," but "scholarship" is more accurate.

17. The definitive study of belles lettres published in Philippson's newspaper is Hans Otto Horch, *Auf der Suche nach der jüdischen Erzählliteratur: Die Literaturkritik der "Allgemeinen Zeitung des Judentums" (1837–1922)* (Frankfurt am Main: Peter Lang, 1985). For a broader treatment on the subject of German-Jewish belles lettres and their place within Jewish newspaper culture, see Itta Shedletzky, "Literaturdiskussion und Belletristik in den juedischen Zeitschriften in Deutschland 1837–1918" (PhD diss., Hebrew University, Jerusalem, 1986).

18. For the general background, see Ulrich Schmid, "Buchmarkt und Literaturvermittlung," in *Hansers Sozialgeschichte der deutschen Literatur vom 16. Jahrhundert bis zur Gegenwart*, vol. 5, ed. Gert Sautermeister and Ulrich Schmid (Munich: Hanser, 1998), 60–93; Wolfgang Beutin, "Historischer und Zeit-Roman," in Sautermeister and Schmid,, *Hansers Sozialgeschichte*, 5:175–194; and Hainer Plaul and Ulrich Schmid, "Die populären Lesestoff," in Sautermeister and Schmid, *Hansers Sozialgeschichte*, 5:313–338. For the way Jewish authors and the Jewish reading public fit into the general trends of the times, see Jonathan M. Hess, *Middlebrow Literature and the Making of German-Jewish Identity* (Stanford, CA: Stanford University Press, 2010), 1–25.

19. Florian Krobb, *Selbstdarstellungen: Untersuchungen zur deutsch-jüdischen Erzählliteratur im neunzehnten Jahrhundert* (Würzburg: Königshausen & Neumann, 2000), 24.

20. On the importance of lending libraries in Germany for the dissemination of novels, see Alberto Martino, *Die deutsche Leihbibliothek: Geschichte einer literarischen Institution (1756–1914)* (Wiesbaden: O. Harrassowitz, 1990).

21. Horch, *Auf der Suche nach der jüdischen Erzählliteratur*, 145. For the institute more specifically see 153–157; and Roemer, *Jewish Scholarship in Nineteenth-Century Germany*, 71–78.

22. Ben-Ari, "1834," 143.

23. Ben-Ari, *Romanze der Vergangenheit*, 45–46.

24. Amos Bitzan, "The Problem of Pleasure: Disciplining the German Jewish Reading Revolution, 1770–1870" (PhD diss., University of California–Berkeley, 2011), 2.

25. Jonathan Skolnik, *Jewish Pasts, German Fictions: History, Memory, and Minority Culture in Germany, 1824–1955* (Stanford, CA: Stanford University Press, 2014), 67. Among the scores of scholarly studies I have consulted in writing this chapter, I am especially indebted to the work of Hans Otto Horch, Florian Krobb, Nitsa Ben-Ari, Jonathan Hess, and Jonathan Skolnik. While I refer to many of the same works of fiction that they do (there is, of course, a finite number of stories), our concerns are different. All four are literature scholars and bring to bear their own considerable methodological skills when approaching these works of historical fiction. Among other things, they are far more concerned than I am with the structure of these novels and short stories, finding parallels between the works of Jewish and non-Jewish authors and judging them as works of literature. As a historian, my task and intent are different. My principal concern is to present some of the different ways Sephardim have been portrayed in these works, examining whether as characters they prove to be true to or renegades from the Jewish people. This leads me to pay

particular attention to the visual images of Sephardim that such literary works conjured up. I am also especially interested in these works as a form of German-Jewish vernacular culture. Finally, while the scholars mentioned above focus almost all their attention on fiction, the literary evidence presented in this chapter is only one of many different aspects to the Sephardicist turn taken by German-Jewish culture in the nineteenth century and should thus be considered as one, albeit it very important, piece of a much larger puzzle. Historical literature, whether fictional or not, was perhaps the foremost medium that contributed to the popularization and concretization among German Jews of a particular aesthetic that they associated with Sephardim and their history.

26. J. C., "Phöbus Philippson. Ein Erinnerungsblat zu seinem hundertsten Geburtstag," *Allgemeine Zeitung des Judentums* 30 (1907): 354–355.

27. Florian Krobb, *Kollektivautobiographien, Wunschautobiographien: Marannenschicksal im deutsch-jüdischen historischen Roman* (Würzburg: Königshausen & Neumann, 2000), 42.

28. Ludwig Philippson, in *Saron*, vol. 5 (Leipzig: Oskar Leiner, 1863), 8. Also quoted in Carsten Schapkow, *Vorbild und Gegenbild: Das iberische Judentum in der deutsch-jüdischen Erinnerungskultur 1779–1939* (Cologne: Böhlau, 2011), 294.

29. Here Philippson may have misread Jewish sentiment in imagining that German Jews would not or should not be interested in reading about traditional Ashkenazic Jews. An entire genre of fiction called "ghetto literature" began to appear in the middle of the nineteenth century and proved to be extremely popular. See Hess, *Middlebrow Literature*, 72–110.

30. Spanish historical novels set during the expulsion of Jews in 1492 and their persecution at the hands of the Inquisition that followed were of particular interest in England, where such representations were, according to Michael Ragussis, "a means of exploring urgent issues of national identity perceived as racial difference in Victorian England." See Michael Ragussis, "Writing Spanish History in Nineteenth-Century Britain: The Inquisition and the 'Secret Race,'" in *Sephardism: Spanish Jewish History and the Modern Literary Imagination*, ed. Yael Halevi-Wise (Stanford, CA: Stanford University Press, 2012), 59–90.

31. Elaine Marks, *Marrano as Metaphor: The Jewish Presence in French Writing* (New York: Columbia University Press, 1996).

32. Krobb, *Kollektivautobiographien*, 46–47. Both quotations appear in Marcus Lehmann, "Eine Seder-Nacht in Madrid," *Der Israelit* 9, nos. 49–52 (December 1868): 911–912, 931–932, 951–952, 967–968. The new *ma nishtana* is to be found on p. 932.

33. See Berthold Auerbach, *Spinoza: Ein historischer Roman* (Stuttgart: Scheible, 1837). For more on Auerbach's Spinoza, see Jonathan Skolnik, "Writing Jewish History between Gutzkow and Goethe: Auerbach's Spinoza and the Birth of Modern Jewish Historical Fiction," *Prooftexts* 19, no. 2 (1999): 101–125; and for a highly critical assessment of Auerbach, see David Sorkin, *The Transformation of German Jewry, 1780–1840* (New York: Oxford University Press, 1987), 140–155. On Spinoza's image, see Daniel B. Schwartz, *The First Modern Jew: Spinoza and the History of an Image* (Princeton, NJ: Princeton University Press, 2012). On da Costa, see the three-act drama by Karl Gutzkow, *Uriel Acosta* (1846), in Karl Gutzkow, *Dramatische Werke*, vol. 5. (Leipzig: Weber, 1847), 113–238; and the response of Hermann Jellinek, *Uriel Acosta's Leben und Lehre. Ein beitrag zur kenntniss seiner moral, wie zur Berichtigung*

der Gutzkow'schen Fiktionen über Acosta, und zur Charakteristik der damaligen Juden (Zerbst: Kummer'schen Buchhandlung, 1847). An author and radical journalist, Jellinek was executed in 1848 at the age of twenty-six for his revolutionary activity. He was the brother of the scholar and rabbi of Vienna's Leopoldstädter Tempel, Adolf Jellinek. As a play Gutzkow's *Uriel Acosta* also became a mainstay of the Yiddish theater. See Seth L. Wolitz, "Translations of Karl Gutzkow's 'Uriel Acosta' as Iconic Moments in Yiddish Theater," in *Inventing the Modern Yiddish Stage*, ed. Joel Berkowitz and Barbara Henry (Detroit: Wayne State University Press, 2012): 87–115. Also on Gutzkow, see Angela Botelho, "Modern Marranism and the German-Jewish Experience: The Persistence of Jewish Identity in Conversion" (MA thesis, Graduate Theological Seminary, Berkeley, 2013), 45–67.

34. Jeffrey L. Sammons, *Heinrich Heine: A Modern Biography* (Princeton, NJ: Princeton University Press, 1979), 45.

35. http://www.staff.uni-mainz.de/pommeren/Gedichte/BdL/DonnaClara.html. As if to underscore the extent to which Heine wanted to inflict maximum hurt with the revelation of his identity, he wrote to his friend Moses Moser, "There is an Abraham of Saragossa, but I found Israel to be more significant." See Israel Tabak, *Heine and His Heritage: A Study of Judaic Lore in His Work* (New York: Twayne Publisher, 1956), 55. Heine's revenge would redound not only to his own honor but to that of all Israel.

36. *Heinrich Heine's Sämtliche Werke*, ed. Adolf Strodtman, vol. 19 (Hamburg: Hoffmann and Campe, 1876), 174.

37. Hess, *Middlebrow Literature*, 59. On the various roles played by women in nineteenth-century German-Jewish culture, see Marion A. Kaplan, *The Making of the Jewish Middle Class: Women, Family, and Identity in Imperial Germany* (New York: Oxford University Press, 1991).

38. Both quotations appear in Hess, *Middlebrow Literature*, 27 and 31, respectively.

39. Ulrike Hönsch, *Wege des Spanienbildes im Deutschland des 18. Jahrhunderts: Von der schwarzen Legende zum "Hesperischen Zaubergarten"* (Tübingen: Niemeyer, 2000).

40. Phöbus Philippson, *Die Marannen*, in *Saron*, ed. Ludwig Philippson, vol. 1 (Leipzig: Leopold Schauss, 1855), 4.

41. Quoted in Skolnik, *Jewish Pasts, German Fictions*, 80.

42. Philippson, *Die Marannen*, 8.

43. Ibid., 34.

44. Ibid., 37–38.

45. Karlheinz Fingerhut, "Spanische Spiegel: Heinrich Heines Verwendung spanischer Geschichte und Literatur zur Selbstreflexion des Juden und des Dichters," *Heine Jahrbuch* 31 (1992): 106–136. Fingerhut misreads Heine's motives in using Sephardic characters, claiming that Heine had no real interest in Spanish Jewry of the Golden Age, and that he merely deployed such figures to combat the Christian triumphalism of German romantics who rejoiced over the Reconquista. My situating of Heine within the larger context of the German-Jewish celebration of all things Sephardic demonstrates that his relationship to Spain was not purely instrumental but of a piece with a larger Jewish cultural trend.

46. Some literary critics consider the work incoherent, if not an outright failure. Nevertheless, for the historian of German Jewry, the incomplete story is a rich and

suggestive source. For a staunch criticism, see Jeffrey L. Sammons, "Heine's *Rabbi von Bacherach*: The Unresolved Tensions," *German Quarterly*, 37, no. 1 (1964): 26–38.

47. Tabak, *Heine and His Heritage*, 45.

48. Following the disappearance of a Capuchin monk, Father Thomas, and his servant, fellow monks and local Christians claimed that Jews had murdered the two men for ritual purposes. When the Jews petitioned the Muslim leader of the city, Sharif ("Sheriff") Pasha, to investigate, the French consul in Damascus, Count Ratti-Menton, suggested to the sheriff that the Jews had killed the two men. Mass arrests followed the ransacking of the Jewish quarter. The day before the disappearance of the two men, a Muslim had threatened to kill Father Thomas for allegedly having blasphemed against the prophet Muhammad. Ratti-Menton had fabricated the story of Jewish guilt because blaming anyone in the Muslim community would have upset France's imperial relations with Muhammad Ali, the Egyptian ruler of Syria. On this history, see Jonathan Frankel, *The Damascus Affair: "Ritual Murder," Politics, and the Jews in 1840* (Cambridge: Cambridge University Press, 1997).

49. On the research Heine did for this novella, see his letters to Moses Moser of June 25, 1824, and October 25, 1824, in Heinrich Heine, *The Poetry and Prose of Heinrich Heine*, ed. Frederic Ewen (New York: Citadel Press, 1948), 354–355 and 364–365. On Heine's Jewishness, see S. S. Prawer, *Heine's Jewish Comedy: A Study of His Portraits of Jews and Judaism* (Oxford: Clarendon Press, 1983); and Tabak, *Heine and His Heritage*.

50. Heinrich Heine, *Sämtliche Schriften*, ed. Klaus Briegleb (Munich: Carl Hanser, 1968), 1:495. Literary scholars have seen in the Abravanel character a reflection of Don Quixote, an interpretation made all the more plausible by the fact that Heine wrote an introduction to a new German translation of Cervantes's masterpiece that appeared in 1837. See Skolnik, *Jewish Pasts, German Fictions*, 63.

51. Prawer, *Heine's Jewish Comedy*, 368.

52. Both quotations appear in Heine, *Sämtliche Schriften*, 2:77. The German original of the first quotation reads: "Dennoch, trotz der barbarischen Pelzmütze, die seinen Kopf bedeckt, und der noch barbarischeren Ideen, die denselben füllen, schätze ich den polnischen Juden weit höher als so manchen deutschen Juden, der seinen Bolivar auf dem Kopf und seinen Jean Paul im Kopfe trägt." See also Jeffrey Grossman, "Heine and Jewish Culture: The Poetics of Appropriation," in *A Companion to the Works of Heinrich Heine*, ed. Roger F. Cook (Rochester, NY: Camden House, 2002), 258–260. Jean Paul Richter (1763–1825) was a romantic author and humorist.

53. Tabak, *Heine and His Heritage*, 5.

54. Heine, *The Poetry and Prose of Heinrich Heine*, 343.

55. Philipp F. Veit, "Heine: The Marrano Pose," *Monatshefte* 66, no. 2 (1974): 145–156, esp. 145–147.

56. Heine, *Sämtliche Schriften*, 1:464.

57. Ibid., 496.

58. Prawer, *Heine's Jewish Comedy*, 367–369.

59. Heine, *Sämtliche Schriften*, 1:498.

60. See the letter to Moses Moser of January 9, 1826: "I am now hated by both Christians and Jews. I regret that I've been baptized. I don't see that it's helped me very much. On the contrary, it's brought me nothing but misfortune." Heine, *The Poetry and Prose of Heinrich Heine*, 370. See also Prawer, *Heine's Jewish Comedy*,

28–43; and Robert C. Holub, "Troubled Apostate: Heine's Conversion and Its Consequences," in Cook, *Companion to the Works of Heinrich Heine*, 229–250. Elsewhere Holub is emphatic that Heine was not a Jew and therefore could not have been a German-Jewish writer. He was, rather, a German writer of Jewish origin. This is an extreme and unconvincing assertion. If Holub believes that Heine's "Jewishness" is an invention of "critics and literature scholars," then surely Holub's claim that Heine was not Jewish also betray the invented claims of a literature scholar. See Jeffrey L. Sammons, *Heinrich Heine: Alternative Perspectives, 1985–2005* (Würzburg: Könighausen & Neumann, 2006), 198.

61. Jocelyne Kolb, *The Ambiguity of Taste: Freedom and Food in European Romanticism* (Ann Arbor: University of Michigan Press, 1995), 115–223. Curiously Kolb does not address the important references to food in *The Rabbi of Bacherach*. She does, however, take seriously Heine's allusions to food, where many other critics have dismissed them as unimportant, as a "key to unlocking political meaning," or even as an example of his poor writing. For the reference to pig's trotters, see Prawer, *Heine's Jewish Comedy*, 368.

62. Heine, *Sämtliche Schriften*, 1:498.

63. Natan Rotenstreich, "Hegel's Idea of Judaism," *Jewish Social Studies* 15, no. 1 (1953): 35–36.

64. Prawer, *Heine's Jewish Comedy*, 42.

65. Heine, *Sämtliche Schriften*, 1:499.

66. "Literarische Nachrichten," *Allgemeine Zeitung des Judentums* 1 (1841): 7–8.

67. Lehmann, "Eine Seder-Nacht in Madrid," 968.

68. See Michael Studemund-Halévy, "Wie Wien zu seinen Sefarden kam: Die wundersame Geschichte des Diego de Aguilar." www.hagalil.com/archiv/2010/07/26/sefarden.

69. http://www.jewishencyclopedia.com/articles/921-aguilar-diego-d.

70. Anton Schlossar, "Frankl von Hochwart, Ludwig August Ritter," in *Allgemeine Deutsche Biographie*, vol. 48 (Leipzig: Duncker & Humblot, 1904), 706–712.

71. Ludwig August Frankel, "Geschichte Diego d'Aguilar's," *Allgemeine Zeitung des Judentums* 50 (1854): 630–634 and 51 (1854): 656–661.

72. Adolf von Zemlinszky, *Geschichte der türkisch-israelitischen Gemeinde zu Wien von ihrer Gründung bis Heute: Nach historischen Daten* (Vienna: M. Papo, 1888).

73. See Anthony Beaumont, *Zemlinsky* (Ithaca, NY: Cornell University Press, 2000), 5–16.

74. Hess, *Middlebrow Literature*, 40–41.

75. Ludwig Philippson, "Die drei Brüder," in *Saron*, ed. Ludwig Philippson, vol. 5 (Leipzig: Oskar Leiner, 1863), 223–224. This story has recently been ably translated into English for the first time by Jonathan Hess and appears in *Nineteenth Century Jewish Literature: A Reader*, ed. Jonathan M. Hess, Maurice Samuels, and Nadia Valman (Stanford, CA: Stanford University Press, 2013), 210–247.

76. Philippson, "Die drei Brüder," 227.

77. Ibid.

78. Ibid., 235.

79. Ibid., 236.

80. Ibid., 256.

81. Hess, *Middlebrow Literature*, 50–52.

82. Miriam Bodian, *Hebrews of the Portuguese Nation: Conversos and Community in Early Modern Amsterdam* (Bloomington: Indiana University Press, 1999), 17–24. The quotations appear on p. 24.

83. Meyer Kayserling, *Sephardim. Romanische poesien der Juden in Spanien. Ein Beitrag zur Literatur und Geschichte der spanisch-portugiesischen Juden* (Leipzig, H. Mendelssohn, 1859), 169. Kayserling referred to *Jakob Tirado* as "Philippson's belletristic masterpiece and also the best work of modern German literature." See Meyer Kayserling, *Ludwig Philippson: Eine Biographie* (Leipzig: Hermann Mendelsohn, 1898), 212; and Hess, *Middlebrow Literature*, 54–61.

84. Quoted in Hess, *Middlebrow Literature*, 67.

85. Bodian, *Hebrews of the Portuguese Nation*, 18–19.

86. Yosef Hayim Yerushalmi, "Sephardic Jewry between Cross and Crescent," in *The Faith of Fallen Jews: Yosef Hayim Yerushalmi and the Writing of Jewish History*, ed. David N. Myers and Alexander Kaye (Waltham, MA: Brandeis University Press, 2014), 153.

87. Yosef Hayim Yerushalmi, *Zakhor: Jewish History and Jewish Memory* (Seattle: University of Washington Press, 1996), 98.

88. See Bitzan, "The Problem of Pleasure, esp. chaps. 4–7.

Chapter Five
Writing Jewish History: The Construction of a Glorious Sephardic Past

1. Ismar Schorsch, "Converging Cognates: The Intersection of Jewish and Islamic Studies in Nineteenth Century Germany," *Leo Baeck Institute Year Book 55* (2010): 3–36. Schorsch makes clear that thanks to the patronage of H. L. Fleischer, founder of the Deutsche-Morgenländische Gesellschaft in 1845, Jewish studies that did not focus on the world of Islam was also incorporated into the larger corpus of German orientalist scholarship.

2. Ismar Schorsch, *From Text to Context: The Turn to History in Modern Judaism* (Hanover, NH: University Press of New England, 1994), 82–83.

3. See Kerstin von der Krone, *Wissenschaft in Öffentlichkeit: Die Wissenschaft des Judentums und ihre Zeitschriften* (Berlin: De Gruyter, 2011).

4. Leopold Zunz, *Die synagogale Poesie des Mittelalters* (Berlin: Julius Springer, 1855), 215.

5. In this respect, nineteenth-century Jewish historians were heirs to a Jewish historiographical tradition dating back to the early modern period wherein Jewish chroniclers from Christian Europe idealized Ottoman rulers thanks to the sanctuary they had offered the Spanish-Jewish refugees of 1492. It is noteworthy that Jewish chroniclers from the Muslim world were sometimes far more critical of Islam. See Martin Jacobs, *Islamische Geschichte in Judischen Chroniken: Hebraische Historiographie des 16. und 17. Jahrhunderts* (Tübingen: Mohr Siebeck, 2004).

6. Edward W. Said, *Orientalism* (New York: Vintage, 1979), 4.

7. Susannah Heschel, *Abraham Geiger and the Jewish Jesus* (Chicago: University of Chicago Press, 1998), esp. 19–21.

8. On Heine's relation to the Verein, see Edith Lutz, *Der Verein für Kultur- und Wissenschaft der Juden und sein Mitglied H. Heine* (Stuttgart: J. B. Metzler, 1997), 101–269.

9. Heinrich Heine, *Sämtliche Schriften* (Munich: Carl Hanser, 1968), 4:258. On Heine's poetry and what it can tell us about the creation of a successful disaporic culture where the subdominant resides comfortably with the dominant, see Bluma Goldstein, "A Politics and Poetics of Diaspora: Heine's *Hebräische Melodien*," in *Diasporas and Exiles: Varieties of Jewish Identity*, ed. Howard Wettstein (Berkeley: University of California Press, 2002), 60–77.

10. Stephen Neill, *Colonialism and Christian Missions* (London: Lutterworth, 1966); Torben Christensen and William R. Hutchison, eds., *Missionary Ideologies in the Imperialist Era, 1880–1920* (Aarhus, Denmark: Aros, 1982).

11. Michael A. Meyer, *Response to Modernity: A History of the Reform Movement in Judaism* (New York: Oxford University Press, 1988), 89–99.

12. Ludwig Geiger, *Abraham Geiger: Leben und Lebenswerk* (Berlin: Georg Reimer, 1910), 17–18, 23. More generally, see Max Wiener, *Abraham Geiger and Liberal Judaism* (Philadelphia: Jewish Publication Society of America, 1962), 3–80.

13. Jacob Lassner, "Abraham Geiger: A Nineteenth-Century Jewish Reformer on the Origins of Islam," in *The Jewish Discovery of Islam*, ed. Martin Kramer (Tel Aviv: Moshe Dayan Center for Middle Eastern and African Studies, 1999), 104; Johann Fück, *Die arabischen Studien in Europa bis in den Anfang des 20. Jahrhunderts* (Leipzig: O. Harrassowitz, 1955), 174–175.

14. Heschel, *Abraham Geiger and the Jewish Jesus*, 51.

15. Suzanne L. Marchand, *German Orientalism in the Age of Empire: Religion, Race, and Scholarship* (New York: Cambridge University Press, 2009), 74–75.

16. Theodore Nöldeke, *Sketches from Eastern History* (Beirut: Khayats, 1963), 61. See also D. Gustav Pfannmüller, *Handbuch der Islam-Literatur* (Berlin: Walter de Gruyter, 1923), 164–196, esp. 172–177, on the representation of Muhammad in the French Enlightenment and German Aufklärung, respectively. See also Alastair Hamilton, "Western Attitudes to Islam in the Enlightenment," *Middle Eastern Studies* 3 (1999): 69–85.

17. Jonathan M. Hess, *Germans, Jews and the Claims of Modernity* (New Haven, CT: Yale University Press, 2002), 51–89; Jonathan Sheehan, *The Enlightenment Bible: Translation, Scholarship, Culture* (Princeton, NJ: Princeton University Press, 2005), 148–240; and Marchand, *German Orientalism in the Age of Empire*, 38–52.

18. For a sweeping study of the way Europeans became disenchanted with the contemporary Orient, see Jürgen Osterhammel, *Die Entzauberung Asiens: Europa und die asiatischen Reiche im 18. Jahrhundert* (Munich: C. H. Beck, 1998).

19. Moses Mendelssohn, *Jerusalem, or on Religious Power and Judaism*, trans. Allan Arkush (Hanover, NH: Brandeis University Press, 1983), 59–60.

20. Abraham Geiger, *Was hat Muhammad aus dem Judenthume aufgenommen?* (Bonn: privately printed, 1833), 35. The page numbers to further references from this work will be cited in parentheses in the main body of the text.

21. Lassner, "Abraham Geiger," 106–107 and 131n14.

22. Quoted in Heschel, *Abraham Geiger and the Jewish Jesus*, 30.

23. Abraham Geiger, *Das Judenthum und seine Geschichte in zehn Vorlesungen: Von dem Anfange des dreizehnten bis zum Ende des sechszehnten Jahrhunderts* (Breslau: Schletter, 1865–1871), 3:21.

24. See for example, Frank Manuel, *The Broken Staff: Judaism through Christian Eyes* (Cambridge, MA: Harvard University Press, 1992); and Aya Elyada, *A Goy Who*

Speaks Yiddish: Christians and the Jewish Language in Early Modern Germany (Stanford, CA: Stanford University Press, 2012).

25. David Moshfegh, "Ignaz Goldziher and the Rise of *Islamwissenschaft* as a 'Science of Religion'" (PhD diss., University of California–Berkeley, 2012), 140–239.

26. My italics. Ludwig Geiger, ed., *Abraham Geiger's Nachgelassene Schriften* (Berlin: Louis Gerschel, 1875), 2:40. For a similar view but one that long predated Geiger, see Salomo Löwisohn, "Abenezra (Aben Ezra) und dessen Schriften," *Sulamith* 4, no. 1 (1812): 217–222.

27. Abraham Geiger, *Divan des Castiliers, Abu'-l-Hassan Juda ha-Levi* (Breslau: J. U. Kern, 1851), 13; and Geiger, *Das Judenthum und seine Geschichte*, 3:20–23.

28. Geiger was deeply engaged in the study of Hebrew and saw it as a central task of *Wissenschaft des Judentums* to study the linguistic structure of Hebrew via a comparative method with cognate languages, the history of Hebrew linguistics, which would entail an engagement with the Sephardic grammarians, and the history of the Hebrew language with a view to plotting its development and change over time. See Geiger, *Nachgelassene Schriften*, 2:39–61.

29. See the letter in Wiener, *Abraham Geiger*, 125. See also Geiger, *Das Judenthum und seine Geschichte*, 1–2:138–148.

30. Geiger, *Das Judenthum und seine Geschichte*, 1:142.

31. The letter to Nöldeke appears in Wiener, *Abraham Geiger*, 130–131.

32. Geiger, *Das Judenthum und seine Geschichte*, 3:96.

33. Geiger, *Nachgelassene Schriften*, 2:307–313; and on Delitzsch's relationship to Geiger, see Heschel, *Abraham Geiger and the Jewish Jesus*, 194–197. Geiger's disappointment with Delitzsch carries echoes of the same crushing disappointment felt by Moses Mendelssohn when his friend Johann Caspar Lavater challenged him to convert.

34. While he was echoing the sentiments of Moses Mendelssohn, more immediately Geiger was especially inspired by the Jewish politician Gabriel Riesser (1806–1863), because of the latter's committed public advocacy of Jewish emancipation. Conversely, he was frustrated by the relative silence of Leopold Zunz, leading light of *Wissenschaft des Judentums*, because of his refusal to speak out publicly on the need for reform within Judaism and its connection to Jewish emancipation. See Geiger's letter to Zunz in Wiener, *Abraham Geiger*, 144.

35. Abraham Geiger, "Der Kampf christlicher Theologen gegen die bürgerliche Gleichstellung der Juden, namentlich mit Bezug auf Anton Theodor Hartmann," *Wissenschaftliche Zeitschrift für Jüdische Theologie* 1, no. 1 (1835): 52–67, 1, no. 3 (1835): 340–357, 2, no. 1 (1836): 78–92, and 2, no. 3 (1836): 446–473.

36. See the letter in Wiener, *Abraham Geiger*, 135–136.

37. Heschel, *Abraham Geiger and the Jewish Jesus*, 105 and 186–228.

38. The Geiger-Titkin affair erupted in 1838 when the Breslau Jewish community sought to hire a new rabbi. When the community board announced that Geiger was one of the finalists, the Orthodox rabbi Solomon Titkin led the charge against Geiger's appointment. Geiger eventually prevailed, becoming assistant rabbi in 1838. Thereafter, the dispute intensified, with the Orthodox faction denouncing Geiger to the government as a political radical. That faction requested that the government annul the election, withhold Prussian citizenship from Geiger, and prevent him from publishing. Titkin's refusal to work with Geiger led to his being suspended

from duties and precipitated an official schism in the community. See David Philipson, *The Reform Movement in Judaism* (New York: The Macmillan Company, 1931), 72–101.

39. Abraham Geiger, "Alte Romantik, neue Reaktion," *Jüdische Zeitschrift für Wissenschaft und Leben* 1, no. 4 (1862): 245–252. The reference to the "absolutism (*unverbrüchlichkeit*) of the *Shulkhan Arukh*" appears on p. 251.

40. Geiger, *Nachgelassene Schriften*, 2:240 and 313.

41. Ibid., 313–321.

42. Ibid., 322–324.

43. Ibid., 156–196.

44. Ibid,. 170.

45. On the political history of this region, see William W. Hagen, *Germans, Poles, and Jews: The Nationality Conflict in the Prussian East, 1772–1914* (Chicago: University of Chicago Press, 1980).

46. Carsten Schapkow, *Vorbild und Gegenbild: Das iberische Judentum in der deutsch-jüdischen Erinnerungskultur 1779–1939* (Cologne: Böhlau, 2011), 214–238. For biographical details on Graetz, see Philip Bloch's essay in Heinrich Graetz, *History of the Jews* (Philadelphia: Jewish Publication Society, 1945), 6:1–86. On Graetz as a historian, see Israel Abrahams, "H. Graetz, the Jewish Historian," *Jewish Quarterly Review* 4 (January 1892): 165–203; Josef Meisl, *Heinrich Graetz; Eine Würdigung des Historikers und Juden zu seinem 100. Geburtstage 31. Oktober 1917, 21. Cheschwan* (Berlin: Louis Lamm, 1917); and Shmuel Ettinger, "Mifalo shel historiografi shel Graetz," in *Historiyonim ve-Askolot Historiyot* (Jerusalem: ha-Hevrah ha-historit ha-Yisre'elit, 1963), 84–92.

47. Marcus Pyka, *Jüdische Identität bei Heinrich Graetz* (Göttingen: Vandenhoeck & Ruprecht, 2009), esp. 87–103.

48. Hirsch Grätz, *Gnosticismus und Judenthum* (Krotoschin: B. L. Monasch, 1846). Graetz still used his Yiddish first name at this stage of his career.

49. See Ismar Schorsch's introduction in Heinrich Graetz, *The Structure of Jewish History and Other Essays*, ed. Ismar Schorsch (New York: Jewish Theological Seminary, 1975), 31.

50. On Graetz's scholarship, see Michael Brenner, *Prophets of the Past: Interpreters of Jewish History* (Princeton, NJ: Princeton University Press, 2010), 53–82; and Michael A. Meyer, *Judaism within Modernity: Essays on Jewish History and Religion* (Detroit: Wayne State University Press, 2001), 57–60 and 64–75.

51. Schorsch, *From Text to Context*, 286–293.

52. Bitzan, "The Problem of Pleasure," chap. 6, p. 4.

53. Heinrich Graetz, *Geschichte der Juden*, (Leipzig: Oskar Leiner, 1897–1911), 5:122.

54. To be sure, Ismar Schorsch is correct to state that, in the early phase of his professional career, "in nearly every significant aspect, Graetz's theory [of Jewish history] ran counter to that propounded by his [Reform] adversaries." Graetz, *Structure of Jewish History*, 38–39. What I am suggesting here, however, is that from the very beginning, Graetz and Geiger were in fundamental agreement on the topic of Islam and the role of Judaism in its development.

55. Graetz, *Geschichte der Juden*, 5:18.

56. Ibid.

57. Quoted in Brenner, *Prophets of the Past*, 66.

58. Entry of October 31, 1898, in *The Diaries of Theodor Herzl*, ed. and trans. Marvin Lowenthal (London: V. Gollancz, 1958), 283.

59. Graetz, *Geschichte der Juden*, 3:281.

60. Ibid., 5:59–61. Indeed, the origins of this myth can be traced back to the Jews of Muslim Spain. See H. H. Ben-Sasson, "The Generation of the Spanish Exiles Considers Its Fate," *Binah: Studies in Jewish History, Culture, and Thought* 1 (1989): 83–98.

61. Some authors have maintained that Muslims and Islam in the play are, in reality, intended to be Jews and Judaism. See Ludwig Rosenthal, *Heinrich Heine als Jude* (Frankfurt am Main: Ullstein, 1973), 113; Hartmut Kircher, *Heine und das Judentum* (Bonn: Bouvier, 1973), 186. For a contrary view, one that regards Heine as an earnest student of Muslim culture and history, see Mounir Fendri, *Halbmond, Kreuz und Schibboleth: Heinrich Heine und der islamische Orient* (Hamburg: Hoffmann und Campe, Heinrich-Heine-Verlag, 1980), 19.

62. The original reads: "Almansor: Wir hörten daß der furchtbare Ximenes, Inmitten auf dem Markte, zu Granada—Mir starrt die Zung im Mund—den Koran in eines Scheiterhaufens Flamme warf! Hassan: Das war ein Vorspiel nur, dort wo man Bücher Verbrennt, verbrennt man auch am Ende Menschen." See Heine, *Sämtliche Schriften*, 1:284–285.

63. Graetz, *Structure of Jewish History*, 52. On orientalism in the Saidean sense, and its relation to the representation of Shabbtai Zvi, see David Biale, "Shabbtai Zvi and the Seductions of Jewish Orientalism," *Jerusalem Studies in Jewish Thought* 16–17 (2001): 85–110.

64. Graetz, *Geschichte der Juden*, 4:308. Later *Wissenschaft des Judentums* scholars, Graetz principal among them, rejected the Hegelian view that because it lacked tragedy in the Greek sense of the term, Jewish history was meaningless. They did so by interpreting the long history of Jewish suffering, especially that which occurred during the First Crusade of 1096, as having been for a higher purpose. See Nils Roemer, "Turning Defeat into Victory: 'Wissenschaft des Judentums' and the Martyrs of 1096," *Jewish History* 13, no. 2 (1999): 65–80.

65. Heinrich Graetz, "The Correspondence of an English Lady on Judaism and Semitism," in *Structure of Jewish History*, 208.

66. Both quotations appear in Graetz, *Geschichte der Juden*, 5:72–73.

67. Ibid., 76–82.

68. Ibid., 100.

69. David B. Ruderman, "Cecil Roth, Historian of Italian Jewry: A Reassessment," in *The Jewish Past Revisited: Reflections on Modern Jewish Historians*, ed. David N. Myers and David B. Ruderman (New Haven, CT: Yale University Press, 1998), 138.

70. Graetz, *Geschichte der Juden*, 11:2–3.

71. Ibid., 7.

72. Ibid., 6:265.

73. Ibid., 11:7.

74. Bitzan, "The Problem of Pleasure," chap. 6., p. 15.

75. Graetz, *Geschichte der Juden*, 11:7.

76. Ibid., 5:371.

77. Both quotations appear in ibid., 370.

78. Ibid., 370–371.

79. Ibid., 10:59.

80. Karl Emil Franzos, "Every Country Has the Jews It Deserves," in *The Jew in the Modern World*, ed. Paul Mendes-Flohr and Jehuda Reinharz (Oxford: Oxford University Press, 1995), 254.

81. Graetz, *Geschichte der Juden*, 10:59–60.

82. Ibid., 11:94–95.

83. Ibid., 11–12.

84. Robert D. King, "The Czernowitz Conference in Retrospect," in *The Politics of Yiddish: Studies in Language, Literature, and Society*, vol. 4, ed. Dov-Ber Kerler (Walnut Creek, CA: AltaMira Press, 1998), 47. History has a funny way of exacting revenge. Graetz's work was translated into many languages, but he refused to countenance a Yiddish translation. After his death several Yiddish versions did appear, but, like the Hebrew translations, they were so heavily reworked so as not to offend readers in Eastern Europe that the negative comments about Yiddish and Eastern European Jews were simply excised. Hasidism was presented as a great spiritual awakening, and its founder, the Ba'al Shem Tov, as a great and sincere religious leader. Brenner, *Prophets of the Past*, 74–75.

85. Leopold Zunz, *Die gottesdienstliche Vorträge der Juden* (Berlin: A. Ascher, 1832), 427.

86. Ibid., 427–435. The quotations appear on 427 and 435.

87. Ibid., 437.

88. Ibid., 438.

89. Ibid., 443–444. Half a century after Zunz, Richard Andree still held to the claim that German Jews had originally, and until the sixteenth century, spoken pure German. Richard Andree, *Zur Volkskunde der Juden* (Bielefeld: Velhagen & Klasing, 1881), 108.

90. Zunz, *Die gottesdienstliche Vorträge der Juden*, 438.

91. Schorsch, *From Text to Context*, 233–254.

92. Zunz, *Die gottesdienstliche Vorträge der Juden*, 437–448.

93. On how the Jewish bibliographer and important figure of *Wissenschaft des Judentums* Moritz Steinschneider approached Yiddish, and Zunz's powerful influence on him, see Diana Matut, "Steinschneider and Yiddish," in *Studies on Steinschneider: Moritz Steinschneider and the Emergence of the Science of Judaism in Nineteenth-Century Germany*, ed. Reimund Leicht and Gar Freudenthal (Leiden: Brill, 2012), 383–409. See also Max Grunwald, the Hamburg rabbi and folklorist, who founded the first Jewish scholarly journal dedicated to the exploration of Jewish folkore. In the first article in the first issue of his newly established journal, Grunwald wrote an article on Jewish languages entitled "Namen und Mundartliches: Sprache der Juden," *Mitteilungen der Gesellschaft für Jüdische Volkskunde* 1 (1898): 17–18, wherein he claims, "Up until their banishment to Poland in the fourteenth century, the Jews in Germany spoke pure German (*reines Deutsch*), admittedly with many made-up Hebrew words unavoidably thrown in" (17).

94. Zunz, *Die gottesdienstliche Vorträge der Juden*, 451–453.

95. Quoted in Schorsch, *From Text to Context*, 234.

96. Hermann Reckendorf, *Die Geheimnisse der Juden*, vol. 5 (Leipzig: W. Gerhard, 1857), 158–159.

97. According to Jeffrey Grossman, the process whereby German Jews changed from Yiddish speakers into German speakers was central to what he calls "the invention of the German Jew." See his *The Discourse on Yiddish in Germany*, 75–113.

98. See, for example, Peter G. J. Pulzer, *The Rise of Political Anti-Semitism in Germany and Austria* (New York: John Wiley, 1964); Jacob Katz, *From Prejudice to Destruction: Anti-Semitism, 1700–1933* (Cambridge, MA: Harvard University Press, 1980), 147–300; and Werner Jochmann, *Gesellschaftskrise und Judenfeindschaft in Deutschland 1870–1945* (Hamburg: Hans Christians, 1988), esp. 13–98.

99. See Walter Boehlich, ed., *Der Berliner Antisemitismusstreit* (Frankfurt am Main: Insel, 1988), for a reprint of the most important and vituperative exchanges. The quotations are on pp. 28 and 80, respectively. For further background, see Meyer, *Judaism within Modernity*, 64–75 and esp. 73n1, which provides a list of the most important secondary sources dealing with the Graetz-Treitschke dispute. See also George Y. Kohler, "German Spirit and Holy Ghost—Treitschke's Call for Conversion of German Jewry: The Debate Revisited," *Modern Judaism* 30, no. 2 (2010): 172–195. Kohler interprets the dispute as a call by Treitschke for Jews to convert to Protestantism.

100. Boehlich, *Der Berliner Antisemitismusstreit*, 45–46.

101. Ibid., 10.

102. This point was made explicitly by Meyer Kayserling in his *Geschichte der Juden in Portugal* (Leipzig: Oskar Leiner, 1867), vi.

103. In a revealing interview conducted in 1988, the distinguished historian of the Arab world Albert Hourani declared that in preparation for a series of public lectures he was to deliver at Cambridge University, he "went deeply into Goldziher because our view of Islam and Islamic culture until today is very largely that which Goldziher laid down." Also according to Hourani, "very few of the works on the Middle East written before the last twenty or thirty years stand up. Of the works on Islamic history, very few except those of Ignaz Goldziher are sound." See Nancy Elizabeth Gallagher, *Approaches to the History of the Middle East: Interviews with Leading Middle East Historians* (Reading, UK: Ithaca Press, 1994), 40 and 42.

104. *Sefer zicharon le-kehilot Székesfehérvár ve-hasvivah* (Jerusalem: n.p., 1997), 11 and 14.

105. Ignaz Goldziher, *Tagebuch* (Leiden: E. J. Brill, 1978), 22.

106. Lawrence I. Conrad, "The Dervish's Disciple: On the Personality and Intellectual Milieu of the Young Ignaz Goldziher," *Journal of the Royal Asiatic Society* 2 (1990): 225–266.

107. Daniel Viragh, "Becoming Hungarian: The Creation of a Hungarian-Language Jewish Cultural Sphere in Budapest, 1867–1914" (PhD diss., University of California–Berkeley, 2014), chap. 2, p. 1.

108. Quoted in Simon Hopkins, "The Language Studies of Ignaz Goldziher," in *Goldziher Memorial Conference*, ed. Éva Apor and István Ormos (Budapest: Library of the Hungarian Academy of Sciences, 2005), 88. See also, in the same volume, István Ormos, "Goldziher's Mother Tongue: A Contribution to the Study of the Language Situation in Hungary in the Nineteenth Century," 203–243.

109. The term *Jargon* was not necessarily a pejorative term for Yiddish, and it was in fact used quite regularly by none other than the great Yiddish author Sholom Aleichem. Quoted in Ormos, "Goldziher's Mother Tongue," 213.

110. Nathaniel Katzburg, "The Jewish Congress of Hungary, 1868–1869," in *Hungarian Jewish Studies*, vol. 2, ed. Randolph L. Braham (New York: World Federation of Hungarian Jews, 1966), 1–33.

111. The fullest account of Hungarian-Jewish language politics, with special emphasis on Goldziher and his family, is found in Ormos, "Goldziher's Mother Tongue," 213 and 223–240.

112. See also Peter Haber, *Zwischen jüdischer Tradition und Wissenschaft: Der ungarische orientalist Ignac Goldziher (1850–1921)* (Cologne: Böhlau, 2006). Haber's study focuses to a great extent on Goldziher's diaries and the personal, as opposed to professional, aspect of his life.

113. Ignaz Goldziher, *Introduction to Islamic Theology and Law*, trans. Andras and Ruth Hamori (Princeton, NJ: Princeton University Press, 1981).

114. Ignaz Goldziher, *Muhammedanische Studien* (Halle: Max Niemeyer, 1889–90); Ignaz Goldziher, *Die Richtungen der islamischen Koranauslegung* (Leiden: E. J. Brill, 1952); Ignaz Goldziher, *Abhandlungen zur arabischen Philologie* (Leiden: Brill, 1896); Ignaz Goldziher, *On the History of Grammar among the Arabs: An Essay in Literary History*, trans. and ed. Kinga Dévényi and Tamás Iványi (Amsterdam: J. Benjamins, 1994); Róbert Simon, *Ignác Goldziher: His Life and Scholarship as Reflected in His Works and Correspondence* (Leiden: E. J. Brill, 1986); and Shimon Federbusch, *Hokhmat Yisra'el be-Ma'arav Eropah* (Jerusalem: Ogen, 1958), 166–181. As further testament to the lasting nature of Goldziher's scholarship, the author of a 1967 study of classical Arabic poetry still employed Goldziher's *Abhandlungen zur arabischen Philologie* (1896) as the point of departure to make his own case; in the end he concludes that "I do not pretend that the observations in this study . . . lead to conclusions that go much beyond those of Goldziher and Gibb." H.A.R. Gibb's study, one of the first to counter some of Goldziher's positions, did not appear until 1948. It is entitled "Arab Poet and Arabic Philologist," *Bulletin of the School of Oriental and African Studies* 12, nos. 3–4 (1947–1948): 574–578. In it he writes that the "general presentation of Goldziher's argument could scarcely be questioned." See Seeger A. Bonebakker, "Poets and Critics in the Third Century A.H.," in *Logic in Classical Islamic Culture*, ed. G. E. von Grunebaum (Wiesbaden: Otto Harrassowitz, 1970), 85–111; Ignaz Goldziher, *A Short History of Classical Arabic Literature* (Hildesheim: Georg Olms, 1966). Interestingly, this book was commissioned by the Imperial and Royal Ministry of Joint Finances of Vienna in 1908. The purpose was to provide a textbook on this subject for classroom use in the Muslim high schools of Bosnia and Herzogovina.

115. Ignaz Goldziher, *Studien über Tanchûm Jerûschalmi* (Leipzig: List and Franke, 1870); Ignác Goldziher, "Die islamische und die jüdische Philosophie," in *Allgemeine Geschichte der Philosophie*, ed. Paul Hinneberg (Berlin: B. G. Teubner, 1909), 45–77; Ignaz Goldziher, *Muhammedanischer aberglaube über gedächtnisskraft und vergesslichkeit, mit parallelen aus der jüdischen literatur* (Berlin: H. Itzkowski, 1903).

116. For both quotations see Goldziher, *Introduction to Islamic Theology and Law*, 3.

117. Goldziher, *Islamischen Koranauslegung*, 2. See also Goldziher, *Introduction to Islamic Theology and Law*, 4. Geiger laid this out most definitively in his *Urschrift und Uebersetzungen der Bibel in ihrer Abhängigkeit von der innern Entwickelung des Judenthums* (Breslau: J. Hainauer, 1857).

118. See Lawrence I. Conrad, "Ignaz Goldziher on Ernest Renan: From Orientalist Philology to the Study of Islam," in Kramer, *The Jewish Discovery of Islam*, 137–180;

and Shmuel Almog, "The Racial Motif in Renan's Attitude to Jews and Judaism," in *Antisemitism through the Ages*, ed. Shmuel Almog (Oxford: Pergamon Press, 1988), 255–278.

119. On the development of the religion and society of biblical Israel, see Ignaz Goldziher, *Mythology among the Hebrews and Its Historical Development*, trans. Russell Martineau (New York: Cooper Square, 1967), 231–259 and 316–336.

120. Ludmila Hanisch, ed., *"Machen Sie doch unseren Islam nicht gar zu schlecht": Der Briefwechsel der Islamwissenschaftler Ignaz Goldziher und Martin Hartmann, 1894–1914* (Wiesbaden: Harrassowitz, 2000), 62–63.

121. Ignaz Goldziher, "Die Fortschritte der Islam-Wissenschaft in der letzen drei Jahrzehnten," in *Ignaz Goldziher: Gesammelte Schriften*, vol. 4., ed. Joseph Desomogyi (Hildesheim: G. Olms, 1970), 444.

122. Moshfegh, "Ignaz Goldziher and the Rise of *Islamwissenschaft*," pt. 2, p. 11.

123. Goldziher, *Mythology among the Hebrews*, 4.

124. For an exposition of Renan's thought on this subject, see Maurice Olender, *The Languages of Paradise: Race, Religion, and Philology in the Nineteenth Century* (Cambridge, MA: Harvard University Press, 1992), 51–81.

125. Moshfegh, "Ignaz Goldziher and the Rise of *Islamwissenschaft*," pt. 2, pp. 33–35.

126. Olender, *Languages of Paradise*, 71.

127. Goldziher sets out his objections to Renan in his *Mythology among the Hebrews*, 1–17. In terms of shared psychology, Goldziher put it thus: "It will then appear that the Hebrew myths, necessarily owing their existence to the same psychological operation as the Aryan or the so-called Turanian, must consequently have the same original signification as these" (14).

128. Moshfegh, "Ignaz Goldziher and the Rise of *Islamwissenschaft*," pt. 1, pp. 231–232.

129. Goldziher, *Mythology among the Hebrews*, 259.

130. In his diary, Goldziher revealed how his father scolded him for his audaciousness in publishing such a book but took the opportunity to egg him on to greater things: "In ten years you will be ashamed of this fruit of your ambition. Still, don't forget to celebrate in 1887 your twenty-fifth jubilee as a writer; until then God willing, you will accomplish great things in Israel." Quoted in Raphael Patai, *Ignaz Goldziher and His Oriental Diary: A Translation and Psychological Portrait* (Detroit: Wayne State University Press, 1987), 15–16.

131. Hungarian Jewry produced some of the foremost orientalists of the nineteenth and twentieth centuries. See Raphael Patai, *The Jews of Hungary* (Detroit: Wayne State University Press, 1996), 392–398.

132. Patai, *Oriental Diary*, 17.

133. Goldziher, *Tagebuch*, 33.

134. Like Geiger and Graetz before him, Goldziher also stressed the "etymological, grammatical, and lexical connection of Hebrew, Arabic, and Aramaic," claiming this to be a product of the "similarity of natural character of those who speak these languages." Goldziher, *Studien über Tanchûm Jerûschalmi*, 22.

135. Goldziher, *Tagebuch*, 75–76. In 1894, Hungary formally recognized Judaism as the legal equal of Christianity, thus making it possible for a Jew to obtain the rank of full professor.

136. Lawrence I. Conrad, "The Pilgrim from Pest: Goldziher's Study Tour to the Near East (1873–1874)," in *Golden Roads: Migration, Pilgrimage and Travel in Medieval and Modern Islam*, ed. Ian Richard Netton (London: Curzon Press, 1993), 110–159.

137. Goldziher, *Tagebuch*, 56–57.

138. Said, *Orientalism*, 105. At the end of his study, Said concludes that "Orientalism failed to identify with human experience" (328).

139. Quoted in Bernard Lewis's introduction to Goldziher's *Introduction to Islamic Theology and Law*, xi.

140. Goldziher, *Tagebuch*, 58–59.

141. In fact, the lecture series was such an unmitigated disaster that he abruptly canceled the series after the sixth lecture "for the sake of my honor." From that moment forward, he decided to work only on subjects to do with Arabic or Islam. Goldziher said that giving the lectures was like casting "pearls before swine." Goldziher, *Tagebuch*, 111–112. On Goldziher's intellectual debt to Geiger, see his *Tagebuch*, 123. The details of the lecture series are laid out in Máté Hidvégi, "Immanuel Löw's Reflections on 'The Essence of and Evolution of Judaism' in His Letters to Ignaz Goldziher in 1888," in Apor and Ormos, *Goldziher Memorial Conference*, 75–77.

142. Patai, *Oriental Diary*, 61.

143. Goldziher, *Tagebuch*, 71.

144. Ibid., 69–72, for a vivid description of his induction into Al-Azhar.

145. On this, see Jacob Katz, *A House Divided: Orthodoxy and Schism in Nineteenth-Century Central European Jewry* (Hanover, NH: University Press of New England, 1998). On the distinction between Hungarian Neologism and German Reform Judaism, see esp. pp. 40–47. Basically, Neologism supported aesthetic changes to the worship service, including the use of university-educated rabbis, but opposed deviations from *Halakhah*, or Jewish law.

146. Patai, *The Jews of Hungary*, 358–441.

147. Goldziher, *Tagebuch*, 80–86.

148. Ibid., 98.

149. In fact, Moritz Wahrmann was the grandson of Israel Wahrmann (1755–1826), chief rabbi of Pest. Goldziher expressed relief, if not satisfaction, on hearing news of Wahrmann's death. See Goldziher, *Tagebuch*, 154–155.

150. Ibid., 71.

151. Ibid., 86–89.

152. Patai, *Oriental Diary*, 30.

153. Conrad, "The Dervish's Disciple," 230 and 265.

154. Patai, *Oriental Diary*, 31.

155. Ibid., 91–92.

156. Ibid., 99–100.

157. As for his self-hatred, Goldziher testified to it when in 1893 he approvingly declared that Renan was "the most dangerous anti-Semite, because he is right." The quotation appears in Conrad, "Ignaz Goldziher," 155. The original reads, "Er [Renan] ist der gefährlichste Antisemit, weil er im Rechte ist." Goldziher, *Tagebuch*, 159.

158. Patai, *Oriental Diary*, 131.

159. Goldziher, *Tagebuch*, 284.

160. Goldziher in *The Jewish Encyclopedia*, vol. 6 (New York: Funk and Wagnalls, 1904), 654.

161. Goldziher, *Tagebuch*, 61.

162. Geiger's book on the Jewish roots of Islam, for example, was in fact translated into English in 1896 by Christian missionaries in Bangalore, in order to win Muslim converts. See Moshe Pearlman's "Prolegomenon," in Abraham Geiger, *Judaism and Islam* (New York: KTAV, 1970), viii.

163. Patai, *Oriental Diary*, 27–28.

164. Goldziher, *History of Classical Arabic Literature*, 159–160.

165. Bernard Lewis, *Islam in History: Ideas, People, and Events in the Middle East* (Chicago: Open Court, 1993), 137–151.

166. See Bernard Lewis's introduction to Goldziher, *Introduction to Islamic Theology and Law*, xi.

167. Said, *Orientalism*, 105.

168. Dirk Hartwig et al., eds., *"Im vollen Licht der Geschichte": Die Wissenschaft des Judentums und die Anfänge der kritischen Koranforschung* (Würzburg: Ergon, 2008).

169. Jonathan M. Hess, "Johann David Michaelis and the Colonial Imaginary: Orientalism and the Emergence of Racial Antisemitism in Eighteenth-Century Germany," *Jewish Social Studies* 6, no. 2 (Summer 2000): 65; Anna-Ruth Löwenbrück, *Judenfeindschaft im Zeitalter der Aufklärung. Eine Studie zur Vorgeschichte des modernen Antisemitismus am Beispiel des Göttinger Theologen und Orientalisten Johann David Michaelis (1717–1791)* (Frankfurt am Main: Peter Lang, 1995).

170. The terms "domination" and "hegemony" are those used by Said to characterize the relationship of Occident to Orient, as well as the attitude of orientalists toward the Muslim world.

EPILOGUE

1. Jonathan Skolnik, *Jewish Pasts, German Fictions: History, Memory, and Minority Culture in Germany, 1824–1955* (Stanford, CA: Stanford University Press, 2014), 147–175. Central European Jews in Palestine also turned to Sephardic themes in the 1930s. At the end of 1938 Max Zweig, a German-speaking refugee from Czechoslovakia, directed a wildly successful and critically acclaimed play entitled *The Marranos*. Realized by the leading theater company, Habimah, the 51 performances in its first season were attended by more than 35,000 people. The play was performed another 30 times before 1948 and the establishment of the state of Israel. See Na'amah Sheffi, "The Jewish Expulsion from Spain and the Rise of National Socialism on the Hebrew Stage," http://www.jewish-theatre.com/visitor/article_display.aspx?articleID=527. Even at this moment there were still German Jews claiming, as Heine and Herzl had claimed previously, to have come from Sephardic stock. In the fateful year of 1933, the German-Jewish author Jacob Wassermann begins his autobiography thus: "I was born and raised in Fuerth, a predominantly Protestant manufacturing city of Middle Franconia, with a large Jewish community consisting principally of artisans and tradesmen.... Jewish settlements are said to have existed there as far back as the ninth century.... [but] they began to flourish only at the end of the fifteenth, when the Jews were expelled from the neighboring city of Nuremberg. Later another stream of refugees—Jews driven out of Spain—came across the Rhine into

Franconia. Among these, I believe, were my maternal ancestors." Jacob Wassermann, *My Life as German and Jew* (New York: Coward-McCann, 1933), 4.

2. Grunwald's ethnographic work even preceded the very important development of Jewish ethnography in Russia, which saw figures such as Simon Dubnow and S. Ansky lead the way, with the establishment of the Jewish Historical and Ethnographic Society in 1908. See Jeffrey Veidlinger, *Jewish Public Culture in the Late Russian Empire* (Bloomington: Indiana University Press, 2009), 229–260.

3. Both quotations are to be found in *Ost und West* 1 (1901): 3–4.

4. See "Beethoven's erste Liebe," *Ost und West* 1 (1901): 69–70.

5. David A. Brenner, *Marketing Identities: The Invention of Jewish Ethnicity in Ost und West* (Detroit: Wayne State University Press, 1998), 17.

6. Martin Buber, "Jüdische Renaissance," *Ost und West* 1 (1901): 7–10.

7. See, for example, Arnold Zweig, *Das ostjüdische Antlitz* (Wiesbaden: Fourier, 1988); Sammy Gronemann, *Hawdoloh und Zapfenstreich* (Königsteim im Taunus, 1984); and Alfred Döblin, *Reise in Polen* (Berlin: S. Fischer, 1926). The best scholarly treatment of this phenomenon remains Steven E. Aschheim, *Brothers and Strangers: The East European Jew in German and German Jewish Consciousness, 1800–1923* (Madison: University of Wisconsin Press, 1982). See also Sander L. Gilman, "The Rediscovery of the Eastern Jews: German Jews in the East, 1890–1918," in *Jews and Germans from 1860 to 1933: A Problematic Symbiosis*, ed. David Bronsen (Heidelberg: Carl Winter, 1979), 338–365.

8. Zweig, *Das ostjüdische Antlitz*, 22.

9. Ibid., 13–14.

10. Franz Kafka, *Letter to His Father* (New York: Schocken, 1966), 79–83.

11. Michael Brenner, *The Renaissance of Jewish Culture in Weimar Germany* (New Haven, CT: Yale University Press, 1996).

12. See, for example, Karl Wilhelm Friedrich Grattenauer, *Erklärung an das Publikum über meine Schrift: Wider die Juden* (Berlin: Johann Wilhelm Schmidt, 1803), 36. Grattenauer, a pathological antisemite, accused the Jews, whom he referred to as an "Oriental, foreign people" (*orientalische Fremdlingsvolke*), of being the "most dangerous nation on earth"; he wanted them expelled from Germany or, short of this, sought the passage of a raft of discriminatory laws that would serve to ghettoize them.

13. The leading Christian pro-emancipationist voice was that of Christian Wilhelm von Dohm, but the premise of his call for emancipation was that the Jews are in some ways defective, and that emancipation would in some measure correct their deficiencies. See his *Über die Bürgerliche Verbesserung der Juden* (Berlin: Friedrich Nicolai, 1781).

Bibliography

Aarsleff, Hans. *From Locke to Saussure: Essays on the Study of Language and Intellectual History*. Minneapolis: University of Minnesota Press, 1982.

———. "The Tradition of Condillac: The Problem of the Origin of Language in the Eighteenth Century and the Debate in the Berlin Academy before Herder." In *Studies in the History of Linguistics: Traditions and Paradigms*, edited by Dell Hymes, 93–156. Bloomington: Indiana University Press, 1974.

Abrahams, Israel. "H. Graetz, the Jewish Historian." *Jewish Quarterly Review* 4 (January 1892): 165–203.

Aebi Farahmand, Adrian. *Die Sprache und das Schöne: Karl Philipp Moritz' Sprachreflexionen in Verbindung mit seiner Ästhetik*. Berlin: De Gruyter, 2012.

Almog, Shmuel. "The Racial Motif in Renan's Attitude to Jews and Judaism." In *Antisemitism through the Ages*, edited by Shmuel Almog, 255–278. Oxford: Pergamon Press, 1988.

Altmann, Alexander. *Moses Mendelssohn: A Biographical Study*. N.p.: University of Alabama Press, 1973.

Andree, Richard. *Zur Volkskunde der Juden*. Bielefeld: Velhagen & Klasing, 1881.

Appelbaum, Diana Muir. "Jewish Identity and Egyptian Revival Architecture." *Journal of Jewish Identities* 5, no. 2 (July 2012): 1–25.

Applegate, Celia. *Bach in Berlin: Nation and Culture in Mendelssohn's Revival of the St. Matthew Passion*. Ithaca, NY: Cornell University Press, 2005.

Aschheim, Steven E. *At the Edges of Liberalism: Junctions of European, German, and Jewish History*. London: Palgrave Macmillan, 2012.

———. *Brothers and Strangers: The East European Jew in German and German Jewish Consciousness, 1800–1923*. Madison: University of Wisconsin Press, 1982.

Attias, Jean-Christophe, and Jane Marie Todd. "Isaac Abravanel: Between Ethnic Memory and National Memory." *Jewish Social Studies* 2, no. 3 (1996): 137–155.

Auerbach, Berthold. *Spinoza: Ein historischer Roman*. Stuttgart: Scheible, 1837.

Auerbach, Elias. "Die jüdische Rassenfrage." *Archiv für Rassen- und Gesellschaftsbiologie* 4, no. 3 (1907): 332–361.

———. *Pionier der Verwirklichung: Ein Arzt aus Deutschland erzählt vom Beginn der zionistischen Bewegung und seiner Niederlassung in Palästina kurz nach der Jahrhundertwende*. Stuttgart: Deutsche Verlags-Anstalt, 1969.

Bacher, Wilhelm. "The Views of Jehuda Halevi concerning the Hebrew Language." *Hebraica* 8, nos. 3–4 (April–July 1892): 136–149.

Backhaus, Fritz. "'Hab'n Sie nicht den kleinen Cohn geseh'n?' Die Bilderwelt antisemitischer Postkarten vom Kaiserreich bis in die NS-Zeit." *Jahrbuch für Antisemitismusforschung* 6 (1997): 313–323.

Baer, Yitzhak F. *Galut*. New York: Schocken Books, 1947.

Bar-Am, Micha and Orna. *Painting with Light: The Photographic Aspect in the Work of E. M. Lilien*. Tel Aviv: Tel Aviv Museum of Art, 1991.

Barnard, Frederick M. "The Hebrews and Herder's Political Creed." *Modern Language Review* 54, no. 4 (1959): 533–546.

———. "Herder and Israel." *Jewish Social Studies* 28, no. 1 (1966): 25–33

Baron, Salo Wittmayer. *The Jewish Community, Its History and Structure to the American Revolution*. Philadelphia: Jewish Publication Society of America, 1942.

———. *A Social and Religious History of the Jews*. 3 vols. New York: Columbia University Press, 1937.

Bartal, Israel. "From Traditional Bilingualism to National Monolingualism." In *Hebrew in Ashkenaz*, edited by Lewis Glinert, 141–150. New York: Oxford University Press, 1993.

Barzilay, Isaac. "From Purism to Expansionism: A Chapter in the Early History of Modern Hebrew." *JANES* 11 (1979): 3–15.

Baumgarten, Alexander Gottlieb. *Theoretische Aesthetik: Die Grundlegenden Abschnitte aus der "Aesthetica" (1750/1758)*. Edited and translated by Hans Rudolf Schweitzer. Hamburg: Meiner, 1983.

Bayerdörfer, Hans-Peter, and Jens Malte Fischer. *Judenrollen: Darstellungsformen im europäischen Theater von der Restauration bis zur Zwischenkriegszeit (Conditio Judaica)*. Niemeyer: Tübingen, 2008.

Beal, Joan C. *English Pronunciation in the Eighteenth Century: Thomas Spence's Grand Repository of the English Language*. Oxford: Oxford University Press, 1999.

Beaumont, Anthony. *Zemlinsky*. Ithaca, NY: Cornell University Press, 2000.

Bedoire, Fredric. *The Jewish Contribution to Modern Architecture, 1830–1930*. Jersey City, NJ: KTAV, 2004.

Beiser, Frederick C. *The Romantic Imperative: The Concept of Early German Romanticism*. Cambridge, MA: Harvard University Press, 2003.

Ben-Ari, Nitsa. "1834: The Jewish Historical Novel Helps to Reshape the Historical Consciousness of German Jews." In *Yale Companion to Jewish Writing and Thought in German Culture, 1096–1966*, edited by Sander Gilman and Jack Zipes, 143–151. New Haven, CT: Yale University Press, 1997.

———. *Romanze mit der Vergangenheit: Der deutsch-jüdische historische Roman des 19. Jahrhunderts und seine Bedeutung für die Entstehung einer jüdischen Nationalliteratur*. Tübingen: Max Niemeyer Verlag, 2006.

Benbassa, Esther, and Aron Rodrigue. *Sephardi Jewry: A History of the Judeo-Spanish Community, 14th–20th Centuries*. Berkeley: University of California Press, 2000.

Benedict, Ruth. "Race: What It Is Not." In *Theories of Race and Racism: A Reader*, edited by Les Back and John Solomos, 113–118. London: Routledge, 2009.

Ben-Gurion, David. *Recollections*. London: MacDonald, 1970.

Bennett, Benjamin. *Beyond Theory: Eighteenth-Century German Literature and the Poetics of Irony*. Ithaca, NY: Cornell University Press, 1993.

Ben-Sasson, H. H. "The Generation of the Spanish Exiles Considers Its Fate." In *Binah: Studies in Jewish History, Culture, and Thought* 1 (1989): 83–98.

Ben-Yehuda, Eliezer. *Ha-khalom ve-shivro*. Edited by Reuven Sivan. Jerusalem: Mossad Bialik, 1978.

Berkowitz, Michael. *The Jewish Self-Image: American and British Perspectives, 1881–1939*. London: Reaktion Books, 2000.

Berlin, Isaiah. *The Roots of Romanticism*. Princeton, NJ: Princeton University Press, 2001.

Berman, Russell A. *Enlightenment or Empire: Colonial Discourse in German Culture*. Lincoln: University of Nebraska Press, 1998.

Beutin, Wolfgang. "Historischer und Zeit-Roman." In *Hansers Sozialgeschichte der deutschen Literatur vom 16. Jahrhundert bis zur Gegenwart*, vol. 5, edited by Gert Sautermeister and Ulrich Schmid, 175–194. Munich: Hanser, 1998.

Biale, David. "Jewish Consumer Culture in Historical and Contemporary Perspective." In *Longing, Belonging, and the Making of Jewish Consumer Culture*, edited by Gideon Reuveni and Nils Roemer, 23–38. Leiden: Brill, 2010.

———. "Shabbtai Zvi and the Seductions of Jewish Orientalism." *Jerusalem Studies in Jewish Thought* 16–17 (2001): 85–110.

"Biographie des Herrn Marcus Herz." *Sulamith* 3 (1811): 77–97.

Bitzan, Amos. "The Problem of Pleasure: Disciplining the German Jewish Reading Revolution, 1770–1870." PhD diss., University of California–Berkeley, 2011.

Blechmann, Bernhard. *Ein Beitrag zur Anthropologie der Juden*. Dorpat: W. Just, 1882.

Bloom, Etan. "Arthur Ruppin and the Production of the Modern Hebrew Culture." PhD diss., University of Tel Aviv, 2008.

Blumenkranz, Bernhard. *Juden und Judentum in der mittelalterlichen Kunst*. Stuttgart: W. Kohlhammer, 1965.

Bodian, Miriam. *Hebrews of the Portuguese Nation: Conversos and Community in Early Modern Amsterdam*. Bloomington: Indiana University Press, 1999.

Boelich, Walter, ed. *Der Berliner Antisemitismusstreit*. Frankfurt am Main: Insel Verlag, 1988.

Bondi, M. "Beitrag zur Geschichte der Herkunft des Gelehrten Hartwig Wessely." *Sulamith* 15, no. 1 (1817): 94–99.

Bonebakker, Seeger A. "Poets and Critics in the Third Century A.H." In *Logic in Classical Islamic Culture*, edited by G. E. von Grunebaum, 85–111. Wiesbaden: Otto Harrassowitz, 1970.

Botelho, Angela. "Modern Marranism and the German-Jewish Experience: The Persistence of Jewish Identity in Conversion." M.A. thesis, Graduate Theological Seminary, Berkeley, 2013.

Botstein, Leon. "The Aesthetics of Assimilation and Affirmation: Reconstructing the Career of Felix Mendelssohn." In *Mendelssohn and His World*, edited by R. Larry Todd, 5–42. Princeton, NJ: Princeton University Press, 1991.

Bourdieu, Pierre. *Distinction: A Social Critique of the Judgment of Taste*. Cambridge, MA: Harvard University Press, 1984.

Breckman, Warren. *European Romanticism: A Brief History with Documents*. Boston: Bedford/St. Martins, 2008.

Brenner, David A. *Marketing Identities: The Invention of Jewish Ethnicity in Ost und West*. Detroit: Wayne State University Press, 1998.

Brenner, Michael. "The Construction and Deconstruction of a Hero: Moses Mendelssohn's Afterlife in Early-Twentieth-Century Germany." In *Mediating Modernity: Challenges and Trends in the Jewish Encounter with the Modern World. Essays in Honor of Michael A. Meyer*, edited by Lauren B. Strauss and Michael Brenner, 274–289. Detroit: Wayne State University Press, 2008.

———. *Prophets of the Past: Interpreters of Jewish History*. Princeton, NJ: Princeton University Press, 2010.

———. *The Renaissance of Jewish Culture in Weimar Germany*. New Haven, CT: Yale University Press, 1996.

Brenner, Michael, and Gideon Reuveni, eds. *Emancipation through Muscles: Jews and Sports in Europe*. Lincoln: University of Nebraska Press, 2006.

Breslauer, Emil. "Die Einweihung der neuen Synagoge zu Berlin." *Allgemeine Zeitung des Judentums* 39 (1866): 622–624.

Breuer, Edward. "Naphtali Herz Wessely and the Cultural Dislocations of an Eighteenth-Century Maskil." In *New Perspectives on the Haskalah*, edited by Shmuel Feiner and David Sorkin, 27–47. London: Littman Library of Jewish Civilization, 2001.

Brocke, Michael, and Christiane E. Müller, eds. *Haus des Lebens: Jüdische Friedhöfe in Deutschland*. Reclam: Leipzig, 2001.

Buber, Martin "Jüdische Renaissance." *Ost und West* 1 (1901): 7–10.

Buchwalter, Andrew. "Is Hegel's Philosophy of History Eurocentric?" In *Hegel and History*, edited by Will Dudley, 87–110. Albany: State University of New York Press, 2009.

Bush, Olga. "The Architecture of Jewish Identity: The Neo-Islamic Central Synagogue of New York." *Journal of the Society of Architectural Historians* 63, no. 2 (June 2004): 180–201.

Butler, E. M. *The Tyranny of Greece over Germany: A Study of the Influence Exercised by Greek Art and Poetry over the Great German Writers of the Eighteenth, Nineteenth and Twentieth Centuries*. Cambridge: Cambridge University Press, 1935.

Cardoso, José Luis, and António de Vasconcelos Noqueira. "Isaac de Pinto (1717–1787) and the Jewish Problems: Apologetic Letters to Voltaire and Diderot." *History of European Ideas* 33, no. 4 (2007): 476–487.

Carrott, Richard G. *The Egyptian Revival: Its Sources, Monuments, and Meaning, 1808–1858*. Berkeley: University of California Press, 1978.

Chamberlain, Houston Stewart. *Foundations of the Nineteenth Century*. London: John Lane, The Bodley Head, 1912.

Charbonnier, Azra. *Carl Heinrich Eduard Knoblauch (1801–1865): Architekt des Bürgertums*. Munich: Deutscher Kunstverlag, 2007.

Chevalier, Tracy. ed. *Encyclopedia of the Essay*. Chicago: Fitzroy Dearborn Publishers, 1997.

Christensen, Torben, and William R. Hutchison, eds. *Missionary Ideologies in the Imperialist Era, 1880–1920*. Aarhus, Denmark: Aros, 1982.

Cloeren, Hermann J. *Language and Thought: German Approaches to Analytic Philosophy in the 18th and 19th Centuries*. Berlin: Walter de Gruyter, 1988.

Coenen Snyder, Saskia. *Building a Public Judaism: Synagogues and Jewish Identity in Nineteenth-Century Europe*. Cambridge, MA: Harvard University Press, 2013.

Cohen, Richard I. *Jewish Icons: Art and Society in Modern Europe*. Berkeley: University of California Press, 1998.

Cohen-Mushlin, Aliza, and Harmen H. Thies, eds. *Jewish Architecture in Europe*. Petersberg: Imhof, 2010.

Collins, Peter. *Changing Ideals in Modern Architecture, 1750–1850*. Montreal: McGill-Queen's University Press, 1998.

"Concurrenz-Eröffnung für Pläne zu einer neuen Synagoge in Berlin." *Zeitschrift für Bauwesen* 7 (1857): 448–450.

Conner, Patrick. *Oriental Architecture in the West*. London: Thames and Hudson, 1979.

Conrad, Lawrence I. "The Dervish's Disciple: On the Personality and Intellectual Milieu of the Young Ignaz Goldziher." *Journal of the Royal Asiatic Society* 2 (1990): 225–266.

———. "Ignaz Goldziher on Ernest Renan: From Orientalist Philology to the Study of Islam." In *The Jewish Discovery of Islam*, edited by Martin Kramer, 137–180. Tel Aviv: Moshe Dayan Center for Middle Eastern and African Studies, 1999.

———. "The Pilgrim from Pest: Goldziher's Study Tour to the Near East (1873–1874)." In *Golden Roads: Migration, Pilgrimage and Travel in Medieval and Modern Islam*, edited by Ian Richard Netton, 110–159. London: Curzon Press, 1993.

Corbin, Alain. *Time, Desire, and Horror: Towards a History of the Senses*. Cambridge, UK: Polity Press, 1995.

———. *Village Bells: Sound and Meaning in the Nineteenth-Century French Countryside*. New York: Columbia University Press, 1998.

Curl, James Stevens. *The Egyptian Revival: Ancient Egypt as the Inspiration for Design Motifs in the West*. New York: Routledge, 2005.

———. *Victorian Architecture: Diversity and Invention*. Reading, UK: Spire Books, 2007.

Danby, Miles. *Moorish Style*. London: Phaedon Press, 1995.

David-Sirocko, Karen. "Anglo-German Interconnexions during the Gothic Revival: A Case Study from the Work of Georg Gottlob Ungewitter (1820–64)." *Architectural History* 41 (1998): 153–178.

Davies, Martin L. *Identity or History? Marcus Herz and the End of the Enlightenment*. Detroit: Wayne State University Press, 1995.

De Breffny, Brian. *The Synagogue*. New York: Macmillan, 1978.

Delitzsch, Franz. *Zur Geschichte der jüdischen Poësie vom abschluss der Heiligen Schriften alten Bundes bis auf die neueste Zeit*. Leipzig: K. Tauchnitz, 1836.

Dickenson, Gregory A., and Aaron J. West. "Imperial Laws and Letters Involving Religion AD 311–364." http://www.fourthcentury.com/index.php/imperial-laws-chart.

Dietler, Michael. "'Our Ancestors the Gauls': Archaeology, Ethnic Nationalism, and the Manipulation of Celtic Identity in Modern Europe." *American Anthropologist* 96, no. 3 (1994): 584–605.

Dittmar, Peter. *Die Darstellung der Juden in der populären Kunst zur Zeit der Emanzipation*. Munich: K. G. Sauer, 1992.

Döblin, Alfred. *Reise in Polen*. Berlin: S. Fischer, 1926.

Dohm, Christian Wilhelm. *Ueber die bürgerliche Verbesserung der Juden*. Berlin: F. Nicolai, 1781.

Döhmer, Klaus. *"In welchem Style sollen wir bauen?" Architekturtheorie zwischen Klassizismus und Jugendstil*. Munich: Prestel-Verlag, 1976.

Dubin, Lois C. *The Port Jews of Habsburg Trieste: Absolutist Politics and Enlightenment Culture*. Stanford, CA: Stanford University Press, 1999.

Du Bois, W.E.B. *Souls of Black Folk*. Oxford: Oxford University Press, 2007.

Dynner, Glenn. *Men of Silk: The Hasidic Conquest of Polish Jewish Society*. Oxford: Oxford University Press, 2006.

Eagleton, Terry. *The Ideology of the Aesthetic*. Oxford: Blackwell, 2000.

Edwards, Elizabeth, ed. *Anthropology and Photography, 1860–1920*. New Haven, CT: Yale University Press, 1992.

Efrati, Nathan. *Mi leshon Yehudim li leshon uma: Ha-dibur ha-Ivri be-Eretz Yisra'el be-shanim 1882–1922*. Jerusalem: Akademyah la-lashon ha-'Ivrit, 2004.

Efron, John M. *Defenders of the Race: Jewish Doctors and Race Science in Fin-de-Siècle Europe*. New Haven, CT: Yale University Press, 1994.

———. *Medicine and the German Jews: A History*. New Haven, CT: Yale University Press, 2001.

———. "Scientific Racism and the Mystique of Sephardic Racial Superiority." *Leo Baeck Institute Year Book* 38 (1993): 75–96.

"Einweihung der neuen Synagoge." *Sulamith* 7, no. 1 (1826): 210–216.

"Einweihung des neuen Israelitischen Bethauses zu Wien. am 9. April 1826 (2 Nissan 5586)." *Sulamith* 7, no. 1 (1826): 267–276 and 290–297.

Eisler, Colin. "Wagner's Three Synagogues." *Artibus et Historiae* 25, no. 50 (2004): 9–15.

Eisler, Max. "Der Seitenstetten Tempel." *Menorah* 3 (1926): 149–157.

Eldar, Ilan. "The Grammatical Literature of Medieval Ashkenazic Jewry." In *Hebrew in Ashkenaz*, edited by Lewis Glinert, 245–266. New York: Oxford University Press, 1993.

Elias, Norbert. *The Civilizing Process*. Vol. 2. New York: Panethon Books, 1982.

Eliav, Mordechai. *Jüdische Erziehung in Deutschland im Zeitalter der Aufklärung und Emanzipation*. Münster: Waxmann, 2001.

Elior, Rachel. "Rabbi Nathan Adler and the Frankfurt Pietists: Pietist Groups in Eastern and Central Europe during the Eighteenth Century." In *Jüdische Kultur in Frankfurt am Main, von den Anfangen bis zur Gegenwart*, edited by Karl Erich Grozinger, 135–177. Wiesbaden: Harrassowitz Verlag, 1997.

Elyada, Aya. *A Goy Who Speaks Yiddish: Christians and the Jewish Language in Early Modern Germany*. Stanford, CA: Stanford University Press, 2012.

Endelman, Todd M. "Benjamin Disraeli and the Myth of Sephardi Superiority." *Jewish History* 10, no. 2 (1996): 21–35.

———. *Jewish Apostasy in the Modern World*. New York: Holmes & Meier, 1987.

———. *The Jews of Georgian England, 1714–1830: Tradition and Change in a Liberal Society*. Philadelphia: Jewish Publication Society of America, 1979.

Enzenbach, Isabel. "Stamps, Stickers and Stigmata. A Social Practice of Antisemitism Presented in a Slide-Show." *Quest. Issues in Contemporary Jewish History. Journal of Fondazione CDEC*, no. 3 (July 2012). www.quest-cdecjournal.it/focus.php?id=307.

Enzenbach, Isabel, and Wolfgang Haney, eds. *Alltagskultur des Antisemitismus im Kleinformat. Vignetten der Sammlung Wolfgang Haney ab 1880*. Berlin: Metropol Verlag, 2012.

Ettinger, Shmuel. "Mifalo shel historiografi shel Graetz." In *Historiyonim ve-Askolot Historiyot*, 84–92. Jerusalem: ha-Hevrah ha-historit ha-Yisre'elit, 1963.

Euchel, Isaac. "Forward." *Ha-Me'assef* 2 (1784): n.p.

Even, Eliezer, and Benjamin Ravid. *The Jews of Szekesfehervar & Its Environs*. Translation of *Z'chor-Emelkezz-Remember Yehdei Szekesfehervar V'Hasviva*. Jerusalem: n.p., 1997.

Federbusch, Shimon. *Hokhmat Yisra'el be-Ma'arav Eropah*. Jerusalem: Ogen, 1958.

Feiner, Shmuel. "From Renaissance to Revolution: The Eighteenth Century in Jewish History." In *Sepharad in Ashkenaz: Medieval Knowledge and Eighteenth-Century Enlightened Jewish Discourse*, edited by Resianne Fontaine, Andrea Schatz, and

Irene E. Zwiep, 1–11. Amsterdam: 2007 Royal Netherlands Academy of Arts and Sciences, 2007.

———. *Haskalah and History: The Emergence of a Modern Jewish Historical Consciousness*. Portland, OR: Littman Library of Jewish Civilization, 2002.

———. *The Jewish Enlightenment*. Philadelphia: University of Pennyslvania Press, 2004.

———. *Moses Mendelssohn: Sage of Modernity*. New Haven, CT: Yale University Press, 2010.

———. *The Origins of Jewish Secularization in Eighteenth-Century Europe*. Philadelphia: University of Pennsylvania Press, 2010.

Feiner, Shmuel, and David Sorkin, eds. *New Perspectives on the Haskalah*. London: Littman Library of Jewish Civilization, 2001.

Fendri, Mounir. *Halbmond, Kreuz und Schibboleth: Heinrich Heine und der islamische Orient*. Hamburg: Hoffmann und Campe, Heinrich-Heine-Verlag, 1980.

Fenves, Peter. "Imagining an Inundation of Australians, or, Leibniz on the Principles of Grace and Race." In *Race and Racism in Modern Philosophy*, edited by Andrew Valls, 73–88. Ithaca, NY: Cornell University Press, 2005.

Ferber, Michael. *Romanticism: A Very Short Introduction*. New York: Oxford University Press, 2010.

Field, Geoffrey C. *Evangelist of Race: The Germanic Vision of Houston Stewart Chamberlain*. New York: Columbia University Press, 1981.

Fingerhut, Karlheinz. "Spanische Spiegel: Heinrich Heines Verwendung spanischer Geschichte und Literatur zur Selbstreflexion des Juden und des Dichters." *Heine Jahrbuch* 31 (1992): 106–136.

Fishberg, Maurice. *Di gefar fun di idishe natsyonalistishe bevegung: In ireh farshidene formen vi di rassenfrage, Tsien-Tsienizm, teritorializm, Ahad-ha-'Am-kulturizm, natsyonalkulturele-oytonomye*. New York: M. Mayzel, 1906.

———. *The Jews: A Study of Race and Environment*. New York: Walter Scott, 1911.

———. *Die Rassenmerkmale der Juden: Eine Einführung in ihre Anthropologie*. Munich: Ernst Reinhardt, 1913.

Fishman, David E. *Russia's First Modern Jews: The Jews of Shklov*. New York: New York University Press, 1996.

Fleming, Katherine. *Greece: A Jewish History*. Princeton, NJ: Princeton University Press, 2008.

Förster, Ludwig. "Das israelitische Bethaus in Wien." *Allgemeine Bauzeitung* 24 (1859): 13–16.

———. "Plan der Bauzeitung und Aufforderung an Männer vom Fache, dieselbe durch Mittheilungen zu bereichern." *Allgemeine Bauzeitung* 1 (1836): 1–3.

———. "Ueber Synagogenbau." *Allgemeine Zeitung des Judentums* 23 (1858): 314–316.

Fränkel, David. "Gallerie schädlicher Mißbräuche, unanständiger Convenienzen und absurder Ceremonien unter den Juden. Ein paar Worte über Denk- und Pressefreiheit." *Sulamith* 1, no. 1 (1806): 222–244 and 319–331.

Frankel, Ernst. "David Friedländer und seine Zeit." *Zeitschrift für die Geschichte der Juden in Deutschland* 6 (1935): 65–77.

Frankel, Jonathan. *The Damascus Affair: "Ritual Murder," Politics, and the Jews in 1840*. Cambridge: Cambridge University Press, 1997.

Frankel, Ludwig August. "Geschichte Diego d'Aguilar's." *Allgemeine Zeitung des Judentums* 50 (1854): 630–634 and 51 (1854): 656–661.

Franzos, Karl Emil. "Every Country Has the Jews It Deserves." In *The Jew in the Modern World*, edited by Paul Mendes-Flohr and Jehuda Reinharz, 253–254. Oxford: Oxford University Press, 1995.

Friedländer, David. *Aktenstücke, die Reform der Jüdischen Kolonieen in den Preussischen Staaten betreffend.* Berlin: Voß, 1793.

———. *Ueber die Verbesserung der Israeliten im Konigreich Pohlen: Ein von der Regierung daselbst im Jahr 1816 abgefordertes Gutachten.* Berlin: Nicolaische Buchhandlung, 1819.

Friesel, Evyatar. *Atlas of Modern Jewish History.* Oxford: Oxford University Press, 1990.

Fuchs, Eduard. *Die Juden in der Karitatur: Ein Beitrag zur Kulturgeschichte.* Munich: Albert Langen, 1921.

Fück, Johann. *Die arabischen Studien in Europa bis in den Anfang des 20. Jahrhunderts.* Leipzig: O. Harrassowitz, 1955.

Gallagher, Nancy Elizabeth. *Approaches to the History of the Middle East: Interviews with Leading Middle East Historians.* Reading, UK: Ithaca Press, 1994.

Gans, Eduard. "A Society to Further Jewish Integration." In *The Jew in the Modern World: A Documentary History*, edited by Paul Mendes-Flohr and Jehuda Reinharz, 240–243. New York: Oxford University Press, 2011.

Gardt, Andreas. *Nation und Sprache: Die Diskussion ihres Verhältnisses in Geschichte und Gegenwart.* Berlin: De Gruyter, 2000.

Gauding, Daniela. "Jüdische Ritualbäder in Berlin." In *Beiträge zur jüdischen Architektur in Berlin*, edited by Daniela Gauding and Aliza Cohen-Mushlin, 33–45. Petersberg: Imhof, 2009.

Gauding, Daniela, and Aliza Cohen-Mushlin, eds. *Beiträge zur jüdischen Architektur in Berlin.* Petersberg: Imhof, 2009.

Gazdar, Kaedan. *Herrscher im Paradies: Fürst Franz und das Gartenreich Dessau-Wörlitz.* Berlin: Aufbau-Verlag, 2006.

Geiger, Abraham. "Alte Romantik, neue Reaktion." *Jüdische Zeitschrift für Wissenschaft und Leben* 1, no. 4 (1862): 245–252.

———. *Divan des Castiliers, Abu'-l-Hassan Juda ha-Levi.* Breslau: J. U. Kern, 1851.

———. *Judaism and Islam.* Edited by Moshe Pearlman. New York: KTAV, 1970.

———. *Das Judenthum und seine Geschichte in zehn Vorlesungen: Von dem Anfange des dreizehnten bis zum Ende des sechszehnten Jahrhunderts.* 3 vols. Breslau: Schletter, 1865–1871.

———. "Der Kampf christlicher Theologen gegen die bürgerliche Gleichstellung der Juden, namentlich mit Bezug auf Anton Theodor Hartmann." *Wissenschaftliche Zeitschrift für Jüdische Theologie* 1, no. 1 (1835): 52–67; 1, no. 3 (1835): 340–357, 2, no. 1 (1836): 78–92, and 2, no. 3 (1836): 446–473.

———. *Urschrift und Uebersetzungen der Bibel in ihrer Abhängigkeit von der innern Entwickelung des Judenthums.* Breslau: J. Hainauer, 1857.

———. *Was hat Muhammad aus dem Judenthume aufgenommen?* Bonn: privately printed, 1833.

Geiger, Ludwig. *Abraham Geiger: Leben und Lebenswerk.* Berlin: Georg Reimer, 1910.

———, ed. *Abraham Geiger's Nachgelassene Schriften.* 5 vols. Berlin: Louis Gerschel, 1875.

Genée, Pierre. *Wiener Synagogen, 1825–1938*. Vienna: Löcker Verlag, 1987.

Gerber, Jane. "Towards an Understanding of the Term: 'The Golden Age' as an Historical Reality." In *The Heritage of the Jews of Spain*, edited by Aviva Doron, 15–22. Tel Aviv: Levinsky College of Education Publishing House, 1994.

Gerhard, Anselm. *Musik und Ästhetik im Berlin Moses Mendelssohns*. Tübingen: Max Neimeyer Verlag, 1999.

Germann, Georg. *Gothic Revival in Europe and Britain: Sources, Influences and Ideas*. Cambridge, MA: MIT Press, 1973.

Gernsheim, Helmut. *The History of Photography from the Camera Obscura to the Beginning of the Modern Era*. London: Thames & Hudson, 1969.

Gesenius, Wilhelm. *Gesenius' Hebrew Grammar*. Oxford: Clarendon Press, 1910.

Gessinger, Joachim. *Sprache und Bürgertum: Zur Sozialgeschichte sprachlicher Verkehrsformen im Deutschland des 18. Jahrhunderts*. Stuttgart: Metzler, 1980.

Gibb, H.A.R. "Arab Poet and Arabic Philologist." *Bulletin of the School of Oriental and African Studies* 12, nos. 3–4 (1947–1948): 574–578.

Gilman, Sander L. *Fat: A Cultural History of Obesity*. Cambridge, UK: Polity, 2008.

———. *Jewish Self-Hatred: Anti-Semitism and the Hidden Language of the Jews*. Baltimore: Johns Hopkins University Press, 1986.

———. *Making the Body Beautiful: A Cultural History of Aesthetic Surgery*. Princeton, NJ: Princeton University Press, 1999.

———. "'Die Rasse ist nicht schön—Nein, wir Juden sind keine hübsche Rasse!' Der schöne und der häßliche Rasse." In *Der Schejne Jid: Das Bild des "jüdischen Körpers" in Mythos und Ritual*, edited by Sander L. Gilman, 57–74. Vienna: Picus, 1998.

———. "The Rediscovery of the Eastern Jews: German Jews in the East, 1890–1918." In *Jews and Germans from 1860 to 1933: A Problematic Symbiosis*, edited by David Bronsen, 338–365. Heidelberg: Carl Winter, 1979.

———, ed. *Der Schejne Jid: Das Bild des "jüdischen Körpers" in Mythos und Ritual*. Vienna: Picus, 1998.

Ginsborg, Hannah. "Kant's Aesthetics and Teleology." *The Stanford Encyclopedia of Philosophy* (Fall 2008 Edition). http://plato.stanford.edu/archives/fall2008/entries/kant-aesthetics/.

Gobineau, Arthur de, comte. *The Inequality of the Human Races*. New York: G. P. Putnam's Sons, 1915.

Godefroid, Susanne. *Bürgerliche Ideologie und Bildungspolitik das Bildungswesen in Preußen vom Ausgang des 18. Jahrhunderts bis zur bürgerlichen Revolution 1848/49. Eine historisch-materialistische Analyse seiner Entstehungsbedingungen*. Giessen: Achenbach, 1974.

Goldfarb, Michael. *Emancipation*. New York: Simon and Schuster, 2009.

Goldstein, Bluma. "A Politics and Poetics of Diaspora: Heine's *Hebräische* Melodien." In *Diasporas and Exiles: Varieties of Jewish Identity*, edited by Howard Wettstein, 60–77. Berkeley: University of California Press, 2002.

Goldziher, Ignaz. *Abhandlungen zur arabischen Philologie*. Leiden: Brill, 1896.

———. *Ignaz Goldziher: Gesammelte Schriften*. Vol. 4. Edited by Joseph Desomogyi. Hildesheim: G. Olms, 1970.

———. *Introduction to Islamic Theology and Law*. Translated by Andras and Ruth Hamori. Princeton, NJ: Princeton University Press, 1981.

———. "Die islamische und die jüdische Philosophie." In *Allgemeine Geschichte der Philosophie*, edited by Paul Hinneberg, 45–77. Berlin: B. G. Teubner, 1909.

———. *Muhammedanischer aberglaube über gedächtnisskraft und vergesslichkeit, mit parallelen aus der jüdischen Literatur*. Berlin: H. Itzkowski, 1903.

———. *Muhammedanische Studien*. Halle: Max Niemeyer, 1889–90.

———. *Mythology among the Hebrews and Its Historical Development*. Translated by Russell Martineau. New York: Cooper Square, 1967.

———. *On the History of Grammar among the Arabs: An Essay in Literary History*. Translated and edited by Kinga Dévényi and Tamás Iványi. Amsterdam: J. Benjamins, 1994.

———. *Die Richtungen der islamischen Koranauslegung*. Leiden: E. J. Brill, 1952.

———. *A Short History of Classical Arabic Literature*. Hildesheim: Georg Olms, 1966.

———. *Studien über Tanchûm Jerûschalmi*. Leipzig: List and Franke, 1870.

———. *Tagebuch*. Leiden: E. J. Brill, 1978.

Gootzé, Marjanne E. "Posing for Posterity: The Representations and Portrayals of Henriette Herz as the 'Beautiful Jewess.'" In *Body Dialectics in the Age of Goethe*, edited by Marianne Henn and Holger A. Pausch, 67–96. Amsterdam: Rodopi, 2003.

Graetz, Heinrich. *Geschichte der Juden*. 11 vols. Leipzig: Oskar Leiner, 1897–1911.

———. *History of the Jews*. 6 vols. Philadelphia: Jewish Publication Society, 1945.

———. *The Structure of Jewish History and Other Essays*. Edited by Ismar Schorsch. New York: Jewish Theological Seminary, 1975.

Graham-Brown, Sarah. *Images of Women: The Portrayal of Women in Photography of the Middle East 1860–1950*. London: Quartet, 1988.

Grattenauer, Karl Wilhelm Friedrich. *Erklärung an das Publikum über meine Schrift: Wider die Juden*. Berlin: Johann Wilhelm Schmidt, 1803.

Grätz, Hirsch. *Gnosticismus und Judenthum*. Krotoschin: B. L. Monasch, 1846.

Green, Roger Lancelyn, ed. *The Works of Lewis Carroll*. London: Hamlyn, 1965.

Grégoire, Henri Jean-Baptiste. *Essai sur la régénération physique, morale et politique des Juifs*. Metz: Impr. de C. Lamort, 1789.

Grimm, Alfred, and Isabel Grimm-Stadelman. *Theatrum Hieroglyphicum: Ägyptisierende Bildwerke im Geiste des Barock*. Dettelbach: Röll, 2011.

Grimm, Harmut. "Moses Mendelssohns Beitrag zur Musikästhetik und Carl Phillip Emanuel Bachs Fantasie-Prinzip." In *Musik und Ästhetik im Berlin Moses Mendelssohns*, edited by Anselm Gerhard, 165–186. Tübingen: Max Neimeyer Verlag, 1999.

Grimschitz, Bruno. *Die Wiener Ringstraße*. Berlin: Angelsachsen Verlag, 1938.

Gronemann, Sammy. *Hawdoloh und Zapfenstreich*. Königstein im Taunus: Jüdischer Verlag Athenäum, 1984.

Grossman, Jeffrey A. *The Discourse on Yiddish in Germany: From the Enlightenment to the Second Empire*. Rochester, NY: Camden House, 2000.

———. "Heine and Jewish Culture: The Poetics of Appropriation." In *A Companion to the Works of Heinrich Heine*, edited by Roger F. Cook, 251–283. Rochester, NY: Camden House, 2002.

Grote, Ludwig, ed. *Die deutsche Stadt im 19. Jahrhundert. Stadtplannung und Baugestaltung im industriellen Zeitalter*. Munich: Prestel Verlag, 1974.

Grunwald, Max. "Durch Spanien und Portugal: Reiserrinerungen an das Frühjahr 1929." *Menorah* 9, nos. 3–4 (1931): 99–118.

————. "Namen und Mundartliches: Sprache der Juden." *Mitteilungen der Gesellschaft für Jüdische Volkskunde* 1 (1898): 17–18.

————. "Wie baut man Synagogen?" *Allgemeine Zeitung des Judentums* (1901): 115–117.

Gutzkow, Karl. *Dramatische Werke*. Vol. 5. Leipzig: Weber, 1847.

Guyer, Paul. "18th Century German Aesthetics." *The Stanford Encyclopedia of Philosophy* (Fall 2008 Edition). http://plato.stanford.edu/archives/fall2008/entries/aesthetics-18th-german.

Haber, Peter. *Zwischen jüdischer Tradition und Wissenschaft: Der ungarische orientalist Ignac Goldziher (1850–1921)*. Cologne: Böhlau, 2006.

HaCohen, Ruth. *The Music Libel against the Jews*. New Haven, CT: Yale University Press, 2011.

Hagen, William W. *Germans, Poles, and Jews: The Nationality Conflict in the Prussian East, 1772–1914*. Chicago: University of Chicago Press, 1980.

Halevi, Judah. *Book of the Kuzari*. Translated by Hartwig Hirschfeld. New York: Pardes Publishing House, 1946.

Halevi-Wise, Yael, ed. *Sephardism: Spanish Jewish History and the Modern Literary Imagination*. Stanford, CA: Stanford University Press, 2012.

Hamilton, Alastair. "Western Attitudes to Islam in the Enlightenment." *Middle Eastern Studies* 3 (1999): 69–85.

Hammermeister, Kai. *The German Aesthetic Tradition*. Cambridge: Cambridge University Press, 2002.

Hammer-Schenk, Harold. "Die Architektur der Synagoge von 1780 bis 1933." In *Die Architektur der Synagoge*, edited by Hans-Peter Schwarz, 157–286. Frankfurt: DAM, 1988.

————. "Edwin Oppler's Theorie des Synagogenbaus. Emanzipationsversuch durch Architektur." *Hannoversche Geschichtsblätter* (1979): 99–117.

————. *Synagogen in Deutschland: Geschichte einer Baugattung im 19. und 20. Jahrhundert, 1780–1933*. 2 vols. Hamburg: H. Christians, 1981.

Hanisch, Ludmila, ed. *"Machen Sie doch unseren Islam nicht gar zu schlecht": Der Briefwechsel der Islamwissenschaftler Ignaz Goldziher und Martin Hartmann, 1894–1914*. Wiesbaden: Harrassowitz, 2000.

Hannaford, Ivan. *Race: A History of an Idea in the West*. Washington, DC: Woodrow Wilson Center Press, 1996.

Haramati, Shlomo. *Ivrit safa meduberet*. Tel Aviv: Misrad ha-bitakhon, 2000.

Harker, Richard, Cheleen Mahar, and Chris Wilkes, eds. *An Introduction to the Work of Pierre Bourdieu: The Practice of Theory*. London: Palgrave Macmillan, 1990.

Harloe, Katherine. *Winckelmann and the Invention of Antiquity: History and Aesthetics in the Age of Altertumswissenschaft*. Oxford: Oxford University Press, 2013.

Harshav, Benjamin. *Language in Time of Revolution*. Berkeley: University of California Press, 1993.

Hart, Mitchell. "Picturing Jews: Iconography and Race Science." In *Studies in Contemporary Jewry*, vol. 11, edited by Peter Medding, 159–175. Oxford: Oxford University Press, 1995.

Hartwig, Dirk, Walter Homolka, Michael J. Marx, and Angelika Neuwirth, eds. *"Im vollen Licht der Geschichte": Die Wissenschaft des Judentums und die Anfänge der kritischen Koranforschung*. Würzburg: Ergon, 2008.

Hau, Michael. *The Cult of Health and Beauty in Germany: A Social History, 1890–1930*. Chicago: University of Chicago Press, 2003.

Haupt, Klaus-Werner. *Johann Winckelmann. Begründer der klassischen Archäologie und modernen Kunstwissenschaften*. Wiesbaden: Marixverlag, 2014.

Heine, Heinrich. "Donna Clara." http://www.staff.uni-mainz.de/pommeren/Gedichte/BdL/DonnaClara.html.

———. *Heinrich Heine's Sämtliche Werke*. Edited by Adolf Strodtmann. Vol. 19. Hamburg: Hoffmann and Campe, 1876.

———. *The Poetry and Prose of Heinrich Heine*. Edited by Frederic Ewen. New York: Citadel Press, 1948.

———. *Sämtliche Schriften*. Edited by Klaus Briegleb. 6 vols. Munich: Carl Hanser, 1968.

Heinemann, Manfred. *Schule im Vorfeld der Verwaltung: Die Entwicklung der preussischen Unterrichtsverwaltung von 1771–1800*. Göttingen: Vandenhoeck und Ruprecht, 1974.

Herder, Johann Gottfried. *The Spirit of Hebrew Poetry*. Translated by James Marsh. Burlington, VT: Edward Smith, 1833.

Herrmann, Wolfgang. *Deutsche Baukunst des XIX. und XX. Jahrhunderts*. Vol. 1. Breslau: Ferdinand Hirt, 1932.

Hertz, Deborah. *How Jews Became Germans: The History of Conversion and Assimilation in Berlin*. New Haven, CT: Yale University Press, 2007.

———. *Jewish High Society in Old Regime Berlin*. New Haven, CT: Yale University Press, 1988.

Hertz, Friedrich. *Race and Civilization*. New York: KTAV, 1971.

Herz, Henriette de Lemos. *Henriette Herz in Erinnerungen Briefen und Zeugnissen*. Edited by Rainer Schmitz. Frankfurt am Main: Insel Verlag, 1984.

Herzl, Theodor. *The Diaries of Theodor Herzl*. Edited and translated by Marvin Lowenthal. London: V. Gollancz, 1958.

Heschel, Abraham Joshua. *Don Jizchak Abravanel*. Berlin: E. Reiss, 1937.

Heschel, Susannah. *Abraham Geiger and the Jewish Jesus*. Chicago: University of Chicago Press, 1998.

Heß, Dr. "Über den Einfluß der Sprache auf's Denken und die Methode des Unterrichts in der Muttersprache." *Sulamith* 7, no. 1 (1825): 232–261.

Hess, Jonathan M. *Germans, Jews and the Claims of Modernity*. New Haven, CT: Yale University Press, 2002.

———. "Johann David Michaelis and the Colonial Imaginary: Orientalism and the Emergence of Racial Antisemitism in Eighteenth-Century Germany." *Jewish Social Studies* 6, no. 2 (Summer 2000): 56–101.

———. *Middlebrow Literature and the Making of German-Jewish Identity*. Stanford, CA: Stanford University Press, 2010.

Hidvégi, Máté. "Immanuel Löw's Reflections on 'The Essence of and Evolution of Judaism' in His Letters to Ignaz Goldziher in 1888." In *Goldziher Memorial Conference*, edited by Éva Apor and István Ormos, 75–81. Budapest: Library of the Hungarian Academy of Sciences, 2005.

Hitchcock, Henry-Russell. *Architecture: Nineteenth and Twentieth Centuries*. Baltimore: Penguin, 1963.

Hodkinson, James, and John Walker, eds. *Deploying Orientalism in Culture and History: From Germany to Central and Eastern Europe*. Rochester, NY: Camden House, 2013.

Holub, Robert C. "Troubled Apostate: Heine's Conversion and Its Consequences." In *A Companion to the Works of Heinrich Heine*, edited by Roger F. Cook, 229–250. Rochester, NY: Camden House, 2002.

Hönsch, Ulrike. *Wege des Spanienbildes im Deutschland des 18. Jahrhunderts: Von der schwarzen Legende zum "Hesperischen Zaubergarten."* Tübingen: Niemeyer, 2000.

Hopkins, Simon. "The Language Studies of Ignaz Goldziher." In *Goldziher Memorial Conference*, edited by Éva Apor and István Ormos, 83–142. Budapest: Library of the Hungarian Academy of Sciences, 2005.

Horch, Hans Otto. *Auf der Suche nach der jüdischen Erzählliteratur: Die Literaturkritik der "Allgemeinen Zeitung des Judentums" (1837–1922)*. Frankfurt am Main: New York: Peter Lang, 1985.

Horowitz, Elliott. "The Early Eighteenth Century Confronts the Beard: Kabbalah and Jewish Self-Fashioning." *Jewish History* 8, nos. 1–2 (1994): 95–115.

Horwitz, Ludwig. *Die Kasseler Synagoge und ihr Erbauer*. Kassel: Vietor, 1907.

Hübsch, Heinrich, et al. *In What Style Should We Build?: The German Debate on Architectural Style*. Translated by Wolfgang Herrmann. Santa Monica, CA: Getty Center for the History of Art and the Humanities, 1992.

Humbert, Jean-Marcel, and Clifford Price, eds. *Imhotep Today: Egyptianizing Architecture*. Portland, OR: Cavendish, 2003.

Hundert, Gershon. *Jews in Poland-Lithuania in the Eighteenth Century: A Genealogy of Modernity*. Berkeley: University of California Press, 2004.

Hundt, Markus. *Spracharbeit im 17. Jahrhundert: Studien zu Georg Philipp Harsdörffer, Justus Georg Schottelius und Christian Gueintz*. Studia Linguistica Germanica, 57. Berlin: De Gruyter, 2000.

Hvattum, Mari. *Gottfried Semper and the Problem of Historicism*. Cambridge: Cambridge University Press, 2004.

Ibing, Brigitte. "Markus Herz, a Biographical Study." *Koroth* 9, nos. 1–2 (1985): 113–121.

Idelsohn, Abraham Z. *Jewish Music: Its Historical Development*. New York: Dover, 1992.

J. C. "Phöbus Philippson. Ein Erinnerungsblat zu seinem hundertsten Geburtstag." *Allgemeine Zeitung des Judentums* 30 (1907): 354–355.

Jacobs, Joseph. *Studies in Jewish Statistics, Social, Vital and Anthropometric*. London: D. Nutt, 1891.

Jacobs, Martin. *Islamische Geschichte in Judischen Chroniken: Hebraische Historiographie des 16. und 17. Jahrhunderts*. Tübingen: Mohr Siebeck, 2004.

Jay, Martin. *Force Fields: Between Intellectual History and Cultural Critique*. Routledge: New York, 1993.

———. *Songs of Experience: Modern American and European Variations on a Universal Theme*. Berkeley: University of California Press, 2004.

Jeitteles, Ignaz. "Bemerkungen eines Reisenden über den Charakter der Einwohner in Galizien. (Eine Rapsodie)." *Sulamith* 1, no. 2 (1807): 182–188.

Jellinek, Hermann. *Uriel Acosta's Leben und Lehre. Ein Beitrag zur kenntniss seiner moral, wie zur Berichtigung der Gutzkow'schen Fiktionen über Acosta, und zur Charakteristik der damaligen Juden*. Zerbst: Kummer'schen Buchhandlung, 1847.

Jersch-Wenzel, Stefi. "Population Shifts and Occupational Structure." In *German-Jewish History in Modern Times*, vol. 2, edited by Michael A. Meyer, 50–89. New York: Columbia University Press, 1997.

Jochmann, Werner. *Gesellschaftskrise und Judenfeindschaft in Deutschland 1870–1945.* Hamburg: Hans Christians, 1988.

Jones, Charles. *English Pronunciation in the Eighteenth and Nineteenth Centuries.* Basingstoke: Palgrave Macmillan, 2006.

Jones, Lindsay. *The Hermeneutics of Sacred Architecture: Experience, Interpretation, Comparison.* Vol. 1, *Monumental Occasions: Reflections on the Eventfulness of Religious Architecture.* Cambridge, MA: Harvard University Press, 2000.

Judt, J. M. *Die Juden als Rasse: Eine Analyse aus dem Gebiete der Anthropologie.* Berlin: Jüdischer Verlag, 1903.

Kafka, Franz. *Letter to His Father.* New York: Schocken, 1966.

Kaiser, Wolfram, and Arina Völker. "Berolina iubilans: Berliner Ärzte als hallesche Doktoranden (V). Markus Herz (1747–1803) und die Berliner jüdischen Ärzte." *Zeitschrift für die gesamte innere Medizin* 42 (1987): 618–623.

Kalmar, Ivan. "Moorish Style: Orientalism, the Jews, and Synagogue Architecture." *Jewish Social Studies* 7, no. 3 (2001): 68–100.

Kalmár, Lajos, Gabor Deutsch, and Vera Farago. *The Dohány Street Synagogue and the Treasures of the Jewish Museum.* Pécs: Alexandra, 2005.

Kaplan, Marion A. *The Making of the Jewish Middle Class: Women, Family, and Identity in Imperial Germany.* New York: Oxford University Press, 1991.

Kaplan, Yosef. *An Alternative Path to Modernity: The Sephardi Diaspora in Western Europe.* Leiden: Brill, 2000.

Kaplan, Yosef, Richard H. Popkin, and Henry Méchoulan, eds. *Menasseh Ben Israel and His World.* Leiden: Brill, 1989.

Karp, Jonathan. "The Aesthetic Difference: Moses Mendelssohn's *Kohelet musar* and the Inception of the Berlin Haskalah." In *Renewing the Past: Reconfiguring Jewish Culture from al-Andalus to the Haskalah,* edited by Ross Brann and Adam Sutcliff, 93–120. Philadelphia: University of Pennsylvania Press, 2004.

Katz, Dovid. *Words on Fire: The Unfinished Story of Yiddish.* New York: Basic Books, 2004.

Katz, Jacob. *From Prejudice to Destruction: Anti-Semitism, 1700–1933.* Cambridge, MA: Harvard University Press, 1980.

———. *A House Divided: Orthodoxy and Schism in Nineteenth-Century Central European Jewry.* Hanover, NH: University Press of New England, 1998.

Katzburg, Nathaniel. "The Jewish Congress of Hungary, 1868–1869." In *Hungarian Jewish Studies,* vol. 2, edited by Randolph L. Braham, 1–33. New York: World Federation of Hungarian Jews, 1966.

Kayserling, Meyer. *Biblioteca Española-Portugueza-Judaica and Other Studies in Ibero-Jewish Bibliography.* New York: KTAV, 1971.

———. *Geschichte der Juden in Portugal.* Leipzig: Oskar Leiner, 1867.

———. *Ludwig Philippson: Eine Biographie.* Leipzig: Hermann Mendelsohn, 1898.

———. "Rabbi Santob de Carrion." *Jershurun* 9 (1856): 484–492.

———. "Sephardim." In *Jewish Encyclopaedia,* 11:197. New York: Funk and Wagnalls, 1905.

———. *Sephardim. Romanische poesien der Juden in Spanien. Ein Beitrag zur Literatur und Geschichte der spanisch-portugiesischen Juden.* Leipzig, H. Mendelssohn, 1859.

Kertzer, David I., and Marzio Barbagli, eds. *The History of the European Family.* New Haven, CT: Yale University Press, 2001.

Keßler, Karin. "Halakhic Rules in Synagogue Architecture." In *Jewish Architecture in Europe*, edited by Aliza Cohen-Mushlin and Harmen H. Thies, 243–256. Petersberg: Imhof, 2010.

Kieval, Hillel J. "Antisemitism and the City: A Beginner's Guide." In *People of the City: Jews and the Urban Challenge*, edited by Ezra Mendelsohn, 3–18. Studies in Contemporary Jewry, vol. 15. Oxford: Oxford University Press, 1999.

Kim, Ransoo. "The 'Art of Building' (*Baukunst*) of Mies van der Rohe." PhD diss, Georgia Institute of Technology, 2006.

King, Robert D. "The Czernowitz Conference in Retrospect." In *The Politics of Yiddish: Studies in Language, Literature, and Society*, vol. 4, edited by Dov-Ber Kerler, 41–49. Walnut Creek, CA: AltaMira Press, 1998.

Kircher, Hartmut. *Heine und das Judentum*. Bonn: Bouvier, 1973.

Klee, Alfred, Rahel Wischnitzer-Bernstein, and Josef Fried. *Gedenkausstellung Don Jizchaq Abrabanel: Seine Welt, Sein Werk*. Berlin: M. Lessmann, 1937.

Knoblauch, Eduard. "Die neue Synagoge in Berlin." *Zeitschrift für Bauwesen* 16 (1866): 3–6.

Knoblauch, G., and Hollin, F. *Die Neue Synagoge in Berlin*. Berlin: Hentrich, 1992.

Knufinke, Ulrich. *Bauwerke jüdische Friedhöfe in Deutschland*. Petersberg: Imhof, 2007.

Kohl, Philip L. "Nationalism and Archaeology: On the Constructions of Nations and the Reconstructions of the Remote Past." *Annual Review of Anthropology* 27 (1998): 223–246.

Kohl, Philip L., and Clare Fawcett, eds. *Nationalism, Politics, and the Practice of Archaeology*. Cambridge: Cambridge University Press, 1996.

Kohler, George Y. "German Spirit and Holy Ghost—Treitschke's Call for Conversion of German Jewry: The Debate Revisited." *Modern Judaism* 30, no. 2 (2010): 172–195.

Kolb, Jocelyne. *The Ambiguity of Taste: Freedom and Food in European Romanticism*. Ann Arbor: University of Michigan Press, 1995.

Kollmann, J. "Schädel und Skeletreste aus einem Judenfriedhof des 13. und 14. Jahrhundert zu Basel." *Verhandlungen der naturforschenden Gesellschaft zu Basel* 7 (1885): 648–656.

Kontje, Todd. *German Orientalisms*. Ann Arbor: University of Michigan Press, 2004.

Kornberg, Jacques. *Theodor Herzl: From Assimilation to Zionism*. Bloomington: Indiana University Press, 1993.

Kostoff, Spiro., ed. *The Architect: Chapters in the History of the Profession*. Oxford: Oxford University Press, 1977.

Krinsky, Carol Herselle. *Synagogues of Europe: Architecture, History, Meaning*. Mineola, NY: Dover, 1996.

Krobb, Florian. *Kollektivautobiographien, Wunschautobiographien: Marannenschicksal im deutsch-jüdischen historischen Roman*. Würzburg: Königshausen & Neumann, 2000.

———. *Selbstdarstellungen: Untersuchungen zur deutsch-jüdischen Erzählliteratur im neunzehnten Jahrhundert*. Würzburg: Königshausen & Neumann, 2000.

Kulenska, Veselina. "The Antisemitic Press in Bulgaria at the End of the 19th Century." *Quest. Issues in Contemporary Jewish History. Journal of Fondazione CDEC*, no. 3 (July 2012). www.quest-cdecjournal.it/focus.php?id=296.

Künzl, Hannelore. "Der Einfluß des alten Orients auf die europäische Kunst besonders im 19. und 20. Jh." PhD diss., University of Cologne, 1973.

———. *Islamische Stilelemente in Synagogenbau des 19. und frühen 20. Jahrhunderts.* Frankfurt am Main: Peter Lang, 1984.

Kuzar, Ron. *Hebrew and Zionism: A Discourse Analytic Cultural Study.* Berlin: Mouton de Gruyter, 2001.

Lassner, Jacob. "Abraham Geiger: A Nineteenth-Century Jewish Reformer on the Origins of Islam." In *The Jewish Discovery of Islam*, edited by Martin Kramer, 103–135. Tel Aviv: Moshe Dayan Center for Middle Eastern and African Studies, 1999.

Lavater, Johan Caspar. *Essays on Physiognomy.* London: D. Blake, 1840.

Le Fanu, Philip, trans. *Letters of Certain Jews to Monsieur Voltaire, Containing an Apology for Their Own People, and for the Old Testament.* Philadelphia: H. Hooker; Cincinnati, G. G. Jones, 1848.

Lehmann, Emil. *Ein Halbjahrhundert in der israelitischen Religionsgemeinde zu Dresden: Erlebtes und Erlesenes.* Dresden: Gustav Salomon, 1890.

Lehmann, James H. "Maimonides, Mendelssohn and the Me'asfim: Philosophy and the Biographical Imagination in the Early Haskalah." *Leo Baeck Institute Year Book* 20 (1975): 87–108.

Lehmann, Marcus. "Eine Seder-Nacht in Madrid." *Der Israelit* 9, nos. 49–52 (December 1868): 911–912, 931–932, 951–952, and 967–968.

Leimdörfer, David, ed. *Festschrift zum hundertjährigen Bestehen des Israelitischen Tempels in Hamburg 1818–1918.* Hamburg: M. Glogau, 1918.

Leket teudot: le-toldot va'ad ha-lashon ve-ha-akademiyah la-lashon ha-ivrit, 1890–1970. Jerusalem: Academy of the Hebrew Language, 1970.

Leroy-Beaulieu, Anatole. *Israel among the Nations: A Study of Jews and Antisemitism.* London: William Heinemann, 1895.

Lessing, Theodor. *Der Jüdischer Selbsthass.* Munich: Matthes & Seitz Verlag, 1984.

Lewis, Bernard. *Islam in History: Ideas, People, and Events in the Middle East.* Chicago: Open Court, 1993.

Liebeschütz, Hans, and Arnold Paucker, eds. *Das Judentum in der Deutschen Umwelt, 1800–1850: Studien zur Frühgeschichte der Emanzipation.* Tübingen: J.C.B. Mohr, 1977.

Lifschitz, Avi S. "From the Corruption of French to the Cultural Distinctiveness of German: The Controversy over Prémontval's *Préservatif* (1759)." *Studies on Voltaire and the Eighteenth Century* (2007:06): 265–290.

———. *Language and Enlightenment: The Berlin Debates of the Eighteenth Century.* Oxford: Oxford University Press, 2012.

Linder, Amnon, ed. *The Jews in Roman Imperial Legislation.* Detroit: Wayne State University Press, 1987.

Lipphardt, Veronika. *Biologie der Juden: Jüdische Wissenschaftler über "Rasse" und Vererbung 1900–1935.* Göttingen: Vandenhoeck & Ruprecht, 2008.

Lipton, Sara. *Dark Mirror: The Medieval Origins of Anti-Jewish Iconography.* New York: Metropolitan Books, 2014.

———. *Images of Intolerance: The Representation of Jews and Judaism in the Bible moralisée.* Berkeley: University of California Press, 1999.

"Literarische Nachrichten." *Allgemeine Zeitung des Judentums* 1 (1841): 7–8.

Litvak, Olga. *Haskalah: The Romantic Movement in Judaism.* New Brunswick, NJ: Rutgers University Press, 2012.

Löffler, Heinrich. *Probleme der Dialektologie. Eine Einführung.* Darmstadt: WBG, 1990.

Lowe, Lisa. *Critical Terrains: French and British Orientalisms*. Ithaca, NY: Cornell University Press, 1991.

Löwenbrück, Anna-Ruth. *Judenfeindschaft im Zeitalter der Aufklärung. Eine Studie zur Vorgeschichte des modernen Antisemitismus am Beispiel des Göttinger Theologen und Orientalisten Johann David Michaelis (1717–1791)*. Frankfurt am Main: Peter Lang, 1995.

Lowenstein, Steven M. *The Berlin Jewish Community: Enlightenment, Family, and Crisis, 1770–1830*. New York: Oxford University Press, 1994.

———. "The Shifting Boundary between Eastern and Western Jewry." *Jewish Social Studies* 4, no. 1 (Autumn 1997): 60–78.

———. "The Yiddish Written Word in Nineteenth-Century Germany." *Leo Baeck Institute Year Book* 24 (1979): 179–192.

Löwisohn, Joseph. "Menasse ben Israel, der glückliche Sachwalter seiner Glaubensgenossen." *Sulamith* 4, no. 2 (1812): 1–5.

Löwisohn, Salomo. "Abenezra (Aben Ezra) und dessen Schriften." *Sulamith* 4, no. 1 (1812): 217–222.

Lund, Hannah Lotte. *Der Berliner "jüdische Salon" um 1800: Emanzipation in der Debatte*. Berlin: De Gruyter, 2012.

Lütteken, Laurenz. "Mendelssohn und der musikästhetische Diskurs der Aufklärung." In *Moses Mendelssohn im Spannungsfeld der Aufklärung*, edited by Michael Albrecht and Eva J. Engel, 159–193. Stuttgart-Bad: Friedrich Fromann, 2000.

———. "Zwischen Ohr und Verstand: Moses Mendelssohn und Johan Philipp Kirnberger und die Begründung des 'reinen Satzes' in der Musik." In *Musik und Ästhetik im Berlin Moses Mendelssohns*, edited by Anselm Gerhard, 135–163. Tübingen: Max Neimeyer Verlag, 1999.

Lutz, Edith. *Der Verein für Kultur- und Wissenschaft der Juden und sein Mitglied H. Heine*. Stuttgart: J. B. Metzler, 1997.

Lutzhöft, Hans Jürgen. *Der Nordische Gedanke in Deutschland 1920–1940*. Stuttgart: Ernst Klett Verlag, 1971.

Manuel, Frank. *The Broken Staff: Judaism through Christian Eyes*. Cambridge, MA: Harvard University Press, 1992.

Marchand, Suzanne L. *Down from Olympus: Archaeology and Philhellenism in Germany, 1750–1970*. Princeton, NJ: Princeton University Press, 1996.

———. *German Orientalism in the Age of Empire: Religion, Race, and Scholarship*. New York: Cambridge University Press, 2009.

Marcus, Ivan G. "Beyond the Sephardic Mystique." *Orim* 1 (1985): 35–53.

Marcus, Jacob Rader, ed. *The Jew in the Medieval World: A Sourcebook, 315–1791*. Philadelphia: Jewish Publication Society, 1960.

Marien, Mary Warner. *Photography: A Cultural History*. Upper Saddle River, NJ: Pearson Prentice Hall, 2006.

Marks, Elaine. *Marrano as Metaphor: The Jewish Presence in French Writing*. New York: Columbia University Press, 1996.

Martino, Alberto. *Die deutsche Leihbibliothek: Geschichte einer literarischen Institution (1756–1914)*. Wiesbaden: O. Harrassowitz, 1990.

Matut, Diana. "Steinschneider and Yiddish." In *Studies on Steinschneider: Moritz Steinschneider and the Emergence of the Science of Judaism in Nineteenth-Century Germany*, edited by Reimund Leicht and Gad Freudenthal, 383–409. Leiden: Brill, 2012.

Maurer, Friedrich. "Mitteilungen aus Bosnien." *Das Ausland* 49 (1869): 1161–1164 and 50 (1869): 1183–1185

McCagg, William O. *A History of Habsburg Jews, 1670–1918.* Bloomington: Indiana University Press, 1992.

Megill, Allan. "The Enlightenment Debate on the Origin of Language and Its Historical Background." PhD diss., Columbia University, 1975.

Meisl, Josef. *Heinrich Graetz; Eine Würdigung des Historikers und Juden zu seinem 100. Geburtstage 31. Oktober 1917, 21. Cheschwan.* Berlin: Louis Lamm, 1917.

Mellinkoff, Ruth. *Antisemitic Hate Signs in Hebrew Illuminated Manuscripts from Medieval Germany.* Jerusalem: Center for Jewish Art, Hebrew University of Jerusalem, 1999.

Mendelssohn, Moses. *Gesammelte Schriften. Jubiläumsausgabe.* Edited by Alexander Altmann and Fritz Bamberger, 25 vols. Stuttgart-Bad Cannstatt: F. Frommann, 1971.

———. *Jerusalem, or on Religious Power and Judaism.* Translated by Allan Arkush. Hanover, NH: Brandeis University Press, 1983.

———. *Moses Mendelssohn: Ästhetische Schriften.* Edited by Anne Pollok. Hamburg: Felix Meiner Verlag, 2006.

———. *Moses Mendelssohn: Selections from His Writings.* Edited and Translated by Eva Jospe. New York: Viking Press, 1975.

———. "On the Question: What does 'to enlighten' mean?" In *Moses Mendelssohn: Philosophical Writings,* edited by Daniel O. Dahlstrom, 311–317. Cambridge: Cambridge University Press, 1997.

Merback, Mitchell B., ed. *Beyond the Yellow Badge: Anti-Judaism and Antisemitism in Medieval and Early Modern Visual Culture.* Leiden: Brill, 2008.

Meyer, Michael A. *Judaism within Modernity: Essays on Jewish History and Religion.* Detroit: Wayne State University Press, 2001.

———. *The Origins of the Modern Jew: Jewish Identity and European Culture in Germany, 1749–1824.* Detroit: Wayne State University Press, 1967.

———. *Response to Modernity: A History of the Reform Movement in Judaism.* New York: Oxford University Press, 1988.

Michaelis, Johann David. *Anfangs-Gründe der hebräischen Accentuation: nebst einer kurtzen Abhandlung von dem Alterthum der Accente und hebräischen Puncte überhaupt: auch einem Anhange, in welchem einige Schrifft-Oerter nach den Regeln der Accentuation untersuchet warden.* Halle: In Verlegung des Wäysenhauses, 1741.

Mies van der Rohe, Ludwig. "Baukunst und Zeitwille." *Der Querschnitt* 4 (1924): 31–32.

Mignot, Claude. *Architecture of the Nineteenth Century in Europe.* New York: Rizzoli, 1984.

Morag, Shelomo. "The Emergence of Modern Hebrew: Some Sociolinguistic Perspectives." In *Hebrew in Ashkenaz,* edited by Lewis Glinert, 208–221. New York: Oxford University Press, 1993.

Morant, G. M., and Otto Samson. "An Examination of Investigations by Dr. Maurice Fishberg and Professor Franz Boas Dealing with Measurements of Jews in New York." *Biometrika* 28, nos. 1–2 (1936): 1–31.

Morris-Reich, Amos. "Arthur Ruppin's Concept of Race." *Israel Studies* 11, no. 3 (2006): 1–30.

Moshfegh, David. "Ignaz Goldziher and the Rise of *Islamwissenschaft* as a 'Science of Religion.'" PhD diss., University of California–Berkeley, 2012.

Mosse, George L. *The Crisis of German Ideology: Intellectual Origins of the Third Reich.* New York: Grosset & Dunlap, 1964.

———. *German Jews beyond Judaism.* Bloomington: Indiana University Press, 1985.

———. *Germans and Jews: The Right, the Left, and the Search for a "Third Force" in Pre-Nazi Germany.* Detroit: Wayne State University Press, 1987.

———. *The Image of Man: The Creation of Modern Masculinity.* Oxford: Oxford University Press, 1996.

———. *Nationalism and Sexuality: Respectability and Abnormal Sexuality in Modern Europe.* New York: Howard Fertig, 1985.

———. *Toward the Final Solution: A History of European Racism.* New York: Harper & Row, 1980.

Mosse, Werner E. "From '*Schutzjuden*' to '*Deutsche Staatsbürger jüdischen Glaubens*': The Long and Bumpy Road of Jewish Emancipation in Germany." In *Paths of Emancipation: Jews, States, and Citizenship*, edited by Pierre Birnbaum and Ira Katznelson, 59–93. Princeton, NJ: Princeton University Press, 1995.

Mosse, Werner E., Arnold Pauker, and Reinhard Rürup eds. *Revolution and Evolution: 1848 in German-Jewish History.* Tübingen: J.C.B. Mohr, 1981.

Müller, F. Max. *Biographies of Words, and the Home of the Aryas.* London: Longmans, Green, and Co., 1888.

Neill, Stephen. *Colonialism and Christian Missions.* London: Lutterworth, 1966.

Neis, Cordula. *Anthropologie im Sprachdenken des 18. Jahrhunderts. Die Berliner Preisfrage nach dem Ursprung der Sprache.* Berlin: De Gruyter, 2003.

Neubauer, Adolf. "Notes on the Race-Types of the Jews." *Journal of the Royal Anthropological Institute of Great Britain and Ireland* 15 (1885): 17–23.

Neubauer, Hans-Joachim. "Auf Begehr: Unser Verkehr: Über eine judenfeindliche Theaterposse im Jahre 1815." In *Antisemitismus und jüdische Geschichte. Studien zu Ehren von Herbert A. Strauss*, edited by Rainer Erb and Michael Schmidt, 313–327. Berlin: Wissenschaftlicher Autorenverlag, 1987.

———. *Judenfiguren: Drama und Theater im frühen 19. Jahrhundert.* Frankfurt: Campus, 1994.

———. "Stimme und Tabu: Was das Theater erfindet und was es vermeidet." In *Judenfeindschaft as Paradigma: Studien zur Vorurteilsforschung*, edited by Wolfgang Benz and Angelika Königseder, 70–78. Berlin: Metropol, 2002.

Nirenberg, David. *Anti-Judaism: The Western Tradition.* New York: W. W. Norton & Company, 2013.

———. *Communities of Violence: Persecution of Minorities in the Middle Ages.* Princeton, NJ: Princeton University Press, 1996.

———. "What Can Medieval Spain Teach Us about Muslim-Jewish Relations?" *CCAR Journal: A Reform Jewish Quarterly* (Spring/Summer 2002): 17–36.

Nöldeke, Theodore. *Sketches from Eastern History.* Beirut: Khayats, 1963.

Nott, J. C., and G. R. Gliddon. *Types of Mankind: or, Ethnological Researches, Based upon the Ancient Monuments, Paintings, Sculptures, and Crania of Races, and upon Their Natural, Geographical, Philological and Biblical History.* Philadelphia: J. B. Lippincott, Grambo, 1854.

Novak, Daniel. "A Model Jew: 'Literary Photographs' and the Jewish Body in Daniel Deronda." *Representations* 85, no. 1 (Winter 2004): 58–97.

Nye, Robert. *Masculinity and Male Codes of Honor in France*. New York: Oxford University Press, 1993.

Oestreich, Gerhard. *Geist und Gestalt des frühmodernen Staates. Ausgewählte Aufsätze*. Berlin: Duncker and Humblot, 1969.

Olender, Maurice. *The Languages of Paradise: Race, Religion, and Philology in the Nineteenth Century*. Cambridge, MA: Harvard University Press, 1992.

Ormos, István. "Goldziher's Mother Tongue: A Contribution to the Study of the Language Situation in Hungary in the Nineteenth Century." In *Goldziher Memorial Conference*, edited by Éva Apor and István Ormos, 203–243. Budapest: Library of the Hungarian Academy of Sciences, 2005.

Osterhammel, Jürgen. *Die Entzauberung Asiens: Europa und die asiatischen Reiche im 18. Jahrhundert*. Munich: C. H. Beck, 1998.

Parfitt, Tudor. "The Contribution of the Old Yishuv to the Revival of Hebrew." *Journal of Semitic Studies* 29, no. 2 (1984): 255–265.

———. "The Use of Hebrew in Palestine, 1800–1882." *Journal of Semitic Studies* 17 (1972): 237–252.

Patai, Raphael. *Ignaz Goldziher and His Oriental Diary: A Translation and Psychological Portrait*. Detroit: Wayne State University Press, 1987.

———. *The Jewish Mind*. Detroit: Wayne State University Press, 1996.

——— *The Jews of Hungary*. Detroit: Wayne State University Press, 1996.

Pelli, Moshe. *The Age of Haskalah: Studies in Hebrew Literature of the Enlightenment in Germany*. Leiden: E. J. Brill, 1979.

———. "'These are the words of the great pundit, scholar and poet, Herder' . . . : Herder and the Hebrew Haskalah." In *Hebräische Poesie und jüdischer Volksgeist: Die Wirkungsgeschichte von Johann Gottfried Herder im Judentum Mittel- und Osteuropas*, edited by Christoph Schulte, 107–124. Hildesheim: Olms, 2003.

Penslar, Derek J. *Shylock's Children: Economics and Jewish Identity in Modern Europe*. Berkeley: University of California Press, 2001.

Perlmann, Moshe. "The Medieval Polemics between Islam and Judaism." In *Religion in a Religious Age*, edited by Shlomo Dov Goitein, 103–138. Cambridge, MA: Association for Jewish Studies, 1974.

Petuchowski, Jacob. *Prayerbook Reform in Europe: The Liturgy of European Liberal and Reform Judaism*. New York: World Union for Progressive Judaism 1968.

Pevsner, Nikolaus. *A History of Building Types*. Princeton, NJ: Princeton University Press, 1976.

———. *An Outline of European Architecture*. Baltimore: Penguin, 1960.

Pfannmüller, Gustav D. *Handbuch der Islam-Literatur*. Berlin: Walter de Gruyter, 1923.

Philippson, Johanna. "Ludwig Philippson und die *Allgemeine Zeitung des Judentums*." In *Das Judentum in der deutschen Umwelt, 1800–1850: Studien zur Frühgeschichte der Emanzipation*, edited by Hans Liebeschütz and Arnold Paucker, 243–291. Tübingen: Mohr, 1977.

Philippson, Ludwig. "Die drei Brüder." In *Saron*, edited by Ludwig Philippson, 5:215–265. Leipzig: Oskar Leiner, 1863.

————. "The Three Brothers." In *Nineteenth Century Jewish Literature: A Reader*, edited by Jonathan M. Hess, Maurice Samuels, and Nadia Valman, 210–247. Stanford, CA: Stanford University Press, 2013.

Philippson, Phöbus. *Die Marannen*. In *Saron*, edited by Ludwig Philippson, 1:3–124. Leipzig: Leopold Schauss, 1855.

Philipsborn, Alexander. "The Jewish Hospitals in Germany." *Leo Baeck Institute Year Book* 4 (1959): 220–234.

Philipson, David. *The Reform Movement in Judaism*. New York: The Macmillan Company, 1931.

Pietsch, Ludwig. "Carl Heinrich Eduard Knoblauch." *Zeitschrift für Praktische Baukunst* (1865): 301.

Pinney, Christopher. *Photography and Anthropology*. London: Reaktion Books, 2011.

Pinney, Christopher, and Nicolas Peterson, eds. *Photography's Other Histories (Objects/ Histories)*. Durham, NC: Duke University Press 2003.

Plaul, Hainer, and Ulrich Schmid. "Die populären Lesestoff." In *Hansers Sozialgeschichte der deutschen Literatur vom 16. Jahrhundert bis zur Gegenwart*, vol. 5, edited by Gert Sautermeister and Ulrich Schmid, 313–338. Munich: Hanser, 1998.

Poliakov, Léon. *The Aryan Myth: A History of Racist and Nationalist Ideas in Europe*. New York: Meridian, 1977.

————. *The History of Anti-Semitism*. 4 vols. New York: Vanguard Press, 1965.

Pollok, Anne. *Facetten des Menschen: Zur Anthropologie Moses Mendessohns*. Hamburg: Feliz Meiner, 2010.

Popkin, Richard H. "Hume and Isaac de Pinto." *Texas Studies in Literature and Language* 12, no. 3 (1970): 417–430.

Prawer, S. S. *Heine's Jewish Comedy: A Study of His Portraits of Jews and Judaism*. Oxford: Clarendon Press, 1983.

Pulzer, Peter G. J. *Jews and the German State: The Political History of a Minority, 1848–1933*. Oxford: Blackwell Publishers, 1992

————. *The Rise of Political Anti-Semitism in Germany and Austria*. New York: John Wiley, 1964.

Pyka, Marcus. *Jüdische Identität bei Heinrich Graetz*. Göttingen: Vandenhoeck & Ruprecht, 2009.

Rabinbach, Anson G. "The Migration of Galician Jews to Vienna, 1857–1800." *Austrian History Year Book* 11 (1975): 43–54.

Ragussis, Michael. "Writing Spanish History in Nineteenth-Century Britain: The Inquisition and the 'Secret Race.'" In *Sephardism: Spanish Jewish History and the Modern Literary Imagination*, edited by Yael Halevi-Wise, 59–90. Stanford, CA: Stanford University Press, 2012.

Rathenau, Walter. "Höre Israel!" In *The Jew in the Modern World*, edited by Paul Mendes-Flohr and Jehuda Reinharz, 814–817. New York: Oxford University Press, 2011.

Ray, Jonathan. "Beyond Tolerance and Persecution: Reassessing Our Approach to Medieval Convivencia." *Jewish Social Studies* 11, no. 2 (2005): 1–18.

Reckendorf, Hermann. *Die Geheimnisse der Juden*. 5 vols. Leipzig: W. Gerhard, 1856–1857.

Reinhold, Josef. "Die verspätete Emanzipation der Juden in Sachsen als legislativer Rahmen. Die Konstituierung der Israelitischen Religionsgemeinde zu Leipzig und die ersten Jahrzehnte ihrer Entwicklung." *Journal Juden in Sachsen* (April 2010): 3–19.

Richarz, Monika. "Demographic Developments." In *German-Jewish History in Modern Times*, vol. 3, edited by Michael A. Meyer, 30–31. New York: Columbia University Press, 1997.

Rickard, Peter. *The Embarrassments of Irregularity: The French Language in the Eighteenth Century*. London: Cambridge University Press, 1981.

Rodrigue, Aron. *Jews and Muslims: Images of Sephardi and Eastern Jewries in Modern Times*. Seattle: University of Washington Press, 2003.

Roemer, Nils. *Jewish Scholarship in Nineteenth-Century Germany: Between History and Faith*. Madison: University of Wisconsin Press, 2005.

———. "Turning Defeat into Victory: 'Wissenschaft des Judentums' and the Martyrs of 1096." *Jewish History* 13, no. 2 (1999): 65–80.

Rohde, Saskia. "Im Zeichen der Hannoverschen Architekturschule: Der Architekt Edwin Oppler (1831–1880) und seine schlesichen Bauten." *Hannoversche Zeitung* (2000): 67–86.

Rohrbacher, Stefan, and Michael Schmidt. *Judenbilder: Kulturgeschichte antijüdischer Mythen und antisemitischer Vorurteile*. Hamburg: Rowohlt, 1991.

Roitman, Alexander. *Envisioning the Temple*. Jerusalem: Israel Museum, 2003.

Rosenau, Helen. "German Synagogues in the Early Period of Emancipation." *Leo Baeck Institute Year Book* 8 (1963): 214–225.

———. "Gottfried Semper and German Synagogue Architecture." *Leo Baeck Institute Year Book* 22 (1977): 237–244.

———. *Vision of the Temple: The Image of the Temple of Jerusalem in Judaism and Christianity*. London: Oresko Books, 1979.

Rosengarten, Albert. *A Handbook of Architectural Styles*. Boston: Longwood Press, 1977.

———. "Die neue Synagoge in Cassel." *Allgemeine Bauzeitung* 5 (1840): 205–207.

Rosenthal, Carl Albert. "In welchem Style sollen wir bauen? (Eine Frage für Mitglieder des deutschen Architektenvereins)." *Zeitschrift für prakitsche Baukunst* 4 (1844): 23–27.

Rosenthal, Donald A. *Orientalism: The Near East in French Painting, 1800–1880*. Rochester, NY: Memorial Art Gallery of the University of Rochester, 1982.

Rosenthal, Ludwig. *Heinrich Heine als Jude*. Frankfurt am Main: Ullstein, 1973.

Rotenstreich, Natan. "Hegel's Idea of Judaism." *Jewish Social Studies* 15, no. 1 (1953): 33–52.

Roth, Cecil. "Jewish History for Our Own Needs." *Menorah* 14, no. 5 (1928): 419–434.

Roth, Norman, ed. *Medieval Jewish Civilization: An Encyclopedia*. New York: Routledge, 2003.

Rozenblit, Marsha L. *The Jews of Vienna, 1867–1914: Assimilation and Identity*. Albany: State University of New York Press, 1983.

Ruderman, David B. "Cecil Roth, Historian of Italian Jewry: A Reassessment." In *The Jewish Past Revisited: Reflections on Modern Jewish Historians*, edited by David N. Myers and David B. Ruderman, 128–142. New Haven, CT: Yale University Press, 1998.

———. *Jewish Enlightenment in an English Key: Anglo-Jewry's Construction of Modern Jewish Thought*. Princeton, NJ: Princeton University Press, 2000.

Ruppin, Arthur. *Briefe, Tagebücher, Errinerungen*. Edited by Schlomo Krolik. Königstein: Jüdischer Verlag Athenäum, 1985.

———. *Die Juden der Gegenwart*. Cologne: Jüdischer Verlag, 1911.

Rürup, Reinhard. "Emancipation and Crisis: The 'Jewish Question' in Germany, 1850–1890." *Leo Baeck Institute Year Book* 20 (1975): 13–25.

———. "The Jewish Emancipation and Bourgeois Society." *Leo Baeck Institute Year Book* 14 (1969): 67–91.

Sáenz-Badillos, Ángel. *A History of the Hebrew Language*. Cambridge: Cambridge University Press, 1993.

Said, Edward W. *Culture and Imperialism*. New York: Knopf, 1993.

———. *Orientalism*. New York: Vintage, 1979.

Salomon, Gotthold. "Rabbi Moses ben Maimon." *Sulamith* 2, no. 2 (1809): 376–412.

Sammons, Jeffrey L. "Heine's Rabbi von Bacherach: The Unresolved Tensions." *German Quarterly* 37, no. 1 (1964): 26–38.

———. *Heinrich Heine: Alternative Perspectives, 1985–2005*. Würzburg: Könighausen & Neumann, 2006.

———. *Heinrich Heine: A Modern Biography*. Princeton, NJ: Princeton University Press, 1979.

Saposnik, Arieh Bruce. *Becoming Hebrew: The Creation of a Jewish National Culture in Ottoman Palestine*. New York: Oxford University Press, 2008.

———. "Europe and Its Orients in Zionist Culture before the First World War." *Historical Journal* 49, no. 4 (2006): 1105–1123.

Schäfer, Julia. "Verzeichnet. Über 'Judenbilder' in der Karikatur als historische Quelle." *Jahrbuch für Antisemitismusforschung* 10 (2001): 138–155.

Schapkow, Carsten. *Vorbild und Gegenbild: Das iberische Judentum in der deutschjüdischen Erinnerungskultur 1779–1939*. Cologne: Böhlau, 2011.

Schatz, Andrea. "'Peoples of Pure Speech': The Religious, the Secular and the Jewish Beginnings of Modernity." In *Early Modern Culture and Haskalah: Reconsidering the Borderlines of Modern Jewish History*, edited by David B. Ruderman and Shmuel Feiner, 169–190. Göttingen: Vandenhoek & Ruprecht, 2007.

———. "Returning to Sepharad: Maskilic Reflections on Hebrew in the Diaspora." In *Sepharad in Ashkenaz: Medieval Knowledge and Eighteenth-Century Enlightened Jewish Discourse*, edited by Resianne Fontaine, Andrea Schatz, and Irene E. Zwiep, 263–277. Amsterdam: 2007 Royal Netherlands Academy of Arts and Sciences, 2007.

———. *Sprache in der Zerstreuung: Zur Säkularisierung des Hebräischen im 18. Jahrhundert*. Göttingen, Ruprecht & Vandenhoeck, 2007.

Schiller, Friedrich. *On the Aesthetic Education of Man. The Project Gutenberg EBook of The Aesthetical Essays*. http://www.gutenberg.org/files/6798/6798-h/6798-h.htm #link2H_4_0031/.

Schlossar, Anton. "Frankl von Hochwart, Ludwig August Ritter." In *Allgemeine Deutsche Biographie*, 48:706–712. Leipzig: Duncker & Humblot, 1904.

Schmid, Ulrich. "Buchmarkt und Literaturvermittlung." In *Hansers Sozialgeschichte der deutschen Literatur vom 16. Jahrhundert bis zur Gegenwart*, vol. 5, edited by Gert Sautermeister and Ulrich Schmid, 60–93. Munich: Hanser, 1998.

Schmidt, Gilya Gerda. *The Art and Artists of the Fifth Zionist Congress, 1901: Heralds of a New Age*. Syracuse, NY: Syracuse University Press, 2003.

Schmidt, Leigh Eric. *Hearing Things: Religion, Illusion, and the American Enlightenment*. Cambridge, MA: Harvard University Press, 2000.

Schoeps, Julius H., and Joachim Schlör, eds. *Bilder der Judenfeindschaft: Antisemitismus Vorurteile und Mythen*. Augsburg: Bechtermünz, 1999.

Scholem, Gershom. *On Jews and Judaism in Crisis: Selected Essays*. Philadelphia: Paul Dry Books, 2012.

Schöner, Petra. *Judenbilder im deutschen Einblattdruck der Renaissance: Ein Beitrag zur Imagologie*. Baden-Baden: V. Koerner, 2002.

Schorch, Grit. *Moses Mendelssohns Sprachpolitik*. Berlin: Walter de Gruyter, 2012.

Schorsch, Ismar. "Breakthrough into the Past: The Verein für Cultur und Wissenschaft der Juden." *Leo Baeck Institute Year Book* 38 (1988): 3–29.

———. "Converging Cognates: The Intersection of Jewish and Islamic Studies in Nineteenth Century Germany." *Leo Baeck Institute Year Book* 55 (2010): 3–36.

———. *From Text to Context: The Turn to History in Modern Judaism*. Hanover, NH: University Press of New England, 1994.

———. *Jewish Reactions to German Anti-Semitism, 1870–1914*. New York, Columbia University Press, 1972.

———. "The Myth of Sephardic Superiority." *Leo Baeck Institute Year Book* 34 (1989): 47–66.

Schorske, Carl E. *Fin-de-Siècle Vienna*. New York: Vintage Books, 1981.

Schottel, Justus Georg. *Ausführlich Arbeit von der Teutschen Haubt-Sprache*. C. F. Zilligern: Braunschweig, 1663. Reprint, Niemeyer: Tübingen, 1967.

Schwartz, Abraham. *Sefer Derekh ha-Nesher ve-Torat ha-Emet*. Vol. 1. Satumare: M. L. Hirsh, 1928.

Schwartz, Daniel B. *The First Modern Jew: Spinoza and the History of an Image*. Princeton, NJ: Princeton University Press, 2012.

Schwarz, Stefan. *Die Juden in Bayern im Wandel der Zeiten*. Munich: Günter Olzog, 1963.

Schwarzer, Mitchell. *German Architectural Theory and the Search for Modern Identity*. Cambridge: Cambridge University Press, 1995.

Schweizer, Hans Rudolf. *Ästhetik als Philosophie der sinnlichen Erkenntnis: Eine Interpretation der "Aesthetica" A. G. Baumgartens mit teilweiser Wiedergabe der lateinischen Textes und deutscher Übersetzung*. Basel: Schwabe, 1973.

Sefer zicharon le-kehilot Székesfehérvár ve-hasvivah. Jerusalem: n.p., 1997.

Segal, Miryam. *A New Sound in Hebrew Poetry: Poetics, Politics, Accent*. Bloomington: Indiana University Press, 2010.

Segall, Jacob. *Die Entwicklung der jüdischen Bevölkerung in München 1875–1905*. Berlin: Verein für die Statistik der Juden, 1910.

Sekula, Allan. "The Body and the Archive." *October* 39 (1986): 3–64.

Semper, Gottfried. "Die Synagoge zu Dresden." *Allgemeine Bauzeitung* 12 (1847): 127.

Seroussi, Edwin. "Beautifying Worship: Music in Early Reform Synagogues of Northern-Germany (ca. 1810–1840)." In *Fasch und die Musik im Europa des 18. Jahrhunderts*, edited by Guido Bimberg and Rüdiger Pfeiffer, 241–252. Weimar: Böhlau, 1995.

Shachar, Isaiah. "The Emergence of the Modern Pictorial Stereotype of 'The Jews' in England." In *Studies in the Cultural Life of the Jews in England*, edited by Dov Noy and Issachar Ben-Ami, 331–365. Folklore Research Center Studies, vol. 5. Jerusalem: Magnes Press, 1975.

———. *The Judensau: A Medieval Anti-Jewish Motif and Its History*. London: Warburg Institute, 1974.

Shavit, Yaakov. "A Duty Too Heavy to Bear: Hebrew in the Berlin Haskalah, 1783–1819: Between Classic, Modern, and Romantic." In *Hebrew in Ashkenaz*, edited by Lewis Glinert, 111–128. New York: Oxford University Press, 1993.

Shedletzky, Itta. "Literaturdiskussion und Belletristik in den juedischen Zeitschriften in Deutschland 1837–1918." PhD diss., Hebrew University, Jerusalem, 1986.

Sheehan, Jonathan. *The Enlightenment Bible: Translation, Scholarship, Culture*. Princeton, NJ: Princeton University Press, 2005.

Sheffi, Na'amah. "The Jewish Expulsion from Spain and the Rise of National Socialism on the Hebrew Stage." http://www.jewish-theatre.com/visitor/article_display .aspx?articleID=527.

Shusterman, Richard. *Surface and Depth: Dialectics of Criticism and Culture*. Ithaca, NY: Cornell University Press, 2002.

Sigal-Klagsbald, Laurence, ed. *Les Juifs dans l'orientalisme*. Paris: Skira Flammarion, 2012.

Simon, Hermann. *Das Berliner Jüdische Museum in der Oranienburger Strasse: Geschichte einer zerstörten Kultustätte*. Berlin: Union, 1988.

———. *Die Neue Synagoge Berlin: Geschichte, Gegenwart, Zukunft*. Berlin: Stiftung Neue Synagoge Berlin—Centrum Judaicum, 1992.

Simon, Róbert. *Ignác Goldziher: His Life and Scholarship as Reflected in His Works and Correspondence*. Leiden: E. J. Brill, 1986.

Simonson, Otto. *Der neue Tempel in Leipzig*. Berlin: F. Riegel, 1858.

Sinkoff, Nancy. *Out of the Shtetl: Making Jews Modern in the Polish Borderlands*. Providence, RI: Brown Judaic Studies, 2004.

Skolnik, Jonathan. *Jewish Pasts, German Fictions: History, Memory, and Minority Culture in Germany, 1824–1955*. Stanford, CA: Stanford University Press, 2014.

———. "The Strange Career of the Abarbanels from Heine to the Holocaust." In *Sephardism: Spanish Jewish History and the Modern Literary Imagination*, edited by Yael Halevi-Wise, 114–126. Stanford, CA: Stanford University Press, 2012.

———. "Writing Jewish History between Gutzkow and Goethe: Auerbach's Spinoza and the Birth of Modern Jewish Historical Fiction." *Prooftexts* 19, no. 2 (1999): 101–125.

Smith, Raoul N. "The Sociology of Language in Johann David Michaelis's Dissertation of 1760." *Journal of the History of the Behavioral Sciences* 12, no. 4 (1976): 338–346.

Snyder, Louis L. *Race: A History of Modern Ethnic Theories*. New York: Longmans, Green and Co., Alliance Book Corporation, 1939.

Sorkin, David. *The Berlin Haskalah and German Religious Thought: Orphans of Knowledge*. London: Vallentine Mitchell, 2000.

———. *Moses Mendelssohn*. London: Peter Halban, 1996.

———. *The Religious Enlightenment: Protestants, Jews, and Catholics from London to Vienna*. Princeton, NJ: Princeton University Press, 2008.

———. *The Transformation of German Jewry, 1780–1840*. New York: Oxford University Press, 1987.

———. "Wilhelm von Humboldt: The Theory and Practice of Self-Formation (*Bildung*), 1791–1810." *Journal of the History of Ideas* 44, no. 1 (1983): 55–73.

Spalding, Almut. *Elise Reimarus (1735–1805), the Muse of Hamburg: A Woman of the German Enlightenment*. Wurzburg: Konigshausen & Neumann, 2005.

Spicer, Joaneath. "The Star of David and Jewish Culture in Prague around 1600, Reflected in Drawings of Roelandt Savery and Paulus van Vianen." *Journal of the Walters Art Gallery* 54 (1996): 203–224.

Spurzheim, Johan Gaspar. *The Physiognomical System of Drs. Gall and Spurzheim*. London: Baldwin, Cradock and Joy, 1815.

Stanislawski, Michael. *A Murder in Lemberg: Politics, Religion, and Violence in Modern Jewish History*. Princeton, NJ: Princeton University Press, 2007.

———. *Zionism and the Fin-de-Siècle: Cosmopolitanism and Nationalism from Nordau to Jabotinsky*. Berkeley: University of California Press, 2001.

Steinschneider, Moritz. *Polemische und apologetische Literatur in arabischer Sprache zwischen Muslimen, Christen und Juden*. Hildesheim: Georg Olms, 1877.

Stern, Eliyahu. *The Genius: Elijah of Vilna and the Making of Modern Judaism*. New Haven, CT: Yale University Press, 2013.

Stevens, Mary Anne, ed. *The Orientalists: Delacroix to Matisse. European Painters in North Africa and the Near East*. London: Royal Academy of Arts, 1984.

Stieda, Ludwig. "Ein Beitrag zur Anthropologie der Juden." *Archiv für Anthropologie* 14 (1883): 61–71.

Stiefel, Barry. "The Architectural Origins of the Great Early Modern Urban Synagogue." *Leo Baeck Institute Year Book* 56 (2011): 105–134.

Stieglitz, Christian Ludwig. *Geschichte der Baukunst der Alten*. Vol. 1. Leipzig: Dykschen Buchhandlung, 1792.

Straus, Jutta. "Aaron Halle-Wolfson: Ein Leben in drei Sprachen." In *Musik und Ästhetik im Berlin Moses Mendelssohns*, edited by Anselm Gerhard, 57–76. Tübingen: Max Neimeyer Verlag, 1999.

Stroumsa, Sarah. "Jewish Polemics against Islam and Christianity in the Light of Judaeo-Arabic Texts." In *Judaeo-Arabic Studies*, edited by Norman Golb, 241–250. Amsterdam: Harwood Academic Publishers, 1997.

Studemund-Halévy, Michael. "Wie Wien zu seinen Sefarden kam: Die wundersame Geschichte des Diego de Aguilar." www.hagalil.com/archiv/2010/07/26/sefarden.

Sulzer, Johann Georg. *Allgemeine Theorie der schönen Künste*. Vol. 1. Leipzig: Weidmannschen Buchhandlung, 1792.

"Sumptuary Laws." In *Encyclopedia Judaica*, 15:515–516. Jerusalem: Keter, 1971.

Suppan, Wolfgang. "Moses Mendelssohn und die Musikästhetik des 18. Jahrhunderts." *Die Musikforschung* 17 (1964): 22–33.

Sutcliffe, Adam. "Can a Jew be a Philosophe? Isaac de Pinto, Voltaire and Jewish Participation in the European Enlightenment." *Jewish Social Studies* 6, no. 3 (2000): 31–51.

"Synagogen in Deutschland." http://www.cad.architektur.tu-darmstadt.de/synagogen/inter/menu.html.

Tabak, Israel. *Heine and His Heritage: A Study of Judaic Lore in His Work*. New York: Twayne Publisher, 1956.

Theilhaber, Felix. *Der Untergang der deutschen Juden*. Berlin: Jüdischer Verlag, 1921.

Thomas, Downing A. *Music and the Origins of Language: Theories from the French Enlightenment*. Cambridge: Cambridge University Press, 1995.

Tieken-Boon van Ostade, Ingrid, ed. *Grammars, Grammarians, and Grammar-Writing in Eighteenth-Century England*. Berlin: Mouton de Gruyter, 2008.

Toepfer, Karl. Empire of Ecstasy: *Nudity and Movement in German Body Culture, 1910–1935*. Berkeley: University of California Press, 1997.

"Toledot ha-Rav Yitzhak Abarbanel." *Ha-Me'assef* 1 (1784): 57–61.

Toury, Jacob. *Soziale und politische Geschichte der Juden in Deutschland, 1847–1871: Zwischen Revolution, Reaktion und Emanzipation*. Düsseldorf: Droste, 1977.

Trachtenberg, Joshua. *The Devil and the Jews: The Medieval Conception of the Jew and Its Relation to Modern Anti-Semitism*. Philadelphia: Jewish Publication Society, 1983.

Trigger, Bruce. "Romanticism, Nationalism and Archaeology." In *Nationalism, Politics, and the Practice of Archaeology*, edited by Philip L Kohl and Clare Fawcett, 263–279. Cambridge: Cambridge University Press, 1996.

Upton, Dell. "Pattern Books and Professionalism: Aspects of the Transformation of Domestic American Architecture, 1800–1860." *Winterthur Portfolio* 19, nos. 2–3 (1984): 107–150.

Van Brunt, Henry. "On the Present Condition and Prospects of Architecture." *Atlantic Monthly* 57, no. 341 (March 1886): 374–384.

van Zanten, David. *The Architectural Polychromy of the 1830's*. New York: Garland, 1977.

Veidlinger, Jeffrey. *Jewish Public Culture in the Late Russian Empire*. Bloomington: Indiana University Press, 2009.

Veit, Philipp F. "Heine: The Marrano Pose." *Monatshefte* 66, no. 2 (1974): 145–156.

Vertinsky, Patricia. "Body Matters: Race, Gender, and Perceptions of Physical Ability from Goethe to Weininger." In *Identity and Intolerance: Nationalism, Racism, and Xenophobia in Germany and the United States*, edited by Norbert Finzsch and Dietmar Schirmer, 331–370. Washington, DC: German Historical Institute; Cambridge: Cambridge University Press, 1998.

Viragh, Daniel. "Becoming Hungarian: The Creation of a Hungarian-Language Jewish Cultural Sphere in Budapest, 1867–1914." PhD diss., University of California–Berkeley, 2014.

Voge, Wilfried M. *The Pronunciation of German in the 18th Century*. Hamburg: Buske, 1978.

Vogel, Hans. "Aegyptisierende Baukunst des Klassizismus." *Zeitschrift für Bildende Kunst* 62 (1928–1929): 160–165.

Vogt, Carl. *Lectures on Man*. London: Longmans, 1864.

Volkov, Shulamit. *Walter Rathenau: Weimar's Fallen Statesman*. New Haven, CT: Yale University Press, 2012.

von der Krone, Kerstin. *Wissenschaft in Öffentlichkeit: Die Wissenschaft des Judentums und ihre Zeitschriften*. Berlin: De Gruyter, 2011.

von Dohm, Christian Wilhelm. *Über die Bürgerliche Verbesserung der Juden*. Berlin: Friedrich Nicolai, 1781.

von Klenze, Leo. *Anweisung zur Architektur des Christlichen Cultus*. Munich: n.p., 1822.

von Treitschke, Heinrich. "Herr Graetz und sein Judenthum." In *Der Berliner Antisemitismusstreit*, edited by Walter Boehlich, 33–47. Frankfurt am Main: Insel Verlag, 1988.

Vyleta, Daniel M. *Crime, Jews and News: Vienna 1895–1914*. New York: Berghahn, 2007.

Wahrman, Dror. *The Making of the Modern Self: Identity and Culture in Eighteenth-Century England*. New Haven, CT: Yale University Press, 2004.

Walter, Silke. "'In welchem Style sollen wir bauen?'—Studien zu den Schriften und Bauten des Architekten Heinrich Hübsch (1795–1863)." PhD diss., University of Stuttgart, 2004.

Wassermann, Jacob. *My Life as German and Jew.* New York: Coward-McCann, 1933.

Weber, Eugen. "Gymnastics and Sports in Fin-de-Siècle France: Opium of the Classes?" *American Historical Review* 76, no. 1 (1971): 70–98.

Weindling, Paul. *Health, Race and German Politics between National Unification and Nazism, 1870–1945.* Cambridge: Cambridge University Press, 1989.

Weisbach, Augustin. "Körpermessungen verschiedener Menschenrassen." *Zeitschrift für Ethnologie* 9 (1877): 212–214.

Weiss, John. *The Politics of Hate: Anti-Semitism, History, and the Holocaust in Modern Europe.* Chicago: Ivan R. Dee, 2003.

Weiss, Thomas. *Infinitely Beautiful: The Garden Realm of Dessau-Wörlitz.* Berlin: Nicolai, 2005.

Weissberg, Liliane. "Weibliche Körperschaften: Bild und Wort bei Henriette Herz." In *Von einer Welt in die andere: Jüdinnen im 19. und 20. Jahrhundert,* edited by Jutta Dick and Barbara Hahn, 71–92. Vienna: Brandstätter, 1993.

Weissenberg, Samuel. "Die Spaniolen: Eine anthropometrische Skizze." *Mittheilung der Anthropologischen Gessellschaft in Wien* 39 (1909): 225–236.

Weitzman, Steven. *Solomon: The Lure of Wisdom.* Stanford, CA: Stanford University Press, 2011.

Wessely, Naphtali Herz. *Divrei shalom ve-emet.* Berlin: n.p., 1782.

———. "Words of Peace and Truth (1782)." In The Jew in the Modern World, edited by Paul Mendes-Flohr and Jehuda Reinharz, 70–74. New York: Oxford University Press, 1995.

———. *Worte der Wahrheit und des Friedens an die gesammte jüdische Nation. Vorzüglich an diejenigen, so unter dem Schutze des glorreichen und großmächtigsten Kaysers Josephs II. wohnen.* Translated by David Friedländer. Berlin: n.p., 1782.

Westerhoff, Jan C. "*Poeta Calculans*: Harsdörffer, Leibniz, and the *mathesis universalis*." *Journal of the History of Ideas* 60, no. 3 (1999): 449–467.

Wiener, Max. *Abraham Geiger and Liberal Judaism.* Philadelphia: Jewish Publication Society of America, 1962.

Wiesemann, Falk. *Antijüdischer Nippes und populäre Judenbilder: Die Sammlung Finkelstein.* Essen: Klartext, 2005.

Wischnitzer, Rachel. *Architecture of the European Synagogue.* Philadelphia: Jewish Publication Society, 1964.

———. "The Egyptian Revival in Synagogue Architecture." In *The Synagogue: Studies in Origins, Archaeology, and Architecture,* edited by Joseph Gutmann, 334–350. New York: KTAV, 1975.

Wistrich, Robert S. *The Jews of Vienna in the Age of Franz Joseph.* Oxford: Oxford University Press, 1990.

———. *A Lethal Obsession: Anti-Semitism from Antiquity to the Global Jihad.* New York: Random House, 2010.

———. "Theodor Herzl: Between Myth and Messianism." In *Theodor Herzl: From Europe to Zion,* edited by Mark H. Gelber and Vivian Liska, 7–22. Tübingen: Niemeyer, 2007.

Wodziński, Marcin. *Hasidism and Politics: The Kingdom of Poland, 1815–1864*. Oxford: Littman Library of Jewish Civilization, 2013.

Wohlwill, Emmanuel. "Bemerkungen über Sprache und Sprachunterricht, als Beförderungsmittel der allgemeinen Bildung." *Sulamith* 7, no. 1 (1825): 25–42, 79–100.

Wojtowicz, David, and David B. Brownlee. "The New Imagery of Public Architecture." In *Friedrich Weinbrenner: Architect of Karlsruhe*, edited by David B. Brownlee, 23–26. Philadelphia: Architectural Archives of the University of Pennsylvania, 1986.

Wolf, Gerson. *Geschichte der Juden in Wien, 1156–1876*. Vienna: Alfred Hölder, 1876.

———. *Vom ersten zum zweiten Tempel: Geschichte der israelitischen Cultusgemeinde in Wien, 1820–1860*. Vienna: Wilhelm Braumüller, 1861.

Wolf, Joseph. "Zweck und Titel dieser Zeitschrift." *Sulamith* 1, no. 1 (1806): 1–11.

Wolf, Kenneth Baxter. "*Convivencia* in Medieval Spain: A Brief History." *Religion Compass* 3, no. 1 (2009): 72–85.

Wolff, Johann Heinrich. "Einige Worte über die von Herrn Professor Stier bei der Architektenversammlung zu Bamberg zur Sprache gebrachten architektonishen Fragen." *Allgemeine Bauzeitung* 10 (1845), Literatur-und Anzeigeblatt für das Baufach. Beilage zur *Allgemeine Bauzeitung* 2, no. 17: 255–270.

Wolitz, Seth L. "Translations of Karl Gutzkow's 'Uriel Acosta' as Iconic Moments in Yiddish Theater." In *Inventing the Modern Yiddish Stage*, edited by Joel Berkowitz and Barbara Henry, 87–115. Detroit: Wayne State University Press, 2012.

Wollny, Peter. "'Ein förmlicher Sebastian und Philipp Emanuel Bach-Kultus': Sara Levy, geb. Itzig und ihr musikalisch-literarisher Salon." In *Musik und Ästhetik im Berlin Moses Mendelssohns*, edited by Anselm Gerhard, 217–256. Tübingen: Max Neimeyer Verlag, 1999.

Yalon, Henoch. *Kuntresim le-inyanei ha-lashon ha-ivrit*. Jerusalem: n.p., 1937.

Yerushalmi, Yosef Hayim. *Assimilation and Racial Anti-Semitism: The Iberian and the German Models*. New York: Leo Baeck Institute, 1982.

———. *From Spanish Court to Italian Ghetto; Isaac Cardoso: A Study in Seventeenth-Century Marranism and Jewish Apologetics*. New York: Columbia University Press, 1971.

———. "Sephardic Jewry between Cross and Crescent." In *The Faith of Fallen Jews: Yosef Hayim Yerushalmi and the Writing of Jewish History*, edited by David N. Myers and Alexander Kaye, 141–156. Waltham, MA: Brandeis University Press, 2014.

———. *Zakhor: Jewish History and Jewish Memory*. Seattle: University of Washington Press, 1996.

Zadoff, Mirjam. *Next Year in Marienbad: The Lost Worlds of Jewish Spa Culture*. Philadelphia: University of Pennsylvania Press, 2012.

Zell, Michael. *Reframing Rembrandt: Jews and the Christian Image in Seventeenth-Century Amsterdam*. Berkeley: University of California Press, 2002.

Zemlinszky, Adolf von. *Geschichte der türkisch-israelitischen Gemeinde zu Wien von ihrer Gründung bis Heute: Nach historischen Daten*. Vienna: M. Papo, 1888.

Zimmels, H. J. *Ashkenazim and Sephardim: Their Relations, Differences, and Problems as Reflected in the Rabbinical Responsa*. London: Oxford University Press, 1958.

Zinberg, Israel. *History of Jewish Literature*. 10 vols. Cincinnati: Hebrew Union College Press, 1976.

Zuckermann, Ghil'ad. "'Abba, why was Professor Higgins trying to teach Eliza to speak like our cleaning lady?': Mizrahim, Ashkenazim, Prescriptivism and the Real Sounds of the Israeli Language." *Australian Journal of Jewish Studies* 19 (2005): 210–231.

Zunz, Leopold. *Die gottesdienstliche Vorträge der Juden*. Berlin: A. Ascher, 1832.

———. *Die synagogale Poesie des Mittelalters*. Berlin: Julius Springer, 1855.

———. *Zur Geschichte und Literatur*. Vol. 1. Berlin: Veit and Comp 1845.

Zweig, Arnold. *Das ostjüdische Antlitz*. Wiesbaden: Fourier, 1988.

Zwicker, Lisa Featheringill. *Dueling Students: Conflict, Masculinity, and Politics in German Universities, 1890–1914*. Ann Arbor: University of Michigan Press, 2011.

Index

◄●►

Abravanel, Don Isaac, 61, 63–64, 202, 214, 255n38
acculturation, 61, 64, 102, 113, 160; and Abravanel, 63; and beauty, 67; capacity for, 69; and Fishberg, 94, 96; and Gans, 161; and Goldziher, 217, 221; and Graetz, 208, 215–16; and Hungarian Jews, 224; and Kayserling, 96; and Marranos, 170; promotion of, 20; and Rathenau, 99; and Reform Judaism, 135; and Sephardim, 14, 93, 161. *See also* assimilation; cultural integration; culture; emancipation; social acceptance; social integration
Adler, Nathan, 39
aesthetics: Arabic as Judaized, 199; and architecture, 112; Baumgarten on, 30–31; and Berlin Neue Synagogue, 158; and bourgeoisie, 4; as discourse of body, 4; and Eastern European Jews, 232, 234; and emancipation, 9; and Friedländer, 34; and German Enlightenment, 30; and German Jewry, 59; and Graetz, 203, 205, 209; and Haskalah, 39; and Hebrew, 31, 38; and Hebrew accent, 42; and Heine, 175, 177; and H. Herz, 61; ideology of, 4; of Jewish peoplehood, 78; judgment vs. production of art in, 44; and language, 7, 9, 21–22, 30–31; and Law, 5; and masculine ideal, 5; and maskilim, 30; and M. Mendelssohn, 31–33, 36, 40, 67; and middle-class/bourgeoisie, 5–6; as narrative, 112; and Neubauer, 89; and physical anthropology, 85; and politics, 4, 5; and purity of biblical Hebrew, 23; response to object in, 44; and self-fulfillment, 7; as sensual cognition, 31; and Sephardim, 1, 4, 53, 61, 66, 162, 163; and social acceptance, 7; and synagogues, 130; and thought, 30–31; and N. Wessely, 40, 43–44; and Zionism, 49. *See also* beauty
African Americans, 6–7

Aguilar, Diego d' (Moses Lopes Pereira), 182, 183, 184
Aguilar, Grace, *Cedar Valley*, 164
Albo, Yosef, 185
Alfonso V, 63
Allgemeine Bauzeitung (General Journal for Construction), 144
Allgemeine Zeitung des Judentums, 166, 169, 182, 187
Alliance Israélite Universelle, 102
Altmann, Alexander, 37, 38
Altona, 39, 44
Americanization, 94, 98
Amorites, 75, fig. 2.3
Amsterdam, 80–81, 129, 187
Andree, Richard, 87
anthropology, 17, 41, 72, 74, 78
anthropology, physical (race science), 24, 67, 85–111
anti-Judaism, 207. *See also* antisemitism
antiquity, 68–78; authenticity derived from, 131; and Förster, 148–49; Jewish claims to, 68; polychromy in, 137–38; reliefs from, 68–78, 257n62; sculpture from, 74; and Sephardim, 77, 84. *See also* archaeology; Assyria; Egyptians, ancient; Greeks, ancient; history; Israelites, ancient; Near East, ancient; Romans, ancient
antisemitism, 1, 228, figs. 2.6–2.9; and accusations of crimes, 79; and aesthetics, 78; and Ashkenazim, 83–84; and beauty, 67; and Berlin Neue Synagogue, 159; and Chamberlain, 74–75, 76, 89–90; and Christianity, 19; and emancipation, 12–13; and Geiger, 200; in Germany, 208, 215–16; and Goldziher, 221, 223, 287n157; and Graetz, 207, 208, 215–16; and Heine, 170, 171; in images and depictions, 78, 79–84; internalization of, 7; and Israelites on ancient reliefs, 69; and Jews as aggressive conspirators, 81; and Judt, 96; and Kayserling, 89;